Statemaking and Territory in South Asia

Statemaking and Territory in South Asia

Lessons from the Anglo–Gorkha War (1814–1816)

BERNARDO A. MICHAEL

ANTHEM PRESS
LONDON · NEW YORK · DELHI

Anthem Press
An imprint of Wimbledon Publishing Company
www.anthempress.com

This edition first published in UK and USA 2014
by ANTHEM PRESS
75–76 Blackfriars Road, London SE1 8HA, UK
or PO Box 9779, London SW19 7ZG, UK
and
244 Madison Ave. #116, New York, NY10016, USA

First published in hardback by Anthem Press in 2012

Copyright © Bernardo A. Michael 2014

The author asserts the moral right to be identified as the author of this work.

All rights reserved. Without limiting the rights under copyright reserved above,
no part of this publication may be reproduced, stored or introduced into
a retrieval system, or transmitted, in any form or by any means
(electronic, mechanical, photocopying, recording or otherwise),
without the prior written permission of both the copyright
owner and the above publisher of this book.

British Library Cataloguing-in-Publication Data
A catalogue record for this book is available from the British Library.

Library of Congress Cataloging-in-Publication Data
The Library of Congress has catalogued the hardcover edition as follows:
Michael, Bernardo A.
Statemaking and territory in South Asia : lessons from
the Anglo-Gorkha War (1814–1816) / Bernardo A. Michael.
pages cm. – (Anthem modern South Asian history)
"This title is also available as an ebook"–Title page verso.
Includes bibliographical references and index.
ISBN 978-0-85728-519-5 (hbk : alkaline paper) – ISBN 0-85728-519-X (hbk : alkaline paper)
1. Nepalese War, 1814–1816. 2. Nation-building–Nepal–History–19th century.
3. Nation-building–Great Britain–History–19th century. 4. Nepal–Colonization.
5. Great Britain–Territorial expansion. 6. Nepal–Boundaries–India.
7. India–Boundaries–Nepal. I. Title.
DS485.N4M47 2012
954.96–dc23
2012036738

ISBN-13: 978 1 78308 322 0 (Pbk)
ISBN-10: 1 78308 322 0 (Pbk)

This title is also available as an ebook.

For
Ammedeus and Nirmala Michael
and
Thomas and Mary Varughese

CONTENTS

List of Maps, Plates and Tables   ix

Acknowledgments   xiii

Abbreviations   xvii

Chapter 1   Statemaking, Cultures of Governance and the Anglo–Gorkha War of 1814–1816   1

Chapter 2   The Agrarian Environment and the Production of Space on the Anglo–Gorkha Frontier   17

Chapter 3   The Champaran–Tarriani Frontier   31

Chapter 4   The Gorakhpur–Butwal Frontier   49

Chapter 5   The Disjointed Spaces of Precolonial Territorial Divisions   67

Chapter 6   Making States Legible: Maps, Surveys and Boundaries   87

Chapter 7   Conclusion   123

Glossary   129

Notes   137

Archival Sources   197

Bibliography   201

Index   221

LIST OF MAPS, PLATES AND TABLES

Book Cover

Military encampment on the banks of the Bagmati River, at the foot of a steep wooded hill. The Gurkha fort of Harriharpur stands on the crown, with smoke from shellfire and tracers from shells between a stockade and a promontory below (1816). 27.5 × 36 cm. Ink and watercolor by John Harris. Inscribed: "Shelling the Goorkahs 1st March at Sun Set, & storm coming on. Harriorpore [*sic*]. J. Harris HM 24th Regt." This battle, fought only 20 miles south of Kathmandu, resulted in the signing of the peace treaty between Sir David Ochterlony and the Gurkhas on 3 March 1816. Reproduced by permission of the British Library © British Library Board.

Source: Prints & Drawings, Hastings Albums, WD4396, India Office Records, Asia, Pacific & Africa Collections, British Library.

Maps

1.1	The Anglo–Gorkha frontier, 1814 CE	4
1.2	"A Map of the Routes by which General Sir David Ochterlony's Army advanced in Three Divisions towards Mukwanpoor (Nipaul) in February 1816," 1820 CE	13
2.1	Sketch of the line of boundary between the Nipaul Tarriani and the Zillah Sarun, 1822 CE	19
2.2	"Map of the Northern Frontier of the District of Goruckpoor, where it touches the Nepaulese Dominions, including the Goruckpoor Turrai and that portion of it ceded to the Nepaulese Government comprehending also a Survey of the Course of the Arrah Nuddee, which forms the Boundary between the Territories of His Excellency the Nawab Vizier on the west, and the Goorkhali Dominions on the east," 1818 CE	20
3.1	The Champaran–Tarriani frontier, 1814 CE	32
3.2	Location and internal divisions of the *pargana/praganna* of (Gadh) Simraon, 1814 CE	39
4.1	The Gorakhpur–Butwal frontier, 1814 CE	50

4.2	*Parganas* and *tappas* on the Gorkahpur–Butwal frontier, 1814 CE	61
5.1	Boundaries and internal divisions of the Mughal Empire, 1650 CE	68
5.2	Sketch showing the kingdoms of Sirmur, Jubal and Otroj, 1815 CE	73
5.3	*Pargana* Majhowa, in *sarkar* Champaran showing detached portions of *tappas* Jaffarabad, Mando and Mudhwal	79
6.1	The *subas* of Lahore and Multan as depicted on a Mughal map of northwestern India and Kabul, 1780 CE	88
6.2	Colonel Jean Baptiste Gentil's map of the *suba* of Bihar, 1770 CE	90
6.3	Map of *pargana* Gurdhan in *suba* Kashmir, 1830s CE	91
6.4	Rough sketch of the Terae lying between the Rivers Raptee and Koosah by Lieutenant John P. Boileau, 1816 CE	97
6.5	Map showing a portion of the district of Jaunpur with detached portions of the kingdom of Awadh and the *parganas* of Raree and Mureeahoo, 1846 CE	101
6.6	Detail from the Revenue Survey of India's "Map of the District of Bhagulpoor," 1852 CE	102
6.7	Detail from a section of the Revenue Survey of India's "Map of the District of Purneah [Purnea]," 1851 CE	103
6.8	Detail from the Revenue Survey of India's "Map of the District of Rangpur including the independent state of Kooch Behar," 1861 CE	104
6.9	Thana divisions of Gorakhpur district showing their detached portions and location of police posts in 1814 CE	106
6.10	Rearrangement of Thana boundaries in District Manbhoom [Manbhum], 1875 CE	108
6.11	A Nepali map of Central Asia, post-1855 CE (?)	113
6.12	Map of Central Nepal in the Hodgson Collection, 1835–1840 CE	114
6.13	Map of a portion of Western Nepal in the Hodgson Collection, 1830–1840 CE	115
6.14	Topographic map of Southeastern Nepal showing rivers, forests and hills, c. 1860 CE	116
6.15	Sketch of District West No. 1 (Dhading) showing detached segments, Nepal, 1957–1959 CE	119

Plates

1.1	Gorkhali prime minister Bhim Sen Thapa, 1806–1837 CE	12
1.2	Portrait of Sir David Ochterlony (1758–1825 CE), 1818 CE	12
2.1	Gorkhali king Pratap Singh Shah's (1775–1777 CE) *lal mohar* (red seal document) to Tharu magnate Hem Chaudhari, 1776 CE	23
3.1	Letter from Raja Ran Bahadur Shah to Bahadur Shah, 1840 BS (1783 CE)	42
6.1	Royal letter from Raja Girbana Juddha Bikram Shah to Chautariya Bam Shah, 1873 BS (1816 CE)	96
6.2	The geo-body of Nepal displaying its non-overlapping and clearly defined divisions as depicted on Nepali notebooks	120
6.3	The geo-body of the Nepali nation as depicted on postage stamps, symbolizing the close connections between territory and Nepali nationhood despite its political transformation from a Hindu kingdom to a federal democratic republic in 2008 CE	121

Tables

1	Total number of disputed villages on the Champaran–Tarriani frontier in 1814 CE	45

ACKNOWLEDGMENTS

Books never start or end – they are textualized entries into ongoing conversations, lives and relationships. It has taken many years for this book to assume its present avatar, and along the way I have accumulated a number of debts. George Varughese prodded me to return to graduate school and saw that I stayed the course then and thereafter. At the University of Hawaii, my teachers Leonard Andaya, Jerry Bentley, Jon Goss, Peter Hoffenberg, Sankaran Krishna, Brian Murton, Idus Newby and the late Jagdish Sharma shared their wisdom while tolerating my missteps. K. Sivaramakrishnan's friendship and scholarship, so generously given, and so hard to emulate, has been an exemplary source of inspiration that will never be fully repaid. Scholars, colleagues and friends from around the world sustained me with encouragement, wisdom and criticism as they gently tried to remind me about the need to complete the book. Now that it is done, I hope they don't regret that decision. They include: Itty Abraham, the late Professor Qeyamuddin Ahmad, Ian Barrow, Raymond Craib, Mary DesChene, Ramesh Dhungel, Matthew Edney, Stewart Gordon, Sumit Guha, Jose K. John SJ, Sankaran Krishna, Sunil Kumar, Michael Mann, Sridevi Menon, Gregory Maskarinec, Louise McReynolds, Pratyoush Onta, Ravi Palat, Damodar Pandit, Bhaveshwar Pangeni, K. N. Pannikkar, Dinesh Raj Pant, Sumathi Ramaswamy, the late Mahesh C. Regmi, Sumit Sarkar, Vivek Sharma, James C. Scott, Deborah Sutton, Nirmal Tuladhar, Tom Trautmann, Dilbagh Singh, T. R. Vaidya, John Whelpton, Damodar Wagle and Michael Witzel. At the Aligarh Muslim University, Professors S. P. Gupta, Irfan Habib, Farat Hasan, Iqtidar Alam Khan and Shireen Moosvi patiently listened to my simple questions while they generously shared their expertise with customary vigor. Participants who attended conferences and workshops on the subject of space at the University of Aberdeen (2001) and Yale (2005) taught me a lot about the theoretical and empirical expressions of that elusive term. When navigating archives and libraries from around the world, many volunteered their time and resources, namely Andrew Cook, Monica Ghosh, Diane Hunsinger, Dr Niraj Pasricha, Jaya Ravindran, Barb Syvertson and Lynette Wageman. My colleagues and students at Messiah College were a source of intellectual sustenance and collegial encouragement while officials at Murray Library, Faculty Services and College Press provided much needed logistical support. Natalie Burack and Megan Keller, my Smith Scholar interns at the college, provided invaluable assistance at various stages of the pre-publication process. Natalie happily entertained innumerable requests and demands on her time, especially when it came to editing the manuscript and securing the images and maps. In Nepal, Basant Gautam kept me connected with a growing circle of friends as he scouted out information and provided valuable logistical assistance. Family members intervened at various junctures to provide much needed relief and support in the form of fellowship, living space and victuals. My thanks go out to the extended Varughese and Michael *khandaans*, the *samast* Rawal *parivar*, Dan and Lee Curran, Kanak Mani Dixit, Ernie and Shirley Ogilvie, Dr Alice Matthew, Shri B. D. Sharma, Deepak Thapa, Rajiv Theodore and Alvin Yoshinaga. Joe Anciong, Jay Kumar, Natalie Burack, Saramma Michael, Sharon Michael and the late Christy Verghese generously shared their computer skills and resources to produce the maps as they stand. A sincere *mahalo* goes out to them all.

Finances matter, and so support from the following sources is gratefully acknowledged: the Department of History and the World Civilizations Program at the University of Hawaii, various scholarships administered by the University of Hawaii Foundation, the American Institute of Indian Studies Junior Research Fellowship, and the Office of Faculty Development and the School of Humanities at Messiah College. A Visitorship from the University Grants Commission of India allowed me to travel to Aligarh Muslim University to consult with their specialists on Mughal India. At Anthem Press, Tej P. S. Sood, Janka Romero, Rob Reddick and Caelin Charge cheerfully handled my questions with a patience and generosity that made working with them a pleasure. The anonymous reviewers made invaluable suggestions on improving the manuscript in its argument, content and organization, and the indexer provided invaluable assistance when it came to preparing the index.

My family witnessed the birth of this book with enthusiasm, consternation and then relief. The increasing demands I made on them were repeatedly met with unconditional love, patience and self-denial. Sharon, David Ano'i and Mary Nirmala suffered my long absences and distractions while my wife Shanti kept me in line, confronting the anxieties and dysfunctions of scholarship with generous doses of sanity and cheer. Together we would like to dedicate this work to our parents, Ammedeus and Nirmala Michael, and Thomas and Mary Varughese. We would never exchange for anything the rich inheritance of wisdom, experiences and worldviews they have given us. Thomas and Mary Varughese introduced us to the joys and responsibilities of teaching, rural fieldwork and liminal living as we trafficked between India, Nepal and the United States. Colleagues, fellow workers and students in Far-Western Nepal taught me much about the meaning of life and service in ways that continue to enrich my life.

I would like to conclude with a word about dates. Unless specified all dates belong to the Gregorian calendar. Besides the Christian era, there are two other calendars observed in Nepal – the Bikram Sambat (BS) beginning in 57 BCE and the Nepal Sambat (NS) starting in 879 AD. Also, in converting the dates from the Bikram Samvat (the calendar followed by the rulers of Gorkha) to the Gregorian calendar, I have refrained from attempting precise technical calculations in favor of using a simpler method of dating. To Bikram Samvat dates falling between 1 January (in the middle of the Nepali month of Paush) and mid-April (approximately Chaitra 32 or the last day in the Nepali year), I deduct 56 to get the Gregorian equivalent. To Bikram Samvat dates falling between mid-April and 31 December, I deduct 57 to get the Gregorian equivalent. If no Nepali months are specified in the document, I deduct 57 to access the Gregorian counterpart. I am grateful to Shri Dinesh Raj Pant for suggesting this method for converting dates.

For transliteration purposes, when using Devanagari words in the text I have dispensed with diacritics to bring words closer in line with the Anglicization commonly used in non-technical writing. No distinction is made between long and short vowels. "Ch" is used for both consonants "c" and "ch" (so for example, "Chudamani," not "Cudamani"). "S" is used for the dental sibilant and "sh" to register sounds stretching anywhere between the "s" in English "sip" and the "sh" in "ship." "B" or "w" is used instead of "v" where this reflects the current Nepali pronunciation (e.g. "Bikram Sambat" not "Vikram Samvat").

ABBREVIATIONS

AA	American Anthropologist
Add.	Additional Manuscripts
AE	American Ethnologist
AHR	American Historical Review
APAC	Asia, Pacific & Africa Collection
BCR	Bettiah Church Records, Church of the Nativity of Our Lady of the Blessed Virgin
BL	British Library, St Pancras, London
BOR	Board of Revenue
BRM	Bettiah Raj Mahfizkhana, Bettiah, Champaran District
BS	Bikram Sambat
BSA	Bihar State Archives, Patna
Capt.	Captain
CE	Common Era
CIS	Contributions to Indian Sociology
CNS	Contributions to Nepalese Studies
Col.	Colonel
Coll.	Collector
Consl.	Consultation
CPC	Calendar of Persian Correspondence
CSSH	Comparative Studies in Society and History
DRM	District Record Room, (DRM) Chapra, Saran District
EPW	Economic and Political Weekly
Eur. Mss	European Manuscripts
FP	Foreign Political
GCR	Gorakhpur Collectorate Records
GDR	Gorakhpur Divisional Records
GTS	Great Trigonometrical Survey
ICS	Institute for Contemporary Studies
IESHR	Indian Economic and Social History Review
IO	Islamic Oriental
IOR	India Office Records
JAS	Journal of Asian Studies
JASB	Journal of the Asiatic Society of Bengal
JBRS	Journal of the Bihar Research Society

JHS	Journal of Historical Sociology
JWH	Journal of World History
KCGT	Kumari Chowk Goswara Tahabil
KRR	Kathmandu Residency Records, 1792–1818
L/P&S/19	Departmental Records/ Political and Secret/ Miscellaneous Series
Lt.	Lieutenant
Lt. Col.	Lieutenant Colonel
Magst.	Magistrate
MRIO	Map Record and Issue Office
NAI	National Archives of India
NAN	National Archives of Nepal, Ramshah Path, Kathmandu
OIOC	Oriental and India Office Collections
PGGCB	Proceedings of the Governor General's Council in Bengal
PIHC	Proceedings of the Indian History Congress
PIHRC	Proceedings of the Indian Historical Records Commission
PRNW	Papers Respecting the Nepal War
Procs.	Processes
RADD	Regional Archives, Dehra Dun
RRC	Regmi Research Collection
RRS	Regmi Research Series
Rs	Rupees
RSA	Regional State Archives, Allahabad
SIH	Studies in Indian History
SINHAS	Studies in Nepali History and Society
SOIR	Survey of India Records
UPSA	Uttar Pradesh State Archives, Lucknow
WBSA	West Bengal State Archives, Calcutta

Chapter 1

STATEMAKING, CULTURES OF GOVERNANCE AND THE ANGLO–GORKHA WAR OF 1814–1816

The word [state] commonly denotes no class of objects that can be identified exactly, and for the same reason it signifies no list of attributes which bears the sanction of common usage.

—George Sabine[1]

[...] we recognise space as the product of interrelations; as constituted through interactions, from the immensity of the global to the intimately tiny.

—Doreen Massey[2]

1. Approaching States and Statemaking

It was the start of a warm day in the month of Jeyt in 2046 BS (May/June 1989 CE) when I awoke at 4.00am to undertake the six-hour trek to the Indian border. I had been living in a small town, in Far Western Nepal, teaching in a public school and now had to travel to Delhi to repair school equipment and purchase textbooks. I trudged along under the weight of a backpack full with nearly thirty mismatched pounds of damaged machine parts, punctured soccer balls and books in need of binding. As the day headed purposefully towards its consummation in a scorching finale of 110 degree Fahrenheit, I broke for a cup of tea along the Mohana River which marked the Indo–Nepal boundary. Always a porous zone of flows, this section of the Indo–Nepal boundary had been a mobile space attracting traders, migrant labor, smugglers and tourists alike. That day, however, the Nepali guards were out, armed, vigilant as they gazed across the river at the outpost of their Indian counterparts. I unpacked my bags for the guards to rummage through. When they discovered I was a teacher, they quickly waved me on. I received the same treatment on the other side of the river where there was an unusual buzz of activity on what should have been a quiet and uneventful day. All of a sudden the border had come alive and the boundary that had been irreverently crossed all these days was now being carefully monitored, especially by the Indian side. This was a tense time in the relations between the two neighbors. The Indo–Nepal Trade and Transit treaties had expired and the Indian government had imposed an economic blockade on Nepal by sealing the borders. At such times a tighter regime of discipline and control ensued with new protocols of crossing, examination, and scrutiny. It felt as if the boundary which had always seemed like an imaginary line on the ground had suddenly been reincarnated into a real wall of separation. Out of all the innumerable boundary crossings I made during my nearly eight year stay in Nepal, these remain most vividly ingrained in my imagination – signifying the boundary as both porous and impermeable.

This book is a historical account of the emergence of the Anglo–Gorkha boundary set against a wider backdrop of colonial territorial formation. It bridges two distinct but dispersed historical junctures where the idea of the modern state as a geographically discernible and territorially circumscribed entity emerged in colonial South Asia. Firstly, it examines the territorial disputes that emerged along the common frontiers of Gorkha (present-day Nepal) and the English East India Company that eventually led to the outbreak of the Anglo–Gorkha War in 1814. I suggest that at the heart of these disputes were questions pertaining to the geographical construction of the state, more specifically the precise location and layout of territorial divisions along the shared frontier of the two states. These disputes coalesced around older tribute, taxation and tenurial claims that left their territories perpetually intermixed with ill-defined boundaries. Following the defeat of the Gorkhalis in 1816, the Company's officials surveyed the frontier to establish a linear boundary that would clearly demarcate their respective territories. Secondly, this book also argues that such exercises in colonial boundary formation formed part of a long-drawn process whereby the colonial state, through various cartographic projects and changes in administrative routines, rearranged its internal administrative divisions in an attempt to create the geographical template of the modern state – occupying a definite portion of the earth's surface and divided into non-overlapping divisions and sub-divisions. The Gorkhali state would initiate similar proceedings only in the twentieth century.

The observation of the historical sociologist Michael Mann, that "societies are much messier than our theories of them," could very easily be applied to the study of the state and the messy middle ground that marks state–society relations.[3] It is at this middle ground, where abstractions such as "state" and "society" break down to reveal their form in terms of process rather than some fixed unyielding structure, that the study of statemaking can be located.[4] Consequently, statemaking calls for the study of the complex embroidery of social forces that make up the middle ground between the state and society and the negotiated and contingent manner in which these forces are produced, sustained and transformed through time.[5] Furthermore, and from the standpoint of this study, the role of culture, power, space and history in shaping processes of statemaking is clearly acknowledged. Such an approach to statemaking reveals the finest local details in all their complexity, while balancing them with broad generalizations of dominant trends and patterns.

Within the specific context of South Asian history the state has been an object of scholarly scrutiny. Many studies traversing the length and breadth of the subcontinent's history have generated a rich palette of histories and interpretations of states and statemaking. Here, states and statemaking have been defined and interpreted in terms of an intersecting array of political, economic, ideological, environmental and cultural forces. This has led to the study of military and bureaucratic institutions, agrarian systems, long-distance trade, nationalism, the environment, colonial constructions of knowledge and subaltern life. Given this context, studies on statemaking emerging from South Asia continue to evolve in new and innovative directions – questioning received wisdom on the subject and pursuing interdisciplinary agendas that are sensitive to the socio-cultural complexity expressed through the nuances, vagaries and varieties of human agency.[6] On this point, the state of history writing in modern Nepal deserves special comment.[7] Over the last fifty years or so, scholars have mined archival repositories to produce historical works on the Nepali state that are varying in their range and quality.[8] These mostly nationalist accounts have explored themes of administration, diplomacy, national unification, politics, war and the activities of famous personalities.[9] The pathbreaking work of historian Mahesh Chandra Regmi has yielded rich descriptions of general administration, land distribution and taxation, the nature of the state, trade, production and resource mobilization commencing from the late eighteenth century onwards.[10] However, there have been few attempts to replicate or expand on his work.[11] These scattered and uneven writings on the Nepali state underscore the continuing need for "greater pluralism in history writing practices" and conversations between its practitioners.[12]

2. Statemaking, Cultures of Governance, Space

Recent studies on statemaking have profited immensely from gains made in theorizing the cultural turn in the humanities.[13] These new approaches have called for a process-oriented view of the state and statemaking discerned in terms of complex intertwined strands of historically unfolding meanings and practices.[14] Such a view rests on a notion of culture that is structurally implicated yet continually emergent, and simultaneously ordered and disordered, as it incessantly triangulates with forces such as power and history.[15] Taking a process-oriented approach to culture blends the older antinomies of continuity and change to conceive of social reality in terms of finely woven, layered and difficult-to-parse webs of signs and meaningful practices – constituting a blurred and boundless world that is given shape by language, institutions and power.[16] The heuristic ambitions of such a view are balanced by a refusal to reinstate an omnibus notion of culture that can be universally applied over time and space. That is, cultural approaches to statemaking need to be carefully designed and calibrated to engage the questions posed by specific research agendas, which in the case of this book is statemaking and the organization of territory along the Anglo–Gorkha frontier in colonial South Asia (see Map 1.1).

Informed by such a perspective, this book seeks to examine how specific cultures of governance – meanings and practices of rule concerning a range of agrarian entitlements – determined territorial organization along the Anglo–Gorkha frontier. Such cultures of governance crystallized around the complex territorializing strategies individuals and groups employed to "affect, influence and control access to [entitlements involving] people, things, and relationships."[17] These entitlements, when viewed in terms of land tenures, may be provisionally divided into *malguzari* (arising out of revenue collection arrangements), *khidmatguzari* (service tenures) and *maafi* (tax-free) tenures. Intricately woven into such rights to "enjoy" the fruits of the land were whole systems of customary privileges concerning rights to exercise authority, exact fees and services, and bear titles, objects, emblems and honors. It follows that these entitlements, which were simultaneously symbolic and material in their manifestations, found expression in maneuverings over resources such as land, labor, water, forests, markets, commodities and capital. Such rights, which went by various names, were enjoyed on a hereditary basis or bestowed by some superior authority or overlord – such as the Mughal emperor, high-ranking officials,

Map 1.1 The Anglo–Gorkha frontier, 1814 CE

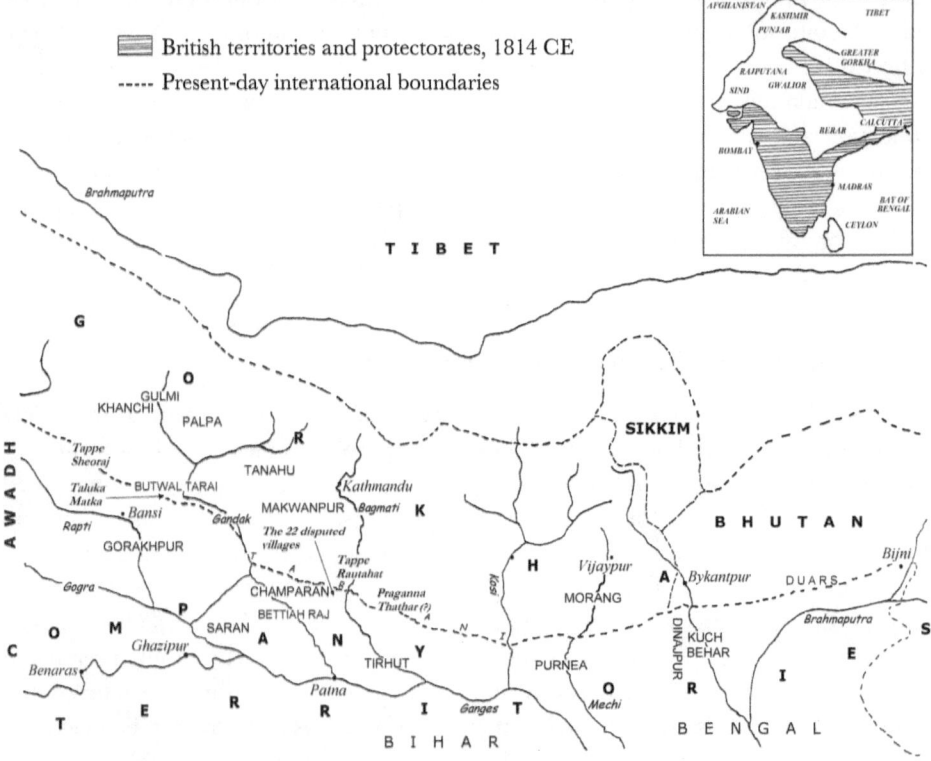

This map is not drawn to scale. Boundaries and the locations of tappes, pragannas, and villages are approximate. Mapwork by Saramma and Sharon Michael.

petty chieftains and landlords. This created hierarchies of political relationships that were prone to frequent realignments arising out of the vagaries of statemaking. Such a conflicted structure of entitlements and shifting hierarchical political relationships formed the deep-seated institutional infrastructure of territorial governance and animated the histories of the little kingdoms that straddled the Anglo–Gorkha frontier, such as Gulmi, Argha, Kanchi, Pyuthan, Tanahu, Makwanpur, Palpa and Bettiah.[18] Consequently, when Gorkha and the Company state acquired the territories of these little kingdoms, they also inherited an older history of entitlements and territorial disputes whose significance for our understanding of the Anglo–Gorkha War has never been fully explored.[19] While colonial and postcolonial scholars have written histories of such agrarian rights and privileges, they have rarely examined them for the spatial or territorial implications arising out of the dynamic ways in which they were accessed, maintained, reconfigured and even lost.[20] Consequently, such rights and privileges remained prone to frequent fluctuations in their definitions, terms and territorial extent.[21] These fluctuations triggered commensurate rearrangements and mutations in the boundaries and layout of the parent territorial units they were housed within. These precolonial territorial divisions such as *parganas, tappas, tarafs,* and *mouzas* came to possess intermixed bodies and discontinuous boundaries. Consequently, in the first half of the book, I seek to trace the connections between such themes and the production of territory along the Anglo–Gorkha frontier.

A crucial dimension of statemaking is manifest in the struggles surrounding the capacity of states and their agents to bind and mark space or territory.[22] Spatiality is the common thread that connects the study of statemaking to cultures of governance and territoriality. In recent years, space, which has for a long time been the compelling object of study for geographers, has witnessed a reassertion in social theory.[23] In this book I define space in terms of the organization and layout of territory, and not some neutral stage or container on or in which life unfolds.[24] Rather, it is a dynamic entity produced out of a shifting ensemble of meanings, practices and interrelationships involving human communities, institutions (such as the state) and struggles to define and control resources. Space is historically produced, being made manifest at distinct times and places by embodied human agents interacting with each other and their environments. Space does not sit apart from and above the local situatedness of place. Rather, the production of space is the history of the thrown-togetherness and interpenetration of space and place.[25] Such a conception of space, as detailed in this book, views the production of territory as a power-laden, culturally determined, contentious process involving access to resources, both material and symbolic, that are derived from agrarian environments. Ultimately, connecting cultures of governance to their agrarian environments through the pursuit of questions of space affords an opportunity to write histories of territory that evade the passive metageographical constructions of area studies approaches.[26]

The existence of this rich body of writing on space has produced a renewed interest in the historical production of territory and especially in the efforts of states to manage, organize and bind territory.[27] Historian Thongchai Winichakul's groundbreaking study of the emergence of Siam as a territorial entity – or "geo-body" – has shown how the Southeast Asian kingdom of Siam completed the colonization of neighboring kingdoms not just through conquest but also by incorporating them into the singular territorial representation of the state on modern maps.[28] This territorial representation became an important symbol of Siamese unity and identity which hid from view its multifarious and contested history of territorial relations with numerous smaller kingdoms, prior to their incorporation into Siam. This book builds on the insights of Thongchai's work, but seeks to go further by taking a closer look at the contested territorial relationships involving various polities along the Anglo–Gorkha frontier. By examining the cultures of governance that produced territory along this frontier, I seek to give greater agency to the local and regional actors who are often lost in the nationalist-driven narratives of the Anglo–Gorkha War or of Siamese state-formation. Such "non-state spaces" – of local power, action and influence – that resisted the centralizing thrust of political elites reveal the highly nuanced and variable character of processes of statemaking.[29] Consequently, the Anglo–Gorkha frontier became a borderland made up of dynamic, shifting and hard-to-govern territories – a fact that has eluded most studies of the war.[30]

To conclude, the notion of cultures of governance was also designed with the intention of creating a framework that would make territorial sense of the structure of entitlements and many multi-cornered contests that took place over agrarian resources along the Anglo–Gorkha frontier. Consequently, the large number of territorial disputes that broke out on this frontier between 1760 and 1814 crystallized mainly around diffuse relationships of power, as they unfolded unevenly across the boundaries of caste, kinship and ethnicity.[31] Numerous agents, located at multiple levels, constantly undertook situational adjustments that produced shifts in existing configurations of culture, power, history and space. Competing agents sought to exploit the indeterminacies of their situations by reinterpreting or redefining the rules that gave them access to and control over agrarian entitlements. Such strategies generated conflict and indeterminacy in social interactions and plasticity in territorial arrangements.[32] They form the subject matter of the next three chapters.

3. Spatiality and the Study of Cartographic History

Ever since the English East India Company acquired territory in 1765, it had been confronted with the persistent puzzle of discovering the layout, internal organization and limits of its territories. Company officials struggled to come to terms with the intermixture, overlaps and fluid boundaries of its territories. Without this territorial knowledge, the colonial state's capacity to tax its subjects, impose law and establish order was severely blunted. This problem was accentuated all along its frontiers with neighboring states, and not just along the Anglo–Gorkha frontier. In 1818, George Dowdeswell, the vice-president of the Company's governing council at Calcutta echoed the sentiments of many Company officials when he observed: "We have almost *daily experience* of the very defective state of our geographical information in many parts of our own territories and of the serious inconveniences and embarassments arising from this cause in the conduct of *ordinary* affairs of the administration."[33] Dowdeswell's comment is a reminder of how colonial anxieties about clearly defined territories reflected a wider and more ubiquitous drive to parse, reorder and systematize life in the colony. At the heart of empire lay a tremendous concern for things spatial – in rearranging territory, relationships, objects and bodies.[34] This book seeks to unearth these spatial anxieties to reveal how they nourished processes of statemaking and territorial production along the Anglo–Gorkha frontier.

In making this argument, I use the theme of spatiality to connect two oft-disconnected bodies of knowledge and inquiry: the study of agrarian entitlements and the history of modern cartography. I argue that colonial anxieties at the time of the Anglo–Gorkha War about the need for accurate geographical information (which ultimately led to the institution of surveys and the delineation of the Anglo–Gorkha boundary) can be fruitfully connected with the spatial history of agrarian entitlements along the frontier. While the spatial effects of agrarian entitlements have been discussed in previous paragraphs, the study of the history of cartography deserves further mention. Long considered neutral and unproblematic representations of the world, and celebrated for their technical qualities, maps have recently come under critical scrutiny. Over the last three decades this critical approach to the history of cartography has, in the fashion of Ariadne's thread, tried to trace the connections between the map viewed purely as a representational artifact and the social world that produced and consumed it. Under the influence of the pioneering work of scholars like Arthur Robinson, David Woodward and John Brian Harley, it became evident that maps are not merely the products of technical skill, but are also awash with the forces of culture, power and history.[35] Harley's work was followed by a spate of writings that have carefully unpacked themes of European imperial domination, the creation of colonial knowledge, the development of modern science, the dynamics of state formation and indigenous mapmaking traditions.[36] More recently, this genre of writing has extended itself to the study of South Asian history, producing rich studies ranging from histories of surveying institutions and endeavors to the ideological and representational effects of maps.[37] Still others have conducted detailed studies of the circulation of geographical knowledge and the formation of the boundaries of modern nation-states such as India and Pakistan.[38]

Such histories of cartography have broadened the study of maps by encouraging greater theoretical innovation and the pursuit of a more inclusive agenda.[39] There is a growing realization that cartographic agendas can be informed by spatial impulses that originate in arenas of social life far removed from the confines of surveying departments and the technicalities and representational effects of mapmaking.[40] For instance, maps are not innocent creations of states and their agents; rather, they are also the product of deep-seated and conflicted social forces far removed from the surveyor's office.[41] A growing chorus of both elite and subaltern agents, inhabiting diverse social landscapes, is now perceived as contributing to the production and consumption of maps. For instance, cadastral mapping may be viewed as the cartographic component of the larger social arena within which various forms of agrarian property rights are defined, organized and regulated. Consequently, this book seeks to trace the elusive dots that connect maps to the wider socio-spatial conditions of their production. It pursues Harley's initial call to "deconstruct" maps with greater vigor and attention, by focusing on the "lived geographies of empire," where such socio-spatial dynamics unfolded.[42] The first half of this book raises the hope that the study of colonial cartography in South Asia can be informed by the inclusion of the highly localized socio-spatial histories of agrarian territories along the Anglo–Gorkha frontier. The inclusion of the rich voices lying along the margins of states helps resist the urge to present simplistic readings, in order to reveal new and valuable counterpoints that have remained underdeveloped in previous studies on the history of cartography, statemaking and spatiality.

Such an approach to the study of the history of cartography has methodological implications as well. It calls for the interdisciplinary pursuit of historical questions that engage fields such as cultural geography and anthropology, history, environmental studies, postcolonial literature and critical cartography. Historians seeking to establish deeper connections between maps than their socio-spatial contexts will need to examine a wider range of archival materials that are not confined to map collections and survey records. Primary source documents on land revenue administration in colonial South Asia lying in provincial and district level archives provide valuable information on the organization of territory and its implications for the cartographic projects of the colonial state. The territorial disputes between the English East India Company and Gorkha in the late eighteenth and early nineteenth centuries provide a richly chronicled example of this. But to write a history that connects these territorial disputes to the cartographic projects of the state requires tedious research that engages materials dispersed over a number of local, regional, national and international archives.

It is clear from a study of these materials that during the first 50 years of colonial rule, officials of the English East India Company increasingly harbored an Icarian vision of clearly demarcated territories that found expression not only in the surveying and mapmaking projects of the state, but also in the routines and practices of everyday governance. For instance during the early years of colonial rule, where in the absence of modern maps, colonial administrators tried to formulate principles that would regulate or dismantle relationships and practices that confounded the establishment of linear boundaries and continuous territories. Thus, Company officials at Calcutta asked their representatives stationed along the Anglo–Gorkha frontier to formulate "fixed principles" to resolve competing territorial claims presented by hill chieftains in the west following the defeat of the Gorkhalis by the British in 1815. Secretary John Adam noted that:

> Without some *fixed principle* for the decision of such questions, it would be extremely embarrassing and difficult if not practicable to undertake the adjustment of the multiplied and conflicting claims of territory arising out of the disturbed state of the country for a long series of years, and the *frequent transition* of particular districts from the authority of one principality to that of another. The period of the Gorkhali invasion is in all respects the most convenient from being of so modern a date as to render evidence easily attainable while with reference to our public declaration and the avowed objects of our interference in the affairs of the Hill Chiefs, namely the restoration of things to the state in which they were at that time, we might be perhaps justly considered to be precluded from taking cognisance of claims originating in the transactions of an antecedent period.[43]

This "fixed principle" of holding a moratorium on all competing territorial claims prior to the Gorkhali invasion was intended to reduce the number and complexity of these claims while simplifying the process of redrawing political boundaries. Another territorial principle Company officials affirmed was a refusal to occupy and govern lands in the hills along the Anglo–Gorkha frontier. This "principle of limitation" was clearly motivated by spatial concerns.[44] First enunciated in 1813, it declared to Gorkhali authorities that "no interference should take place in the proceedings of Nipaul in the hills and on the other hand the Nipaulese authority should on no account be extended below the hills."[45] The aim of this "principle" was to put a halt to the interminable territorial disputes that peppered the political relations between the Gorkhali commanders in the hills and their Indian counterparts in the plains. That is, hill and plain chieftains were asked to renounce all claims on each other's territories and align the political boundaries of their states with the natural separation of the hills from the plains. In this manner, the messy realities of the political boundaries of these states were subordinated to the convenient and arbitrary fiction of a geographic boundary that the Company was increasingly imposing on South Asian kingdoms. In another instance, the competing territorial claims of Sikh chieftains in the area were "frozen" in principle by notifying them that the political status quo between them was to be preserved as it stood in 1805, the year the Company's official Charles Metcalf undertook his preliminary survey of that area.[46] Once again, the administrative exigency of disentangling itself from long-standing territorial disputes and the need to establish linear boundaries drove Company officials to make such spatial adjustments.[47]

Elsewhere, this territorial vision gradually trickled down to the record-keeping practices of the English East India Company. While the British had always depended on indigenous records to collect information on land revenue, property rights and the administrative geography of its territories, they increasingly realized that this information did not yield images of compact, contiguous and well-bounded administrative divisions. In 1800, colonial surveyors like Francis Buchanan-Hamilton expressed this anxiety in their observations on precolonial taxation surveys in Mysore:

> The principal native officer here says that people are now employed in measuring the lands which belong to all the villages in this lately acquired division of Major Mcleod's district. The measurement, however, will by no means be complete; as large hills and wastes are not included within the boundaries of any village and will not be comprehended in the accompts [sic]. Even within the village boundaries it is only the lands that are considered arable, or as capable of being made so, that are actually measured, steep and rocky places are taken by conjecture.[48]

Buchanan-Hamilton's anxiety arose out of his belief that in order for a survey to be *complete* it had to take into account *all* the topographical features, both within and beyond the boundaries of a village. Company officials were quick to notice this "confusion" and "disorganization" in the revenue records. Without the aid of modern maps to orient them, and in a rather ill-coordinated fashion, they called for efforts to bring about a greater alignment between the geographical frame of its territories and practices of record keeping. Consequently, information pertaining to land rights, revenue administration and record keeping became increasingly organized with the intention of creating territorially compact administrative divisions. For instance, in 1773 J. I. Kieghly, the Collector of Tirhut District (along the Anglo–Gorkha frontier) tried to systematize the unwieldy revenue accounts of each *pargana* division under his charge, in order to make the "Purgunnnah as complete as possible."[49] The inability of the Company during the early years of its rule to distill the administrative geography of its territorial possessions might arguably have compromised the work of bodies such as the Amini Commission. Active between 1776 and 1778, the Amini Commission was tasked by the Company to undertake one of the most detailed investigations into the revenue records of its provinces in order to make sense of this data. Its sponsor, Governor-General Warren Hastings, explained that the Commission's mandate was "[t]o collect these different accounts and methodize them for our guidance in forming a new settlement."[50] This was due to the fact that the records of each district "underwent considerable and annual alterations, having in many instances been augmented and in others diminished."[51] However, in 1778, having spent two years gathering a vast corpus of materials, the Commission was disbanded for reasons that are still unclear.[52]

Company officials became increasingly sensitive to the representation of territorial divisions in the revenue records. Efforts were made to systematize these records by ensuring that territorial divisions were insulated from mutations in the revenue records. In 1789, the Board of Revenue instructed Archibald Montgomerie, the Collector of

Saran District in Bihar, to take careful note of administrative divisions and sub-divisions (such as *parganas* and *tappas*) when making revenue settlements.[53] In 1791 the Amended Code of Regulations for the Decennial Settlement of Bengal and Bihar instructed the collector of every district in Bengal and Bihar to establish a fixed arrangement of divisions such as *parganas*, *tarafs*, *taluks* and *kismuts* within each *zamindari*. *Zamindars* and *taluqdars* were also disallowed from making any alterations to these divisions, regarding their extent, designation or disposition. These regulations also stipulated that the revenue accounts were to be systematized according to *parganas*, with the accounts of the internal divisions of a *pargana* being inserted into the account register of that particular *pargana*, and not any other.[54] Similar attempts were made to preserve territorial continuity in record keeping in the North-Western Provinces. In 1815, when the Company decided to allow the reappointment of *patwaris* (village accountants) in these provinces, it added the caveat that these *patwaris* should either be appointed to separate villages or any number of *contiguous* villages.[55] Later, in 1820, it was decided that every *pargana* would have three registers for recording information pertaining to estates (*mahals*), rent-free lands (*lakhiraj*) and villages (*mauzas*).[56] By the 1840s, the arrangement of records witnessed further systematization. In 1840 the Sadr Board of Revenue in the North-Western Provinces issued instructions to its Commissioners of Revenue about the maintenance of records and registration, which can be gleaned from selections in the handbook titled *Circular Orders by the Sudder Board of Revenue, North West Provinces Addressed to Commissioners of Revenue on Records and Registration* (1840):

> In preparation of Reports intended for the Boards Office, or for transmission to Government from your divisions, you are requested to adopt the arrangement of collectorates which is given in the Appendix. This geographical arrangement has been enjoined by orders of government to ensure facility of reference.[57]
>
> The records are to be kept parganawar and mauzawar [...] A separate shelf or space is to be set apart for each pergunnah, and the name of the pergunnah is to be clearly and durably written both on the outside of the door or the press and on front of the shelf or shelves on which the records of that pergunnah may be arranged.[58]

Such measures highlight the Company's determination to carefully reiterate the geography of its territories in the organization of its records. Therefore, even prior to the mapping exercises of the nineteenth century, Company officials tried to put a halt – *in the revenue record* – to the back-and-forth movement of villages from one *tappa* or *pargana* to another. They had realized that these records did not allow them to grasp the contours, layout and internal divisions; in a word, the *complete* architecture of the territories they had acquired. It took time for this realization to dawn on them, as the Company's slow progress in this area was marked not by any inherent teleology but by contests, dissonances, contradictions and contingencies. In fact, the insertion of this distinct spatial vision into the Company's revenue records (or those of other indigenous states) constitutes a potential area of study in its own right, which falls outside the scope of this present investigation. Indeed, I would suggest that these exercises must not be quickly dismissed as instances of administrative "rationality" or "reform;" rather, they announced the casting of a distinct territorial order into the organization and maintenance of governmental records. Such an expression of territory outside the cartographic medium of maps formed part of a process by which a new territorial archive was created in South Asia – whereby the territories of the colonial state came to be viewed as a unified and emboxed whole.[59] Under colonial rule, the patchy, discontinuous, ill-defined and overlapping territories of precolonial states in South Asia would be gradually rearranged in an effort to constitute the continuous and well-defined geographical frame of the modern state – perfectly consistent in all its parts.[60] In doing this, the colonial state created a new grid of intelligibility – of governmentality – whereby state power was exercised through new routines, procedures, instruments, tactics, technologies and vocabularies to control space, populations and resources.[61]

The territorial disputes that led to the Anglo–Gorkha War reveal how struggles over agrarian entitlements and political power informed processes of statemaking and the constitution of territory. We need an expanded notion of cartographic agency that is not confined to the work of mapmakers and surveying institutions but embraces elite and subaltern agents inhabiting times and places that have not always been included within the dominant narratives of nations, states, kingdoms and their surveying departments.[62] It is social agents such as these that co-produced the cultures of governance of the time that in turn produced the disjointed territories and geographies of the early colonial state. The English East India Company, in order to render these territories legible, was forced to initiate an ultimately ill-coordinated and even incomplete project of territorial reordering that would persist well into the twenty-first century, long after the demise of British power in the subcontinent. Consequently, the latter half of this book will then move away from a discussion of the territorial politics of the Anglo–Gorkha frontier to examine the spatial qualities of precolonial territorial divisions and the measures that both the colonial and the Gorkhali state took to reconstitute their territories.

4. The Anglo–Gorkha War (1814–16)

In the second half of the eighteenth century both the English East India Company and the Himalayan state of Gorkha witnessed a period of rapid territorial expansion. By 1814, Gorkha's territorial possessions stretched between the River Tista in the east and the Sutlej in the west. In the process it conquered or reduced to a state of dependency a number of hill kingdoms such as Lamjung, Parbat, Kaski, Tanahu, Makwanpur, Kumaon and Garhwal.[63] In 1765, when the English East India Company acquired the right to collect revenue (*diwani*) from the provinces of Bihar and Bengal, its territorial frontier stretched across the foothills of the Himalayas to nestle alongside Gorkha's Tarai possessions, while including a number of little kingdoms such as Palpa and Bettiah.[64] Following this, there arose numerous territorial disputes along the Anglo–Gorkha frontier that became particularly acrimonious between 1800 and 1814. While the Anglo–Gorkha boundary disputes were varied in their expression, history and duration, this study will only explore the disputes that arose at two places: the Champaran–Tarriani and the Gorakhpur–Butwal sections of the frontier (see Map 1.1).[65] These disputes proved to be particularly intractable despite the series of

Plate 1.1 Gorkhali prime minister Bhim Sen Thapa, 1806–1837 CE

Source: William Wilson Hunter, *Life of Brian Houghton Hodgson, British Resident at the Court of Nepal* (London: John Murray, 1896), 131.

Plate 1.2 Portrait of Sir David Ochterlony (1758–1825 CE), 1818 CE

79 × 72.5 cm. Oil on canvas by Robert Home (1752–1834). Reproduced by permission of the British Library © British Library Board.
Source: Prints & Drawings F1063, India Office Records, Asia, Pacific & Africa Collections, British Library.

investigations and diplomatic efforts undertaken by the two states. Finally, in October 1814, Gorkhali troops launched an attack on the Company's police stations along the Gorakhpur–Butwal frontier, killing a number of its police officers. Shortly after, on 1 November 1814, the English East India Company declared war on Gorkha. After facing some initial setbacks, the Company's forces gradually wrested territories from the Gorkhalis and by April 1815 had ousted them from their western territories of Kumaon and Garhwal. By the end of that year, the Gorkhalis had sued for peace, and the Treaty of Sugauli was concluded in December 1815. However, the failure of the authorities at Kathmandu, led by Prime Minister Bhim Sen Thapa, to ratify this treaty led to a resumption of hostilities in January 1816 (see Plate 1.1). Under the leadership of Major-General David Ochterlony (see Plate 1.2), the Company's forces made rapid advances through Gorkha's Eastern Tarai districts, capturing the forts of Hetauda, Makwanpur and Hariharpur. Alarmed by the sudden advance of the Company's armies on the capital, the Gorkhalis capitulated and hastily ratified the Treaty of Sugauli on 4 March 1816, bringing the war to an end. The Treaty of Sugauli resulted in the loss of Gorkha's western dominions and most of its Tarai lands in the south. The British also established a permanent presence in Nepal through the appointment of a Resident at Kathmandu. Subsequently, and more significantly, they commenced demarcating the Anglo–Gorkha boundary in 1816. For the next five years its officials would painstakingly etch this linear boundary on the ground, marking it with masonry pillars that survive to this day.

Map 1.2 "A Map of the Routes by which General Sir David Ochterlony's Army advanced in Three Divisions towards Mukwanpoor (Nipaul) in February 1816," 1820 CE

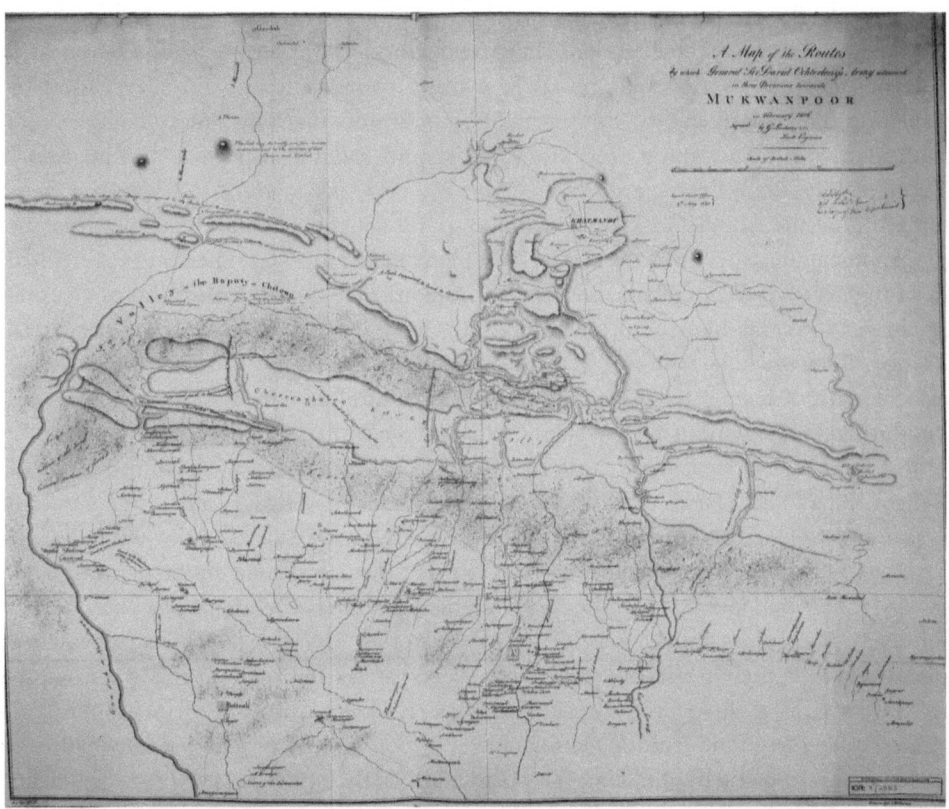

By Lt. G. Lindesay. 68.6 × 81.3 cm. Scale = four miles to one inch. Forests are shown in color with important places in red. Reproduced by permission of the British Library © British Library Board. Source: India Office Map Collection X/2983, Indian Office Records, Asia, Pacific & Africa Collections, British Library.

The Anglo–Gorkha War (1814–16) has attracted considerable attention from historians who have studied it largely from military, political and diplomatic perspectives, with a strong focus on narratives of military engagements, diplomatic maneuverings and nationalist sentiments.[66] Most historians of Nepal have viewed the war as the culmination of modern Gorkha's territorial expansion, which came to an end in 1816 with the defeat of Gorkha.[67] However, less stated is the view that the disputes surrounding the Anglo–Gorkha War (1814–16) also offer a unique opportunity to explore questions of statemaking and spatiality. To be fair, potential connections between questions of spatiality and the Anglo–Gorkha War have been suggested, albeit fleetingly, by scholars such as Ludwig Stiller and Mary Des Chene. Stiller briefly discusses the contested notions of political territory that the two states grappled with, and the subsequent attempts of the British to devise linear boundaries.[68] Mary DesChene's cultural history of the "Gurkhas" makes the astute observation that "Neither the idea of connected territory nor the concept of a 'line of frontier' entered into the Gorkhali understanding of possessions."[69] However, barring these interventions, scant attention has been paid to the spatial dynamics that underwrote the cultures of governance and process of statemaking along the Anglo–Gorkha frontier.

As a first step in that direction, the Anglo–Gorkha War needs to be viewed as a "diagnostic event" – one that reveals the ongoing dismantling and/or creation of structures. Because diagnostic events might be indicators that other more complex and hard-to-discern forces are at work, they will require careful inspection and analysis.[70] Extrapolating from this, I argue, once the rhetoric surrounding the war has been cleared, that the Anglo–Gorkha territorial disputes actually encoded struggles over the geographical construction of the state. Our understanding of the war needs to be liberated from the neat typologies of current military, diplomatic and nationalist histories so that it can yield insights into the production of territory that are framed within a cultural history of statemaking, war and space. Consequently, the Anglo–Gorkha disputes serve as a signpost of deeper territorial dynamics and cultural transformations being worked out during the long arc of British colonial rule on the Indian subcontinent.[71]

In South Asia, the English East India Company's acquisition of the provinces of Bengal, Bihar and Orissa in 1765 inaugurated its formal engagement with questions pertaining to the organization and knowledge of its territories. It would take the Company many decades to fully grasp the fact that the precolonial entitlements to land, loyalty, tribute and taxes it had inherited from the Mughals had undeniable consequences for the organization and knowledge of its territories. Company officials increasingly discovered that their territorial possessions were patchy, discontinuous and constantly shifting, with ill-defined boundaries. They perceived a growing need to simplify and make legible these fluid territories using a host of policies and practices that would later include surveying and mapmaking. The Gorkhalis, on their part, asserted their territorial claims not in terms of some fixed unchanging naturalized geographical template for the state, but against a shifting panoply of agrarian entitlements and practices they laid claim to, and that had for a long time organized territory in the South Asian world. The Anglo–Gorkha War provides a unique opportunity to diagnose questions pertaining to the changing geographical construction of states in early colonial South Asia. The war was one of those contentious markers that inaugurated a colonial project of territorial redrawing that has persisted to this day in South Asia. The long-drawn process used the tool of modern surveying to generate a firm geographical framework for the state that was capable of representation on maps. The establishment of the Anglo–Gorkha boundary following the cessation of hostilities in 1816 upheld and enforced this new principle of territorial representation and organization on the subcontinent.

5. Structure of the Book

Statemaking and Territory in South Asia has been arranged into seven chapters including a conclusion. This opening chapter presents the central arguments of the book concerning the cultural constitution of territory, while drawing on disciplines such as history, human geography and cultural anthropology. The premise of the book is that examining the territorial disputes leading to the Anglo–Gorkha War provides a promising entry point to explore the cultures of governance that produced the entangled territories of the two states. Chapter 2 unpacks the environmental relationships that informed the constitution of territory along the Anglo–Gorkha frontier. More specifically, it explores the relationships between land, labor and agrarian activity, all of which left their imprint on the organization of territory. Chapters 3 and 4 explore how relationships concerning tribute, taxation, landed tenures and other agrarian entitlements produced disjointed and entangled borderlands along the Champaran–Tarriani and the Gorakhpur–Butwal sections of the Anglo–Gorkha frontier. Historically, such relationships had created a multiplicity of claims to patches of land at multiple scales – local, regional and interstate. Various regional, petty kingdoms and the English East India Company would find themselves entangled within the web of such conflicting claims and rights. Chapter 5 shifts the focus of the narrative away from the Anglo–Gorkha frontier to make broader observations of the variables, operating at many scales, that produced the dispersed bodies and fluid boundaries of South Asian states. These territorial divisions were a composite of various forms of knowledge and practice that did not constitute the coherent continuous geographical envelope that Company officials were so anxious to discern. The colonial state then initiated a long-drawn, ill-coordinated and largely incomplete process of territorial reorganization that would uphold the now-dominant principle that states possessed well defined and immutable geographical frames. Consequently, Chapter 6 shifts gear to focus on the projects of territorial reorganization undertaken by both the colonial state in North India and the Gorkhali (later Nepali) government in the nineteenth and twentieth centuries. The history of colonial cartography then surfaces not as an overdrawn homogenous metropolitan project-in-the-making that was thrust on a passive, colonized landscape. Rather, the work of surveying departments was complemented, confounded and sometimes even preceded by the work of numerous agents, drawn from a variety of locations, as they co-produced the space of the state. In the end, this book seeks to connect the dots between two narratives: the first about how certain forms of territorial organization precipitated the Anglo–Gorkha War, which in turn fed a second longer narrative about the emergence of a specific colonial vision of territory that would gradually try and overshadow other, older arrangements in South Asia.

Chapter 2

THE AGRARIAN ENVIRONMENT AND THE PRODUCTION OF SPACE ON THE ANGLO–GORKHA FRONTIER

1. Introduction

While territories are socially produced spaces, the role of the environment in their constitution cannot be overlooked. In recent decades an environmentalist paradigm has captured the historical imagination to reveal the mutual transformations that characterize the relationship between the environment and human beings.[1] The varied literature that has developed on this theme of environmental history has restored the environment to the center stage of history. Within the South Asian context, recent studies of the environment have examined the role of climate, health and disease and forests in the social, political and economic history of the subcontinent.[2] This chapter builds on these insights in order to gain a better understanding of the connections between the environment and the socio-political forces acting on them that ultimately mediated the production of territory.[3] In order to better understand the spatial dimensions of processes of state formation on the Anglo–Gorkha frontier, the relationships between the environment, land and labor in the production of territory needs to be emphasized.[4] Interactions between human beings and their environment shaped the cultures of governance on this frontier in important ways, producing fluctuating histories of land control. The agency of the environment, along with a host of local actors, has all too frequently been ignored by historians of the Anglo–Gorkha War. Part of the problem has been methodological, because information on such questions can only be gleaned by analyzing data from a variety of local and regional – and not just national – archival repositories. Consequently, scant attention has been paid to agrarian life, the lived experiences of the inhabitants – including the paucity of labor – and their engagement with the densely forested environment that marked the shared frontier of Gorkha and the English East India Company. The dynamism and struggle that was forged within these agrarian environments produced unique signatures in terms of the territorial layout and organization of the Anglo–Gorkha frontier.[5] In the following sections I will examine the forested environment and society of Gorkha's Tarai, the persistent shortage of labor, shifting patterns of land use and the localized struggles over agrarian resources that impacted the organization of territory along the frontier. These variables combined to leave unclear the layout and boundaries of the administrative districts (*parganas* and *tappas*) along the Anglo–Gorkha frontier. The mutually transformatory relations that shaped the agrarian environment and territory would provide an indispensable context for the outbreak of war between the English East India Company and Gorkha in 1814.

2. The Tarai: Environment and Society

The Nepali Tarai took nearly a hundred years (from 1775–1875) to crystallize in its present form.[6] In eighteenth-century Gorkhali documents, it finds initial reference as the "Tarriani" – a narrow strip of thickly-forested plains covering the districts of Chitwan (formerly Marjyadpur), Parsa, Bara, Rautahat, Saptari and Mahottari.[7] At its greatest extent it stretched for over 2,000 kilometers from the district of Naini Tal in the west to Arunachal Pradesh in India's northeast.[8] It varied in breadth from a few kilometers to over 50 kilometers. At various places it straddled administrative divisions belonging to both states, which included the Champaran–Tarriani and Gorakhpur–Butwal sections of the Anglo–Gorkha frontier. At the time of the Anglo–Gorkha War, the Champaran–Tarriani section was formed by the northern reaches of *sarkar* Champaran and Gorkha's Eastern Tarai districts, including the *tappa* of Rautahat (see Maps 2.1, 3.1 and 3.2). Champaran, which had been under the rule of the East India Company since 1765, was divided into four *parganas* – Majhowa (the largest), Mehsi, Babra and Simraon.[9] Gorkha's Eastern Tarai districts – formed of the lands formerly belonging to the hill kingdoms of Makwanpur, Tanahun and Chaudandi – were made up of the following districts (*zillas*), from west to east: Parsa, Bara, *tappa* Rautahat, Mahottari, Saptari, Sarlahi and Morang. Each district was further subdivided, rather haphazardly, into a number of *parganas*, *tappas*, *tarafs* and *mouzas* (or villages which constituted the basic revenue unit), in – though not always – descending order.

The Gorakhpur–Butwal section of the Tarai was formed by a stretch of territory that straddled the northern portions of *sarkar* Gorakhpur and the plains of Butwal, belonging to the petty hill kingdom of Palpa (see Maps 2.2 and 4.1). In November 1801, the *nawab* of Awadh concluded a treaty with the East India Company, ceding the *sarkar* of Gorakhpur to the latter.[10] In 1801, Gorakhpur encompassed an enormous tract of land that included the present day districts of Gorakhpur, Basti and Deoria – a total of 48 *parganas*.[11] Along the northern reaches of *sarkar* Gorakhpur and lying largely within the Company's territories lay the *parganas* of Ratanpur Bansi, Tilpur and Binayakpur (see Map 4.2). On the other side of the frontier lay (from west to east) the *tappas* of Sheoraj, the *taluqas* of Khajahani and Matka (Matuka) and the *pargana* of Binayakpur. These lands which had traditionally been held by the petty hill principalities of Palpa, Pyuthana, Gulmi, Argha and Khanchi had fallen into Gorkhali hands by the end of the eighteenth century. In 1804, the Gorkhalis imprisoned the ruler of Palpa at Kathmandu, and forcibly incorporated his territories lying in the Gorakhpur–Butwal area.[12] In this manner, Gorkha and the English East India Company came to share a common frontier that straddled the *sarkars* of Gorakhpur and Champaran.

This shared frontier formed an intersection of ecological, agrarian, social and political regimes whose extent, though often overlapping, was never constant.[13] The entire region was dissected by numerous rivers and streams, draining from north to south to form the vast drainage system of the Indo–Gangetic plains. The stretch of land lying immediately

Map 2.1 Sketch of the line of boundary between the Nipaul Tarriani and the Zillah Sarun, 1822 CE

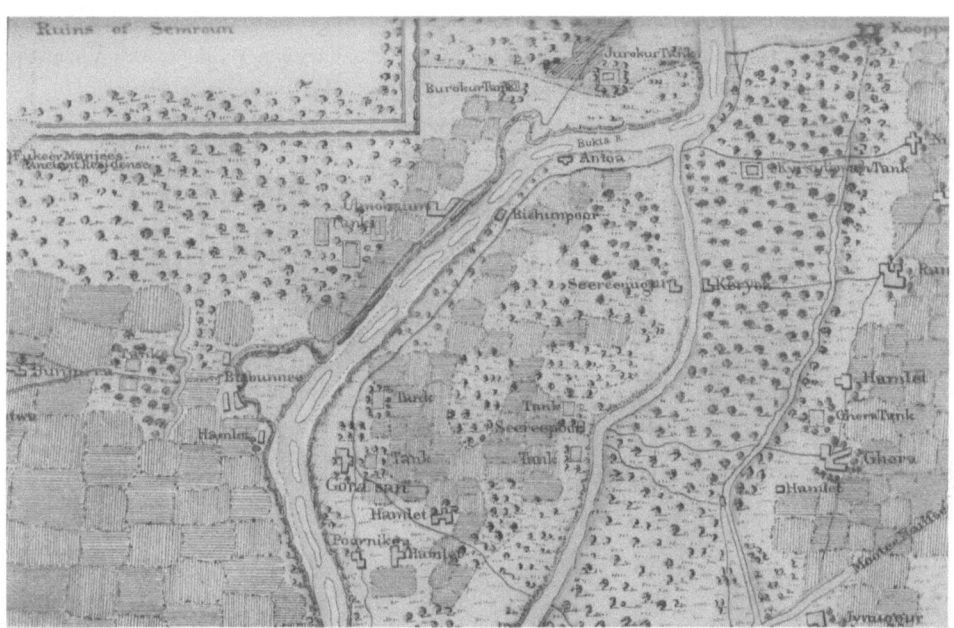

Reproduced by permission of the Surveyor-General of India © The Survey of India.
Source: R. H. Phillimore, Historical Records of the Survey of India, 1815–30 (Dehra Dun, 1954), vol. 3, plate 4.

adjacent and south of the foothills was typically swampy, thickly carpeted with forests and hosting a variety of wild animals, their cover occasionally broken by patches of tall grasslands and valleys (*duns*) which formed potentially rich agricultural niches. The transitional region between the hills and the plains proper, known as the Bhabar, was a zone of alluvial fans composed of highly porous gravels, rocks and sands washed down from the hills. Lying to the north were the foothills that grew progressively in height, ultimately forming the high mountains of the Himalayas.

The soil in these parts was varied in its composition. In the more densely forested areas the soil, being "virgin" (*kalabanjar*), was rich in nutrients. Where the elevation was lower, as in the northern half of Champaran, it was composed of hard clay (*bangar*).[14] Being so, this kind of clayey soil required irrigation in order to cultivate crops such as rice and opium. Along the Gorakhpur–Butwal frontier the surface texture of the soil was usually a combination of loam (*doras*), clay (*matyar*) and sand (*balua*).[15] The northern reaches of Gorakhpur, being at a low level and with moist and clayey soil, possessed numerous *jheels* or lakes which filled up during the rainy season.[16] In the dry season the land would be covered with reeds and remain in an uncultivated state. With a low water table of two to four meters and abundant rainfall, agriculture in these parts did not face the same problems of irrigation as experienced on the Champaran–Tarriani frontier. The harvest months were usually those of Bhadau (August–September) for *rabi* (summer) crops, and Phagun (February–March) and Chait (March–April) for *kharif* (winter) crops.[17]

Map 2.2 "Map of the Northern Frontier of the District of Goruckpoor, where it touches the Nepaulese Dominions, including the Goruckpoor Turrai and that portion of it ceded to the Nepaulese Government comprehending also a Survey of the Course of the Arrah Nuddee, which forms the Boundary between the Territories of His Excellency the Nawab Vizier on the west, and the Goorkhali Dominions on the east," 1818 CE

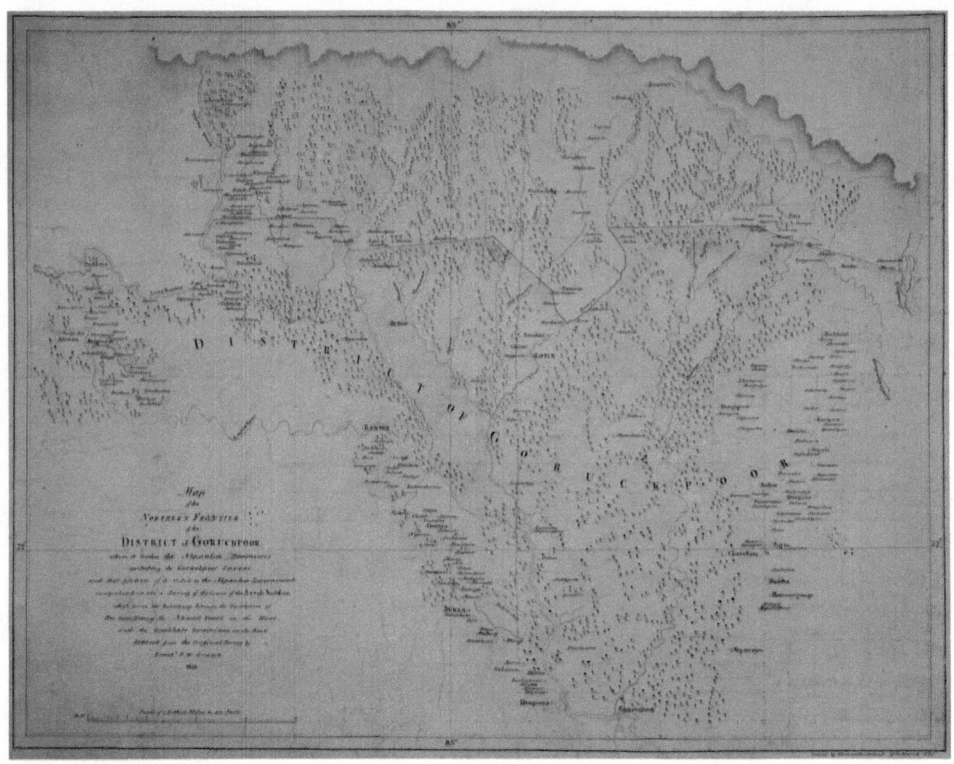

Surveyed by Lt. P. W. Grant. 55.9 × 68.6 cm. Scale = four miles to one inch. Color on cloth-backed paper. Reproduced by permission of the British Library © British Library Board.
Source: India Office Map Collection IOR/X/1432/2, Asia, Pacific & Africa Collections, British Library.

The thick forests that covered this frontier were made up of large sections of mixed trees dominated by *sal* (*Shorea robusta*) and *sisum* (*Dalbergia sisoo*) species. In 1813, forests about a mile thick extended from the foothills of Butwal (*pargana* Binayakpur) into the Tarai.[18] Company officials were aware of the economic value of this timber, which along with rice formed the major exports of the Tarai. Alexander Fraser, an English surgeon stationed at Gorakhpur, noted that in 1813 5,000 straight *sal* trees, 20,000 crooked *sals* and over 60,000 trees of other types were cut from the forests of Gorakhpur. In the same year nearly 8,000 straight *sals* and 3,000 *sisum* timbers alone were cut from the forests of the Butwal Tarai. Given the high value of timber, Fraser recommended that the forests should be brought under the direct management of the government.[19] These forests were also particularly rich in wildlife such as elephants, tigers, monkeys, musk deer, as well as a variety of birds and forest products such as pepper, wax, honey, resins, lac and grass.[20] Like the preceding little kingdoms of the Tarai, the Gorkhalis were also known for collecting revenues from the capture of wild elephants, which in 1793 might have totaled 200–300 elephants.[21] Cattle raising was another source of revenue for the Gorkhalis, with considerable movement of herds from the Company's territories into the Tarriani during the dry season (October-March).[22] The presence of malaria (*aul*) made these forests difficult for human habitation, and between May and October every year, when the disease was rampant, most inhabitants would relocate to more hospitable regions till the summer had passed. Only forest communities such as the Tharu, who through their long residence had developed resistance to malaria, remained. Consequently, malaria discouraged extensive immigration into the region, and severely curtailed the activities of government officials to the few months of the cold season.[23] During the summer months, the raja of Palpa, along with his followers, would abandon the town of Butwal and ascend to cooler places such as Nayakot in the hills.[24] The same was also true of traders and travelers who left the town to return again in the cooler winter months. The added presence of robbers, forest tribes and the reputation of the Tharu for practicing sorcery rendered this frontier region a zone of danger and fear in the popular imagination.

A variety of social groups inhabited the Anglo–Gorkha Tarai. The Tharu formed a sizeable community of pioneer cultivators. In fact, in 1812, out of the estimated population of 124,000 in Gorkha's Eastern Tarai approximately half were Tharu. The other half was a mixture of other cultivating castes such as Ahirs and Kurmis, with a sprinkling of Brahman, Rajputs and Kayasths.[25] In addition to these were a number of mobile groups such as the Banjaras, forest tribes such as the Banturs, and Bhars, who probably practiced non-sedentary "shifting" agriculture and collected forest products.[26] The Banturs, while practicing shifting farming, also supplemented their income by selling charcoal, firewood and other forest products to the villages that lay along this frontier. The Bhars were knows to have collected resins (*damar*) from the *sal* tree. The inhabitants along this sparsely populated frontier practiced a mixed economy of shifting cultivation combined with reliance on forest products and activities such as fishing. A mobile mix of cultivating, pastoral and service castes emerged whose fortunes followed the vagaries of their existence on the Anglo–Gorkha frontier.

3. Labor

In the late eighteenth and early nineteenth centuries, the Champaran–Tarriani and Gorakhpur–Butwal sections of the Tarai formed an expanding agrarian frontier with a growing population. At the time of the advent of the English East India Company's authority, the population of Champaran was estimated to have doubled from 12 lakhs in the 1790s to approximately 25 lakhs in 1811.[27] The Bengal famine of 1769–70 also induced large-scale migration into the Tarriani from Champaran.[28] The extent of land under cultivation increased from around 3 percent at the end of the sixteenth century (in 1594) to over 10 percent at the beginning of the eighteenth century (from 1707–20).[29] By the end of the eighteenth century, this figure seems to have then risen to 25 percent.[30] On the Gorakhpur–Butwal and Champaran–Tarriani frontiers agricultural labor was drawn from numerous cultivating groups such as the Tharus, Ahirs and Kurmis, and mobile "tribes" such as the Domkatars, Bhars, Musahars and Banjaras.[31]

Eager to exploit the agrarian resources of the Tarai, the Gorkhalis made grants of taxable and tax-free lands and issued contracts for the collection of revenue. Local landed magnates, cultivating groups like the Tharu and even ascetic orders of Gosains were the recipients of such state patronage.[32] The Gosains and other ascetic groups received tracts of tax-free lands in order to set up and support their monastic orders in the Tarai. For instance, the ascetics and abbots of the Vaisnavite Ramanandi sect were given extensive tax-free lands around the modern town of Janakpurdham in Gorkha's Eastern Tarai.[33] State officials hoped that such land grants would preserve existing tax collection arrangements while extending cultivation into new areas. Consequently, many Gorkhali land grants in the Tarai were made up of both cultivable and waste lands. For example, the lands granted by Gorkhali kings to the Hanumanagar Monastery (1781) and Ram Chandra Monastery (1807) had a cultivable to waste land ratio of 1:1 and 1:3 respectively.[34] There is now ample evidence to suggest that the political formations on this frontier pursued long-standing strategies of partnering with these mendicant orders to further agrarian expansion, stabilize governance and promote interregional trade.[35]

Despite the growing intensification of agrarian activity and rising population figures at this time, there was an acute shortage of labor in the Tarai lands along the Anglo–Gorkha frontier. Malarial forests and the seasonal character of cultivation and residence, combined with the periodic outbursts of war in the latter half of the eighteenth century produced frequent dislocations in labor supply that were hard to overcome. In fact, so serious was this shortage of labor that Kathmandu frequently issued clear instructions to its Eastern Tarai officials to do everything in their power to attract cultivators. Thus, while agrarian contractors were forbidden from bringing labor from revenue paying lands (*malko raiti nabasaunu*) they were encouraged to import cultivators (*raiti*) from Moglan or even from other lands assigned to Gorkhali officials in lieu of cash salaries (*jagir*) or on an inheritable basis (*birta*).[36] For instance, in 1810 *sardar* Gaj Singh Khatri was ordered to procure respectable persons (*bhala manis*) and cultivators (*ryots*) from Moglan to retain and settle culturable forest lands (*kalabanjar*) in Morung.[37] And again, in 1805 CE (1862 BS) *jagirdars* and *birtadars* of Bara and Saptari Districts (in Gorkha's Tarai) invited cultivators from India in order to replace local revenue-paying peasantry on *kalabanjar* lands.[38] In neighboring Gorakhpur, cultivators shifted from one place to another, irrespective of the government in power, in order to take advantage of available tax concessions or to elude excessive demands.[39] Consequently, there were many instances of desertion as labor was enticed away by promises of low rental rates. Perhaps it is for these very reasons that in 1803 the Palpali king, Prithvipal Sen, lamented the loss of the *taluqa* (or estate) of Matka caused by the migration of its *raiyats* (cultivators) to Gorakhpur District.[40] Moreover, cultivating groups such as the Tharus resisted any undue exactions by voting with their feet. In 1791, the Gosains and Tharus of *pargana* Koradi (Mahottari District), who had fled to India (Moglan) following oppression by *amils* (revenue collectors), were asked to return and restore the *pargana* to its former state.[41] Again, in Mahottari District shortages of labor in the eighteenth century induced a number of Vaishnavaite abbots holding *kusa birta* (rent-free) grants from the kings of Makwanpur (and later reconfirmed by Gorkha) to take responsibility for the (more lucrative) collection of revenue on crown lands.[42] In 1762 following the conquest of Makwanpur by Gorkha, many Tharus fled the Eastern

Plate 2.1 Gorkhali king Pratap Singh Shah's (1775–1777 CE) *lal mohar* (red seal document) to Tharu magnate Hem Chaudhari, 1776 CE

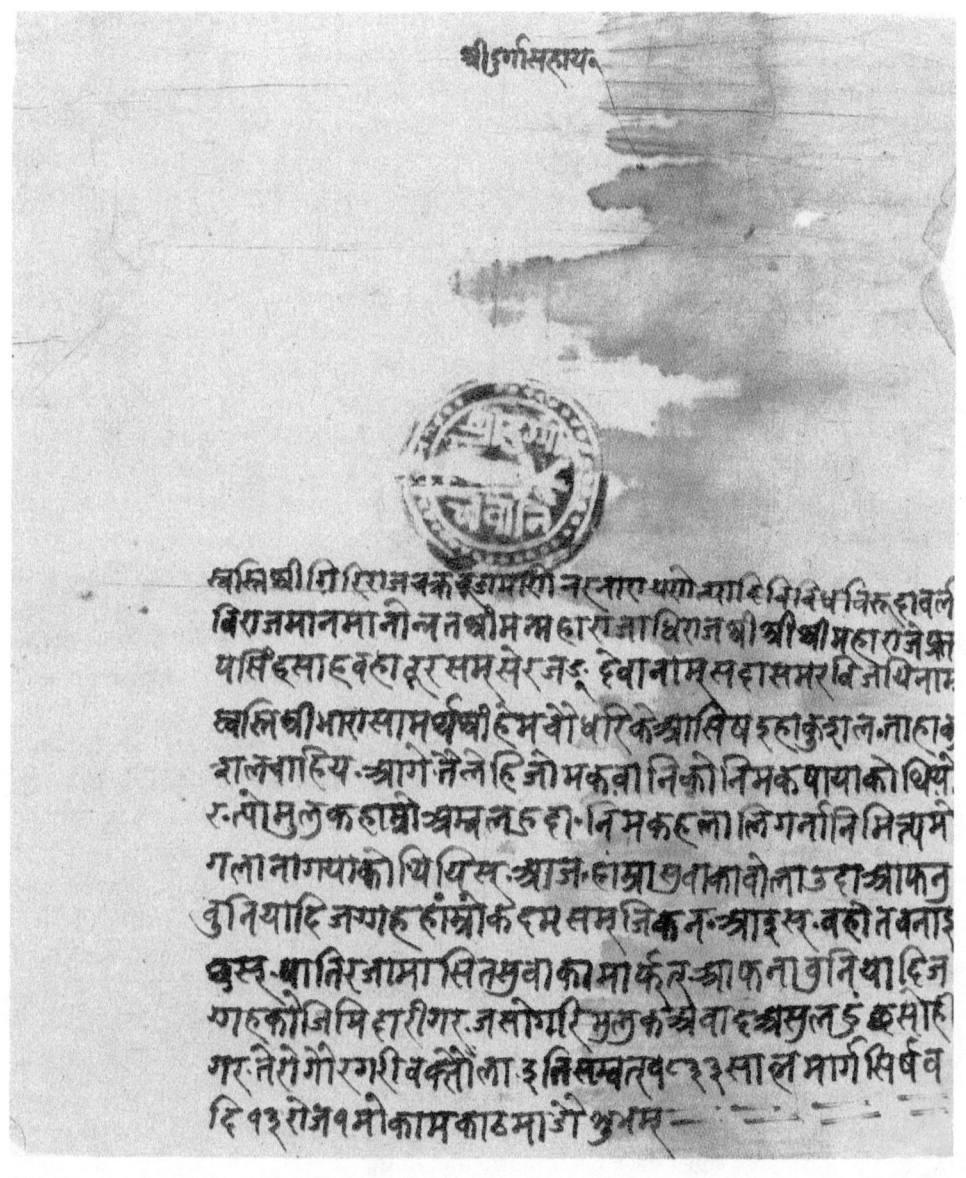

This document reconfirms Hem Chaudhari's revenue collection rights in the territories of the Makwani kingdom following its conquest by Gorkha in 1762. Reproduced by permission of Kurt Meyer and Pamela Deuel Meyer.
Source: Giselle Krauskopf, Tej Narain Panjiar and Tek Bahadur Shrestha, eds, *The Kings of Nepal and the Tharu of the Tarai: The Panjiar Collection of Fifty Royal Documents from 1726–1971* (Los Angeles: Rusca Press; Kirtipur: Centre for Nepal and Asian Studies, 2000), Document 2, pp. 118–19.

Tarai regions to the safety of Champaran. Later, Kathmandu recalled them promising to restore them to their former holdings (see Plate 2.1).⁴³ Elsewhere, the arrest of the Palpali raja in Kathmandu in 1804 created a panic in the Butwal Tarai, which induced the flight of labor from the Butwal area to the Company's territories.⁴⁴ At the same time, large numbers of cultivators migrated from Awadh to the Company's territories in order to escape the heavy assessments imposed upon them by the *amils* of that kingdom.⁴⁵ Such a shortage of labor also gave rise to stiff competition, resulting in disputes over entitlements to appropriate taxes, crops, forest and water resources, and boundaries. Given these dynamics, there was much back-and-forth movement of labor between the territories of Gorkha and those of the Company.⁴⁶ The agrarian landscape pulsated in sync with these flows of labor as patches of land fell in and out of cultivation.

Thus for a variety of reasons land on the Anglo–Gorkha frontier cycled between cultivation, commons and waste, depending on the availability of agricultural labor and the concessions offered or exactions imposed by agrarian elites and state officials. In 1814, the *tappas* that marked the northern boundary of Gorakhpur consisted of Dhebrua, Khajahani, Banjaraha and Dholia Bandar (belonging to *pargana* Ratanpur Bansi); Bhatipar, Mirchwar, Sirsia and Nagwa (lying in *pargana* Binayakpur); and Sukrahar, Khas and Domakhand (in *pargana* Tilpur). The lands constituting these *tappas* registered frequent fluctuations between their use for cultivation, commons and waste. An instance of this can be found in the case of *tappa* Dhebrua which lay across the disputed Gorkhali *tappa* of Sheoraj and at one time was made up of 60 *mauzas* (villages). While most of the lands lay in a state of "waste" from 1752, they increasingly came under cultivation after 1792, and by 1811 amounted to 48 *mauzas*.⁴⁷ On many occasions, it became difficult for Company officials to distinguish between lands that lay under their jurisdiction and those that belonged to Gorkha. Commenting on this, D. Scott, the acting magistrate of Gorakhpur in 1811, noted that since uncultivated lands remained more in "a state of commons than of private pasture grounds, it becomes in many cases a matter of difficulty to ascertain what waste land has been hitherto subject to the British government and what has been usurped by the Nypalese."⁴⁸ Such dynamism produced the illegible agrarian landscapes of the Anglo–Gorkha frontier, making it hard for officials from both the East India Company and Gorkha to discern and manage what was really taking place on the ground.

It is possible that on the Anglo–Gorkha frontier such patterns of flexible and shifting cultivation indicated the availability of a class of *pahikasht* cultivators – or persons who cultivated lands in a village other than to the one to which they belonged.⁴⁹ The presence of such mobile labor must have been substantial in this region, at least on the northern fringes of the district where the most barren tracts lay. English surveyor and traveler Francis Buchanan-Hamilton noted the presence of just under 20,000 persons who would qualify as *pahikasht* and who were active in the northern police jurisdictions (*thanas*) of Bansi, Dholiya Bandar, Pali, Lotan and Nichlaul.⁵⁰ In fact around the late eighteenth century these northern tracts remained predominantly *pahikasht* holdings. *Pahikasht* cultivators were constantly on the move, drawn to cultivate *Banjar* lands on short-term leases for up to three years, after which they would move on in search of new lands to cultivate.⁵¹ Historian Christopher Bayly's observations on the phenomenon of *pahikasht* cultivation in northern India are relevant to the argument here, when he notes that "Cultivators of this sort [i.e. *pahikasht*] provided a shifting population of agrarian servants and specialists whose movements in response to political change could rapidly transform an area from high cultivation to wilderness, or vice-versa."[52] Commenting on the synergistic relationship that existed between *pahikasht* labor and the land in the northern tracts of Gorakhpur, historian Meena Bhargava concludes that "the ability of the economy of Gorakhpur to repeople, recycle and revive agriculture speaks for its resilient, adaptive and flexible nature."[53] Bhargava's comments about the northern reaches of Gorakhpur District echo similar patterns unfolding elsewhere on the Champaran–Tarriani frontier. Thus, the agrarian environments of the Anglo–Gorkha frontier created a tract of land rich in forest and resources for cultivation that interacted dynamically with mobile populations and extractive agrarian regimes. These human agents engaged with their environment to forge a field of activity that was marked by negotiations and contests as they sought to gain access to and control over the rich agrarian resources of the Anglo–Gorkha frontier. Frequent contests over such resources were one of the marked features of cultures of governance on this frontier. Such dynamism in the agrarian environment had an ebb and flow-like quality which left its impression on the organization and layout of the territory, resulting in the creation of a mosaic of forests, fields and waste lands on the Anglo–Gorkha frontier.

4. Forest–Field–Waste Mosaics on the Anglo–Gorkha Frontier

A discussion of agrarian spaces needs to consider the presence of "waste lands," a term that occurs frequently in East India Company records. The use of this term in Company records was in some ways misleading because it minimized the crucial role these lands played in the reproduction and transformation of the agrarian landscapes of the region. "Waste" as a category did not signify a permanent condition for lands to lie in; rather, it denoted a variety of land-use patterns that over time embraced forests, grasslands, and farms that were invariably shaped by local and supra-local systems of power.[54] So the generic category of "waste lands" could in reality encapsulate lands that for various reasons (transhumance, warfare or famine) shifted back and forth between cultivation, commons, fallow and waste.[55] Unpacking the category of "waste lands" calls for its historicization, which then makes it possible to discern the various environmental and social factors that ultimately led to shifting patterns of "waste land" use. For purposes of governance, states – both indigenous and colonial – were aware of the fluid character of these waste lands, their implications for tax collection/evasion and the synchronization between their ebb and flow and the structure of territory. That land lay to "waste" was not due to the indolence of cultivators or the despotism of local rulers. Rather, the diversity of waste land types encoded dynamic patterns of local struggles over land, resistance to the tax claims of ruling authorities, shifting patterns of land use and shortages of labor, all of which caused lands to fall in and out of the category of "waste." The actual extent of these waste lands eluded the prying eyes of the Company state during the first 50 years of colonial rule (1765–1815).[56] This section will only look at the question of "wastelands" along the Anglo–Gorkha frontier; a fuller account of their polyvalent histories and contributions to territorial dynamism remains to be written and lies beyond the scope of this book.

In the Company records there are considerable references to patches of land lying in an uncultivated state along the Champaran–Tarriani frontier. For example, in Champaran over half the area of the northern *tappas* of Rajpur Soharria, Jamauli, Chigwan Batsara and Manpur Chowdand were covered with forest, grasslands and uncultivated "waste land." In 1788, Archibald Montgomerie, the Company-appointed Collector of Saran District noted that *sarkar* Champaran contained an "immense" quantity of wastelands that were fit for cultivation, and which for the most part lay along the border of the Nipal [Nepal] territories.[57] In fact, the entire northern reaches of the Raj Ramnagar (*tappas* Chigwan, Jamauli and Ramgir) were covered by grassland.[58] The existence of such grasslands triggered a regular sequence of cattle movements, with grazers from the neighboring districts of Gorakhpur, Azamgarh and Saran bringing in their cattle to graze on these lands.[59] Over a period of time such "waste lands" came to represent a complex composite of various types of cultivable wastes (fallow lands that could either be forest fallows or grass fallows), uncultivable wastes, forest lands (cultivable or uncultivable) and common lands.

A substantial number of Gorkhali land grants that pertained to the Eastern Tarai included uncultivated forest lands (*kalabanjar zamin*). Grantees were instructed to clear the forest, establish settlements and encourage cultivation (*abad gulzar garnu*).[60] Tharu communities played a crucial role in such projects of agrarian expansion and recent documents bear testimony to this fact.[61] However, the physical extent of these forests was never static as they might have been cleared for cultivation, only to return to forest or a state of "waste." Such developments and their attendant spatial implications unfolded in the area of *pargana* Simraon, where 22 villages fell under dispute at the time of the Anglo–Gorkha War in 1814. This area contained a sizeable quantity of "waste lands." In 1815, Lt. Col. Paris Bradshaw, the Company's political agent to Nepal, noted that the areas east of Bara Garhi and *pargana* Simraon were "surprisingly" barren.[62] While Bir Kishor Singh, the raja of Bettiah, had claimed these lands, he had never included them in the revenue settlement of his estate with the British in 1799.[63] The raja may have tried to conceal information relating to the resources and revenue-yielding capacity of these 22 villages by claiming them as lying in a state of waste, a practice widespread among landholders of the region who had always tried to elude the claims of superior authorities. In the meantime, the lands might have been cultivated by various client groups with unstable allegiances to Gorkha or the East India Company. Whatever the circumstances, it might be reasonable to suggest that for a variety of reasons, patches of land could slip between cultivation and "waste" with their "ownership" and visibility in the historical record determined by the local arrangements of agrarian power and the success or failure to resist the tax claims of superior authorities. Shifts in the supply of labor would have hastened this unfolding dialectic to produce the pulsating "waste lands" of the region, a process that would extend well into the nineteenth century.[64]

Elsewhere on the Anglo–Gorkha frontier, a considerable portion of Gorakhpur District – amounting to as much as 50 percent in some areas – remained *wairan* (waste). Writing in 1810, Mufti Ghulam Hazrat noted that *wairan* lands could be found mainly in the *tappas* of Anowla, Bansi, Sylhet, Basti, Maghar and Gorakhpur, either due to the presence of thick forests, the depredations of wild animals (such as wild elephants) or even the scarcity of tenants.[65] A similar situation prevailed in the lands lying along the Gorakhpur–Butwal frontier. Gorakhpur's first English Collector, John Routledge, in his initial survey of the district in 1802, noted the presence of uncultivated waste lands, with a high incidence of migration to areas like Butwal.[66] The *tappa* of Dholiya Bandar (also known as Birdpur Ghaus) was probably the most desolate of the *tappas* on Gorakhpur's northern frontier, and was described as "poorly cultivated, interspersed with stretches of waste land which is partly clear and partly covered with withered long grass and partly occupied by ugly bushes and thorns."[67] The *thanas* of Lotan and Nichlaul, and to a lesser extent *thana* Parrona, also exhibited the same tendencies.[68] The *pargana* of Bansi in the northern reaches of Gorakhpur District had a total of 1,289,680 Calcutta *bighas* out of which only 280,840 were cultivated; the remaining *bighas* (over one million) were left uncultivated for various unspecified reasons. The British surveyor Francis Buchanan-Hamilton, after studying the records of accountants (*quanungos*), concluded that this *pargana* possessed 2,332 *mauzas*, of which only 1,118 were occupied. Even rent-free lands, which had a higher incidence of cultivation, had as much as one-fourth remaining uncultivated. Moreover, the northern *tappas* of Dhebrua and Khajahani along the Anglo–Gorkha frontier had very few villages in cultivation in 1801, and it was only in 1813 that the Company made a direct settlement (*kham*) with Sarabjit Singh, the raja of Bansi.[69] Such a state of affairs persisted even after the conclusion of the Anglo–Gorkha War and well into the second decade of the nineteenth century. For instance, in 1817 Gorakhpur District had a total *raqba* (measured area) of 3,821,819 *bighas*, of which 1,326,400 *bighas* were fit for cultivation and 1,200,616 were deemed waste. Even so, out of all the *bighas* fit for cultivation, only 748,498 *bighas* were actually cultivated.[70] At the time of the Anglo–Gorkha War, the lands of the Gorakhpur–Butwal Tarai remained sparsely populated, poorly cultivated and composed of a mix of "waste lands" and forests. The Company and its predecessor regimes were very aware of this situation and offered various incentives to promote cultivation. For instance, the rulers (*nawabs*) of Awadh granted allowances (*nankar*) to the rajas of Bansi and Amorha as reward for their efforts in clearing the forest for cultivation.[71] The Company confirmed these rights on its accession, and issued *jangalbari pattas* which allowed cultivators to reclaim waste lands on concessional terms.[72]

5. Conclusion: Agrarian Environments and the Production of Space

The Anglo–Gorkha frontier afforded its inhabitants a vast zone of possibilities, especially for individuals and groups seeking to exert their agrarian agency in the presence of political regimes and landed magnates. The agrarian environment of the frontier created dynamic and fluid cultures of governance where groups of mobile cultivators, forest dwellers, bandits and other subaltern groups blunted the ruling elite's ability to extract taxes, tribute and other material and symbolic entitlements. The frontier became a potential zone of refuge from, and resistance to, state power while at the same time attracting agrarian entrepreneurs and revenue contractors to invest in the productive potentials of the land. Frequent political realignments and conflicts produced changes in tenurial, taxation and customary arrangements (see Chapters 3 and 4). The shortage of labor was a perennial concern for these entrepreneurs and managers, who made every effort to secure access to this scarce resource through enticements, coercion, violence and forced conscription. This, combined with the added variable of malarial forests, ultimately gave rise to an ebb and flow in patterns of land use.[73]

The dynamic interactions of ecology, land use and labor flows produced the mobile agrarian spaces of the Anglo–Gorkha frontier. Lands lying along this frontier were subject to considerable fluctuation as patches slipped back and forth between forest, pasture, fallow, cultivation and uncultivated waste. It is not always easy to discern the complexity of land-use patterns along the Anglo–Gorkha frontier through a passive reading of the official records of the East India Company and Gorkha, since they tend to gloss over the social and ecological tensions that may have been involved in the production of lands that were deemed as "waste" or "barren." Under certain conditions, such as the availability of labor, water and political will, "waste" lands were transformed into cultivated tracts. On the other hand, the lack of labor, combined with political instability, famine and malaria could result in the discontinuation of cultivation for varying lengths of time. In spatial terms, patches of land kept slipping back and forth between cultivation and "waste," as the case may be. On the Anglo–Gorkha frontier processes of statemaking and cultures of governance unfolded within a context of such flexible human–environment interactions and arrangements that it in turn produced a fluctuating layout of forests with dispersed fields and wastelands.[74]

Histories of such shifting land-use patterns can provide important insights into the changing architecture of the administrative divisions to which these lands must have ultimately belonged. One conclusion that emerges is that since lands kept falling in and out of cultivation they must have also have affected the territorial layout and boundaries of an administrative division (whether *tappa*, *pargana*, or *mauza*). Typically, the basic unit of these divisions was the village (*mauzas*) and its attached lands. While these lands would be entered into the account books as attached to some administrative division (such as a *pargana* or *tappa*) in one year, it was highly likely that they would fall into a state of waste the next year and then subsequently be removed from the account registers for that year. Furthermore, because cultivation depended on the availability of labor and some organizing authority, lands frequently tended to shift back and forth between agents belonging to different states. In this case, cultivated patches of land from an administrative unit along the Anglo–Gorkha frontier could come under the extractive levies of some local magnate or petty chief in one year, remain waste in another, and then revert to cultivation in the third, only this time in the hands of some new source of political authority. While the physical land did not actually shift back and forth, it most certainly did in the account registers as well as in the structure of agrarian entitlements that combined to represent and constitute territory along the frontier.

All this left the Anglo–Gorkha frontier a fuzzy, incoherent zone of territorial divisions. For officials from both states these mobile spaces eluded state control and posed problems of legibility for governing authorities. The actual extent, boundaries and internal organization of many frontier administrative divisions remained fluid, discontinuous and intermixed. In many instances, and especially along the frontier, the boundary separating the Company's territories from Gorkha was difficult to discern, and so, for instance, in 1811 the Magistrate of Bareilly noticed quite by accident that Gorkhali officials had built a fort in Kheri on the Anglo–Gorkha frontier. The Magistrate was certain that the Gorkhalis had not occupied these tracts of lands two years previously. He observed that, "Such is the undefined boundary between the two governments and our want of local information of the extent of our territories in the unexplored tract of country along the foot of the hills, that doubts may be entertained whether even the acquisitions of the Nepalese which are stated to appertain to the pergana [sic] of Kherigarh can be pronounced encroachment on our territories."[75] While the case of the boundary at Kheri remained a trifling one, the situation along the Champaran–Tarriani frontier took on a more ominous tone. It is to this that we must now turn.

Chapter 3

THE CHAMPARAN–TARRIANI FRONTIER

[…] the British possessions, […] as classed by governments and revenue or judicial divisions, must be considered only *approximations to truth* on a subject, in its nature of great difficulty, and which has hitherto not received from the Indian authorities the degree of attention which its *practical value* and importance is entitled to.

—John Crawfurd[1]

1. Introduction: The Constitution of Order on the Champaran–Tarriani Frontier, 1765–1814

Between 1765 and 1814, Gorkha and the English East India Company witnessed a phase of territorial expansion which culminated in the outbreak of serious territorial disputes along the Champaran–Tarriani frontier. This section of the Anglo–Gorkha frontier stretched across Gorkha's Eastern Tarai districts and the northern reaches of the district of Champaran (in Bihar) that fell under the jurisdiction of the Company (see Map 3.1).[2] Gorkha's Eastern Tarai, which was made up of the districts of Chitwan (formerly Marjyadpur), Parsa, Bara, Rautahat, Saptari and Mahottari, was placed under the charge of officials who exercised civil, military and judicial powers.[3] During the reign of King Girbana Juddha Bikram Shah (1799–1816), numerous land grants were issued conferring new rights or reconfirming preexisting arrangements that had been instituted by the preceding Sen rulers of Makwanpur, Tanahu, Chaudandi and Bijaypur. Kathmandu's ruling elite became increasingly invested in establishing institutional arrangements for the collection of revenue and establishing law and order. High-ranking Gorkhali officials participated in the creation of an institutional order that would enable them to gain access to the agrarian resources of the Tarai.[4] Gorkhali officials at Kathmandu, despite their differences, had a strong interest in preserving their claims vis-à-vis the East India Company, which had also been trying to establish its administration in the region.[5] In *sarkar* Champaran, the East India Company had instituted revenue settlements, such as a nine year settlement in 1791 and finally the Permanent Settlement in 1793, by which time the revenue obligations of landholders were fixed in perpetuity.[6]

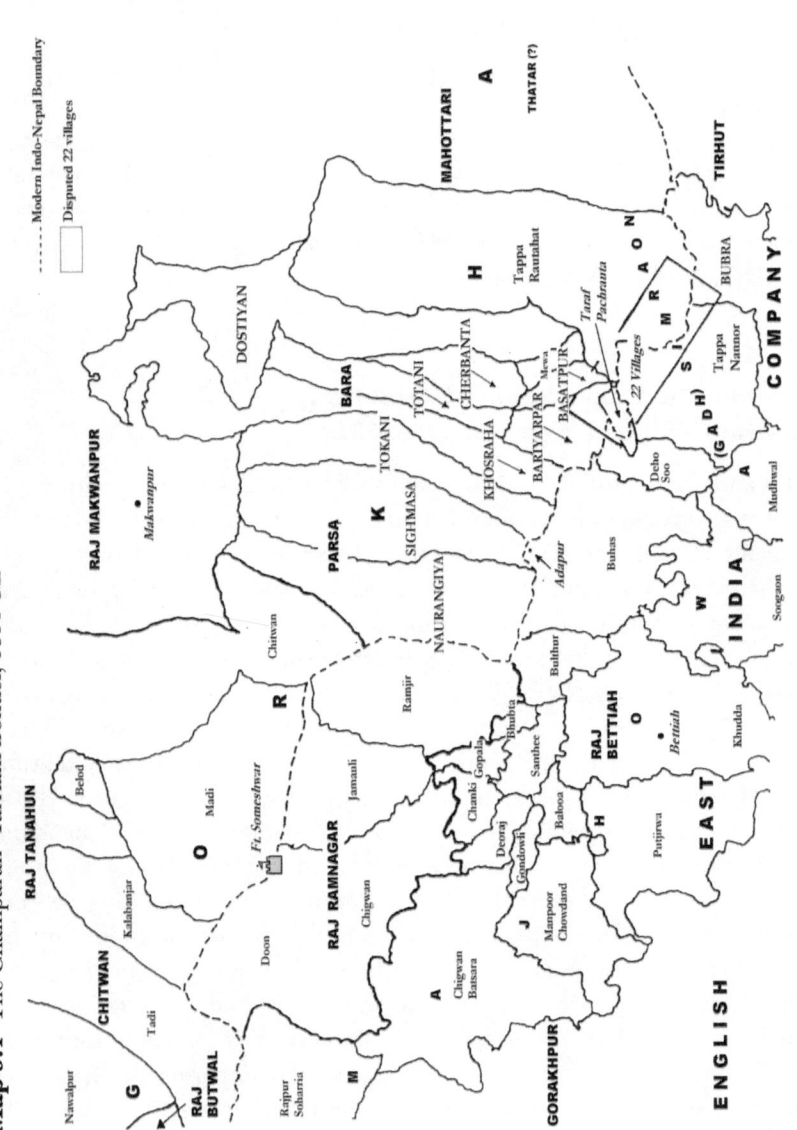

Map 3.1 The Champaran–Tarriani frontier, 1814 CE

Mapwork by Bernardo A. Michael.

2. Cultures of Governance and Illegible Landscapes on the Champaran–Tarriani Frontier

The growing presence of Gorkhali and East India Company officials along their shared frontier produced cultures of governance that were heavily informed by local factors, including the territorial dynamics of little kingdoms. On the Champaran–Tarriani frontier, they were unable to exact compliance from local officials or landholders in the faithful representation of the resources under their jurisdictions and in the submission of revenue. Such uncertainty in landed affairs posed considerable problems of legibility for central authorities. Given the presence of dynamic local forces, these illegible landscapes constituted a persistent feature of processes of statemaking along the Anglo–Gorkha frontier. These local forces refracted, resisted, compromised and subverted the initiatives of central authorities. At the same time, the frequent changes and contests involving the structure of entitlements concerning rights to land, agrarian authority, taxation and tribute produced territories with shifting, intermixed bodies and unclear boundaries. On the Anglo–Gorkha frontier this meant that neither Gorkhali nor Company officials had any precise information about the actual location, layout, resources and boundaries of the administrative divisions lying along and across this frontier. Commenting on this state of affairs Sir John Shore, a high-ranking Company official, made the following observation in 1785:

> I may venture to pronounce that the state of the districts is now less known and the revenue less understood than in 1771. Since the natives have had the disposal of accounts, since they have been introduced as agents and trusted with authority, intricacy and confusion have taken place [...] The simplest matters of fact are designedly covered with a veil through which no human understanding could penetrate.[7]

Such a state of affairs persisted up to the time of the outbreak of the war in 1814. In fact, between 1765 and 1793 revenue engagements involving Company officials and local landholders were based mostly on conjecture, due to the lack of necessary information and also due to the manipulations of local officials and landholders. There are numerous instances of this. Within the district of Champaran, a petition presented in 1808 by of one of the sons of a big *zamindar*, Sri Krishen Singh, vividly recalled the kind of maneuvering that went on prior to the conclusion of the decennial settlement in 1791. In fact, so widespread were such instances of local negotiation that English officials at the time of the Permanent Settlement in 1793 had little idea of what was actually transpiring around them.[8] The Permanent Settlement of 1793, which fixed in perpetuity the land revenue for British provinces in Eastern India, was made without any specification of the available resources or actual extent of the Company's territories. This was the situation in frontier districts like Champaran.[9] The importance of understanding the Permanent Settlement against this background of territorial illegibility has never been fully acknowledged in the literature on the subject.[10]

Gorkhali officials at Kathmandu encountered similar problems of legibility when it came to setting up institutions for the administration and collection of revenue in the districts of the Eastern Tarai. Here Gorkhali officials crafted two broad sets of institutional arrangements for the regular collection of revenue – either by entering into contracts with collectors (*ijara*) or by Gorkhali officials themselves undertaking direct collections of taxes (*amana*t).[11] Between 1780 and 1814, the *ijara* system prevailed, with the *amanat* system replacing it in the years 1793–1800, and again in 1814 when all Eastern Tarai districts were once again brought under the *amanat* system, with the exception of the districts of Saptari–Mahottari. From the very outset the reclamation of land and the maximization of revenues were the twin thrusts of the land revenue policies formulated at Kathmandu. In 1793, 1797, 1805, 1810 and 1813 officials were deputed to inquire into details of revenue administration in the Eastern Tara districts.[12] The reclamation of "waste" lands was encouraged in many areas of the Eastern Tarai.[13] At the same time high ranking officials in the Gorkhali court like Bhim Sen Thapa, Dal Mardan Shah, Gajraj Mishra, Chandrashekhar Upadhyaya, Shri Krishan Pandit and Ranganath Pandit were awarded grants of land in the Eastern Tarai.[14] Again, between 1780 and 1799, the Gorkhali *vakil* (envoy) Dinanath Upadhyaya held numerous revenue collection contracts (*ijara*) in Gorkha's Eastern Tarai districts.[15] Members of Gorkha's ruling elite who received revenue contracts in the Eastern Tarai often had important offices conferred upon them.[16] It is highly likely that members of the Gorkhali court would have aggressively pushed for the preservation of their territorial claims along the Anglo–Gorkha frontier. That the Gorkhali state was internally riven with rivalries is clear from correspondence and the clandestine meetings that East India Company officials were holding with Gorkhali commanders like *budakaji* (elder *kaji*), Amar Singh Thapa and Hasti Dal Shah on the western front. Amar Singh indicated that if the Eastern Tarai lands belonging to rival courtiers like Ranganath Pandit, Dalabhanjan Pande and their allies were to be relinquished to the British, the Anglo–Gorkha War could have been terminated. The role of factional politics at the court in Kathmandu in leading to the Anglo–Gorkha War cannot be conclusively ruled out.[17]

However, it was not just high-ranking courtiers at Kathmandu but local officials as well who contributed to the territorial illegibility along the frontier. They enjoyed considerable freedom in their day-to-day activities and became the subjects of frequent complaints of oppression, over-taxation and misappropriation of revenues, which incurred the censure of authorities at Kathmandu. In 1800 CE Kathmandu wrote to district chief (*subba*) Brahmanand Padhya and military commander (*fauzdar*) Mahima Khawas who were also revenue contractors (*ijaradar*) of Saptari district saying:

> We have granted the Ijara to you so that you may make the country populous and prosperous, collect the prescribed taxes and levies from the ryots on the basis of the lands allotted to them and not to oppress them. We have not appointed you as Ijaradar so that you may dispossess the Chaudharis, Kanugoyes and Mokaddams of Saptari of whatever they have. Some ryots have now fled to Moglan [the plains of North India], while others have come to us, complaining that oppression is rampant there. We have promulgated regulations in your name so that you may act justly. But you have not maintained the sanctity of our signature [on the regulations]. Why then did you accept these regulations? You have indulged in oppression, and made forcible collections in different areas.[18]

Some Gorkhali officers, based in the Eastern Tarai, were particularly notorious for such activities despite Kathmandu's repeated warnings to them to desist. For instance, one Achal Thapa received eight censures from Kathmandu for indulging in various "illegal" practices, including unauthorized collections, during his four years as *subba* of Saptari-Mahottari 1810–15.[19] Similar injunctions were passed against other officials like *subba* Dashrath Khatri, *subba* Chandra Bir Thapa and *sardar* Parshuram Thapa.[20] Such charges of misappropriation were also made against officials at the highest levels of the Gorkhali administration. A charge of misappropriation of state funds was made by former Gorkhali ruler Ran Bahadur Shah against his half-brother *chautariya* (a high-ranking minister) and royalty Sher Bahadur Shah, and senior administrators (*kaji*) Tribhuwan Khawas and Narsing Gurung, which then precipitated his assassination by Sher Bahadur Shah in 1806.[21]

Thus, between 1765 and 1814, Gorkha's governance in the Eastern Tarai districts was administratively ineffectual, yielding irregular and sometimes declining revenues, and being prone to local (re)negotiation and dispute.[22] Gorkhali officials, landholders, merchants and cultivators jostled to form all kinds of coalitions aimed at appropriating the rich resources of the Tarai, while authorities at Kathmandu occasionally tried to regulate such practices by instituting commissions of inquiry while threatening to punish the guilty.[23] In a number of instances lands were brought under the direct management of the state through salaried officials specially deputed for this purpose (*amanat*) or farmed out (*ijara*) to local landholders and agrarian managers. However, such measures met with little success, and authorities in Kathmandu struggled to create stable arrangements for the collection of revenue in the decades leading to 1814 CE.

Further complicating the picture were jurisdictional conflicts that broke out between Gorkhali administrators. For instance in 1805, when complaints of oppression had reached a particularly high level in the Tarai, judges were dispatched from Kathmandu to look into them. But a jurisdictional conflict arose between the judges and *ijaradars*. The latter complained that the jurisdiction of the judges affected their (the *ijaradars*') income and prevented them from meeting their contractual obligations. The authorities at Kathmandu relented and asked the judges not to interfere in the judicial functions of the *ijaradars*, but only to hear complaints made against them.[24] Complicating this picture was the unfixed and fluctuating nature of official jurisdictions, which did not always overlap with existing territorial divisions. While on the one hand single offices could be shared by two or more people, on the other hand an official holding a single office had a jurisdiction that covered more than one district.[25]

Thus, by 1814, practices of governance on the Anglo–Gorkha frontier were characterized by innumerable instances of unauthorized exactions, jurisdictional trespass and stiff competition to control land and labor. Multi-cornered contests created a plastic set of institutional arrangements that characterized cultures of governance, leaving Kathmandu and Calcutta's control over their Tarai districts provisional and incomplete. This view steers away from simplified accounts of the Anglo–Gorkha War that understand the conflict in terms of the rivalries of two monolithic states without giving due recognition to the active role of the highly localized and regional forces that limited the vision of central authorities. Between 1765 and 1814 these forces included a number of little kingdoms that became increasingly entangled in the territorial disputes that emerged along the Champaran–Tarriani frontier.

3. The Little Kingdoms of Bettiah and Tanahu

The little kingdoms that straddled the Champaran–Tarriani frontier were all too frequently involved in longstanding territorial disputes whose origins and persistence deserve further study. Take, for instance, the little kingdom of Bettiah, which was formed in the fifteenth or sixteenth century by Bhumihar–Brahman lineages, and became a key player in the Anglo–Gorkha disputes along the frontier.[26] By the eighteenth century it had become subject to internal disputes that ultimately led to the partitioning of the kingdom among the descendants.[27] When Bettiah became a part of British territory in the eighteenth century it had long been a refractory dependent of the *nawabs* of Bengal, who had sent repeated military expeditions to subdue its kings.[28] Such military expeditions and shifts in political overlordship often produced changes in the structure of political authority as one set of overlords replaced another, and this usually unleashed numerous and competing claims (both fresh and long-standing) to territorial entitlements and political privileges. For instance, in 1794 Bir Kishor Singh, the raja of Bettiah, filed a suit against one Kalyan Singh Bahadur claiming he was entitled to an allowance (*malikana*) of Rs 8000 for the *tappa* of Belwa (*pargana* Majhowa), which the latter had held as *jagir*. Bir Kishor claimed that this practice was established during the time of his father raja Jugal Kishor, who had received a *malikana* for Belwa from Kalyan Singh's father Shitab Rai. While Bir Kishor's claim was ultimately dismissed by the British provincial court at Patna, his claim had spatial implications.[29] It established both a hierarchical relationship between Bir Kishor and Kalyan Singh and a joint claim to the *tappa* of Belwa. Because such entitlements were established, reestablished and dissolved on a frequent basis, they produced frequent shifts in the tenurial arrangements and territorial location of divisions such as *tappa* Belwa. Such disputes were widespread in the kingdom of Bettiah, and in the 1790s there were at least 9 claimants to the 13 *tappas* that made up its territories.[30]

Neighboring hill principalities like Tanahu also laid claim to a number of *tappas* in the northern reaches of Champaran.[31] The Tanahu raj emerged out of the kingdom of Palpa lying to its west sometime in the sixteenth century. By the early eighteenth century, Tanahu's influence extended over 15 *tappas* of Champaran, including the *tappas* of Chigwan, Jamauli and Ramgir (see Map 3.1). Tanahu's territorial claims to these *tappas* were contested by the rajas of Bettiah and consequently the ownership of these *tappas* repeatedly changed hands.[32] In 1731 Alivardi Khan, the *nawab* of Bengal, granted the three *tappas* of Chigwan, Jamauli and Ramgir to Raja Dhrub Singh of Bettiah.[33] Later Dhrub Singh's son Jugal Kishor entered into a pact with Har Kumar Dat Sen, the raja of Tanahu, by which the lands were restored to the latter.[34] In 1767 the agents of the Tanahu raja concluded revenue engagements for the 13 *tappas* with the English agent at Bettiah, one Mr Golding and his *amil*, Mohammad Ashraf Khan (1768–1774). In 1768, for reasons unknown, the Tanahu raja lost control over 10½ *tappas*, retaining only Jamauli, Ramgir and half of Chigwan, which were attached to the Fort of Someshwar.[35] In 1769, the Company's *amil* Mohammad Ashraf Khan, along with Abdhut Singh, the *zamindar* of Mehsi, carried out military expeditions in this area, and withdrew only when the Tanahu raja's brother made a gift of some "presents."[36] From the 1770s onwards, the rising influence of Gorkha whittled away Tanahu's political power, and in 1777 it lost the Fort of Someshwar (along its southern frontier) to the former. However, the 2½ *tappas* remained in Champaran, and so in 1777 the raja of Gorkha began to claim them, by virtue of his conquest of Tanahu.[37] In 1781 Someshwar's Gorkhali commander Dinanath Upadhyaya sent a memorandum to authorities in Calcutta claiming the aforementioned *tappas* by virtue of his being the new *killadar* (commandant) of that fort.[38] In the meantime, in 1782, the Bettiah raja, Jugal Kishor, took control of 12½ *tappas* formerly belonging to the Tanahu raj while the *tappas* of Rajpur, Chigwan and Batsara were rented out to the raja of Palpa.[39] However, in 1797 a dispute broke out between Bettiah and Palpa over the payment of arrears in rent and the sharing of elephants.[40] The Palpali kingdom, which was a dependent of Gorkha, was simultaneously paying rent to the Company for some lands it held in the Tribeni area (until at least 1803). In this fashion, a number of *tappas* and *parganas* on the Champaran–Tarriani frontier, belonging to various little kingdoms, became involved in multi-cornered relationships and disputes that left their territories mutually entangled. In the eighteenth century the situation underwent further complications as these little kingdoms were incorporated into the territories of Gorkha and the English East India Company. This threw up a whole new set of disputes about overlordship, authority and power that would ultimately set the stage for the outbreak of the Anglo–Gorkha War in 1814.

4. The Makwani Raj and *Pargana* Tauter/Thathar[41]

In the mid-eighteenth century, the hill principality of Makwanpur controlled the Tarai districts of Bara, Parsa, Rautahat, Saptari and Mahottari, as well as a sizeable chunk of the lucrative market and credit networks that linked the Ganjetic plains to the Kathmandu valley and beyond into Tibet.[42] In 1762, the Gorkhali king Prithvinarayan Shah conquered Makwanpur. By 1768, after successfully resisting two incursions from North India into the Makwani territories, the Gorkhalis began to lay claim to a number of Tarai *parganas*, including the *zamindari* of Bettiah.[43] The most serious disputes revolved around *pargana* Tauter and *tappa* Rautahat in Makwanpur's Tarai. While *pargana* Tauter has never been conclusively identified, it was probably made up of a cluster of 23 non-contiguous revenue paying lands (*mahals*) dispersed over the Gorkhali districts of Mahottari, Sarlahi, parts of Rautahat and the northern parts of *sarkar* Tirhut (in Bihar), lying within the East India Company's territories.[44] That is, *pargana* Tauter straddled the territorial possessions of Gorkha and the East India Company. According to tradition, the kings of Makwanpur paid tribute to their overlords – the rajas of Tirhut, who in turn reciprocated by granting two horses and two pieces of cloth as a marks of honor (*khillats*). This practice was continued by the rajas of Gorkha into the 1770s.[45]

The rights of possession to the Tauter *pargana* had never remained constant; in the sixteenth and seventeenth centuries, *pargana* Tauter, while possessed by the kings of Makwanpur, remained under the overlordship of the *fauzdars* (military commanders) of Tirhut. The rajas of Makwanpur paid an annual *peshkash* (tribute) in elephants (of a minimum height of 8½ hands) at the *fauzdar's* office at Darbhanga. Geographically, the Tauter *pargana* became a part of the Makwani territories while at the same time being a dependency of the district of Tirhut within the province of Bihar. When Makpwanpur was incorporated into the Gorkhali Empire in 1762 and Bengal came under British rule in 1765, *pargana* Tauter fell under their joint overlordship. In 1771 Dinanath Upadhyaya, the Gorkhali *vakil*, arrived at Darbhanga to present Gorkha's claims to the Tauter *pargana*. The *vakil* indicated that in return for the recognition of Gorkha's rights to Tauter his government would continue the payment of tribute, in the form of elephants, to the British. The Company recognized the former relationship of dependency existing between the Tauter *pargana* and its parent district of Tirhut and accepted this proposal. In doing so, the Company unwittingly conceded to sharing its authority over the Tauter *parganas* with the Gorkhali state. At this time, the Company lacked the necessary geographical information about the location of these *parganas*, and was probably unaware of the spatial effects of such relationships of overlordship, which caused the authority of states to overlap, in this case with the Tauter *pargana*. In 1801 the commercial treaty signed between Gorkha and the Company annulled the payment of tribute in elephants. The Tauter *pargana* gradually disappeared from both Gorkhali and British records after the first decade of the nineteenth century when it was dissolved and then integrated into the existing administrative divisions of the two states. In the nineteenth century, the Company became increasingly unwilling to share its territorial sovereignty with indigenous powers. Thus, when the Gorkhalis made a similar proposal to pay tribute for the Company-held lands of the Butwal Tarai in 1804, the Company rejected the offer outright, claiming it had exclusive jurisdiction over those lands. Such cases of territorial overlaps and intermixture could be found all along the Anglo–Gorkha frontier, and possibly throughout the subcontinent.[46]

5. The (Re)constitution of *Tappa* Rautahat, *Pargana* (Gadh) Simraon

In late eighteenth century, the frontier *tappa* of Rautahat figured prominently in a long-standing dispute between Gorkha and the English East India Company. Along with *tappa* Nannor, it at one time made up the old Mughal *pargana* of (Gadh) Simraon.[47] Rautahat was subdivided into seven *tarafs* that included the "dependent" *taraf* of Pachrauta. In Company records the term "dependent" was usually used in reference to land that, while belonging to an administrative division, physically stood detached from it. That is, Pachrauta, while being a subdivision of *tappa* Rautahat, remained physically detached from it (see Map 3.2). Such detachments in territorial layout and organization were usually the product of some political, tenurial or taxation relationship that had found expression in the precolonial revenue record. Such records were invariably constructed without any reference to modern maps, with their penchant for showing contiguous and non-overlapping territories. *Tappa* Nannor, which lay south of Rautahat, fell within the territories of the East India Company. Thus, in 1814, just prior to the outbreak of the Anglo–Gorkha War, the *pargana* of (Gadh) Simraon was for all practical purposes divided between the Gorkhalis and the East India Company.

In the eighteenth century, Rautahat underwent a number of rearrangements regarding its political, taxation and tenurial relationships that merit further investigation. In 1743,

Map 3.2 Location and internal divisions of the *pargana/praganna* of (Gadh) Simraon, 1814 CE

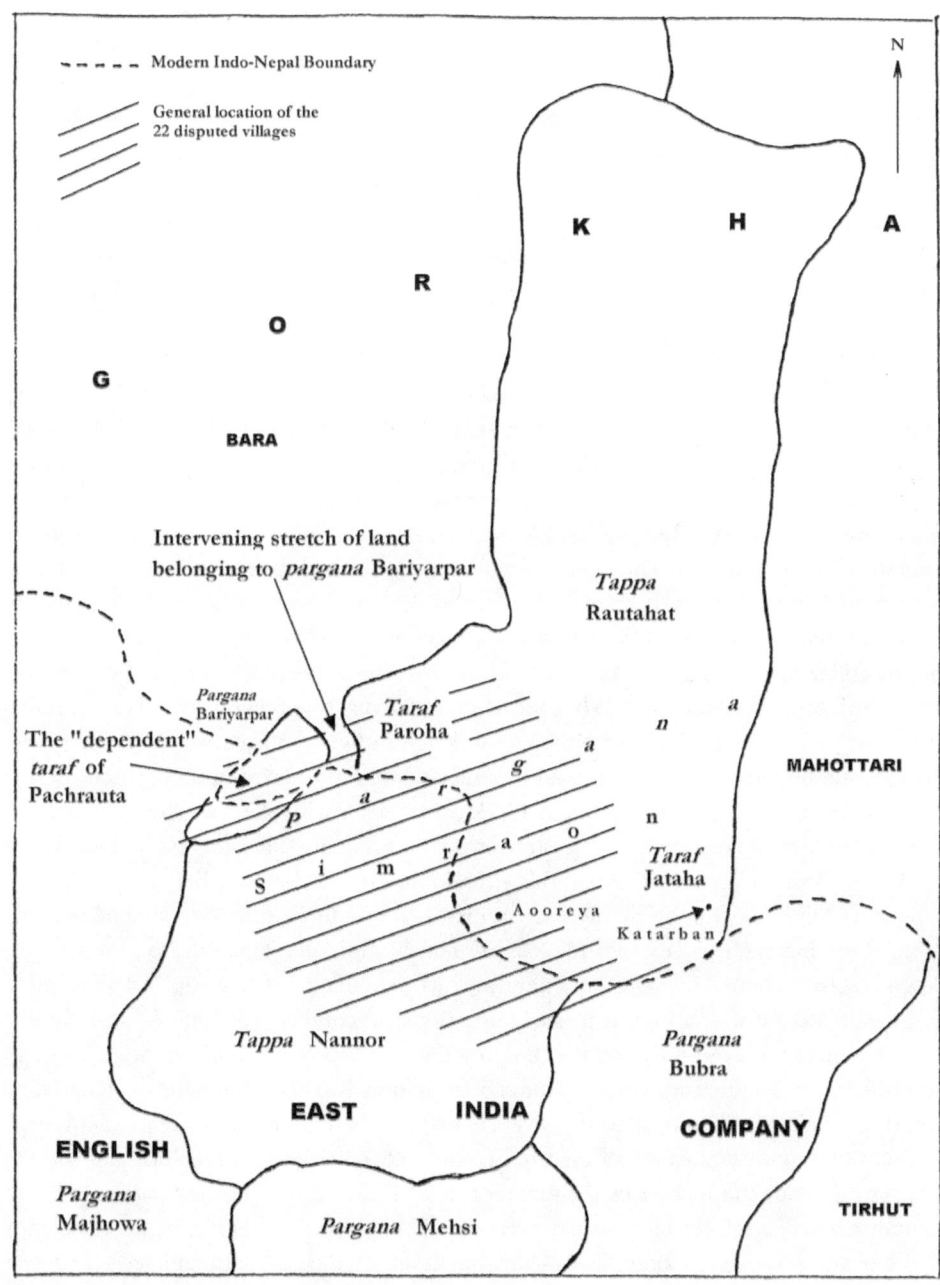

Mapwork by Bernardo A. Michael.

it was conferred as an inheritable rent-free land grant (*birta*) to one Qulb Ali Beg by Hem Karna Sen, the erstwhile raja of Makwanpur as a reward for military services rendered.[48] Hem Karna Sen's royal grant (*syahamohar*) was inscribed in copper and read thus:

> Whereas, I have given the *pargana* of Simraon together with the *tappas* Rautahat, Butkee[?] etc. in all seven *tarafs* cultivated and desolate to Mirza Kulb Ali Beg, son of Ali Quli Khan including the _____[illegible] *mal* [revenue due to the state], *jalkar* [tax due on water based resources], *bankar* [tax on forest products], and *sayer* [customs and excise duties], as long as I and my descendants shall be in possession of my raj, so long let this engagement be in force, and whilst both parties enjoy the revenues, let good faith be preserved between them. Dated 1800, the first day of the moon's increase, Bhadau. *Mokam* [camp] Hariharpur.[49]

From 1743–83, the status of *tappa* Rautahat underwent further changes that left its tenurial status unclear. From the very outset, the raja of Bettiah had claimed the *tappa*. He argued earlier that Ali Quli Khan had obtained a *sanad* from the Bettiah raja Dhrub Singh confirming the former's right to Rautahat. This could only have transpired if the raja of Bettiah had been Ali Quli Khan's overlord and thereby enjoyed a superior claim to Rautahat.[50] It also appears that when Dhrub Singh confirmed the grant, he did not renew its original rent-free terms. Rather, he confirmed the land on a *jagir* (service) basis, which meant it could be resumed at the Bettiah raja's pleasure. This reduced Ali Quli Khan and his descendants, who had originally enjoyed these lands on tax-free terms, to the status of dependents of the Bettiah raja.[51] While the truth underlying these claims is hard to ascertain, they clearly point to the flexible nature of land rights along the frontier and the frequent changes they underwent. Such claims and counter claims ended up rearranging many of the administrative divisions along the Anglo–Gorkha frontier, leaving them territorially unstable and amenable to fluctuations in ownership, layout, internal organization and boundaries.

Political instability also added to this situation of territorial flux. Between 1760 and 1764, Ali Quli Khan and his family were imprisoned by Mir Kasim, the *nawab* of Bengal. *Tappa* Rautahat then passed into the *nawab's* hands, and later Jugal Kishor, the raja of Bettiah, seized control of *tappa* Rautahat and its dependency Pachrauta.[52] Following a trend that was all too common in such situations of conflict, Ali Quli Khan's family tried to counter this move by seeking the protection of a powerful patron. So, sometime in 1765, they obtained an order (*parwana*) from one Kasim Ali Khan, of Rajmaha, ordering officials in Champaran to leave the *tappa* of Rautahat and its dependent *taraf* of Pachrauta in the possession of Ali Quli Khan, in accordance with the original copper plate grant, made in his favor by the former raja of Makwanpur. The *parwana* noted that Rautahat had been struck off (*kharij*) the records of the central accountants (*sadr quanungos*) of Bihar and rendered independent of the tax claims of the government (*nizamat*). *Tappa* Rautahat and its dependencies were thereby restored to Ali Quli Khan's family. Between 1765 and 1770, Ali Quli Khan and his successor Mirza Abdulla Beg obtained a number of *parwanas* from the *nawab* of Bengal and East India Company officials, like Shitab Rai and Edward Golding, that confirmed their original claims to Rautahat and Pachrauta, and that these divisions had been struck off the accounts of Bihar.[53]

In the meantime, *tappa* Rautahat continued to grow in size. In 1765, Mirza Abdulla Beg was renting ten villages in *tappa* Nannor (lying on its boundary with *tappa* Rautahat) from Jugal Kishor Singh, the raja of Bettiah. In 1767, when British forces expelled Jugal Kishor from the region, Abdulla Beg quietly added these ten villages to the *tappa* of Rautahat.[54] Later, when the Company recognized Gorkha's claim to *tappa* Rautahat in 1783, these ten villages, originally belonging to the raja of Bettiah, also fell into Nepali hands and continued to be sequestered from the *tappa* of Nannor. Such opportunistic practices of sequestering non-contiguous villages from one *tappa* to another had tremendous spatial implications because they left discontinuous the bodies of the administrative divisions they were attached to. British colonial records would make frequent references to such territorial intermixture, which was a product of the shifting and contested history of landed entitlements that marked the cultures of governance along the Anglo–Gorkha frontier.

But there is more to this complicated story. It appears that sometime between 1762 and 1781, Mirza Abdulla Beg secured Gorkhali confirmation of his entitlement to *tappa* Rautahat.[55] If this is correct, then the Beg might have followed custom by getting his rights to land confirmed by the Gorkha raja, who had become his overlord after the conquest of Makwanpur. According to Bikha Chaudhari, the Tharu leader from this area, the Gorkha raja Prithvinarayan Shah, had confirmed Mirza Abdulla Beg's grant sometime in 1770.[56] The raja of Bettiah claimed that this came about because the Gorkhali representative, Dinanath Upadhyaya, had bribed Mirza Abdulla Beg's agent to give testimony in favor of Gorkha's territorial claims over Rautahat.[57] In any case, between 1770 and 1780 the relationship between the Gorkha and the Beg soured. The Gorkhalis claimed (as did the raja of Bettiah) that Rautahat had been confirmed as *jagir* tenure that could be resumed and that the copper plate grant Abdulla Beg had produced was nothing but a forgery.[58] There also seems to have been a flight of labor from the Mirza's lands to the nearby Gorkhali villages of Bijay and Burwa where a Gorkhali police post had been established. We know this from a *parwana* that was issued by the court (*adalat*) at Saran in 1778, commanding the Mirza's officers to be more careful in preventing *ryots* from deserting his *jagir* and taking refuge in villages Barwa and Bijay.[59] Gorkhali officials further claimed that sometime around 1781 the Mirza turned against Gorkha and went to Patna, informing authorities there that Rautahat was part of the *suba* of Bengal.[60] Mirza Abdulla Beg now changed strategy to argue that the Gorkha raja had no right to resume the *tappa* which had never been attached to the territorial possessions of the kingdom of Makwanpur. Abdulla Beg argued that Rautahat had "*for many years before his* [Prithvinarayan Shah's] *conquest remained kharige* [*kharij*] *or separate from it* [the kingdom of Makwanpur]."[61] The Beg's claim rested on an assumption that the territories of a state were visible in its tax-yielding lands and that tax-exempt lands, irrespective of their actual location, were islands of autonomy. Such a claim generated its own unique spatial signature, as patches of rent-free lands could be attached or separated from the spatial frame of a state, creating all kinds of territorial intermixture, attachments and detachments. Whatever the case might have been, the Gorkhalis were decided about one thing – the Beg would have to relinquish his right to *tappa* Rautahat and its dependent *taraf* of Pachrauta[62] (see Plate 3.1). Thus, it appears that, by 1780, Mirza Abdulla Beg's

Plate 3.1 Letter from Raja Ran Bahadur Shah to Bahadur Shah, 1840 BS (1783 CE)

Reference is made to Mirza Abdullah Beg's receipt of a *parwana* from Thomas Brooke (Vuruk sahib) at Patna. While Gorkhali authorities were determined to oust Abdulla Beg, they were concerned about the possibility of the Company intervening on his side. Reproduced by permission of the National Archives of Nepal © The National Archives of Nepal.
Source: Historical Letters, *Kausi Tosakhana Collection*, no. 85, National Archives of Nepal.

entitlement to *tappa* Rautahat was redefined from an inheritable *birta* to a resumable *jagir*, as he was increasingly drawn into the logic of his struggles with emerging local and regional forces.

The Company's response was contradictory. On 28 September 1781, the governor-general-in-council (Revenue Department) decided to recognize the Beg's claim. However, this decision was sidelined by the events surrounding the rebellion of Raja Chait Singh of Banaras. In the meantime, on 20 February 1782, William Brooke, the English revenue chief at Patna who was unaware of the Council's earlier decision, issued an order (*parwana*) to the Gorkhalis, recognizing their claim over Rautahat. Brooke later rescinded the *parwana*, probably when he learned of the earlier decision of the governor-general-in-council.[63] The Gorkhalis viewed this about-turn as an attempt to deprive them of their legitimate claims over Rautahat.[64]

In October 1783, Warren Hastings settled this impasse in a minute where he concluded that,

> whatever may be the right of Mirza Abdulla Beg and however unjust the conduct of the Raja of Nepal in depriving him of his Jagheer, it is a point not cognizable by this Government, *since the lands comprising it do not appertain to our jurisdiction*. I there recommend that the orders of 28 September 1781 and 25 February 1783 be repealed, our sepoys recalled, and Mirza Abdulla left to the mercy or Justice of his own Sovereign.[65]

Processes of statemaking on the Champaran–Tarriani frontier unfolded precisely at the sites of such complex negotiations between multiple actors located at many levels, which ended up reconstituting territorial relationships, such as Mirza Abdulla Beg's rights to *tappa* Rautahat. The Beg remained a small "yam" squeezed between two "boulders" (Gorkha and the Company), who struggled to preserve his entitlement to Rautahat at a time of political uncertainty on the frontier, when the region was buffeted by many forces, from within and from beyond.[66]

The spatial implications of all this merit further reflection. The cultures of governance along the Champaran–Tarriani frontier were marked by frequent political instability and military conquests that only served to create an unstable hierarchy of land rights and entitlements that were prone to frequent dissolution and/or redefinition. Historically, the *tappa* of Rautahat had always been located within such a shifting hierarchy of tenurial entitlements, arranged by their ties to local and regional political overlords. The complicated and procrustean nature of land rights, along with their tendency for renegotiation, had serious consequences for a landholder's location within a hierarchy of agrarian entitlements and relations. The practices of confirming and reconfirming land grants became a highly charged open-ended performance, rich in meanings and productive of territorial ambiguity and conflict. Such dynamics reconstituted social relationships, landed entitlements *and territories* which serves as a reminder that the study of land grants needs to be sensitive to the ethnographic and spatial dimensions of their history. And given the number of times Mirza Abdulla Beg's family got their claims processed from various authorities (at least seven times between the years 1743 and 1783) the amount of semantic, spatial and social rearranging that followed in the wake of this entire corpus of practices rendered the physical space of Rautahat and Pachrauta extremely incoherent. In the end, by 1783, Rautahat had been incorporated into the Gorkhali Empire. However, the problems of spatiality would persist as a new series of disputes would crop up in the first decade of the nineteenth century, this time along the common boundary of the *tappas* of Rautahat and Nannor.

6. The Entangled Edges of *Tappa* Rautahat and Nannor: The Twenty-Two Disputed Villages

Between 1783 and 1814, 22 villages lying along the boundary of *tappa* Rautahat became the subject of dispute involving Gorkhali and East India Company officials. While the former maintained that these 22 villages belonged to *tappa* Rautahat, Bir Kishor Singh, the raja of Bettiah (a subject of the East India Company), claimed that they formed an integral part of his possessions, lying within the *tappa* of Nannor. In 1811 the disputes took a violent turn when Gorkhali *subba* Laxman Giri was killed in a skirmish with subjects of the Bettiah raja.[67] From 1813 to 1814, the entire question of the 22 villages' ownership became the subject of a number of official investigations on both sides. The Company's investigations were conducted by John Young, the acting magistrate of Saran, in 1812, by Lt. Col. Paris Bradshaw, political agent on the Nepal frontier in 1813 and, finally, by Persian Secretary John Monckton, who re-evaluated the case in early 1814.[68] The Gorkhalis, too, conducted a number of investigations to establish the boundary between the two states and resolve village disputes in the area.[69] At the end of his investigations, Young was unable to make any sense of the claims and counterclaims being made and turned in a report minus any observations and translations. Company officials in Calcutta were obviously dismayed to see this undigested mass of material and asked Young to submit a formal report. Young then prepared a largely inconclusive report in January 1813. In the meantime, the Gorkhalis concluded that Young had clearly recognized their rights to the disputed villages, though it is unclear as to how and why they might have arrived at such a conclusion. What actually transpired between Young and his Gorkhali counterparts may never be known, having become a part of the hidden transcripts that informed Anglo–Gorkhali communications concerning the territorial disputes along this frontier. There is no consensus in the East India Company reports prepared on the subject by officials like Young, Monckton and Bradshaw about the number and place-names of the 22 villages under dispute.[70] Bradshaw's report mentions 24½ disputed villages while mentioning only 16 by name. Monckton's report lists ten new villages that find no mention in Young's report. In addition, there were territorial disputes taking place along the Champaran–Tarriani frontier involving as many as 42 villages, if not more.[71] The following table bears this out.

The official discourse surrounding the 22 villages might actually be misleading about the true extent of the territorial disputes taking place along this frontier. Out of the 60 villages apparently occupied by Gorkha, approximately 42 lay on or near the Raj Bandh, an embankment constructed by the Bettiah raja Dalip Singh (1695–1715). Company officials who were eager to resolve these disputes searched for some signs of a material boundary separating Gorkha from the Company's territories and quickly latched on to this idea of the Bandh constituting the ancient limits of *sarkar* Champaran. Even

Table 1 Total number of disputed villages on the Champaran–Tarriani frontier in 1814 CE [72]

Tappas	Total no. of villages in 1776, taken from a document under the seal of Quazi Nur-ul Haq, 1178 fasli era (1770 CE).	Villages occupied by Gorkha from 1781 onwards.	Out of the villages occupied by Gorkha, the number of villages lying on or near the Raj Bandh.
tappa Buhas	113	32	30
tappa Bulthur	51	12	9
tappa Nannor	159 ½	16	3
Total (*sarkar* Champaran)	323 ½	60	42

so, East India Company officials were unable to make any progress in resolving these complicated disputes. They possessed little understanding of local boundaries or the territorial intricacies of local land rights in this area. The witnesses produced by both sides gave conflicting testimonies, though it appears that those produced by Bettiah raja fared better in making coherent claims. Perhaps nearly 50 years of colonial rule gave the Bettiah raja better insight into the political and juridical significance of the investigations being conducted by Company officials, with their peculiar questions about fixed linear boundaries and stable longstanding land rights and other entitlements. This familiarity would have allowed the Bettiah raja, Bir Kishor Singh, to school his witnesses accordingly. Gorkhali witnesses on their part had little idea of what exactly the British officials were attempting to establish during the course of these investigations – which was the location of a long-standing, stable and linear Anglo–Gorkha boundary, and the legitimacy of Gorkhali claims to collect taxes in the disputed villages. These witnesses affirmed the Gorkhali rights to the disputed villages without reference to linear boundaries or territorial continuity. Thus, Bassun Raut, the Ahir leader and key Gorkhali witness, made potentially unhelpful statements claiming that the disputed 22 villages now claimed by Gorkha had at one time (in 1791), been under the charge of Bir Kishor Singh. He would further clarify that, of the 22 villages, 7 had for a long time belonged to the English government, while the remaining 15 had been recovered from a state of barrenness and brought under cultivation during the tenure of the English. Such statements convinced British officials that these Gorkhali claims lacked credibility because it showed that they had never enjoyed these lands in the past. No attempt was made to understand the flexible nature of cultivation, land rights and entitlements all along the forested and malarial frontier (see Chapter 2). Furthermore, none of the witnesses could arrive at a consensus about the exact location of the boundary separating the *tappas* of Rautahat and Nannor, let alone that separating the two states.[73]

Company officials were unwilling to admit that the administrative divisions they had inherited from the Mughals were prone to overlaps, intermixtures and entanglements that were in turn the spatial outworking of a body of political, taxation and property relationships. They ignored the lived experiences and testimonies of indigenous elites and subalterns that confirmed the fact that revenue collection rights remained inconstant, given the vagaries of ecology, politics and history. The depositions of witnesses such as Bikha Chaudhari, Bassun Raut and others clearly reveal that along the frontier, various groups belonging to both states were collecting revenues from the disputed 22 villages in a highly irregular fashion.[74] Even so, the basis of the raja of Bettiah's claims to these lands are unclear, as he had never made any mention of these alleged 22 villages in any of his revenue engagements with the Company in 1791. Their ownership through time and their actual state (of cultivation or waste) was never satisfactorily resolved. Most of the witnesses were more concerned with representing who possessed the right (*de facto* or *de jure*) to collect revenue and promote cultivation and seemed disinterested in delineating linear boundaries.[75] Spatially, this meant that landholding, tribute and revenue collection rights were prone to frequent fluctuations that often followed the ebb and flow of power struggles between competing claimants to entitlements. The villages to which they belonged could, either in whole or in part, shift back and forth between different collecting authorities dispersed over different kingdoms and their attendant districts. Consequently, it became virtually impossible to disentangle the mutually intertwined territories of the two states along the Champaran–Tarriani frontier.

7. Additional Territorial Disputes and the Role of Local Agency

Studies of the Anglo–Gorkha War have rarely addressed the role of local agency in shaping the territorial disputes that ultimately resulted in the outbreak of the war. Most of the disputes found in the documentary record involved actors displaying considerable local initiative and agency. Disputes over issues of crop harvesting, water sharing, revenue collection and the boundaries of rivers were fuelled by the maneuverings of local actors such as the petty *zamindars*, officials, Gosains and cultivators. Such local agency and initiative was responsible for the frequent constitution and reconstitution of agrarian territories along the frontier. In 1813, further disagreements over territory arose between Gorkha and the East India Company. One instance involved the lands that the rajas of Makwanpur had assigned to one Shivnath Singh the *quanungo* (registrar) of the old Makwani districts of Bara and Parsa in the Eastern Tarai. These lands, amounting to 32 *tolas* (supplementary hamlets), were attached to the village of Narkattia, and Shivnath Singh had held these lands under a *nankar* tenure as compensation for his service as *quanungo*. It is unclear which administrative unit these lands fell under (presumably Bara-Parsa?), and it appears that they shifted back and forth between forest and cultivation. At the time of the Gorkhali takeover of Makwanpur in 1762, these lands constituted a forested pepper *mahal* (that is, yielding a tax on pepper). Around 1802, Gorkhali authorities abolished the office of the *quanungo* for the districts of Bara-Parsa and resumed the 32 *tolas* that were "dependent" on the village of Narkattia.[76] The now-ousted descendants of Shivnath Singh (by now deceased) disputed the claims of Gorkha to Narkattia and its dependant *tolas* and presented their case to Company officials. By 1813, these *nankar* lands appear to have been included in the possessions of the Bettiah raja, lying within the *tappa* of Buhas in *pargana* Majhowa.[77]

However, officials at Kathmandu disputed this and claimed these lands as belonging to Gorkha by virtue of its conquest of the hill kingdom of Makwanpur. The maneuverings of Shivnath Singh and his descendants cannot be overlooked in the outbreak of such territorial disputes. Moreover, Shivnath Singh may have been employed as a *quanungo* for both the Gorkhali and Company governments.[78] Similarly, local cultivators played a prominent role in other disputes along the frontier involving the villages of Bounra-Bounree in the Company's territory, and the villages of Ghewra, Tehoki, Jaimangalpur and Boodgaon within Gorkha's territories.[79] Such disputes often went unreported and Company officials became aware of them only through the series of special investigations conducted in the region between 1812 and 1814 (as discussed earlier).

8. Conclusion

The above-mentioned cases are only samples of the frequent changes taking place in the structure of agrarian entitlements along the Champaran–Tarriani frontier, a fallout of the numerous situational adjustments being undertaken by holders to such entitlements. Their agency is suggestive of many things. It exposed the flexible and bundled nature of agrarian entitlements and of their constitution and reconstitution within local contexts of conflict. It was these multi-cornered tussles between Gorkhali officials, petty *zamindars*, revenue contractors and cultivators in the region that came to characterize the cultures of governance and statemaking along the frontier. Gorkhali officials such as *subba* Laxman Giri, who were deputed to the frontier from Kathmandu, were often dragged into the vortex of these localized struggles. Laxman Giri's death at the hands of the Bettiah raja's supporters in 1811 has to be understood against this background of local initiative and struggle. It was this, rather than some innate cultural logic or blueprint, which underwrote the outbreak of territorial disputes along the Champaran–Tarriani frontier. The localized moorings of these disputes acknowledge the formative role of power in the organization of territory. The complicated and multifarious disputes taking place along the Champaran–Tarriani frontier resist any neat conception of state power flowing outwards from the center. Rather, any study of these struggles must admit to the discontinuities, contradictions and multi-directional flows of power that were energized by the role of local agents. Such territorial dynamics spilled over into the spaces of neighboring states to produce their intermixed territories (at least that is how they appeared to central authorities). Local agents in their pursuit of agrarian entitlements and resources were less concerned about preserving the integrity of a linear boundary or the connectedness of territory. Rather, such agents strove to secure the diverse portfolio of agrarian investments they had assembled along the shared boundary of the two states. Landholders along the frontier all too often entered into multi-cornered disputes that crisscrossed state boundaries.[80] As central authorities belonging to both states became increasingly drawn into the dynamics of these local conflicts, these disputes were rearticulated in the form of formal interstate conflicts with their commissions of inquiry and strategies of war-making.

Territorial disputes along the Champaran–Tarriani frontier were not the blunt outcome of "official" action or misadventure. Rather, they were diagnostic of *locally* calibrated products of dynamic agrarian conflict that characterized cultures of governance, statemaking and territorial reconstitution. On the Anglo–Gorkha frontier, this had the effect of rendering administrative districts patchy, possessing intertwined and overlapping bodies with unclear boundaries. This chapter has tried to discern the varied historical moments that produced the fluid and intertwined territories that made up the Champaran–Tarriani section of the Anglo–Gorkha frontier. Territorially the frontier was organized around a flexible structure of agrarian entitlements that peppered the landscape with a plethora of rights and claims to various kinds of resources – mainly rights of access to and control over land in its material and symbolic avatars. The administrative divisions and sub-divisions that straddled this frontier were yoked to this shifting ensemble of agrarian rights and relationships. As these rights and relationships changed under the influence of local and regional systems of power they produced commensurate changes in administrative divisions such as *parganas*, *tappas*, and *mauzas* (either in whole or in part), leaving their bodies discontinuous, dispersed and intermixed in many places. A similar set of developments would characterize territorial production elsewhere, along the Gorakhpur–Butwal section of the Anglo–Gorkha frontier.

Chapter 4

THE GORAKHPUR–BUTWAL FRONTIER

Should it therefore please your Lordship [the English governor-general] to order the delivery of those [disputed] places to the officers of the Gurkha government upon the same terms they are retained by the Raja of Palpa, they shall without hesitation submit to the affixed tribute, or if the retention of the different places in the possession of either state independent of each other is preferred, it would be just and proper since the object of either of those proposals is to remove all misunderstandings [...] God almighty has conferred the extensive territories of Hindustan long governed by foreigners on the British Nation. In like manner has he bestowed the territories on the hills on the Gurkhas and both nations have at length reached the banks of the Sutlej to give stability to ancient customs.

—Girbana Juddha Bikram Shah, the raja of Gorkha
to the governor-general, August 1814[1]

1. Introduction

In the eighteenth century the Gorakhpur–Butwal frontier, which was formed of a patchy collection of forests, waste lands, marshes and cultivated fields, straddled the kingdoms of Awadh and the hill principalities to its north. The authority of Awadh's *nawabs* was tenuous at best, and the system of revenue administration made up of loose and flexible arrangements. In November 1801, the English East India Company acquired territories along this frontier when the *nawab* of Awadh ceded the *sarkar* of Gorakhpur to the Company (see Map 4.1).[2] From the very inception of their rule, the British experienced territorial anxieties at the level of everyday governance. For instance, the 1801 cession did not constitute the transfer of a continuous block of territory; some tracts of land, such as the seven *parganas* forming Khairigarh, lay detached from Gorakhpur, separated by the Nawab's territories of Awadh. Moreover, along the northern reaches of Gorakhpur, many *parganas*, *tappas* and *taluqas* possessed unclear boundaries and entangled bodies, which were caused by the frequent reconstitution of political relationships and entitlements to land (both tax yielding and tax free) and the payment of tribute. Furthermore, when the Company took over Gorakhpur, it possessed little knowledge of the territory and its resources, making it difficult to govern effectively.[3] In 1807, Edward Colebrooke, a senior Company official, noted:

The objections alleged by several of the collectors, as well as by the late Commissioners, against the immediate conclusion of a permanent settlement, are principally the

Map 4.1 The Gorakhpur–Butwal frontier, 1814 CE

Mapwork by Bernardo A. Michael and Sharon Michael.

imperfect knowledge yet acquired of the resources of the country, the inequality of the present assessment, the great proportion of the uncultivated lands, estimated at general at a fourth of the arable lands, the deficiency of population, and want of capital to extend the cultivation, the existing restrictions on commerce, land yet unascertained, […] the general uncertainty, [… and] the doubtful value of the standard coin.[4]

Colebrooke's lament applied particularly to the Company's inability to collect revenue from the little hill kingdom of Palpa lying along the Gorkhpur–Butwal frontier. In 1802, the Company entered into a three-year revenue settlement with the Palpali *diwan*, Lal Ran Bahadur Sen, for lands in the Butwal Tarai at an annual rate of Rs 30,000.[5] However, when the Palpali raja was unable to honor his obligations and make payments of revenue, the settlement was revoked and the lands of the Butwal *zamindari* were placed under the direct management of government (*kham tehsil*) for eight years (1803–10 CE).[6] At the same time, the rajas of Palpa fell into arrears in their payments of tribute to the *nawab* Vazir of Awadh. The Butwal rajas had paid their tribute directly to the *nawab* at Lucknow and not through his revenue collectors (*amils*) of Gorakhpur. Three-quarters of the tribute was delivered in the form of elephants, musk and other forest products, and one-quarter was paid in cash. By 1802, Palpa had fallen into arrears in its tribute obligations and even tried to get the Company to intercede on their behalf to secure a remission of these arrears due to the *nawab*.[7] In 1806, the situation reached a stalemate when Palpa was forcibly incorporated into the Gorkhali Empire following the assassination of the Palpali raja Prithvipal Sen in Kathmandu.[8]

After 1806, the Palpali territories were placed under the military governorship of *kajis* Amar Singh Thapa and Dalbhanjan Pande.[9] They immediately set about the task of establishing Gorkha's authority, by overseeing the work of general administration and revenue collection, while reinstating a number of former Palpali officials, and (re)confirming land grants.[10] In 1807, Amar Singh Thapa built the Amar Narayan Temple at Tansen in the hills above Butwal – a symbolic statement of his newly established authority in the region.[11] In the Tarai areas bordering the district of Gorakhpur, Tharu cultivators were allowed to cultivate wastelands on concessional terms.[12] Efforts were also made to catalog and verify the existence of a large number of *maafi* (rent-free) grants. Gorkhali officials were keen on resuming such grants and diverting their revenues for state-building activities. For instance, in the Butwal area, *maafi* grants made to Jaisi Brahmans were resumed by *kaji* Amar Singh Thapa in order to secure fresh lands for the payment of Gorkhali troops.[13] The involvement of local frontier officials and agents in the process of Gorkhali consolidation in the Butwal area, along with their investments in local struggles, cannot be underestimated. For instance, Maniraj Bhaju, the Gorkhali *fauzdar* of Butwal, possessed some cultivable lands along the disputed boundary between *tappas* Dhebrua (*pargana* Bansi) and Sheoraj. He was actively involved in the Anglo–Gorkha territorial disputes along this frontier, and, in 1814, he personally led the Gorkhali attack on the Company's police posts in the Butwal Tarai.[14] The role of such local agents in the governance and constitution of territory along the Gorkhapur–Butwal frontier merits further discussion in the pages that follow.

2. The Sources of Social Power on the Gorakhpur–Butwal Frontier: Rajas, *Talukdars*, *Birtias* and *Maafidars*

On the Gorakhpur–Butwal frontier, centuries of statemaking had resulted in the strengthening of highly localized systems of social power and their cultures of governance. The dominant landholding groups in Awadh belonged to the Rajputs, (Bhumihar) Brahman castes, as well as some Muslim families who coexisted alongside a number of lower and in some cases, dominant, service castes such as Ahirs, Kurmis, Koris, Bania, Chamars and "Trookia" Muslims.[15] Commenting on the social profile of the landed groups of Gorakhpur, Mufti Ghulam Hazrat, writing in 1810, noted that there were three types of *zamindars* in the district of Gorakhpur – absolute proprietors (rajas), *talluqdars* and *birtias*.[16] These landholders became key local players and enjoyed a range of entitlements forged out of complex composites of tribute, taxation and tenurial relationships. Regional and trans-regional rulers had to navigate the authority and influence wielded by such local elites when making arrangements for governance. Taken together, in the post-Mughal world of the eighteenth century, these local, and often opposing, elements constituted a diffuse and dynamic terrain of power along the Gorakhpur–Butwal frontier.

High on the scale of *zamindars* were the rajas. On the basis of custom, they claimed a hereditary and proprietary right in the soil, sometimes covering whole or partial *parganas*. For example, in 1807, Rajput rajas like Prithipath Singh, Sarabjit Singh and Pahalman Singh possessed considerable lands in the *parganas* of Amorha, Ratanpur Bansi, and Haveli Gorakhpur respectively. Such rajas derived their authority from being customarily treated as the ancient proprietors of their holdings, and enjoyed a range of entitlements.[17] They, in turn, were and *talluqdars*, followed by a host of intermediary and smaller *zamindars*.[18] When the East India Company took over the district of Gorakhpur in 1801, it faced the daunting prospect of dealing with these dispersed holdings of local power and the complex expressions of landed rights (like *birt* and *maafi*), prerequisites (the levy of *malikana* and *nankar*) and privileges (the collection of customary dues, and distribution of honors and services) that they had always enjoyed.[19]

The Gorakhpur–Butwal frontier also witnessed the presence of a substantial class of *birt* landholders.[20] A *birt* signified a tenure originally granted by a chieftain to a dependent on account of kinship or services rendered, and subject to an annual payment. It could apply to assignments of both money and land, and could be resumed at the end of a grantee's lifetime or given away on an inheritable tax-free basis. In the eighteenth century they constituted a substantial class of interested landholders in Gorakhpur and along the Gorakhpur–Butwal frontier where large areas of the Butwal and Satasi *zamindaris* were held under such grants.[21] A varied class of landholders, the *birtias*, had to contend with the superior claims of the rajas, *taluqdars* and *zamindars* who had conferred these rights and privileges in the first place.[22] Furthermore, many *birtias* were unable to keep their lands under continuous cultivation, causing them to move back and forth between cultivation and waste, producing fluctuating land-use patterns in the Butwal Tarai.[23] This caused frequent rearrangements in the tenurial structure of the region as various groups competed to preserve their rights or exert power to establish new claims to land and other entitlements.

Maafi (rent-free) grants constituted another substantial class of tenures. Usually, such grants were conferred on a subject by a superior landholder or sovereign as a reward for loyalty and service rendered, or for displaying exceptional learning or saintly repute. Grantees enjoyed the right to collect land revenue while being exempt from paying any taxes to the state or its officials on a lifetime basis or in perpetuity.[24] In the latter half of the eighteenth century, the *nawabs* of Awadh had conferred a large number of *maafi* grants throughout the kingdom. These holders of *maafi* grants became a numerous class of landholders as well as a powerful social prop for the ruling regime in Awadh.[25] *Maafi* grant holders presented a powerful group of interested landholders who could support, subvert, resist and even overthrow their overlords. In the eighteenth century the *nawabs* of Awadh conducted intensive investigations into these landholdings but failed to dislodge these tenure-holders who, at times, assumed the tenure, titles and other entitlements of powerful independent landholders (*zamindars*).[26] As the power of the *nawabs* of Awadh waned in the late eighteenth century, these landholders flexed their muscles as they tenaciously held onto their lands. The *nawabs* had made numerous rent-free grants in the district of Gorakhpur, particularly within the northern *parganas* of Bansi and Rasulpur Ghaus. For instance, in *pargana* Bansi, over 50 percent of the villages were held on a *maafi* basis. By 1811, nearly 5½ million *bighas* of land in Gorakhpur were *maafi*, many being granted not by the *nawabs*, but by local elites (landholders and officials) such as the kings of Palpa, who had replicated the *nawabi* practice.[27] The beneficiaries of such grants in turn replicated this practice as they tried to create a corps of loyal dependents. Such patterns of statemaking characterized the cultures of governance along this frontier, creating multiple and competing centers of power and authority that were prone to dispute and conflict.

The presence of substantial rent-free lands along the Anglo–Gorkha frontier (especially in the Butwal Tarai), is confirmed by Company records.[28] In 1804, around 41 percent of the Butwal Tarai (made up of the *parganas* of Tilpur and Binayakpur, and including the *taluqas* of Khajahani and Matka) was subsumed under rent-free tenures.[29] By 1804, out of the total value of *maafi* grants conferred in this area, the *nawabs* of Awadh accounted for 14 percent of such grants in *pargana* Tilpur and 11 percent in *taluqa* Khajahani Bhandar and *tappa* Matka. 33 percent of the *nawab*'s rent-free grants in the Butwal Tarai were made to the rajas of Palpa and their dependents. This practice was then replicated by the rajas of Palpa who conferred 86 percent of the rent-free grants in the Butwal Tarai, especially between 1789 and 1801. Of this, 48 percent of Palpali *maafi* lands were held by the raja's family and immediate relations.[30] Within the *pargana* of Binayakpur, under the Company's control, an estimated total of 36 percent of income-yielding lands were given out on a rent-free basis. At the same time, after the Gorkhalis occupied parts of *pargana* Binayakpur in the first decade of the nineteenth century, they too issued numerous rent-free grants in the area – possibly as high as 70 percent of the total value of lands under their control. Creating new lines of loyal supporters seems to have been a characteristic pattern of governance along the frontier, as local elites jostled to buttress their claims against one another and their immediate overlords.[31]

When the East India Company acquired Gorakhpur in 1801, it included the *zamindari* of Butwal, valued at Rs 40,000. By 1805 the Company was able to recover only 36 percent of this amount, given the high incidence of *maafi* tenures and uncultivated lands. Collections must have fallen further after Gorkhali advances into the Butwal Tarai in 1806.[32] Eager to increase its revenues, the Company began to take measures to resume undocumented *maafi* lands. Under Regulations 31 and 36 of 1803, grants that lacked documentation or were acquired through the connivance of local officials were considered invalid. In 1805, the Collector of Gorakhpur recommended that they be resumed and "their assets considered as forming a part of the available resources of the District."[33] The presence of a large number of undocumented *maafi* tenures in the area points to a culture of governance where it was customary to indulge in ad hoc practices of making such rent-free grants, which included fictitious claims to such entitlements. The Company tried to stall this process through the Regulation of 1812, which ordered all *maafi* tenures to be registered. This only caused *zamindars* and *quanungoes* to insert their names as *maafi* landholders in official records in even greater numbers, a practice the Regulation had sought to check in the first place. P. Warden Grant, a surveyor along this frontier, noted that, between 1802 and 1812, the number of *maafi* tenures doubled, with many that paid revenue also being included in this number.[34] Palpa's Butwal Tarai had its own share of undocumented *maafi* grants. In 1817, the former Palpa raja Rattan Sen claimed 103 rent-free villages in the *parganas* of Tilpur and Binayakpur that were originally granted to his grandfather Mahadat Sen by *nawab* Asafauddaulah (1775–97) of Awadh. However, no documentary evidence could be found to support his claim. The only *sanad* (royal decree) presented was one from the *nawab* Asafuddaulah (dated 1785 CE) to Prithvipal Sen (Rattan Sen's father) and his wife, which made no mention of the villages concerned. Repeated investigations failed to yield any further information. The problem was accentuated by the fact that the *parganas* of Tilpur and Binayakpur had been settled with Prithvipal Sen until 1803 by the Company, without any reference to rent-free or assessed estates – that is, in the gross. Rattan Sen's claims, which would have severely reduced the Company's revenue claims, were never recognized and the lands were ultimately resumed by the Company in 1817, on the grounds that there was no proof of their ownership.[35]

The Company's officials also tried to sift through the plethora of claims to rent-free lands and discern if they were hereditary or non-hereditary. As far as the frontier district of Gorakhpur went, in 1813, Company officials recognized the right of the *nawabs* of Awadh to issue rent-free grants but were reluctant to recognize similar rights for the lesser rajas and *zamindars*. In 1813, the Company's commissioner on the Nepal frontier, Major Paris Bradshaw, investigated the status of *maafi* lands in the disputed Butwal Tarai. He observed that there were two types of *maafi* grants. First, were those made by a raja or *zamindar* to some of their relatives in lieu of cash payments for services rendered. The second class of *maafi* tenures were those made for the advancement of agriculture and for bringing waste lands under cultivation. Such grants were made to compensate the holders for the labor and expense incurred. Bradshaw considered both grants as non-hereditary, the former reverting back to the superior lord on the death of the *zamindar*, and the latter on the expiration of the *zamindar*'s *kabuliyat* (deed consenting to the terms for the engagement of revenue). Bradshaw further felt that a hereditary gift of land could only be made by the sovereign, who in Prithvipal Sen's case was the *nawab* Vazir of Awadh, the raja of Nepal being only a "pretended sovereign." Since there was no clear evidence of the Vazir having made any *maafi* grants to the Butwal raja, Bradshaw treated the claims of the Gorkhali commissioners as belonging to the *maafi* tenures of the second type. Needless to say, Bradshaw's representations were mere simplifications of the complexities involved in *maafi* land grants, and had the net effect of easily justifying the Company's claims to these lands.[36] The Gorkhalis too had expressed similar concerns as they undertook investigations aimed at discerning the legitimacy of such rent-free grants. For instance, in 1811, *bakshi* (military supervisor) Dashrath Khatri and *kaji* Bahadur Bhandari were deputed by authorities at Kathmandu to settle Garhwal in the far west. All rent-free estates in the hands of individuals were resumed, and if not, a document signed by these commissioners was given to the favored grantee.[37] In any case, both the East India Company and the Gorkhali state made determined efforts to identify and authenticate the rent-free lands in their possession.

The proliferation of rent-free land grants along the Gorakhpur–Butwal frontier has implications for our understanding of statemaking and spatiality. Traditionally, these grants provided powerful patrons with a means to reward loyal clients and build up powerful bases of local support. At the same time, the holders of rent-free lands were never passive recipients of royal largesse; they wielded considerable local influence that could potentially blunt the demands of their immediate overlords, including diminishing their tax base. Holders of rent-free grants would invariably strain to reformulate the terms of their original grant when any opportunity offered itself, such as during times of political turmoil, regime change or rebellion. Thus, the presence, absence, increase or decline of rent-free grants over time was usually indicative of variations in patterns of statemaking – as states and local and supralocal landholders jostled to build alliances or reclaim lands in an effort to extend their influence. In spatial terms, agrarian entitlements such as rent-free lands were perceived as islands of autonomy within the larger tax-yielding territories of a kingdom. For instance, in 1813, Gorkhali officials rejected the Company's claims to sole proprietorship of the Butwal lands, on the grounds that the *maafi* grants conferred by the *nawabs* of Awadh and the rajas of Palpa were *to all practical purposes separated from the fiscal accounts of the pargana to which they were attached*.[38] To prove this claim, the Gorkhalis presented a Palpali deed of assent (*ikrarnamah*) from 1798, addressed to the Gorkhali raja, stating that no revenue for the Butwal *zamindari* had been paid to the *nawab* of Awadh; rather the Butwal raja had held the *zamindari* in *maafi* (rent-free) *from the raja of Gorkha*.[39] In short, the Gorkhalis claimed that the Butwal *zamindari* did not belong to the Company's district of Gorakhpur.[40] That is, these *maafi* lands were perceived as islands of tenurial autonomy (alienated from the district of Gorakhpur) that the Gorkhalis had now inherited by virtue of conquest of the little kingdom of Palpa. The Gorkhalis on their part were more concerned with their inheritance of these landed entitlements without reference to territorial contiguity or linear boundaries – variables the British were trying to uphold. As self-perceived sole legal heirs to the *nawabs*' authority, Company officials were increasingly unwilling to surrender or even share authority with the Gorkhalis over patches of rent-free land lying dispersed within its territories. They believed that these lands belonged to the Company by virtue of the terms of the 1801 treaty with the *nawab* of Awadh.

3. Cultures of Governance and Illegible Landscapes on the Gorakhpur–Butwal Frontier

The only way that the Company state and the Gorkhalis could have accessed the territorial realities of their lands on the Gorakhpur–Butwal frontier was through detailed topographic and cadastral surveys. However, human and financial limitations prevented them from accomplishing this during the early decades of colonial rule. Also, at the time of the cession of Gorakhpur to the Company in 1801, the records of the district were not demanded from the Awadhi capital, Lucknow. The Company was forced to depend on the *pargana* registers furnished by the district officials. However, centuries of statemaking had produced a culture of governance where local officials and landed magnates had resisted the surveillance of central authorities by refusing to divulge accurate information about the internal resources and revenue-yielding potentials of their territories. In one instance, the Awadh *nawab* Shujauddaulah (1732–75) discovered, on one of his inspection tours, that local *quanungos* kept two kinds of account registers – one a fabrication and the other the original.[41] The same could be said for the account books of local officials throughout North India.[42] In a similar vein, Buchanan-Hamilton noted that officials at Lucknow were very good at engineering all kinds of "usurpations," "defalcations" and "forgeries" in the records at their disposal.[43] Numerous villages and waste lands never found mention in the records, and there was a frequent tendency for landholders, in connivance with local officials, to represent rich agricultural lands as waste or rent-free in order to secure tax concessions from the state.[44] In the early decades of colonial rule, more than half of Gorakhpur's *maafi* lands lay in the hands of *quanungos* and their families, and about 1½ *lakh bighas* of land in Gorakhpur escaped assessment (*taufir*), while tax monies went into the pockets of revenue officials.[45] Cultivators were often enticed from revenue-paying lands to work in such waste and rent-free lands, resulting in considerable loss to government.[46] Furthermore, the Company was unable to determine the authenticity of the large number of *birt* and *maafi* land grants made in the region, unless documented by the *nawab* of Awadh, whom it considered to be the only legal sovereign of Gorakhpur district.[47] In addition to this, neither Gorkha nor the Company was able to gain any accurate insight into the actual physical extent, boundaries or internal resources of the districts that lay on the Gorakhpur–Butwal frontier. So, for example, when village disputes arose in 1809 in the *taluqa* Khajahani and the *tappa* of Dhebrua between one Pahalwan Singh and Jurawan Chaudhari, the acting Collector of Gorakhpur was unable to locate a single disputed village, primarily because the *quanungoes* would not divulge their locations.[48] The reluctance of local officials to divulge this information created a situation that made it difficult for both states to discern with accuracy the tenurial portfolios of their respective territories. Cultures of governance along this frontier were also characterized by loose and flexible sets of arrangements for establishing multiple overlordships and the collection of tribute. For instance, the *taluqa* of Matka had been subject to the overlordship of multiple kingdoms, great and small, like Awadh, Gorkha, Palpa and Gulmi. In addition to this, Matka had also been attached to the *parganas* of Ratanpur Bansi and Binayakpur along the northern reaches of Gorakhpur. Consequently, by 1814, prior to the Anglo–Gorkha War, the diverse political and fiscal attachments of *taluqa* Matka had created a plethora of claims on both sides of the Gorakhpur–Butwal frontier that left it intertwined between the territories of the East India Company and Gorkha.

A large number of disputes – "of a most intricate nature and too numerous to be decided upon" – over rights to land, water and forest resources also informed the cultures of governance and formation of territories along the Gorakhpur–Butwal frontier.[49] Many *birtia* tenures, which, in 1801, numbered about 10,000, were steeped in such long-standing disputes.[50] In the 1800s, a few years prior to the Anglo–Gorkha War, the raja of Palpa was engaged in multi-cornered boundary disputes with the rajas of Satasi and Bettiah.[51] In another instance, the raja of Butwal's brother, Survir Sen, disputed the right of one Moorid Beiji Sing[h], an official of the neighboring Satasi estate, to three villages.[52]

Such disputes were present within Gorkha's Tarai possessions as well. In one instance, in 1812, a dispute broke out between the *amils* of Sheoraj and one *kaptan* (Captain) Chandra Bir Kunwar over their rights to certain lands. The latter had been given some villages on a *bekh buniyadi* (inheritable land grant) basis, which had then been encroached upon by the *amils* of *tappa* Sheoraj.[53] There was a high incidence of boundary disputes as well, which left the edges of many *tappas* and *parganas* along the Gorakhpur–Butwal frontier ill-defined.[54] Ultimately, such disputes also spilled over into the territories of Awadh, the Company and Gorkha. In the first decade of the nineteenth century the Gorkhalis were involved in a number of boundary disputes with the British. In addition to the one over the Butwal Tarai, the Gorkhalis also laid claim to the *taluqa* of Sheokhor and *tappa* Dhebrua, which were jointly attached to *pargana* Ratanpur Bansi. *Taluqa* Sheokhor, while belonging to *pargana* Bansi, had for many years been in the possession of the raja of Butwal. This led Gorkhali authorities to lay claim to it after Butwal was incorporated into the Gorkhali Empire. Consequently, administrative divisions along the Gorakhpur–Butwal frontier remained entangled in these complicated territorial disputes that left much of the frontier illegible.[55]

Governance in this part of the frontier reflected extraordinary levels of decentralization, coupled with wide fluctuations in revenue collection. Gorkha's ruling elite was heavily dependent on the revenues from the Tarai. However, while nearly 80 percent of the Gorkhali state's income in the early nineteenth century came from directly assessed (*jagera*) lands in the Eastern Tarai, the Western Tarai (lying east of Gandaki River) accounted for less than one-fifth of the total *jagera* land tax revenue.[56] Such trends reflect variations in processes of statemaking in Gorkha's Tarai possessions, as the centralizing vision of these states was refracted through a dense terrain of dispersed power that coalesced around local elements such as rajas, *zamindars*, *talukdars*, *birtias*, *maafi* holders, local officials, village headmen, cultivators and mobile labor. Given the presence of such powerful and resistant cultures of governance, Gorkhali and Company officials gained little knowledge about the actual extent, layout and internal resources of the districts under their administration. At the same time, these officials were increasingly drawn into the conflicted histories of the *parganas*, *tappas* and villages – the building blocks of the regional states and little kingdoms – on the Gorakhpur–Butwal frontier. In 1814, when war broke out between the Company and Gorkha, the Gorakhpur–Butwal frontier had, from the viewpoint of effective governance, become an epistemological puzzle for both states, whose efforts to render their territories legible by reining in local forces and collecting revenues had met with little or no success.

4. The Palpa Raj: A Yam between Three Boulders?

The hill kingdom of Palpa, whose Tarai lands in the vicinity of Butwal had become a focal point of the disputes along the Gorakhpur–Butwal frontier in 1814, merits further scrutiny. Very little is known about the origins of Palpa's Sen rulers. They were reputed to be Chauhan Rajputs who migrated to the area in the fourteenth century following the invasion of North India by Islamic rulers.[57] One of them, Mukund Sen I (1518–53 AD), is said to have founded the town of Butwal in the fourteenth century.[58] Following Mukund

Sen's death, his sons partitioned the kingdom among themselves, with one Vinayak Sen taking charge of a large stretch of territory west of the Gandaki River.[59] The disputed *pargana* of Binayakpur derives its name from this Vinayak Sen. Palpa's rulers competed with neighboring little kingdoms, like Bansi, Gulmi, Argha-Khanchi and Bettiah, to exercise a tenuous control over the forest and agrarian resources of the Tarai.[60] Sometime in the early eighteenth century, the rulers of Palpa submitted to the overlordship of the *nawabs* of Awadh. The Palpali ruler Mahadat Sen (1782–93) became a favorite of *nawab* Asafuddaulah who during one of his frequent hunting trips to the Butwal Tarai reconfirmed the former's lands in the plains while reducing his revenue obligations from Rs 60,000 to Rs 40,000.[61] However, by the end of the eighteenth century, the weakening of Awadh saw Palpa lose an important protector and become increasingly vulnerable to new intrusive powers like Gorkha and the East India Company.

The relations between Palpa and Gorkha deserve further comment. Palpa stood in the way of Gorkhali plans for westward expansion after their conquest of the Malla kingdoms of Kathmandu in 1769. In 1784, the Gorkhalis occupied the territories of Palpa, compelling its ruler Mahadat Sen to flee. However, shortly thereafter the Gorkhalis evacuated these territories after being pressured by the hill rajas of Satahun and Parbat.[62] Palpa's close connections with the *nawabs* of Awadh also continued to discourage any overt attempts to incorporate it into the Gorkhali Empire.[63] In 1784, the Palpali ruler Mahadat Sen, in a move to strengthen relations, gave his daughter to the Gorkhali Regent, Bahadur Shah, in marriage, following which a treaty was signed between the two kingdoms.[64] The details of this political arrangement (or at least the Gorkhali version of it) were that the raja of Palpa had by a petition (*arzee*) proposed to supply troops and money to finance Gorkhali military expeditions against the western confederation of 22 states (*baise rajya*). The Gorkha raja (the minor Ran Bahadur Shah and his regent-uncle Bahadur Shah) then confirmed the Palpali raja's possessions of the *zamindari* (of Butwal?).[65] As we have seen in the previous chapter, such reconfirmation of land grants usually led to the reconstitution of political relations between overlords and dependents, at least from the perspective of some of the agents. We know this as a fact because the Gorkhalis would later use this treaty to argue that this act of reconfirmation had reduced Palpa's status to that of a dependency of Gorkha, making the Gorkhalis the overlords and rightful heirs to Palpa's territorial possessions.

In any case, Gorkha–Palpa relations remained close during Bahadur Shah's regency (1785–94).[66] Palpa supported the Gorkhali military campaigns against the hill kingdoms of Gulmi, Argha, Khanchi, Dhurkot, Isma, Parbat, Pyuthana, Dang and Rolpa. In return for the assistance provided, the Palpali ruler Mahadat Sen was conferred a golden umbrella, turban and various other symbols of royal authority (*sampurna rajchinnha*), including jewels, pearls, clothes, 101 elephants, 1,001 pure-bred horses and money, along with the three hill kingdoms of Argha, Gulmi and Khanchi.[67] Such gifts were actually exchanges, which while conferring honor and authority on the Palpali raja simultaneously affirmed Palpa's dependent status vis-à-vis Gorkha. By 1780, Palpa had become a dependent of *both* the *nawabs* of Awadh and the rajas of Gorkha. This fact of Palpa's double dependency was confirmed nearly two decades later by W. Scott, the Company's Resident at Lucknow.[68] In 1797, the Gorkhalis sought to reassert their superiority over the Palpali kingdom by forcibly securing an *ikrarnamah* (deed of consent) from the Palpali raja stating that the Gorkhali raja was his absolute lord. The document stated that "The Huzoor is master over my country, my fortunes, my life. Let him do with each whatever best pleases him."[69] By 1802, the Gorkhalis were claiming Palpa as an "ancient dependent."[70] In 1804, *kaji* Damodar Pande, a close ally of the Palpa raja, was executed and the Palpali raja, Prithvipal Sen, was recalled and confined at Kathmandu. In 1806, he was executed, following the assassination of former Gorkhali ruler Ran Bahadur Shah, and his kingdom forcibly incorporated into the Gorkhali Empire.[71] This heralded the abrupt end of a little kingdom that had dominated the political landscape of the mid-hills of central Nepal and its immediate plains for nearly three centuries.

In 1806, the Gorkhalis sent letters to the governor-general seeking the right to farm the Butwal *zamindari* on the same terms that the former rulers of Palpa had done.[72] The Gorkhalis claimed that their conquest of the Palpa raj had made them heirs to all its territories and entitlements.[73] In 1814, just prior to the outbreak of the Anglo–Gorkha War, the raja of Gorkha reiterated this request, stating that

> should it therefore please your Lordship [the English governor-general] to order the delivery of those [disputed] places to the officers of the Gurkha government upon the same terms they are retained by the Raja of Palpa, they shall without hesitation submit to the affixed tribute, or if the retention of the different places in the possession of either state independent of each other is preferred, it would be just and proper since the object of either of those proposals is to remove all misunderstandings [...] God almighty has conferred the extensive territories of Hindustan long governed by foreigners on the British Nation. In like manner has he bestowed the territories on the hills on the Gurkhas and both nations have at length reached the banks of the Sutlej to give stability to ancient customs.[74]

The Gorkhali request outraged Company officials, who believed that the treaty with the *nawab* of Awadh in 1801 had given them full sovereignty and exclusive territorial rights over the lands that the Gorkhalis sought to pay tribute for. Since the Gorkhali claims were based on conquest, the Company viewed them as inferior to its own territorial claims that were confirmed by legal treaty. Such pronouncements were indicative of the Company's emerging vision concerning the juridical basis and exclusive character of its territorial sovereignty.[75] During the first century of colonial rule, this vision crystallized in a very ill-coordinated fashion as the Company pursued an aggressive program of territorial expansion through conquest and treaties. Thus, between 1750 and 1806 Palpa's status was like that of a soft yam (or *tarul*, which was also a Gorkhali metaphor for a weak state) squeezed between large boulders (*dhungo*, or powerful states) like Awadh, Gorkha and, after 1801, the English East India Company.[76] Like many little kingdoms across the subcontinent that lay squeezed between more powerful kingdoms, Palpa's days were numbered and by 1806 no trace of it would remain on the frontier.

5. The Structure of Territory on the Gorakhpur–Butwal Frontier: *Taluqas*, *Parganas* and *Tappas*

The lands straddling the Gorakhpur–Butwal frontier were carved into a number of *parganas*, *taluqas* and *tappas* that had traditionally been subject to the overlordship of the *nawabs* of Awadh (see Map 4.2). These ancient divisions were organized around a shifting ensemble of relationships involving entitlements to overlordship, tax collection and other agrarian resources. As these relationships evolved over time they produced commensurate changes in the layout, organization and boundaries of these divisions, leaving many of them fuzzy and dispersed with overlapping boundaries. For example, *talluqdari* estates, which varied in size, were "for the most part fortuitous collections of villages wrested from the nawab's revenue officers a few at a time, and lumped together arbitrarily in a single revenue engagement."[77] British and Gorkhali officials had limited knowledge of the actual tenurial status, internal divisions and subdivisions of the lands lying along their shared frontier, thanks to local initiative and resistance to the colonizing gaze of these states. A brief historical sketch of these administrative divisions is necessary to better understand the spatial dynamics that informed their creation and evolution.

The Butwal Tarai

Palpa's lands in the Butwal Tarai were largely constituted out of the two *parganas* of Tilpur and Binayakpur. The *pargana* of Binayakpur comprised three divisions: the *pargana* of Binayakpur itself and the *taluqas* of Matka and Khajahani Bhandar.[78] There is no unanimity in the written record concerning the organization, layout and boundaries of these divisions. For instance, Matka had been variously described as a *tappa* or a *taluqa*.[79] British officials themselves were confused about the exact location, layout and structure of the various *taluqa*, *pargana* and *tappa* divisions straddling the Gorakhpur–Butwal frontier (see Map 4.2).

The case of *taluqa* Matka merits further scrutiny. This *taluqa*, made up of 18 or 19 *tappas*, was attached to the *pargana* of Ratanpur Bansi, lying in Gorakhpur.[80] Before 1786 the *taluqa* of Matka belonged to the hill kingdom of Gulmi. Sometime in 1768, the raja of Palpa offered to collect and remit revenues, and officials at Bansi transferred the rights of the *taluqa* to him. The raja of Gulmi complained about the manner in which this came about, alleging that the Palpali raja Mukun Sen II (1752–82) had wrested the *taluqa* from him by paying a *nazrana* (gift) to the *amil* of *pargana* Bansi, under whose charge the *taluqa* lay.[81] This meant that *taluqa* Matka, while attached to the *pargana* of Bansi, was transferred from the territorial possessions of the kingdom of Gulmi to those of Palpa.[82] In 1786, Gulmi, along with the hill kingdoms of Khanchi and Argha, was incorporated into the Palpali raj as a reward for the Palpali assistance provided to Gorkha's western campaigns.[83] This arrangement would have included the Tarai possessions of these kingdoms as well, including Matka. The 1786 grant to the Palpalis severed the fiscal connections that till then had existed between the *taluqa* and the *pargana* of Ratanpur Bansi. From 1786 onwards, the *taluqa* of Matka remained attached to the resources of the Butwal Tarai, more specifically the *pargana* of Binayakpur. Sometime between 1786 and 1793, the Palpa raja Mahadat Sen

Map 4.2 *Parganas* and *tappas* on the Gorakhpur–Butwal frontier, 1814 CE

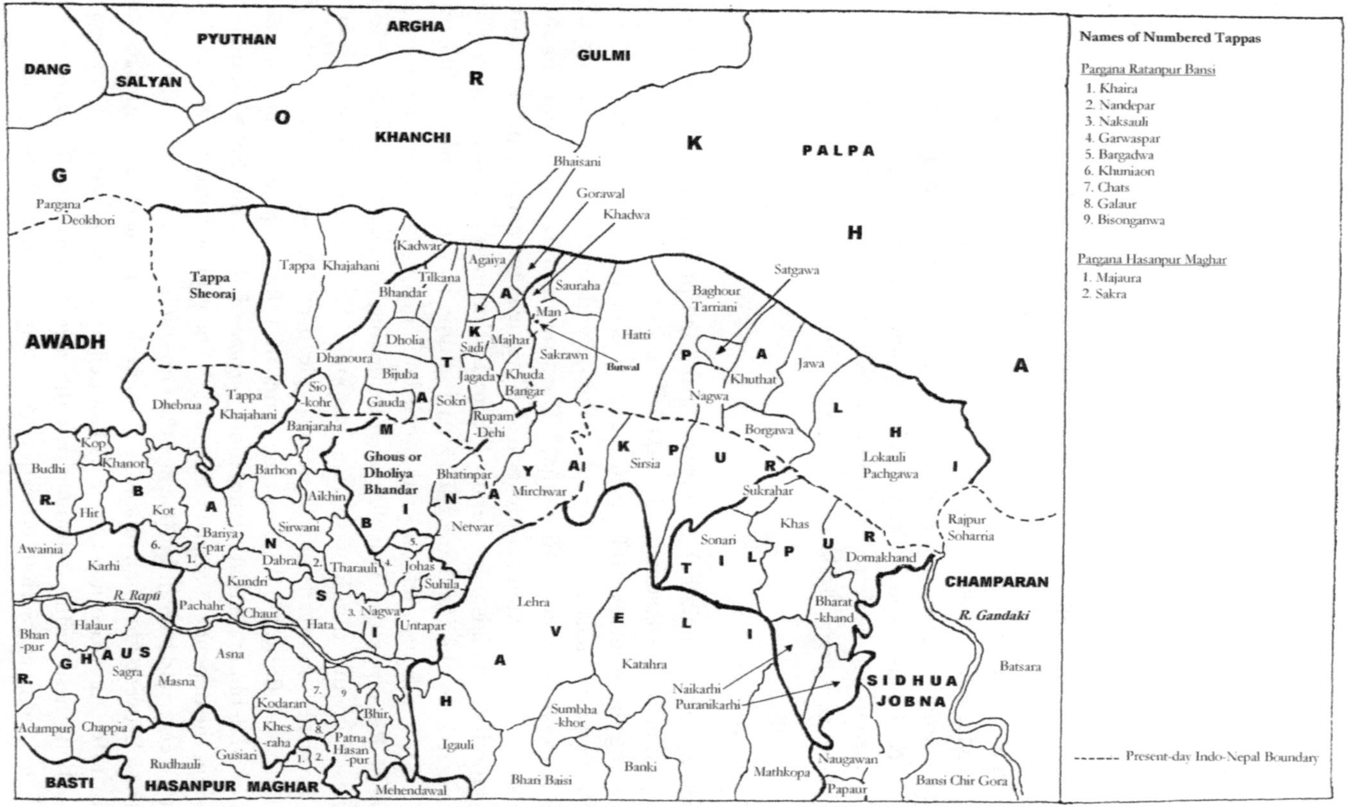

This map is not drawn to scale. The names, location, layout, and boundaries of administrative divisions may vary.
Mapwork by Bernardo A. Michael and Saramma Michael.

got his rights to the *taluqa* of Matka confirmed by Awadh's *nawab* Asafuddaulah, which was then included in the settlements of the *parganas* of Tilpur and Binayakpur. Neither the rajas of Gulmi nor the revenue collectors of Bansi were necessarily pleased with these maneuvers and disputed Palpa's claims.[84] In 1799, the Palpali raja's possessions were confirmed by the Gorkha raja.[85] At the time of the secession of Gorakhpur to the East India Company (in 1801), the *taluqa* was included in the *parganas* of Tilpur and Binayakpur. In 1803, the Gulmi raja, seeking the restoration of Matka, petitioned his sister, who was in charge of the Gorkhali government at Kathmandu.[86] Kathmandu honored the Gulmi raja's request. The Palpali raja, unable to resist this move, reluctantly consented by giving a *razeenamah* (certificate of surrender) to that effect. He even sent word to Company officials that from henceforth the revenues for Matka would be the responsibility of the Gulmi raja.[87] However, he never gave up his claim to this *taluqa* and actively resisted the efforts of the Gulmi raja's officials to take control of it. In 1804, the Gorkhalis reinstated the Palpali raja rights to Matka, which was then valued at Rs 460.[88] No formal grant was issued, and it appears the order given was a verbal one.[89] However, shortly thereafter the Palpali raja was killed in Kathmandu and his kingdom incorporated into Gorkha territories.[90] *Taluqa* Matka remained under the direct management (*kham*) of the East India Company, which was unwilling to accept any Gorkhali claims to the Butwal Tarai.[91]

Tappa *Sheoraj*

Tappa Sheoraj had for long been attached to the hill principality of Pyuthana, and formed a part of its possessions in the plains.[92] As in the case of most administrative divisions along the Anglo–Gorkha frontier, there is confusion as to whether Sheoraj was a *tappa*, *pargana* or *taluqa*. In November 1786, Pyuthana was forcibly incorporated into the territorial possessions of Gorkha.[93] The growing Gorkhali presence in Sheoraj saw increased efforts to extend cultivation and organize tax collection.[94] For instance, in 1795, Gorkhali officials were deputed from Kathmandu in order to survey those lands mortgaged by the Pyuthana raja.[95] At the time of the takeover of Sheoraj by Gorkha in 1786, the *tappa* fell under the jurisdiction of the revenue collectors (*amils*) of *pargana* of Ratanpur Bansi, at that time belonging to Awadh. In addition to this, the *tappa* itself lay mired in long standing disputes. The seventeenth-century French traveler Tavernier observed an intense struggle over this *tappa* between the rajas of Pyuthana and Butwal.[96] At the same time, in 1782, Raja Kirtibam of the hill kingdom of Malebhum (Parbat) claimed the *pargana* of Ratanpur Bansi (and possibly by extension, the dependent *tappa* of Sheoraj).[97] The raja of Palpa too had laid some claim to this *tappa*, and later in 1790, when the Gorkhalis took possession of the *tappa*, a dispute arose between Gorkhali officials stationed there and *amils* of *pargana* Ratanpur Bansi.[98] In 1791, the Governor-General's Council at Calcutta informed the Court of Directors about these "trifling" disputes over the *tappa* of Sheoraj, stating that they are "not likely to lead to any serious consequences or embarrassing consequences," since these lands were, at that time, not under the authority of the Company.[99] However, once the Company acquired territories in this region after the treaty of 1801, it was unable to escape the conflicted histories of these divisions. When this happened, as it did ten years later, the tone of the Company's officials would turn into righteous indignation.

In August 1804, when Sheoraj's taxation arrears (payable at Bansi) began to mount, Bansi's revenue collectors demanded payment of these outstanding dues from the Gorkha raja. The *nawab* of Awadh too had sent a complaint to Company authorities that outstanding arrears were due from the authorities of Sheoraj for the years prior to its cession.[100] The Gorkha raja rejected this demand, arguing that Pyuthan's incorporation into Gorkhali territories in 1786 included its dependent territories such as Sheoraj. There seems to be some truth in this, as Gorkhali records after 1797 refer to Sheoraj as belonging to *zilla* Pyuthana.[101] However, Sheoraj finds mention as a *pargana* and not a *tappa*, as traditionally held. In yet another Gorkhali document, Sheoraj is combined with the neighboring district of Deokhori to form the *pargana* of Deokhori-Sheoraj.[102] However, while I have been unable to discover the nature of the connection between *tappa* Sheoraj and *pargana* Deokhori, it is clear that some kind of connection existed between the two, at least in the revenue records for 1796. Company officials also conducted an investigation into the matter and concluded that *tappa* Sheoraj, by virtue of being attached to *pargana* Ratanpur Bansi, actually formed a part of the Company's possessions. However, Company officials also admitted that the *tappa* of Sheoraj had been in the possession of the Gorkhalis prior to the cession of Gorakhpur to the Company in 1801.[103] Given Gorkha's long connection with Sheoraj, the then governor-general (Lord Minto) surrendered all claims to Sheoraj in 1810, on the condition that the Gorkhalis would refrain from "encroaching" anywhere else on the Gorakhpur–Butwal frontier. The Gorkhalis never seem to have responded to this offer.

Evidence from the Company's records about the fiscal ties between the *tappa* of Sheoraj and its "parent" *pargana* of Ratanpur Bansi between 1786 (when the Gorkhalis first obtained control of it) and 1801 (when the English East India Company first began to claim it) reveals the following information. During these 15 years, the revenue collectors of Bansi were able to collect diminishing revenues for 8 years. No revenues were collected for the remaining 7 years. In the meantime, between 1790 and 1794, some of Gorakhpur's *parganas* like Ratanpur Bansi, Maghar and Rasulpur Ghaus were included in the accounts of the district of Bahraich, though it is not clear if Sheoraj was included in this list. In 1795, they reverted back to Gorakhpur.[104] In addition to the Anglo–Gorkha disputes over Sheoraj, the *tappa* was also wracked by a number of local disputes along its common border with the neighboring *tappa* of Dhebarua, lying in *pargana* Bansi. In the first decade of the nineteenth century, the Tharu revenue collector (*malguzar*) of *tappa* Dhebarua, one Jurawan Chaudhari, was involved in a protracted multi-cornered dispute with Gorkhali officials and local landholders.[105] Jurawan Chaudhari's possessions straddled the Gorakhpur–Butwal frontier, making him a subject both of the East India Company and of Gorkha. The recurrence of such disputes along the Gorakhpur–Butwal frontier worried Company officials. In late 1811, one Captain Williamson was dispatched with a military force to locate the boundary between the *tappas* of Sheoraj and Dhebrua along this frontier. During the course of this investigation, Williamson, who tried to demarcate a straight, linear boundary, was asked by the Gorkhali *fauzdar* stationed there to draw the boundary around certain rice fields that the *fauzdar* was cultivating.[106] Williamson found the request "irregular" and denied it.¹⁰⁷ Williamson, like many of his colleagues, was unwilling to recognize the multiplicity of similar claims that peppered the Anglo–Gorkha frontier, leaving discontinuous the boundary between the two states. Maniraj, like other Gorkhali officials who had been granted lands along the Gorakhpur–Butwal frontier, was unable to fully grasp the rationale of an abstract linear boundary that remained divorced from the various kinds of entitlements they enjoyed (obtained *de facto* or *de jure*) to agrarian resources.¹⁰⁸ It was these social energies, drawn from localized systems of power, influence and claims to agrarian entitlements, which fuelled boundary disputes all along the Anglo–Gorkha frontier. Largely ignored by historians of the Anglo–Gorkha War, they would form a persistent theme and crucial prelude that would inform the eventual outbreak of war in 1814.

In fact, local initiative was so unchecked that even Kathmandu was uncertain about what its officials were doing on the frontier. The Gorkhali commander on the Gorakhpur–Butwal frontier, *kaji* Amar Singh Thapa, discovered, when investigating the dispute over Sheoraj, that the Gorkhali *chaudharis* of Sheoraj had been giving gifts to officials at Bansi.¹⁰⁹ The *chaudharis* insisted that such gifts were customary exchanges made during their meetings and that they had never remitted taxes to Bansi ("*mamilat hoina bhetghat hunda sar saugad diyako ho*").¹¹⁰ The Gorkhali commander was unsure about the exact context of such "gift" exchanges and how they might have informed the relationship between the *chaudharis* of Sheoraj and officials at Bansi. Ultimately, the *kaji* dismissed these claims, as they had never been sanctioned by the authorities at Kathmandu. This suggests that the assessment, collection and remittance of revenues in the area of Sheoraj were in the nature of temporary arrangements made between various revenue officials and landholders/cultivators, usually without the knowledge of authorities at Kathmandu. Despite such local maneuvering, it was clear that senior Gorkhali officials were unwilling to consider Sheoraj anything less than a part of Gorkha's territorial possessions ("*ajasamma aafnu ambal bhayako jaga*").¹¹¹ Consequently, in 1814, the raja of Gorkha sent two letters to firmly reassert Gorkha's claims to this *tappa*.¹¹²

Thus, in 1813, *tappa* Sheoraj had become an illegible patch of territory, wracked by powerful local forces that eluded the centralizing thrust of both Gorkha and the Company. Between 1780 and 1814 it lay entangled with a number of *parganas* (Bansi and Deokhori), little kingdoms (Pyuthana, Butwal and Bansi) and powerful states (like Awadh, Gorkha and the English East India Company). Company officials who were unwilling to relinquish their claims to Sheoraj and other lands in the Butwal Tarai claimed that:

> No documents which have yet been submitted to the Governor-General, afford the least sanction to the authority which the raja of Napaul claims the right of introduction into the lowlands of Bootwal upon the ground of ancient usage, nor does the Governor-General admit the pretention of the Raja to the management of that [Butwal] zamindaree upon any principle of Justice or of equity founded upon the authority which he exercises over the raja of Palpa, as a subject of the Government of Napaul. As a matter of right, therefore the Governor-General is resolved not to accede to the introduction of the authority of Napaul, into the zamindaree in question [...] [T]he Governor-General is of the opinion that the British Government would possess no security for the regular

payment of the revenue by the officers of the Napaul state should the lowlands of Bootwal be entrusted to the Rajah in farm (*theka*).[113]

The Company was only willing to admit Gorkha's territorial claim if it had a juridical basis that was supported by documentary evidence, and not because of its claims to overlordship over Palpa. It was only after the conclusion of the Anglo–Gorkha War and the formal demarcation of the Anglo–Gorkha boundary that the *tappa* of Sheoraj was handed over to the Gorkhalis. Following this, the claims of the rulers of Pyuthana, to whom this *tappa* originally belonged, were forever silenced.[114]

Other Tappas

A similar dynamic unfolded in a number of other fiscal divisions such as the *tappa* of Majhar, which was disputed by the rajas of Palpa and Gulmi. The Palpali raja claimed that Majhar belonged to the *pargana* of Binayakpur, while the latter claimed that it had been attached to the *taluqa* of Matka, then under his possession.[115] Surveyors (*amins*) deputed by Kathmandu were unable to resolve this dispute.[116] The same was the case for the *taluqa* of Khajahani Bhandar, the *pargana* of Ratanpur Bansi and the *tappa* of Dholiya Bhandar. The *taluqa* of Khajahani Bhandar was disputed between the hill kingdoms of Khanchi and Palpa. Khajahani, which was originally held by the hill rajas of Khanchi, was transferred to Palpa in 1786 in return for its assistance in Gorkha's military campaigns in the west.[117] At various times it had also been attached to the *parganas* of Ratanpur Bansi and Binayakpur.[118] However, the *quanungo* records of the period indicate that the *taluqa* was included in the *tappa* of Sheoraj, which had been for some time attached to the *pargana* of Bansi.[119] In another instance, the British surveyor Francis Buchanan-Hamilton noted that the *tappa* of Dholiya Bhandar, lying to the north of *pargana* Bansi, had in the past been attached to the *pargana* of Binayakpur.[120] Similarly, the *pargana* of Tilpur was the subject of a dispute between the rajas of Palpa and Bansi, being attached to various kingdoms on the Gorakhpur–Butwal frontier. Thus, by 1814, and for reasons described in the previous pages, the lands belonging to these administrative divisions had witnessed frequent changes in their tenurial and taxation relationships that made it hard to discern any continuity in their territorial layout and organization. British officials along the frontier found it impossible to disentangle these territories and establish neat, continuous and linear boundaries between them.

6. Conclusion

The developments outlined in this chapter form the ingredients of a spatial history of the Anglo–Gorkha frontier. On the Gorakhpur–Butwal section of the frontier, the Tarai lands of Butwal stood at the center of the Anglo–Gorkha territorial disputes that preceded the war of 1814. These lands remained entangled within a regime of shifting agrarian entitlements and disputatious cultures of governance which created multiple and ever-shifting loci of authority with discontinuous and overlapping jurisdictions. Multi-directional flows of taxes and tribute, along with varied and shifting tenurial arrangements, adequately represented in the records of the time, gave further complexity to the territorial dynamics unfolding along the frontier, leaving many administrative divisions ill-defined, intermixed and contested. The presence of a large number of *birt* and *maafi* grants in the Gorakhpur–Butwal area significantly multiplied the role of local agency in processes of statemaking. Rent-free lands, in particular, became islands of autonomy within the tax-yielding lands along the frontier. Consequently, the territories of most kingdoms – large and small – along the Gorakhpur–Butwal frontier remained mutually entangled and interlocked with discontinuous and fuzzy boundaries. While local communities and states had always lived within such contexts of socio-spatial flux, officials of the East India Company experienced growing anxiety about such territorial illegibility and its implications for the collection of revenue and maintenance of order. By 1814 too much was at stake for both for the Gorkhalis and the British to relinquish their respective territorial claims. With no resolution in sight, a violent conflict seemed imminent. On 29 May 1814, in a surprise dawn attack, Gorkhali troops struck at the Company's police posts (*thanas*) of Biswarea, Chitwa and Sourah in the Butwal Tarai, killing a number of its policemen stationed there. This attack was led by none other than the Gorkhali *fauzdar* of the Butwal Tarai, Maniraj Bhaju. The *thanadar* of Chitwa, one Kashinath, was captured and on Maniraj's orders, tied to a tree and shot to death with arrows. This became the immediate cause of the war, and very soon the questions of territoriality that had plagued the relations between the two states receded into the background, as Company officials responded to this attack by declaring war on Gorkha.

Chapter 5

THE DISJOINTED SPACES OF PRECOLONIAL TERRITORIAL DIVISIONS

Territorial relationships between different polities possessed the characteristic forms of the property system, but on the largest possible scales. Thus, at their edges territorial jurisdictions began to intermingle, while the revenues of some reign – sometimes of whole polities – might well be shared, both parties more than likely organizing their own administrations in the regions concerned. This closely mirrored the tendency of military leaders in the Deccan to hold properties under the jurisdictions of more than one power, and of each holder of fiscal rights in a particular locus to have his own collectorate, a plurality of such collectors descending on the countryside at harvest time.

—Frank Perlin[1]

The boundaries of this state [of Jhansi, in North India] which consist of so many parts cannot be described in aggregation.

—Capt. J. Franklin[2]

There is a very extraordinary variety between Pergannahs and even Talooks on every point on which comparison can be made, and the circumstances combined with the undoubted habit of the royts to migrate from place to place renders it indispensable that every statistical enquiry to be correct should be recent in date and narrowed in locality. General results to any practical purpose would be fallacious.

—Major P. Vans Agnew on the *suba* of Chattisgarh[3]

1. Introduction: Precolonial Administrative Divisions in South Asia

Drawing from evidence gathered in previous chapters on the constitution of territorial divisions along the Anglo–Gorkha frontier, this chapter will inventory the variables that tugged at their spatial frame to produce their discontinuous territories and fuzzy boundaries. In South Asia, precolonial states possessed clearly discernible geographical bodies that were divided and sub-divided into a number of territorial divisions. Mughal provinces (*suba*) were frequently divided into *sarkars*, *parganas*, *tappas* in – though not always – descending order (see Map 5.1).[4] The *parganas* constituted the basic administrative unit of the Mughal Empire and its successor states, both for purposes of general administration and revenue collection.[5] There was no unanimous rationale in

Map 5.1 Boundaries and internal divisions of the Mughal Empire, 1650 CE

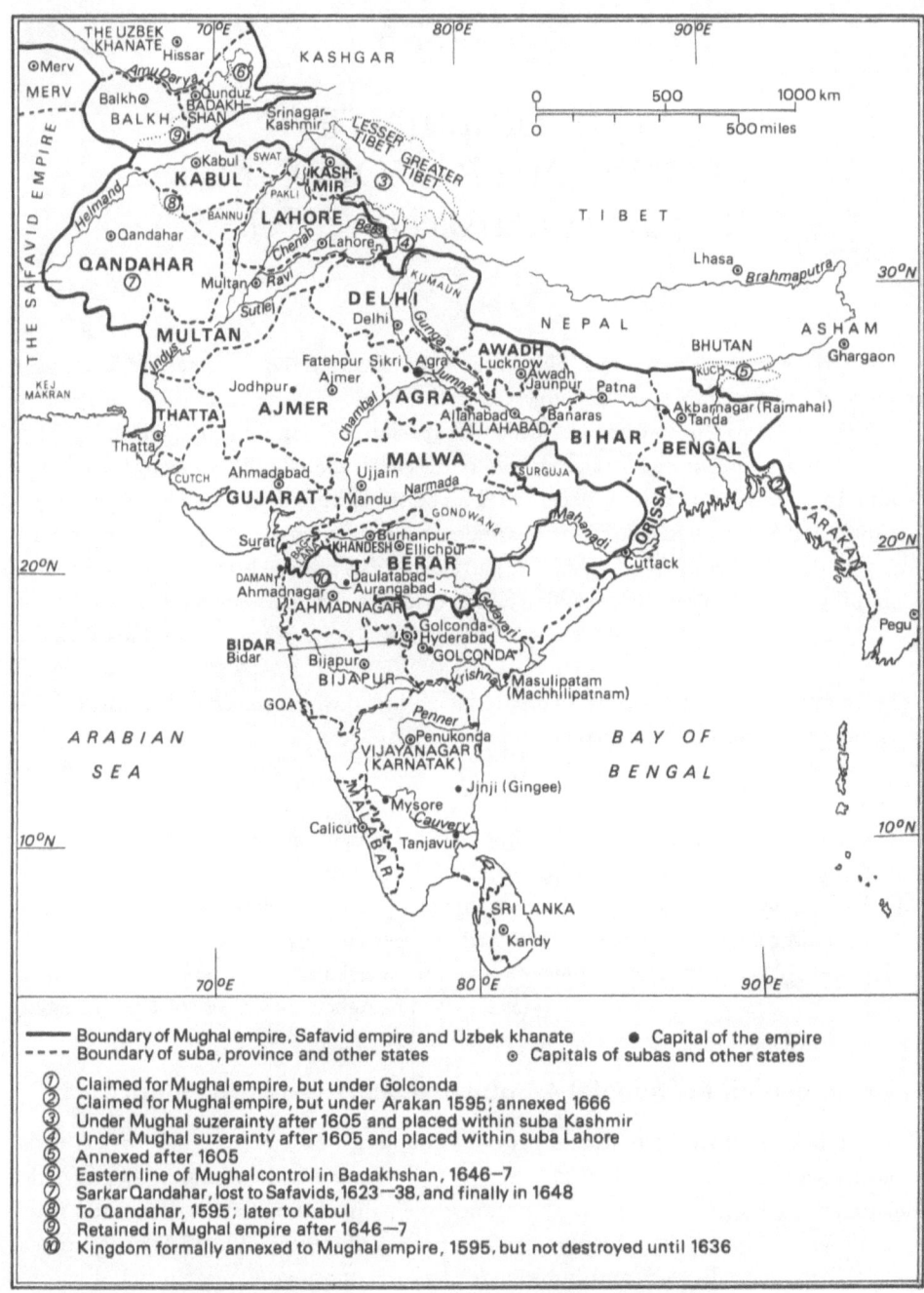

Reproduced with permission from *An Atlas of the Mughal Empire* by Irfan Habib and published by Oxford University Press, New Delhi © 1982, Oxford University Press.

the size or internal organization of these divisions.[6] However, under the Mughals, an attempt was made to organize *parganas* around *dasturs* (areas bound by shared customs, usage and a schedule of uniform crop rates).[7] In general, *parganas* were subdivided into *tappas* and *tarafs*, which were in turn made up of individual *mauzas* (villages). *Mauzas* could be further classified under categories such as *asli*, *dakhili*, *raiyati* and *taluqa*.[8] The term "*asli*" generally signified a village that had its original habitation intact. The term "*dakhili*" applied to a village that, for purposes of revenue collection, was treated as a dependency of an *asli* village. Such relationships were prone to frequent reconstitution as both *asli* and *dakhili* villages, for a variety of reasons, became attached, detached and reattached to one another. For example, in the district of Saran (Bihar), local custom held that when an *asli* village was sold in auction or private sale, attached *dakhili* village(s) were also included in the sale unless their boundaries were already ascertained.[9] *Raiyati* villages were those where the government directly dealt with the landholders (*zamindars*), while a *taluqa* referred to a collection of, usually dispersed, villages formed into an estate for which a single individual had engaged to collect revenue.[10] This description of the hierarchy of territorial divisions is by no means complete, and varied from region to region.[11] Such territorial divisions and arrangements would, as we shall see, register discontinuities in their layout, internal organization and boundaries.

A host of officials supervised the collection of revenue, the administration of justice and the preservation of law and order in the above-mentioned divisions. Officials such as the *fauzdar*, *amalguzar*, *kotwal* and *qazi* were to be found at the level of the *sarkar*, while officials such as the *shiqdar*, *amil*, *quanungo* and *patwari* could be found at the level of the *pargana*. Scholars like W.H. Moreland and P. Saran have debated whether the jurisdictions of these officials neatly overlapped with the territorial limits of an administrative division. Moreland pointed out that there were two broad types of divisions in the Mughal Empire – fiscal and administrative – and the officials placed in charge of these divisions had distinctive territorial jurisdictions that did not always coincide. Saran, on the other hand, argued that the Mughal Empire was divided into fiscal and administrative divisions that overlapped.[12] While entering into the technicalities of the debate is beyond the mandate of this work, Moreland's, rather than Saran's, views seem to fall in line with the findings of this book. Moreover, many jurisdictions, such as the *fauzdari* not only did not overlap, but lay dispersed in a highly irregular fashion across administrative districts.[13] This trait might have been accentuated within certain ecological niches such as the wastes of Haryana, north of Delhi, where the Mughals had "imposed several overlapping jurisdictions on the area as a result of which it belonged to several subas, sarkars, dastur circles and fauzdaris, all without clearly marked rights or boundaries."[14] Under the successor states to the Mughals, revenue-collection jurisdictions must have witnessed greater fluctuations thanks to the practice of regional rulers' (for example, the *nawabs* of Awadh) issuing short-term *ijara* or revenue-farming contracts to officials such as *amils* and *fauzdars*.[15]

To date, the best attempts to locate and map Mughal fiscal divisions have been made by colonial officials such as H. M. Elliot, John Beames and H. Blochmann, and more recently the historians of Mughal India such as Jadunath Sarkar and Irfan Habib.[16] Mughal administrative divisions were prone to frequent changes and the works of Elliot and Beames provide innumerable instances of *mahals* whose names and layout had changed – often drastically – making it impossible to determine their contours, and in many instances even their actual location.[17] This pattern was replicated all along the Anglo–Gorkha frontier where territorial divisions such as *parganas*, *tappas* and *mauzas* were prone to frequent changes in their layout, internal organization and boundaries. This was largely due to their lands shifting back and forth following the ebbs and flows of military conquest and struggles over honor, authority and access to agrarian entitlements. Within Gorkha too, territorial fluctuations did take place, but the evidence is less forthcoming due to the paucity of sources.

Given this history of flux, territories could be understood as *shifting spaces produced by the ebb and flow of dynamic social forces*. Such an understanding has not always found expression in the studies of the historical geography of these administrative divisions. While such accounts begin correctly by taking into account the role of dominant lineages in the production of territory, they end up depicting *parganas* and *tappas* as organic social spaces – the geographical expression of dominant social groups.[18] In this manner, a convenient convergence between kin and territorial boundaries is facilitated that is undisturbed by other variables such as ecology, the changing structure of agrarian entitlements and disputatious cultures of governance and economic forces. Stewart Gordon and John F. Richards' work on kinship and *pargana* in eighteenth-century Adilabad (in Khandesh, Maharashtra) provides a timely corrective by recognizing the role played by variables such as revenue administration and a highly monetized economy in the development of *pargana* organization.[19] The emergence of the state, the land market and monetary economy in the seventeenth and eighteenth centuries further dissolved the continuity between caste, kin and territorial boundaries in North India.[20] B. R. Grover has observed that widespread sale transactions altered the original caste basis of the older *zamindari* villages in the seventeenth century, resulting in "the shuffling of the old caste or clan based zamindari settlements in various villages in North India" to create new "composite settlements and villages."[21] Thus, by the eighteenth century variables such as the environment, the growth of new centers of regional power, the contracting and subcontracting of revenue collection rights by the state and the movement of goods, capital and other resources had broken any neat continuity between the boundaries of states and social groups. Succeeding centuries must have witnessed further intensification of these trends and processes.

2. The Environment, Labor and Shifting Patterns of Land-Use in the Constitution of Territory

Administrative divisions such as *tappas* and *parganas* were also spaces marked by the relationship between humans and their environments. Chapter 2 explored how the environment and dynamic land-use patterns created the mobile territorial spaces of the Anglo–Gorkha frontier, which was made up of thick malarial forests at the edge of an expanding zone of agrarian activity. Administrative divisions lying along this frontier witnessed expansions and contractions in their size and boundaries as land-use patterns shifted under the influence of environmental and human factors. The shortage of labor along the frontier produced shifting patterns of labor mobility which, during the

Mughal period (1526–1707), constituted "one of the most striking features of the social and economic life of the times."[22] This was clearly evident all along the Anglo–Gorkha frontier where the presence or absence of labor produced shifting patterns of land-use which caused territorial divisions such as *tappas* and *parganas* to pulsate in their layout and organization as lands fell in and out of cultivation (see Chapter 2).[23] These divisions fluctuated in size – being inserted in the documentary record when yielding taxes and then disappearing when they fell out of cultivation and were classified as "waste." One recorded instance serves as an exemplar of this. Sometime towards the end of the eighteenth century, the Palpali raja Prithvipal Sen (1793–1806) gave the *tappa* of Mirchwar as a *maafi* (rent-free) grant to his brother, Nadir Shah. The latter then added to *tappa* Mirchwar nine new villages he had established in the neighboring uncultivated *tappa* of Netwar. In this manner, these nine villages (created out of "waste" lands) became detached from the *tappa* of Netwar and attached to the resources of *tappa* Mirchwar. While the aforementioned *tappas* lay within the *pargana* of Binayakpur, such attachments and detachments took place with little consideration for maintaining the territorial continuity and boundaries of the concerned *tappas*.[24] Such fluctuating patterns of (waste)land-use has prompted some scholars to treat them as some kind of "intermediate space," lying between cultivation and forest and denoting a variety of land-use types – cultivable, fallow, pasture or barren.[25] Unearthing such examples from the historical record in order to write a detailed and differentiated spatial history of waste lands on the subcontinent would be a long-drawn task that certainly deserves further attention.

3. Cultures of Precolonial Governance and the Production of Territory

The study of colonial encounters and governance in South Asia has generated much discussion, research and writing. This book seeks to connect this body of knowledge with the writings on spatiality and the production of territory that have emerged largely in studies of the history of cartography and cultural geography. The notion of cultures of governance furnishes a conceptual framework that examines agrarian entitlements and practices for their spatial content. South Asian states were composed out of such a structure of entitlements to agrarian resources which resulted in the creation of multiple and overlapping administrative and political jurisdictions with shared sovereignties. Such cultures of governance produced the dispersed and discontinuous agrarian territories of precolonial states in South Asia which were organized around "conflict and remained essentially open ended instead of becoming territorially circumscribed."[26] The remaining sections of this chapter will review some of the forces that produced the territorial open-endedness of precolonial regimes in South Asia that the Anglo–Gorkha War initially helped to diagnose.

Agrarian Entitlements and the Production of Territory

The study of agrarian entitlements in South Asia over the last two hundred years presents a field full of rich pickings and goes back to the first attempts of the English East India

Company to collect information on this subject in the eighteenth century. Entitlements to land and its derivative resources in eighteenth-century South Asia, emerged from the post-Mughal agrarian order. They were organized in complex *interlocked hierarchies of mutually co-existing* rights to access, allocate and appropriate material and symbolic resources like land, water, forests, taxes, tribute, markets, service, status, honor, authority, and so on. Such rights could be bundled together. For instance, *zamindari* rights, as Irfan Habib has observed, "did not [merely] signify a proprietary right over land. It co-existed with other rights and claims on the produce of the soil."[27] Such rights were sanctioned by custom but subject to frequent changes given the vagaries of power struggles that frequently rearranged the social hierarchies out of which such rights flowed.[28] Such rights were zealously guarded, keenly contested and subject to frequent (re)negotiation. Military (re)conquests and (re)settlement invariably rearranged the alignments of political clients, giving rise to new claims and counter-claims to these entitlements. Entitlements that remained unenforced could lapse. This became very clear when Company officials inquired from officials of Gulmi about Gorkha's connection to the *taluqa* of Makta. These officials indicated that the rights of possession over this *taluqa* had fallen on Gorkha, since its actual owners – the *nawabs* of Awadh had never made any attempt to enforce their claims.[29] Such unscripted and contingent practices complicated any neat and easy attempts to define such entitlements either in language or legislation.

The right to collect taxes and/or tribute had everything to do with issues of honor and authority as well. During periods of political instability these rights could frequently be redefined. Here the case of the little kingdom of Otroj in the Western Himalayas is illuminating. This kingdom bordered the states of Sirmur and Jubal (see Map 5.2).[30] Otroj, a tiny principality made up of a few villages and a dependency of the hill state of Sirmur, is referred to as a *pargana* in the revenue records of the period. Between Otroj and Sirmur lay the kingdom of Jubal, superior to Otroj, but inferior in political status to Sirmur. Before the introduction of Gorkhali rule in the area (1806–14), Otroj's revenues to Sirmur were remitted through Jubal, signifying the former's inferior status to both Jubal and Sirmur. Jubal in turn paid its revenues to Sirmur, signifying its ties of dependency with Sirmur.[31] Under Gorkhali rule, the three principalities were placed under the charge of two different Gorkhali commanders, with Sirmur and Otroj under *kaji* Ranjor Thapa and the Jubal under *budakaji* (elder *kaji*) Amar Singh Thapa.[32] Under this new dispensation, Otroj's ties of dependency with Sirmur were reaffirmed, but its relationship with Jubal became ambiguous since Otroj now no longer paid its revenues through Jubal. In this manner, its older relationship of dependency with Jubal was dissolved. Questions about this relationship surfaced when the British attempted to conduct political and revenue settlements in the area, following their conquest of these Western Himalayan states in 1815. Captain Birch, the English officer in charge of the Company's settlement operations, soon found himself trying to disentangle these relationships constructed around taxation and honor, but now complicated by the fallout of the Gorkhali invasion. Birch found that in the revenue records of the kingdom of Sirmur, Jubal and Otroj were mentioned as constituting a single revenue-paying unit (*Joobul mye Ootraj*, or Otroj revenues being customarily remitted through authorities at Jubal).[33] In this manner, Jubal, Otroj and Sirmur were

Map 5.2 Sketch showing the kingdoms of Sirmur, Jubal and Otroj, 1815 CE

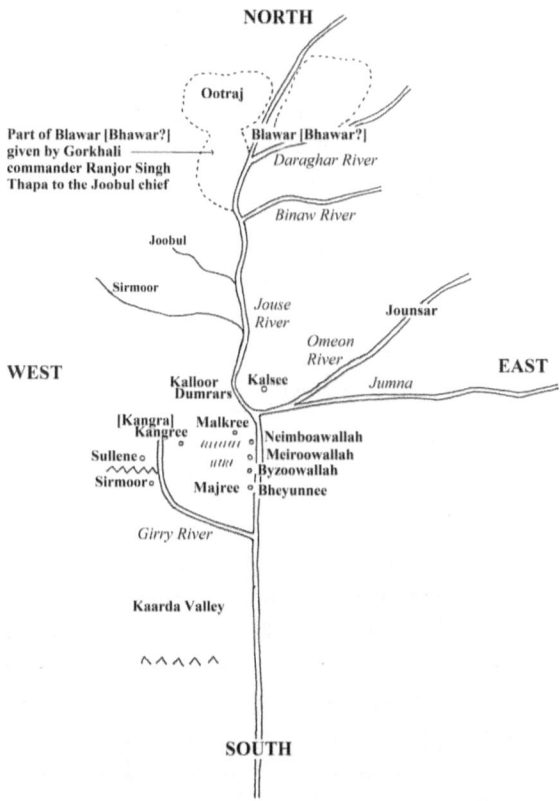

Mapwork by Bernardo A. Michael and Natalie Burack.
Source: Adapted from Captain Birch's "Sketch of the Relative Locations of the Kingdoms of Sirmur, Jubal, and Otroj in the Western Himalayas" (1815). Extract of a letter from Captain Birch, Assistant Agent to the Governor General, to C. T. Metcalf, Resident at Delhi, 7 December 1815, Settlement of the Districts of Joobul and Ootraj, in Boards Collections F/4/570 no. 13993, p. 7, India Office Records, Asia, Pacific & Africa Collections, British Library.

sutured together by such relations and claims to material and symbolic entitlements. Similar instances of this can be found elsewhere. For instance, the raja of Palpa paid his taxes for Butwal directly to the *nawab* of Awadh's treasury in Fyzabad and not to his officials stationed at nearby Gorakhpur. This honor symbolically signified the Palpa raja's favored connection with the *nawab* and his superiority to officials at Gorakhpur. Fiscal relationships such as these were "total" or polyvalent in their constitution – being composed out of symbolic variables concerning status, honor and authority, and not just restricted to material forces such as taxes or tribute.[34] Such shifting political and tenurial relationships, along with their attendant tribute and tax flows, stitched together patches of (at times discontinuous) territory to produce the contorted bodies of many precolonial states in South Asia. Such territories remained prone to frequent fluctuations as political elites jostled to make favorable rearrangements of their locations, relationships and jurisdictions.

The dynamic histories of such entitlements radiated distinctive spatial effects because they were firmly yoked to the territorial frame of precolonial states. They produced an ebb and flow in landholding patterns and territorial claims as *mauzas*, *tappas* and entire *parganas* cycled back and forth between various claimants. These were duly inscribed in the revenue record, land documents, official orders and letters, usually without any attempt being made to keep territories contiguous, coherent or neatly bounded. Spatially anxious colonial officials quickly found that any attempt to protract a modern map from this information would be impossible, as they left administrative divisions such as *parganas* riddled with overlaps, intermixtures and unclear boundaries. Colonial observers like Charles Elliott were quick to make the connection between these shifting entitlements and the constitution of territory. He noted that in the district of Oonao (Unnao, in modern day Uttar Pradesh), the "limits of a Pergunnah hardly ever coincide with physical or geographical boundaries, and the only other cause for their irregular tracing seems to be proprietary right."[35]

Rent-Free (Maafi) Grants

Most South Asian kingdoms possessed territories that were peppered with rent-free landholdings. Such rent-free grants were variously called *aimma*, *altamgha*, *birta*, *inam*, *lakhiraj*, *madad-i-mash* and *maafi*.[36] Within Gorkha, these rights went under the names of *kusa birta*, *sarb ank maaf birta*, *sankalp birta* and *guthi*. Despite the varieties of rent-free grants, for purposes of convenience, the term *maafi* has been used in this book as a generic term to cover all these grants. Traditionally, South Asian rulers had granted such tax-free rights to their subjects in recognition of some service performed (such as assistance in war or personal valor in combat), or some meritorious quality displayed (such as saintliness or learning). Such grants signified the practice by which rulers and elites shared their authority and resources in an effort to build bodies of loyal dependents, clients and supporters as they pursued projects to preserve and expand their respective interests. It is through such practices of sharing their sovereignty that South Asian rulers were able to constitute and reconstitute their political authority. However, there was a tendency among *maafi* holders to convert their holdings into inheritable tenures to which rulers responded by undertaking periodic surveys and resumptions. Thus, while rent-free grants were at once signs of the power and influence of South Asian overlords, they were also indicative of the limits to their authority. The dynamics surrounding such rent-free grants of land formed an integral characteristic of processes of precolonial state formation in South Asia.[37]

Such rent-free land grants could be found all along the Anglo–Gorkha frontier. In the disputes that surfaced along the frontier, frequent references can be found characterizing these grants as being autonomous of lands entered into the tax rolls of the state. Such a notion of the tenurial distinction of rent-free grants allowed individuals and states to assert claims to these lands irrespective of their geographical location and distribution. In other words, *maafi* lands became little islands of tenurial autonomy that jostled with other types of land tenures that could still be bundled around the geographical possessions and revenue collection mechanisms of the state. This point has been noted by anthropologist Richard Burghart who, in an important article on royal gifts of land, concluded that holders of such grants "were completely *outside* the revenue system of Nepal."[38] Mirza Abdulla Beg would make such a claim concerning his tax-free entitlement to *tappa* Rautahat, while the Gorkhali government would lay claim to the *maafi* lands bestowed by the *nawabs* of Awadh on the kings of Palpa. The spatial fallout of such rhetoric suggests that the conflicted discourse surrounding rent-free grants permitted the continual packing and unpacking of a kingdom's territories. Such a spatialized discourse around rent-free lands was at work along the Anglo–Gorkha frontier and formed an important context to the territorial disputes that preceded the war. However, more research needs to be done in order to understand its workings in other regions of South Asia.

Landholders often had their entitlements to lands reconfirmed, in many instances, by multiple overlords. Weaker landholders used this as a strategy to preserve continued access to their cache of material and symbolic entitlements during times of political uncertainty. Such moves were not without some distinct spatial effects. When more than one political superior (re)confirmed a client's rights to a resource, this led to multiple overlords with claims to that resource. Consequently, the physical spaces of precolonial states could overlap, as they did in the cases of *pargana* Tauter, *taluqa* Matka and *tappa* Rautahat along the Anglo–Gorkha frontier. Such practices of reconfirmation were also occasions for reinterpreting the terms of the original grant, as the new overlords sought to eventually resume the grant while the original holders tried to cling to their entitlement on the original or most advantageous terms. Thus, recall Mirza Abdulla Beg applying to the rajas of Bettiah and Gorkha to confirm his rent-free rights to *tappa* Rautahat and the rajas in turn trying to redefine the terms of the grant by reconfirming it on a resumable *jagir* basis (see Chapter 3). Needless to say, tenurial dynamics of this kind invariably translated into the reconstitution of territory as well.

Territorial Rearrangements

Territories were also reconstituted through official fiat that was driven by political and administrative compulsions. Under the Mughals, the *sarkar* of Orissa was constituted into a distinct *suba* (province) while the *sarkar* of Rohtas (*suba* Bihar) was bifurcated into two *sarkars* – Rohtas and Shahbad.[39] This seems to have occurred not only in order to facilitate better political and administrative control, but also to allow for the extension of cultivation.[40] Elsewhere, the *pargana* of Khuronsa was at around this time transferred from *sarkar* Khariabad to *sarkar* Gorakhpur, and, in 1730, the *pargana* of Sidhua Jobna (at one time forming a part of *sarkar* Saran) was transferred to *sarkar* Gorakhpur where it remained until Gorakhpur's union with the East India Company's territories in 1801.[41] In eastern Rajasthan we hear of *tappas* and *parganas* being constituted, reconstituted and consolidated as their constituent villages were attached to, and detached from, the various revenue divisions they belonged to – often in a highly discontinuous fashion. In a number of cases, *tappas* were rendered *parganas*, and vice-versa. For instance, in 1756 the *pargana* of Bhangarh was treated as a *tappa* of *pargana* Ajabgarh for a few months. *Pargana* Ajabgarh itself was in the same year incorporated in *pargana* Ghazi ka Thana.[42]

A similar fate befell many *tappas* and *parganas* along the Anglo–Gorkha frontier prior to 1814. The *taluqa* of Khajahani and the *tappa* Dholiya Bhandar are two instances, among many, of territorial divisions that witnessed numerous mutations and entanglements with the kingdoms of Khanchi, Palpa, Awadh, Gorkha and the East India Company (see Chapter 4). In the eighteenth century, the district of Gorakhpur witnessed frequent transfers within the revenue registers of Awadh. Between 1789 and 1791, it was joined to the district of Azamgarh and thereafter kept separate. Between 1790 and 1794, some of Gorakhpur's *parganas* (like Ratanpur Bansi, Maghar and Rasulpur Ghaus) were included in the accounts of the district of Bahraich. They reverted back to Gorakhpur in 1795.[43] On occasion, even lakes and ponds were subject to such transfers in the revenue record; in 1774, disputes broke out between the *zamindars* of *tappa* Haveli Harhara (*pargana* Mehsi) and *tappa* Butsilla (*pargana* Bissara) over the produce of a lake that, between 1767 and 1773, lay with the former, and thereafter was forcibly taken over by the *zamindars* of the latter *tappa*.[44]

In South Asia, such frequent reconstitutions of territory were also caused by the conflicted constitution of precolonial states. Commenting on the Mughals, one writer observed that, "war was the principal business of the Mughal emperors, who committed by far the bulk of their resources to the military."[45] Such conflict induced frequent territorial reconstitutions not just between states, but between rajas, *zamindars* and other local and supra-local elites as well. Along the Anglo–Gorkha frontier, the *pargana* of Silhet (in Gorakhpur district) originally formed a part of the *pargana* of Haveli Gorakhpur. Around 1683, it emerged as a separate *pargana*, following a protracted contest between the rajas of Haveli Gorkahpur and Majhauli.[46] In the seventeenth century, the eastern part of the *pargana* of Babra (originally belonging to *sarkar* Tirhut) was transferred to *sarkar* Champaran after its conquest by the rajas of Bettiah.[47] Elsewhere, along the Anglo–Gorkha frontier, the *tappa* of Chigwan belonged to the hill kingdom of Makwanpur, until its conquest by Gorkha in 1762. Subsequently, the Gorkhalis took control of the northern half while the southern half fell within the Company's territories and the latter steadfastly refused to surrender it over to the Gorkhalis.[48] Similarly, during the Mughal period, the *pargana* of Kathila (in Gorakhpur district) was renamed Bansi when the raja of Kathila was killed by the Bansi raja. Later it was combined with a portion of *pargana* Ratanpur Maghar to form the new *pargana* of Ratanpur Bansi, while the remaining portion of Maghar, in the eighteenth century, became the *pargana* of Hasanpur Maghar.[49] In the early nineteenth century, numerous territorial disputes arose along the Tirhut-Sarlahi and Purnea-Morung sections of the Anglo–Gorkha frontier.[50] Such disputes involved conflicting claims to shifting riverain boundaries and a host of agrarian, forest and taxation resources, which left contested the boundaries and territorial structure of villages and districts.[51] This probably took place not just along the Anglo–Gorkha frontier, but throughout the length and breadth of the East India Company's territorial possessions.[52] Similar disputes unfolded within Gorkha's Tarai districts, although more work needs to be done to discern their territorial implications.[53]

This conflicted constitution of territory formed the "inner logic" of the political systems operating on the Anglo–Gorkha frontier. It generated considerable *plasticity* in institutional arrangements for governance.[54] The constitution of this kind of plasticity in institutional arrangements formed a persistent theme in processes of statemaking in the North Indian plains. Local agents enjoyed considerable freedom to negotiate, rearrange and redefine institutional arrangements for governance. Landholders, officials and cultivators consistently attempted to pare down the state's taxation demand using a variety of strategies such as defalcation, manipulation of records and even flight.[55] Practices of bribing were also widespread and used for securing offices, service-tenures, revenue contracts and land grants. In fact, it might be asserted that negotiations, rule bending, compromise and free-riding were characteristic practices that marked the assessment and collection of revenue. The Regmi Research Collection and Regmi Research Series reveal a large number of complaints against Gorkhali officials being presented at Kathmandu. These complaints revolved around unauthorized exactions, false claims, acceptance of bribes, harassment of cultivators, withholding of revenues due to the state, and so on.[56] Ad hoc arrangements, such as the farming out of revenue collection rights (*ijaras*), which became increasingly widespread in Awadh and Gorkha's Tarai in the late eighteenth and early nineteenth centuries, further contributed to the creation of flexible institutional arrangements.[57] In the end, neither the Company nor Gorkha were able to enforce their strictures and minimize the territorial slippage that ensued.

Documenting Territory

In precolonial South Asia, states possessed well-established discourses and practices of record keeping. Detailed records were maintained pertaining to almost every aspect of general administration, revenue collection, proprietary rights, crops and trade, as well as intelligence gathering and social communication.[58] While these revenue records referred to administrative divisions, such as *suba*, *sarkar*, *pargana*, *tappa* and *mauza*, it was hard to reconstruct the administrative geography of these divisions in terms of linear boundaries and continuous territories. Mughal land-survey documents (*raqbabandi* documents) provided detailed information on landholders and their rights and obligations, the details of fields under cultivation (*khasra*) and crops and soil types, but made no attempt at producing maps.[59] These *raqbabandi* documents were largely in the nature of village lists organized under *tappa* and *pargana* heads *without any attempt at preserving the layout and spatial integrity of the concerned administrative divisions*.[60] Representing the *pargana* as a *whole* or getting a fix on it as a continuous block of territory was not the pressing concern of record keepers and their practices of record keeping.

In such a statistically rich document as the *Ain-i-Akbari* (1595), this is all too evident. The *Ain* provides detailed statistics on the *sarkars* and *parganas* of the Mughal Empire – their social composition, revenues, crops and even their measured area figures (*arazi*). It is the reliability of the *arazi* figures that is relevant to this discussion.[61] Even today scholars are divided in their opinions about the exact nature of the *arazi* figure; whether they represented the entire area (inclusive of cultivated lands and cultivable and uncultivable wastes), only the net cultivable area (including cultivable wastes), or only seasonal data pertaining to the winter (*kharif*) or summer harvests (*rabi*). At the same time, half the Mughal Empire, including the provinces of Bihar and Awadh, remained unsurveyed as late as the reign of Aurangzeb (r. 1658–1707).[62] The *Ain* offers no *arazi* statistics at all for the entire *suba* of Bengal and parts of the *suba* of Bihar.[63] While the technicalities of the debate are beyond the scope of this work, the *arazi* figures probably do not refer to the total land area of the empire's *mahals*. Mughal officials were, in any case, unable to acquire such detailed information, given the costs in terms of time, money and the unpopularity of such measures.[64] The inability of officials to closely monitor the oscillations whereby lands fell under cultivation or waste made it virtually impossible to ensure the collection of detailed, comprehensive and accurate statistical information on land. Perhaps the *Ain*, like other contemporary records, was not so concerned with drawing up a modern administrative map of the empire; rather, it was more concerned with displaying the revenue-yielding capacities of a district. Moreover, the Mughal government and its agencies did not possess the institutional capacity or power to conduct detailed cadastral or topographic surveys, a necessary precursor to the creation of modern maps.

Consequently, precolonial land records documented territory without the usual deference for spatial integrity and territorial order of the kind seen in modern maps. These records were more in the nature of lists of villages showing the larger fiscal divisions and sub-divisions that they were attached to. Mutations in the record were frequently made without consideration for preserving the territorial continuity of an administrative division. It was virtually impossible to compile information needed to create coherent and well-defined outlines of administrative divisions, in the manner of a modern map. Some examples from the Anglo–Gorkha frontier reveal this. Between 1782 and 1789, the ownership of the *taluqa* of Sangrampur changed hands, attaching it at various times to the *tappas* of Mando and Soogaon (both in *pargana* Majhowa, Champaran). Throughout this time, Sangrampur remained geographically detached from these parent *tappas* (see Map 5.3).[65] Elsewhere, the raja of Gorakhpur possessed a *taluqa* consisting of three whole *tappas* (in *pargana* Haveli Gorakhpur) and a few detached villages spread over the *parganas* of Bhowapar, Sylhet and Dhuriapar. Between 1685 and 1728, the raja's *taluqa* villages were included in the general accounts of the *pargana* of Haveli Gorakhpur. But, in 1729, these villages were separated from the accounts of the several *parganas* and constituted into a separate *mahal* (revenue-yielding unit). In this manner, the *taluqa* of the raja was detached from the fiscal resources of four *parganas* to constitute a new revenue-paying unit that continued to remain dispersed over these *parganas*.[66] This move may have been initiated by the raja of Gorakhpur in order to free him from the influence of local officials and landed magnates competing for control over those *parganas*.[67] The district records of North India are littered with countless such examples of mutations taking place in the fiscal records without any attempt at preserving territorially compact administrative divisions. The reasons for doing this were often connected with the formation of new revenue engagements and conferment of new land rights, or the result of routine contests between landed magnates. Moreover, details about such territorial rearrangements were not uniformly recorded by local (*mofassil*) and central (*sadr*) officials, such as was the case with *tappa* Sheoraj. Barring local officials, no records for *tappa* Sheoraj were found in the *nawab* of Awadh's record room in Lucknow.[68] The same applied to villages and their lands. Village lands were frequently attached or detached from their parent administrative divisions without any regard for preserving the territorial integrity of the division concerned. Indigenous revenue records frequently display such kinds of attachments and detachments that were the product of political, social, economic and ecological forces. Over time, such mutations caused villages and their lands or even

Map 5.3 *Pargana* Majhowa in *sarkar* Champaran showing detached portions of *tappas* Jaffarabad, Mando and Mudhwal

Mapwork by Bernardo A. Michael and Natalie Burack.
The *taluqa* of Sangrampur, belonging to *tappa* Mando, lies between the *tappas* of Sukhwa and Dowlatta.

entire *tappas* and *parganas* to be arbitrarily lumped together in a discontinuous fashion. On other occasions these divisions were broken up and then rearranged. In the end, it was under colonial rule that new regulations would be introduced for the systematization of procedures of record-keeping in a manner that would uphold a coherent and singular territorial framework (see Chapter 1).

At times divisions such as *parganas* and *taluqas* were nothing more than a collection of dispersed villages that were cobbled together under a name in the revenue records. The *pargana* of Athgaon (literally meaning "eight villages") in *sarkar* Benaras was a case in point.[69] Elsewhere, in the district of Gorakhpur, the *taluqa* of Satasi (meaning "eighty-seven") got its name from the extent of the estate in *coses* (a *cos* being approximately equal to two miles).[70] The *taluqa* of Hamrah was disputed by the rajas of Ramnagar, and Bettiah was made up of 85 dispersed villages spread over 13 *tappas* in Champaran District.[71] At times there were disagreements about the internal divisions that made up a *tappa*, *pargana* or *taluqa*, as happened in the case of *taluqa* of Matka along the Gorakhpur–Butwal frontier. The rajas of Palpa and Gulmi disagreed on whether it was made up of 18 or 19 *tappas* (see Chapter 4).[72] The kings of Gulmi and Palpa also disputed each other's claims to the *tappa* of Majhar, the former claiming it belonged to *pargana* Binayakpur while the latter insisting it had been attached to the *taluqa* of Matka.⁷³ Because precolonial territorial divisions possessed such irregular and discontinuous bodies that were shot through with these territorial claims, the English East India Company's acquisition of territories did not always result in the transfers of cohesive blocks of territory. The East India Company's Treaty of Cession with the *nawab* of Awadh in 1801 is a good example of this. The Company received the entire *suba* of Allahabad and the *sarkar* of Gorakhpur, along with a number of other *mahals*.⁷⁴ However, taken together these lands did not comprise a single coherent entity. Patches of territory remained separated from the main body of the territories ceded, such as the seven *parganas* of Khairigarh and six *parganas* belonging to the *chakla* of Nawabgunj. It took the Company's officials some years to discover this fact and, consequently, in 1802, the seven *parganas* of Khairigarh were detached from Gorakhpur District and attached to the contiguous district of Shahjahanpur.⁷⁵

Administrative divisions such as *parganas* and *tappas* were prone to changes in their nomenclature, a fact noticeable in the documentary record. Take the case of Sheoraj: while records at Bansi treat Sheoraj as a *tappa* belonging to *pargana* Bansi, Gorkhali records would sometimes treat it as a single *pargana* or combine it with a neighboring district such as Deokhori to form the *pargana* of Deokhori-Sheoraj.⁷⁶ In some instances, even the names of villages were changed to suit the convenience of competing landholders. In the nineteenth century, the rajas of Ramnagar and Bettiah were involved in a protracted land dispute over the village of Rani Pakeer. The latter argued that the village was actually Rani Pakur alias Jora Joree, and not Rani Pakeer as claimed by the raja of Ramnagar. The Ramnagar raja countered by stating that there was no village called Rani Pakur alias Jora Joree. Rather, there were two distinct villages – Jora Joree and Pakree Khas, both owned by the raja of Bettiah, but *distinct and separate* from the Rani Pakeer claimed by Ramnagar. The Ramnagar raja further alleged that the Bettiah raja had changed the name of Rani Pakeer to Rani Pakur alias Jora Joree and attached the village lands of Pakree Khas to it. Another interesting aspect of this case involved a dispute over the actual location of the village of Seherwa. The raja of Ramnagar claimed this village to be in *tappa* Chankee and his by right, while the Bettiah raja argued that it was in the neighboring *tappa* of Chigwan, in the Ramnagar raja's lands. Other witnesses noted that it lay in neither of the two *tappas*, but in the *tappa* of Jamauli. The Ramnagar raja later clarified that the Seherwa pointed out by the Bettiah raja lay in *tappa* Chankee–Gopala, and was distinct from that claimed by him, which also lay in *tappa* Chankee. It is clear that there were at least two villages with the name Seherwa in the *tappa* of Chankee and one with the same name in the *tappa* of Jamauli.⁷⁷ These land disputes reveal the intricate maneuvers involving the (re)naming of villages taking place along the Anglo–Gorkha frontier. Such practices repeatedly befuddled colonial administrators who, even with the help of modern maps, were unable to resolve such cases. The long-standing practice of local officials, such as *quanungos*, *patwaris* and *amils*, inserting these names at will into the land records must have added to this confusion.⁷⁸ On the Champaran tarriani frontier, former Gorkhali employees, like Ram Baksh Singh, accused senior Gorkhali officials, like Ranganath Pandit, of falsely inserting 22 villages lying along the frontier, and within the Company's possessions, into the village lists of the Gorkhali *tappa* of Rautahat. These 22 villages would later become the subject of dispute between Gorkha and the Company.⁷⁹

The Gorkhalis on their part alleged that it was the "deceitful and treacherous" Ram Baksh Singh who had tried to influence the British by forging documents.[80] Ultimately, precolonial territories found documentary expression in the revenue record, which faithfully registered this dynamism and conflict. Initially, at least, colonial officials had no option but to view their territorial possessions through this vast corpus of documents. Gradually, they came to realize that this documentary record would not yield the kind of spatially coherent information needed to establish continuous and emboxed territorial divisions with linear boundaries.[81] The Company then took measures to standardize record-keeping practices in order to revise the form and content of the vast archive of records that it had inherited and added to, and in a manner that more faithfully reflected its conception of territorial order. That sense of territorial order would endure through the formal surveys of the nineteenth century, which would create a geographical template for the state that was internally consistent in its parts and visible on modern maps.

The Territorial Significance of Forts

Forts also played an important role in the organization of the territory. They constituted nodes for resource control where local rajas, tax collectors and their officials resided, along with their armed retainers. Strategically located, usually on the top of hills or along important routes, forts allowed elites to enforce authority, command, manage and defend agrarian resources, and protect trade. Usually commanded by a *killadar*, forts possessed varying histories and cultural traditions.[82] They were sources of symbolic authority, and the loss of a fort usually invited dishonor. For their maintenance, forts were allotted the revenues (either in cash or in kind) and other resources (labor, priests, guards) of villages lying in their vicinity. On occasion, such villages were clubbed together to form a *mahal* or *pargana*. Such lands often assumed the name of the concerned fort. For example, the *parganas* of Hatin and Punahanah (*sarkar* Tijrah), Pailani (*sarkar* Kalanjar) and Bahadurgarh (*sarkar* Delhi), and the *tappa* of Saktisgarh (*sarkar* Allahabad) all derived their names from forts possessing the same name.[83] On the Champaran–Tarriani frontier the *pargana* of Gadh (fort) Simraon took its name from the ancient fort of Simraongarh. On the crest of the Someshwar foothills along the Anglo–Gorkha boundary lay the fort of Someshwar, which was maintained by the revenues of *tappas* Jamauli and Ramgir and half of *tappa* Chigwan. When the Gorkhalis wrested the fort from the hill kingdom of Tanahu in 1777 they found that the fort's dependent *tappas* now lay in the Company's territories. In 1781, Fort Someshwar's Gorkhali *killadar* (commander), Dinanath Upadhyaya, presented the Gorkhali claims to these two-and-a-half *tappas* to English officials, who denied the petition, arguing that the disputed *tappas* formed an integral part of *sarkar* Champaran that had been granted to the Company by the Mughal emperor in 1765.

While forts played a critical role in managing the agrarian resources of the countryside, they were also symbols of power and sites of struggle. Take for example the siege of a fort, which was no simple military operation. It was always accompanied by hectic parleys, negotiations and practices of bribing between the besieged and besiegers, and even *among* the besiegers. Questions of status, honor, authority and money invariably surfaced during times of siege. The case of the Gorkhali commander *budakaji* Amar

Singh Thapa's efforts to capture the fort of Kangra will bear this out.[84] The Gorkhali commander's opponents at Kathmandu alleged that he had deliberately dragged out the siege of the fort of Kangra and kept up a pretense of fighting after being bribed by Sansar Chand (the besieged ruler of Kangra) to leave an opening for supplies to enter the fort. In the meantime, Gorkhali authorities at Kathmandu, impatient with the *budakaji's* "failure" to break the deadlock, deputed Nyan Singh Thapa (the brother of the prime minister, Bhim Sen Thapa) to Kangra. Nyan Singh Thapa, anxious to secure credit for the conquest of this fort, sealed it off but was killed during an attack on the fort (though the exact circumstances of his death remain unclear). Then, in 1806, Kathmandu deputed two senior officials, Rudra Vir Shah and Dalabhanjan Pande, who were opposed to the Amar Singh Thapa.[85] In the meantime, the Kangra ruler, Sansar Chand, offered a bribe of Rs 5,000 to the Sikh ruler, Ranjit Singh, and asked him to intervene, which he then did. However, Amar Singh Thapa persuaded him to return by offering him the Rs 5,000 that Sansar Chand had originally offered. Meanwhile, a worried Sansar Chand opened negotiations with Dalabhanjan Pande and Rudra Vir Shah; the latter did not inform the *budakaji* of this development, and instead reported matters directly to Kathmandu. Amar Singh Thapa responded by complaining to authorities at Kathamandu that the new Gorkhali commanders had been paid a huge bribe (by Sansar Chand) in return for which they had ended the siege of Kangra Fort. He requested that these Gorkhali officials be withdrawn and that he be given another chance to retake Kangra. In 1808, the two Gorkhali commanders were withdrawn and Parsuram (Thapa?) and Bhairav Bali were sent in their place. However, in August 1809, Ranjit Singh broke the stalemate by forcibly occupying the fort of Kangra. It is unclear if either Gorkhalis or Sansar Chand had offered him bribes at this stage.[86] In this sense, forts and their attached lands became powerful markers and producers of territory which became enmeshed in intricate territorial arrangements and disputes involving multiple domains of authority and power. Ultimately, forts and their attached lands generated territorial dynamics that broke the coherence and continuity of the administrative divisions they were attached to.

4. The Representation of *Parganas* in Everyday Life

I have argued that precolonial administrative divisions can be viewed as forms of knowledge and practice that found historical expression within a dynamic regime of agrarian entitlements along with their documentary record. However, they also found rich expressions in the everyday lives and imaginations of communities and individuals. A *pargana* could evoke ties of affection and a sense of place among its inhabitants. In the nineteenth century, John Beames had to draw on the historical memory of local people while attempting to plot the location of older Mughal *parganas*. He noted: "That so many of the parganahs are still traceable today is due more to the *conservative* instincts of the people, than to any care that has been bestowed upon the matter by those in authority."[87] Such identification with one's *pargana* has persisted in the geographical imagination of people even today. For instance, in some parts of Bihar many older people still recall the *parganas* to which they belonged.[88] Local inhabitants often retained a memory of such *pargana* divisions that recalled some (artistic, linguistic, ecological or agricultural) quality. *Sarkar* Silhat (*suba* Bengal) was remembered as the land of witches and wizards and a major supplier of eunuchs as late as the twentieth century.[89] Colonial officials like H. M. Elliot noted the presence of old *pargana* sub-divisions in North India, called *chaurasi* (literally meaning "eighty-four"), in popular memory that drew inspiration from the "whole scheme of the Hindu, Buddhist, and Jain religions, cosmogonies, rituals, and legendary tales."[90] In some instances, *parganas* were objectified in historical writings (*khyat*) such as Munhta Nainsi's *Marwar ra Parganan ri Vigat* (1664). The *Vigat* contained a detailed history of the seven *parganas* of the kingdom of Marwar including topics such as geography, crop production, revenue collection, and social composition. Probably modeled on the Mughal courtier Abul Fazl's sixteenth century gazetteer of the Mughal Empire (the *Ain-i-Akbari*), Nainsi obtained his information from a variety of historical sources, oral and written, that allowed him to give these *parganas* substance and form.[91]

Sometimes, local communities recalled such territorial divisions in terms of their physical geography. The inhabitants of *pargana* Hajipur (*sarkar* Tirhut) described the topography of their *pargana* in terms of two divisions – "Dearehs" (lowlands subject to inundation) and "Oopurwar" (highlands above the high bank of the Ganges). The inhabitants would often possess local information about the *pargana* of their residence and provide details pertaining to soil, water and productive potentials.[92] Thus, one colonial writer noted that in many instances divisions such as *tappas* were co-extensive with the "natural divisions of soil, or with limits marked off by other natural boundaries."[93] Sometimes *parganas* were associated with their agricultural or animal products: the *parganas* of Ratanpur Bansi and Hasanpur Maghar gave their names respectively to the high quality of rice and wheat grown there (*Bansi ka dhan, Hasanpur ka gehun*); *pargana* Hajipur, in Bihar, was known for its prized mangoes;[94] and the *pargana* of Sureysa (*sarkar* Tirhut, *suba* Bihar) was renowned for its horses.[95] In yet other instances, these divisions memorialized important personages: the *pargana* of Mansurnagar Basti (*sarkar* Gorakhpur) derived its first name from Mansur Ali Khan, the father of *nawab* Shuja-ud-daula (1754–75) of Awadh;[96] and *sarkar* Muazzimabad was a new division created out of *sarkars* Gorakhpur and Saran to commemorate the visit of Prince Muazzim (later Emperor Bahadur Shah) to Gorakhpur at the end of the seventeenth century.[97] On another note, it appears that some territorial divisions might have been coextensive with linguistic regions or identified with sacred places. Again, John Beames suggested that the *sarkars* of Rohtas, Saran and Champaran (in *suba* Bihar) corresponded broadly with the Bhojpuri speaking area, while those of Hajipur and Tirhut with the Maithili speaking area, and the *sarkar* of Bihar with the Magadhi speaking area.[98] Elsewhere, the *pargana* of Deoghar (lying in the Bhawar country, west of the Tons River in the Western Himalayas) was supposedly composed of sacred ground, with a temple dedicated to a deity on it.[99]

In this manner, divisions such as *parganas* and *tappas* were not merely entitlements inscribed in the revenue record; their semantic materials were crafted out of discordant forms of knowledge concerning topography, agricultural productivity, language, local history, social memory and religious practice that were sedimented in the everyday meanings and routines of their inhabitants. It is said that even today in some areas of the North-Western Provinces (lying in the state of Uttar Pradesh), some district level officers are referred to as *pargana hakims*, while school children still recite the names of the *parganas* in their districts and identify the one they belong to.[100] Clearly, the memory of the old *pargana* divisions still persists in various parts of North India. The history of this territorialization of memory and the memorialization of territory in South Asia certainly merits further exploration and study.

5. Conclusion

In South Asia, precolonial territorial divisions were incarnated through multiple forms of knowledge and practice. Their territorial design was embroidered around a number of jostling variables that operated at many levels of agrarian social life – political, tenurial, documentary, cultural, quotidian and imaginative. These territorial divisions were formed out of dynamic agrarian environments, shaped by multiple and shared political sovereignties, shifting patterns of land-use and a complex composite of symbolic and material ingredients. Frequent disputes between various rights-holders provided added lubrication to this loose structure of territorial arrangements and relationships. The situation was further complicated by the presence of rent-free lands which peppered the landscape where ruling elites alienated their rights to land and its resources, creating little islands of "non-state" spaces that were provisionally autonomous of the tax-claims of the state. The anthropologist Richard Burghart perhaps came closest to articulating a sophisticated model that grasped the symbolic and material variables that produced the territories of precolonial kingdoms; in an influential article he argued that the kingdom of Nepal was constituted by three overlapping, but not always coincident spaces – possessions, realm and country. The first two spaces represented the tenurial and ritual authority of the king respectively, while the last represented ethnoterritorial units, each bearing a particular ecological setting and its constituent human communities. The king's territorial possessions were pockmarked with rent-free lands or islands of local influence that were freed from the taxation claims of the state. Together, these spaces formed the macro-space of Gorkha, which in the nineteenth and twentieth centuries became coterminous, resulting in the creation of the unified territory of the modern (nation-)state.[101] Burghart's model is sophisticated for its ability to view the Gorkhali state as being made up of a multiplicity of spaces and also for its sensitivity to indigenous perspectives. Burghart's king-centered model is clearly an advance over prevailing ethnosociological theories because it attributes greater indigenous agency in the production of space. However, it can be broadened to include other variables, discussed in this and previous chapters, such as the structure of entitlements and privileges and the agency of subaltern groups.[102] Consequently, the king's tenurial and ritual authority was never as complete as Burghart had suggested. It was invariably shared with competing power-holders whose claims to material and symbolic entitlements, and their territorial expressions, remained incomplete due to the intervention of various ecological, political and even subaltern agents (see Chapters 2–4). The administrative template of indigenous states remained firmly yoked to this regime of entitlements organized minimally around tribute, taxation and tenurial relationships. Fluctuations in these relationships were transmitted to the surface of these divisions, causing their bodies to overlap, disperse and intermix, leaving them discontinuous in their layout and boundaries. Such a pulsating regime of entitlements and relationships characterized the cultures of governance all along the Anglo–Gorkha frontier, and left their fingerprints on the organization of territory. Consequently, these divisions remained discontinuous spaces shaped by an array of forces that were more concerned with the preservation of rights and relationships than with linear boundaries or territorial continuity. Precolonial territorial divisions were also spaces produced out of a variety of ecological, political and social forces that remained etched in the memories and imaginations of local communities. It would take modern cartography and its technology of the map to prepare a stable image of contiguous territory and linear boundaries that would be maintained or manipulated only by the state and its agents. In South Asia colonial cartography and its technologies of representation would render simple, legible and visually comprehensible the complex, produced geographies of the precolonial territories that the British had inherited. This exercise in marking space would unfold in the nineteenth and twentieth centuries, albeit in a highly uncoordinated fashion. The final chapter will explore this in greater detail.

Chapter 6

MAKING STATES LEGIBLE: MAPS, SURVEYS AND BOUNDARIES

But it is the case, I believe, that we would not have had empire itself, as well as many forms of historiography, anthropology, sociology, and modern legal structures, without important philosophical and imaginative processes at work in the production as well as the acquisition, subordination, and settlement of space.

—Edward W. Said[1]

European states made their power visible not only through ritual performance and dramatic display, but through the gradual extension of "officializing" procedures and routines, through *the capacity to bound and mark space*, to record transactions such as the sale of property, to count and classify their populations, to gradually replace religious institutions as the registrar of the life-cycle facts of birth, marriage, and death, and finally to become the natural embodiment of history, territory, and society.

—Bernard S. Cohn and Nicholas B. Dirks[2]

1. Introduction: Indigenous Maps and Representations of Territory

This book has tried to spin a shared spatial thread to join two dispersed narratives. The first examines the spatial substance of the Anglo–Gorkha disputes in order to better understand the organization of territory along that frontier. The defeat of the Gorkhalis by the East India Company meant the gradual insertion of the second narrative, whereby a specific colonial vision of territory gradually overshadowed older ways of organizing state territories in South Asia. This vision found its material expression in modern surveying and mapmaking exercises undertaken initially by the colonial state and then by succeeding postcolonial regimes. This chapter will examine in some detail the unfolding of the second narrative, which will need to be prefaced by some discussion of maps and mapmaking traditions. Maps, which may be broadly defined as "graphic representations that facilitate a spatial understanding of things, concepts, conditions, processes, or events in the human world" have been employed by societies throughout human history.[3] Within South Asia, the impulse to map has a long history and has found expression in a variety of forms such as architectural plans, astronomical charts, cosmographical and topographic maps.[4] However, maps of political formations, kingdoms and petty principalities are hard to come by. While Mughal rule witnessed the collection of an impressive array of statistical data, no attempt was made by the state or its departments to produce an atlas or its equivalent that depicted the empire.[5]

Map 6.1 The *subas* of Lahore and Multan as depicted on a Mughal map of northwestern India and Kabul, 1780 CE

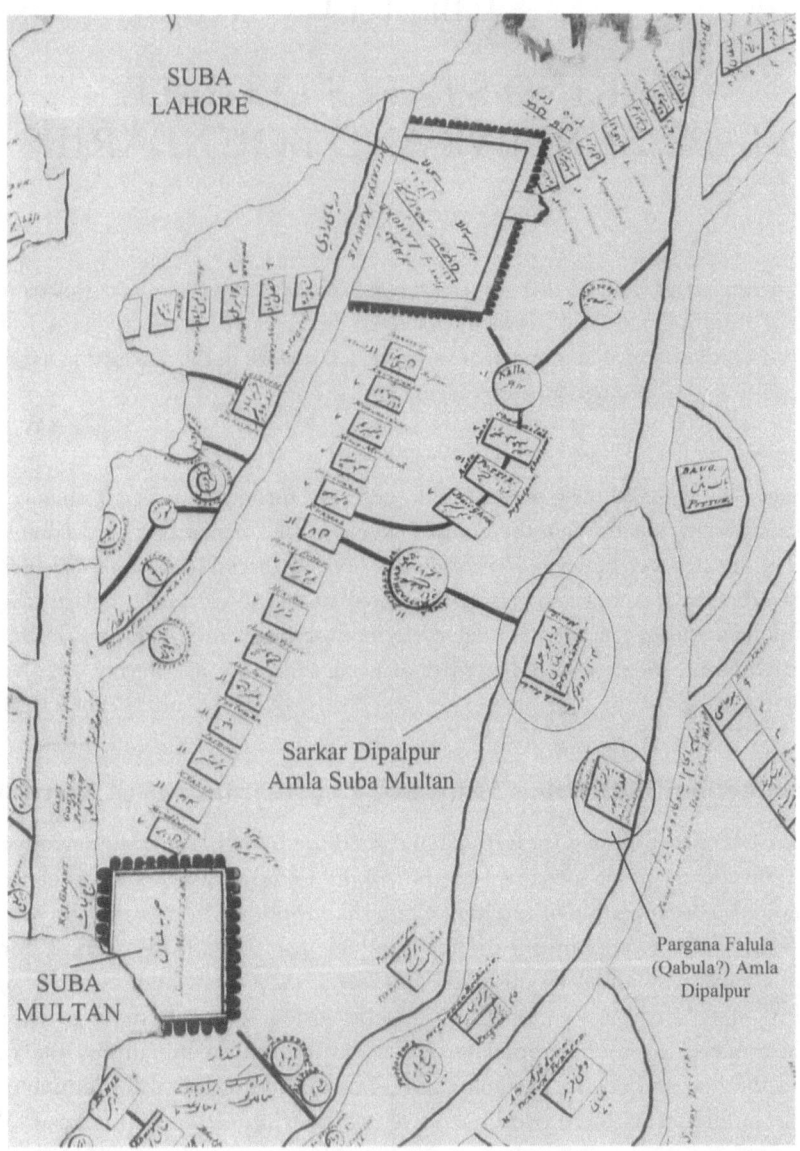

2 sh. 390 × 420 mm. Photographs, reduced, of an MS map owned by the Survey of India. The map is a copy of a Mughal map dated between 1650 and 1730. The map extends from Delhi to Kabul and from Kashmir to the Sea. The names are in Persian script with an English transliteration added. Note the *subas* of Multan and Lahore are represented by the location of forts and not through the demarcation of boundaries. The constituent subdivisions are not emboxed within each other but are shown as separate with territorial attachments indicated by the use of the term *amla* (belonging to). Hence *sarkar* Dipalpur and *pargana* Falula (Qabula?) have the words *amla* Multan and *amla* Dipalpur revealing their respective connections to those superior divisions. Compare with the bounded representations of the same *subas* in a recent map of the region in Irfan Habib's *An Atlas of the Mughal Empire* (see below). Reproduced by permission of the British Library © British Library Board.
Source: Cartographic Items Maps 188.i.2.(4.), British Library.

Map 6.1 *Continued.* The *subas* of Lahore and Multan as depicted in Irfan Habib's *An Atlas of the Mughal Empire*

Reproduced with permission from Irfan Habib, *An Atlas of the Mughal Empire*, published by Oxford University Press, New Delhi © 1982, Oxford University Press.
Source: John F. Richards, *The New Cambridge History of India: The Mughal Empire*, Cambridge: Cambridge University Press 1993. Map 1, p. 7.

There is no evidence that Mughal elites were interested in preparing maps of the kind Christopher Saxton was making in England in the sixteenth century.[6] Mughal maps like the one covering a large portion of northwestern South Asia, and made sometime between 1650 and 1730, seem to bear this out (see Map 6.1). This map displays over 500 settlements, forts, rivers, deserts, tanks, tombs and administrative divisions such

Map 6.2 Colonel Jean Baptiste Gentil's map of the *suba* of Bihar, 1770 CE

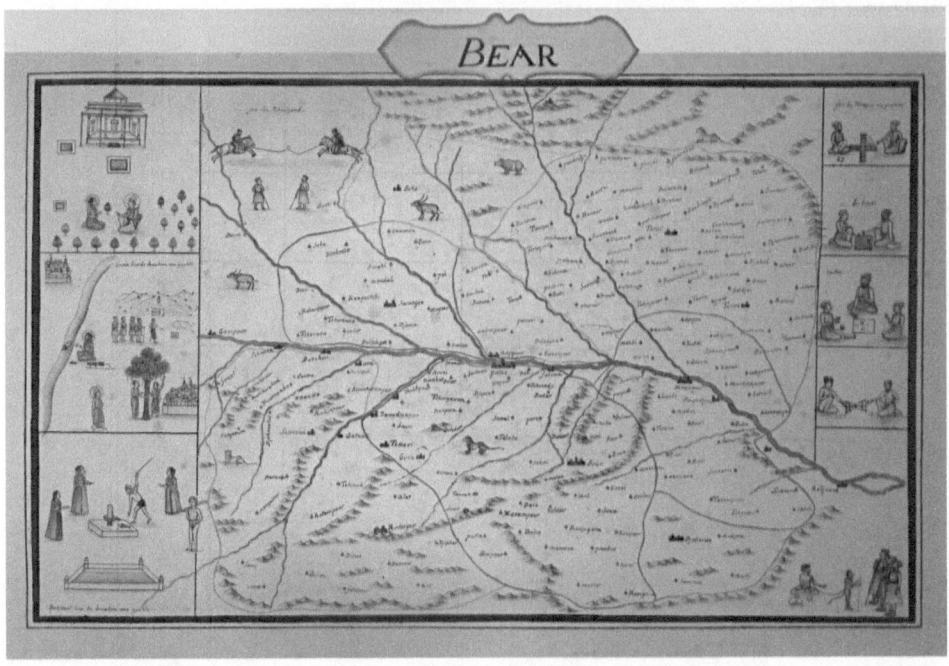

37.5 × 54.5 cm, watercolor and ink. *Sarkar* boundaries are depicted while *parganas* are mentioned only by name without boundaries. *Sarkar* Champaran is erroneously placed in South Bihar when it should be in the north. Scenes from daily life adorn the edges of the map. Reproduced by permission of the British Library © British Library Board.
Source: Prints and Drawings, IOR/Add Or. 4039, folios 15–16, India Office Map Collection, Asia, Pacific & Africa Collections, British Library.

as *subas* and *parganas*.[7] These administrative divisions and sub-divisions did not appear as spatially distinct entities, neatly contained within each other, with well-defined boundaries. For instance, the *suba* of Multan is not represented as a whole division with the *sarkar* of Dipalpur and *pargana* of Falula (Qabula?) lying *within* it, as would have been the case with a modern map. Rather, its dependent parts are shown distinct and separate from each other. Territorial attachments between divisions were signified by the accompanying term "*amla*" ("under the authority/jurisdiction of"). Thus, next to *sarkar* Dipalpur we have the words "*amla* Multan," and next to *pargana* Falula (Qabula?) we have the words "*amla* Dipalpur," signifying that this *pargana* belonged to *sarkar* Dipalpur, which in turn was dependent on the *suba* of Multan.[8] This map depicts the *suba* of Multan in terms of topographic, administrative and travel information rather than being concerned with displaying geographically continuous administrative divisions containing neatly emboxed sub-divisions.[9] Possibly, the first atlas of the Mughal Empire was prepared in 1770 by Jean Baptiste Joseph Gentil (1726–99), the Agent for the French government stationed at the court of *nawab* Shuja-ud daula of Awadh (see Map 6.2). Gentil used statistical data from the *Ain* to construct this atlas, with individual plates depicting 21 provinces.[10] For reasons unclear, Gentil did not combine them in an index

Map 6.3 Map of *pargana* Gurdhan in *suba* Kashmir, 1830s CE

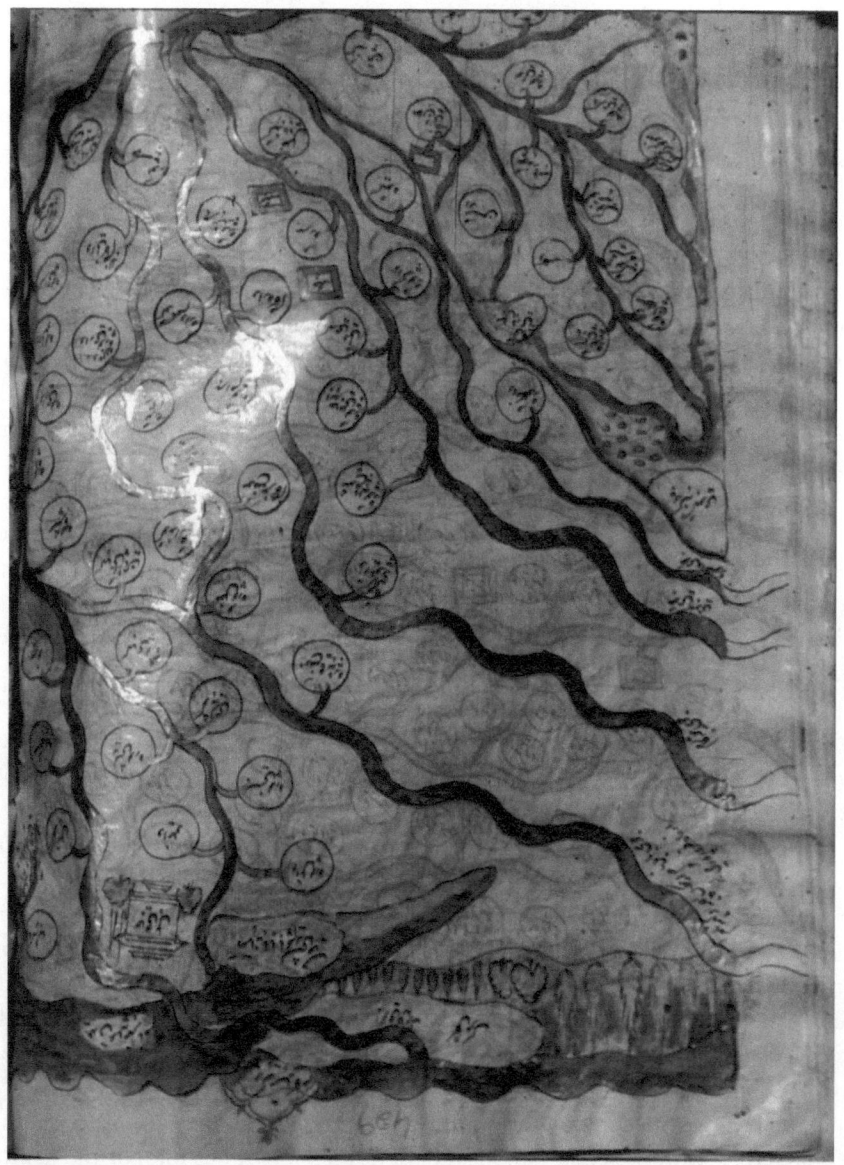

38 × 54 cm, Persian, paper. Amritsar: The map belongs to a collection of *pargana* maps of Kashmir found in the 858-page *Tarikh-i-Qal'ah-i- Kashmir*. The map shows detailed information on Gurdhan's villages (which appear as circles), rivers, bridges, mountains and hills. Reproduced with permission of the Trustees of Columbia University.

map to present a composite image of the Mughal Empire. However, Gentil's atlas is remarkable, because it represents one of the earliest attempts by a South Asian kingdom to represent the Mughal state as a naturalized geographical entity.[11]

Among indigenous maps, of particular interest are a number of Maratha maps from Western India, made between 1750 and 1820.[12] Varying in style, and covering extensive areas of Peninsular India, they depict human settlements, revenue and political relationships, military campaigns, villages, forts, vegetation, temples and sometimes decorative motifs such as animals and fish. The maps, in terms of their content, were designed to provide information on routes or topography. The political jurisdictions that villages and forts fall under are emphasized through the use of distinct color codings along with the term "*amal*", or "under the jurisdiction of." Examples of this include Amal Bavdekar or Amal *firanghi* ("under foreign jurisdiction" – in this case, that of the Portuguese). Administrative divisions such as *taluqas*, *mahals*, and *parganas* are depicted without the use of scales or boundaries.[13] It is difficult to say if these were "purely" Maratha maps, devoid of European agency, in their design and execution. The attempt to flatten the landscape in order to include topographical information suggests some European intervention, and indeed R.H. Phillimore has suggested that this map was made for the first British Collector of Kanara.[14] Similar representations of territory can be found in the *pargana* maps of the province of Kashmir (in North India) prepared between 1819 and 1839 for the Sikh ruler Ranjit Singh.[15] As in the case of the Maratha maps, the Kashmiri *parganas* (like Gurdhan) are not defined by linear boundaries but by their constituent villages, which appear as circles (see Map 6.3). These maps need to be subjected to further scrutiny to reveal both their indigenous and possibly European influences. However, given the information unearthed all along the Anglo–Gorkha frontier, these Kashmiri *parganas* may have been no different from *parganas* elsewhere – dispersed territories defined by various kinds of rights rather than linear boundaries. Indigenous mapmakers were more concerned with displaying this information than revealing coherent and territorially continuous administrative divisions possessing linear boundaries. Elsewhere, the 12 route maps found in the *Chahar Gulshan* (1759–60), a short history of Mughal India, show the stages of several routes in the Deccan. The towns are shown in circles or squares according to their size, with no actual roads being marked. The data is usually spread out in a tabular format, two columns to a page, with no attempt at topographical accuracy or the use of scale. The maps merely provide a *general sense* of the places and topographic features that lay along these routes, leading Susan Gole to conclude that these maps were "little more than tables abstracted from the text of the itineraries."[16] Their tabular construction displays similarities to Gorkhali maps collected by Brian Hodgson, the British Resident at Kathmandu in the nineteenth century (see below).

Such a view was not unique to South Asia and could be found in other times and places, including Europe. Peter Sahlins mentions an anonymous map of the Cerdanya area (on the Franco–Spanish frontier in the Pyrenees), probably dating to the1680s, showing the domination of the king over patches of territory rather than whole territories. In this map (and in a remarkably similar fashion to the South Asian maps discussed previously), French villages were marked blue while Spanish villages were marked red. Another map showed a mix of both jurisdictions and territories along with (mostly inaccurate) boundary lines.[17] But could Asian regimes have developed uses for maps as instruments of rule, as happened in Europe? Asian states were eminently capable of grasping the strategic value of modern maps as the rulers of China and Siam did in the eighteenth and nineteenth centuries, respectively.[18]

That they did not do so in greater numbers meant that they faced unique situations and challenges. The inability of centralizing state elites to infiltrate local systems of authority and power, along with the shifting, overlapping and intertwining structure of agrarian entitlements, combined to produce cultures of governance that denied indigenous states the institutional capacity and social reach to pursue modern cartographic projects – projects that would have provided an Icarian view of the state – complete and perfectly consistent in all its parts. The absence of modern maps in South Asian cultures had little to do with South Asians being more concerned with cosmic or ideological realities; rather, it might have had more to do with the institutional and practical realities of precolonial governance on the subcontinent.[19] European states, on their part, would rearrange their territories through national cartographic projects that proceeded hand-in-hand with European nation-state formation in the eighteenth and nineteenth centuries. The rest of this chapter will examine some of the cartographic activities of the colonial state – expressed in the delineation of linear boundaries, the employment of formal surveys and the rearrangement of territorial divisions throughout the nineteenth and twentieth centuries. The same took place within Gorkha, though much later in the twentieth century. Through these exercises these states and their agents produced new, coherent and territorially circumscribed images of their state.

2. Demarcating the Anglo–Gorkha Boundary

The idea of a boundary conveys a meaning that is distinct from that of the frontier. While the former evokes a precise linear division and the latter connotes a zone, the "movement from the zonal frontier to the linear boundary has been seen as an important element in the growth of the modern state."[20] In North India strips of wasteland, tanks, temples, forts, watersheds, forests, wood and stone pillars marked the territorial boundaries of villages, administrative divisions and even states.[21] Within Gorkha, too, the importance of boundaries was officially recognized. In the seventeenth century King Rama Shah (1606–36) decreed that lands endowed to Brahmans were to be measured and clearly demarcated.[22] In 1793 the Gorkha raja Ran Bahadur Shah deputed Purnanda Upadhyaya to make detailed inquiries about Gorkha's boundary with Sikkim, including its relationships with other kingdoms.[23] In the Administrative Regulations for areas between the Kanka and Mahakali Rivers (1806 AD), Gorkhali officials were asked to determine the boundaries (*sandh simana*) of illegally held lands using the service of a Dogol (a caste proficient at surveying). Excess lands were to be confiscated and the guilty punished.[24] There is plenty of evidence of Gorkhali officials being deputed to make inquiries, determine boundaries and settle disputes.[25] Embankments and rivers formed linear boundaries separating agricultural fields and administrative units, respectively.[26] However, even rivers which formed convenient linear boundaries were prone to frequent changes in their courses, giving rise to riverain boundary (*diara*) disputes.[27]

The spatial structure of the Anglo–Gorkha frontier crystallized out of the expression of sovereignty in jurisdictional rather than territorial terms. The frontier was formed out of a multiplicity of jurisdictions, defined by a host of claims and privileges which created their own distinct boundaries. In some respects this was very similar to the situation in Europe. Historian Peter Sahlins' observations about the Old Regime states of Europe are relevant to this discussion when he notes that:

> Generally conceived, sovereignty consisted of the exercise of authority within a wide range of domains: military affairs, justice, ecclesiastical policies, commercial and economic activities, and taxation. Each of these jurisdictional domains was an administrative circumspection with its own boundaries; these boundaries often failed to coincide, and they remained distinct from the political boundary of the kingdom.[28]

Similarly, precolonial states in North India were made up of such multiple domains that did not coincide with the political boundaries of a kingdom. British officials charged with overseeing the administration of the East India Company's Indian territories became increasingly anxious about this lack of clearly discernible political boundaries, especially along its frontiers with other states. In 1818, the military secretary to the Court of Directors summed up the situation, saying:

> The Court [of Directors] have formerly had occasion to point out to the Governments in India the expediency of ascertaining with precision the true boundaries of our dominions. It is almost unnecessary to observe, that this is a duty which ought never to be neglected by any government that values its own rights or has a due respect for those of its neighbors. It is therefore desireable in the first place to possess an accurate *outline* of the several cessions which have from time to time been made to the East India Company by the several Governments and Chiefs of India, and which will of course give the general boundary of our dominions.
>
> Next in importance, I conceive, is the obligation of gaining the best possible information respecting the frontiers of those states whose dominions we are bound by treaty to protect against foreign aggression. I am aware, that from the *lax habits* of the native governments, the frequent *intermixture* of their respective territories, and indeed, the intentional indefiniteness which prevails among them in respect to boundaries, this is a branch of Indian Geography which cannot be acquired without considerable difficulty.[29]

During the nineteenth century colonial officials became increasingly obsessed with such a perception of "imperial space," or territory that was defined by linear boundaries.[30] This became evident when, following the Anglo–Gorkha War (in 1816), the Company took firm steps to demarcate the common boundaries of the two states. As early as December 1815, the Company's officials stationed along the frontier were instructed thus: "In determining the limits of the respective states, attention must be paid to the selection in all possible cases of natural and well defined boundary marks not liable to alterations or decay – when these cannot be had, as from the general course of the rivers in the Teraiee and the distance of the forests, as His Lordship apprehends will be the case, artificial boundary marks must be resorted to."[31] Following the cessation of hostilities in March 1816, negotiations began on the demarcation of boundaries and it was decided that the new boundary would be drawn 2 *cos* (about 4 miles) from the southernmost point of the old frontier.³² The line was to be a straight one. Where indentations occurred, exchanges of territory were to be made to keep the line direct.³³ Furthermore, it was stated by Company authorities that:

Another object of some importance with a view to obviate causes of future difference is to prevent such a division of private property as shall place individuals in the condition of subjects of *both* states. When this shall be found to be the case, it will be desirable, if practicable to effect such an interchange of territory, as may throw the property of individual land holders, altogether within the limits of *one* state (emphasis mine).³⁴

The demarcation proceedings dragged on until 1821.³⁵

Throughout the boundary proceedings that followed the end of the war in 1816, Gorkhali officials struggled to understand Company officials' obsession with linear boundaries. This was because the notion of modern boundary lines, which drew from European traditions of mapmaking and statecraft, was a concept alien to the Gorkhalis, who were more concerned with the control of villages.³⁶ This view seems to be confirmed when examining the proceedings of the Anglo–Gorkha boundary demarcations of 1816. A recurrent theme in these proceedings (at least on the Champaran–Tarriani frontier) was the inability of the Gorkhalis to grasp the *logic* of the proceedings, and for the most part they just followed the instructions of the British or remained mute observers (see Plate 6.1).³⁷ The Gorkhali commissioners knew that a boundary needed to be laid down, but were then horrified to see that the British officers, in their zeal to keep the boundary straight, were proceeding to slice through former Gorkhali possessions. These possessions were defined not by abstract straight lines on the ground but by claims to tax, property and tribute. Gorkhali commissioners like *taksari* Chandra Shekhar Upadhyaya, who owned lands in these parts, were visibly upset, and not too happy with the exchanges of territory that were made to keep the boundary straight.³⁸ The British commissioners remained baffled by this tendency of the Gorkhalis to involve themselves in what the British considered "petty" land disputes, all the while forgetting that the "great object" at stake was the creation of a linear boundary – the line that would put an end to years of disputes along the frontier.³⁹ Finally in October 1818, when J. P. Boileau commenced his surveying operations on the Champaran–Tarriani frontier (see Map 6.4), the Gorkhali commissioners withdrew from the proceedings, claiming that their input was never valued and that the British commissioners seemed determined to demarcate the boundary on their own terms. A similar story was repeated on the Morang–Purnea frontier to the east. What really concerned the Gorkhalis was the preservation of their jurisdictional rights to tax villages, and not the drawing of some straight line that tended to slice through such jurisdictions.⁴⁰ For similar reasons, the Company's own subjects expressed dissatisfaction with the Company's new penchant for drawing linear boundaries to mark out the territories of states. For instance, petty chieftains such as Chattar Singh of Tirhut, Uday Pratap Sen of Makwanpur, Tej Pratap Sen of Ramnagar and the raja of Bettiah would all claim lands lying beyond the boundary, in Gorkha. Their claims were dismissed by the Company, though they were compensated for their losses with grants of land or remissions in revenues due.⁴¹

These developments expose one of the crucial moments in the geographical construction of the colonial state in South Asia – in the redefinition of its frontiers into linear boundaries. These

Plate 6.1 Royal letter from Raja Girbana Juddha Bikram Shah to Chautariya Bam Shah, 1873 BS (1816 CE)

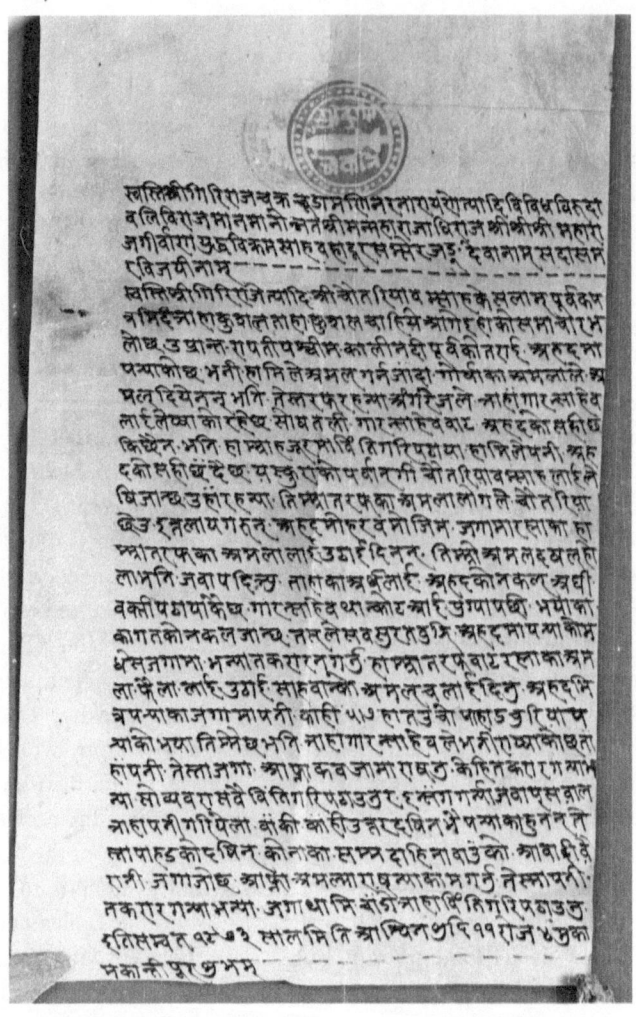

Bam Shah is instructed to oversee the handover of territories west of the Rapti and east of the Kali, to avoid conflict with the English and refer all contentious territorial claims to Kathmandu. Reproduced with permission of the National Archives of Nepal © The National Archives of Nepal.
Source: Historical Letters, Kausi Tosakhana Collection, National Archives of Nepal, no. 555.

linear boundaries were the product of mathematical and surveying calculations that would be drained of local human interventions.[42] The remainder of British rule saw the continued assertion of this principle, as linear boundaries were gradually established all along the colonial state's common frontier with indigenous states through surveys and the subsequent exchange of territories.[43] Furthermore, the notion that individuals along the boundary could owe allegiance, taxes and obedience to one government *only* was gradually enforced. This project of colonial boundary formation was an ill-coordinated project that put in place a fundamental organizing principle – *that states occupy a definite portion of the Earth's surface, and are divided into non-overlapping divisions and sub-divisions*. The colonial state's efforts to rearrange territories and

Map 6.4 Rough sketch of the Terae lying between the Rivers Raptee and Koosah by Lieutenant John P. Boileau, 1816 CE

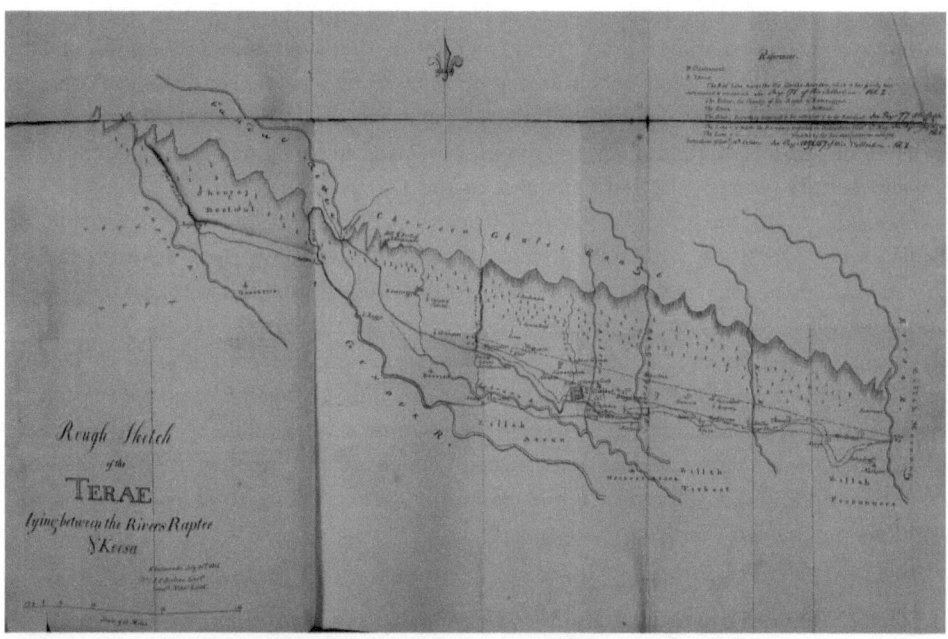

66.5 × 51.5 cm. "Negotiations with the Nipaulese for obtaining possession of the Districts ceded by the treaty concluded with that State." Reproduced by permission of the British Library © British Library Board. Source: Boards Collections, F/4/550, no. 13375, p. 72, India Office Records, Asia, Pacific & Africa Collections, British Library.

demarcate a linear boundary put an end to a number of older relationships concerning tribute, taxation and property. However, this unfolded unevenly across the nineteenth and twentieth centuries as some of these older relationships survived long after the boundary was demarcated. For instance, the Ramnagar raja, while a subject of the Company, continued to maintain close links with Gorkha, even asserting that he was a dependent of Gorkha.[44] It also appears that, in 1839. the rajas of Ramnagar, while residing in the Company's territories, were collecting taxes in *tappa* Chitwan (in Gorkha) through one Kashi Gurau Tharu.[45] All this suggests that while the British tried to enforce and preserve the sacredness of the boundary line, local agents found ways to continue the enjoyment of older entitlements on both sides of the border. Such practices seem to have persisted well into the twentieth century and a history of these cross-border flows remains to be written.[46]

While such cross border flows, relationships and engagements continued to persist, as they invariably do, the colonial state would brook no blatant violations of the sanctity of the boundary. For instance, the British used force to expel the Gorkhalis when the latter forcibly occupied 11 villages in the Ramnagar area in 1839.[47] In another instance, in the 1860s, when the Gorkhali prime minister Jang Bahadur Rana complained to the British Resident at Kathmandu that the British no longer honored the terms of a Gorkhali religious land grant in Kedarnath (Kumaon–Garhwal area), he was told, "You can do what you like on lands situated in your territory; we can do what we like on ours."⁴⁸ In this manner, the reality of the boundary was gradually driven home to the Gorkhalis. The story of this relationship between the creation of colonial boundaries and the rearrangement of indigenous regimes of agrarian entitlements is a long-drawn one with many variations and nuances. While recounting that story in its fullness lies outside the scope of this book, it has been touched upon by some writers. For instance, historian Ajay Skaria shows how colonial notions of exclusive territorial sovereignty replaced indigenous notions of shared sovereignty in the Dangs in Western India. There, during the nineteenth century, the hill chieftains in the Dangs became British subjects while still considering the neighboring Gaekwadi rulers of Baroda as their patrons. While the British recognized these overlapping claims they would not allow the Gaekwads to deal directly with these hill chieftains and a colonial official was appointed to collect these taxes and remit them to Baroda. In doing this the colonial state asserted its claims to exclusive territorial sovereignty over the Dangs. The formal boundary between the state of Baroda and British territories was finally delineated in the 1890s.⁴⁹ Such cartographic projects became the vehicle through which the British colonial state would survey and delineate its boundaries and internal divisions through much of the nineteenth and twentieth centuries, while at the same time adjudicating the various claims to older privileges and entitlements that invariably cropped up.

3. The Colonial State and its *Naqsha* Compass Projects in North India⁵⁰

The Company's cartographic projects need to be contextualized within wider developments taking place in Europe – of the Enlightenment, overseas exploration, colonization and cross-cultural encounters. A desire to describe, quantify, order, systematize, measure and calculate marked the efforts of European explorers, scientists and administrators, giving rise to elaborate and systematic representations of the world.⁵¹ These developments, coupled with a new drive towards the exploration of the interiors of continents, resulted in what Mary Louise Pratt has called a shift in "planetary consciousness" that would lock geography, science and empire in a mutually transformatory embrace.⁵² What followed was an unprecedented investigation, whereby the details pertaining to the politics, society, space, history and culture of colonized populations were excavated, arranged and rearranged for the consumption of both the colonizer and colonized. The appropriative character of this enterprise is evident from nineteenth-century definitions of geography in South Asia as "the science which describes the surface of the globe; the various divisions of that surface, both natural and artificial; the inhabitants of the earth, and variety of its productions; together with the various *lines*, real and imaginary, which are drawn or supposed to be drawn upon it."⁵³ Nowhere was this interventionist project more apparent than in the case of European mapmaking, when from the sixteenth century onwards maps became the tools of government, both for policy formulation, general administration and the consolidation of nationalist sentiment.⁵⁴ European states like France and England began to represent their territories as bounded entities, even if that was not the reality on the ground.⁵⁵

It is against this background of growing "map-mindedness" that the English East India Company acquired its territories in South Asia in 1765.⁵⁶ Despite the Company's growing interest in mapmaking, when its foremost surveyor James Rennell left India in 1777, it possessed only the most general maps, often based on guesswork and on the administrative divisions that made up its territories.⁵⁷ It is highly likely that Rennell's maps had more propaganda value than any utility for colonial administrators on the ground.⁵⁸ From the late eighteenth century onwards the Company conducted a variety of surveys (route, topographic, cadastral and trigonometrical) in South Asia with the intention of gaining new information about its territories.⁵⁹ By 1820, the Company's Surveying Department was unified and placed under the command of the surveyor-general of India at Calcutta. One of the central objectives of this office was to produce accurate maps of the subcontinent based on scientific procedures recently inaugurated by the Great Trigonometrical Survey (GTS) in 1799.⁶⁰ While the GTS was founded on mathematical principles and sought to present a "perfect" picture of the space of India, it was unable to resolve the problem of outlining the districts and other subdivisions that this space of India would be carved into. The GTS was not followed by detailed cadastral surveys that would fill details into the framework put in place by triangulation.⁶¹ Local surveys lagged due to shortages of money and trained personnel, and consequently close coordination with the GTS was not always possible. Thus, during the early decades of colonial rule, the Company continued to experience an inability to discover the actual layout, internal organization and boundaries of the territories they had acquired. Without this information it became difficult to create any new coherent administrative divisions in its territories. Walter Hamilton, who, in 1820, produced a two-volume descriptive account of Hindustan and its neighboring countries, summed the problem accurately when he noted:

> The map [of India] prefixed exhibits the large geographical divisions, but being constructed on so small a scale, it was found impossible to distinguish either the petty native states, whose territories are much *intermixed*, or the different districts into which the British provinces have been partitioned. With respect to the first, no native state has yet been brought to understand the advantages we are accustomed to see in a *compact* territory and uninterrupted frontier; and with regard to the latter, the limits of none can be considered as finally *adjusted*, the judicial and police arrangements requiring frequent revisal of boundaries, and various surveys being still in progress, with the view of obtaining more accurate geographical and statistical information than the Indian governments at present possess. Owing to these imperfections a town may be frequently assigned to one jurisdiction which in reality belongs to another, but the mistake is of no essential importance, and many such corrections must hereafter be required, the limits of no district having yet attained such precision and arrangement as to preclude the necessity of future alteration.⁶²

Hamilton's predicament is clear – he did not possess a "perfect" geographical framework on which he could peg the information he already possessed.⁶³ The geographical framework he sought to discern was that of the state – bounded, and partitioned into non-overlapping divisions and sub-divisions. Such "cartographic anxiety" is also discernable in the observations of an English surveyor Robert Kelly (1738–90) who noted that "the Natives of India never think of surveying large territories, or of settling their boundaries in anything like straight lines; [...] in the center of a district fifty or sixty miles broad it is common to meet with villages belonging to the neighboring states."⁶⁴

The Revenue Surveys[65]

At the beginning of the nineteenth century very little was known about the internal resources, taxation potentials and actual status of landed property rights within the Company's districts. On 7 August 1822, through Regulation 7, the Company decided to break this impasse by instructing its officials to henceforth undertake land revenue settlements that would be based on detailed and systematic surveys.[66] Later, Regulation 9 of 1833 reconfirmed this measure and called for detailed village-by-village cadastral surveys, which would gather information on land rights, natural resources, topography and finally the boundaries of villages.[67] The village was to constitute the basic building block for the reconstruction of the Company state's administrative districts. The revenue surveys were conducted across the Company's dominions, albeit in a phased manner, throughout the nineteenth and early twentieth centuries. These surveys represented the colonial state's claim to sovereignty, insofar as it delegated to itself the right to represent its territories.[68]

We need not be distracted by the historical development, technical details or struggles and contests that invariably characterized these revenue surveys. The revenue surveys are important for another, oft-ignored reason. For the first time, the revenue surveys uncovered detailed information on the old *pargana* divisions that were displayed on maps (see Maps 6.5–6.8). These *pargana* maps exposed the intermixed bodies and discontinuous boundaries of these divisions. Sometimes this phenomenon would be very pronounced throughout the body of an entire district, leaving it almost impossible to reconstruct their layout (see Map 6.7).[69] While these *pargana* maps can still be found in many survey offices in North India, they have for long been ignored by historians, even though their usefulness had been commented on some time ago.[70]

While Company officials were initially reluctant to indulge in the wholesale tampering of *pargana* divisions, they soon realized that their dispersed bodies were "unnatural." The Resolution of the Revenue Department of 30 October 1837 made the observation that "it does not appear that under preceding governments the limits of these divisions were always kept unchanged. Private interests or temporary purposes frequently occasioned the severance of a mouzah from one Pergunnah to which it *naturally* belonged, and its annexation to another more distant one."[71] Company officials increasingly articulated a *naturalized* vision of territory where it remained continuous and without overlaps in its layout, while being enclosed by linear boundaries. Consequently, this resolution also recommended the reordering of these *parganas* while bearing in mind uniformity in tenures, compactness of territory and well-defined boundaries. *Parganas* that were too intermixed to separate were to be united under their joint names. Furthermore, care was to be taken to make the limits of *parganas* coincide with the limits of police (*thana*), revenue (*tehsil*) and judicial (*munsifi*) divisions, which were then made to correspond to the newly fixed limits of districts.

Every effort was made to keep the intermixed layout and sinuous boundaries of *parganas* hidden from view in these maps.[72] Only those detached portions of land that were too large to gloss over were shown.[73] In fact, later maps of British districts showed increasingly compact divisions, until all elements of intermixture and sinuous boundaries were eliminated.[74] This becomes apparent on an examination of the maps of the district

Map 6.5 Map showing a portion of the district of Jaunpur with detached portions of the kingdom of Awadh and the *parganas* of Raree and Mureeahoo, 1846 CE

Mapwork by Bernardo A. Michael and Natalie Burack.
Source: *Map of the District of Jounpoor* [Jaunpur], 1846 CE. India Office Records, X/1419/1, Historical Map Collection, Asia, Pacific & Africa Collections, British Library.

of Purnea. This district was organized around *thana* (police divisions) which were erected over the older *pargana* divisions. To ensure that the *thana* divisions remained territorially coherent, the bodies of their constituent *parganas* were rearranged to become continuous with linear boundaries. The terribly intermixed *parganas* of Powakhalee and Futtehpur Singheea were gradually "adjusted" to eliminate this intermixture (see Map 6.7). In fact, by 1897 these two *parganas* had disappeared, leaving in their place the new division of Kishungunj.[75] In the end, every attempt was made to "mend" the scarred, bent, mutilated, entangled and patchy bodies of these *pargana* divisions. Over time these efforts assumed the shape of a massive colonial project that silently reorganized the Company's territories on new lines, as it underwrote the territorialization of the Company's power.[76] An apt summary of the colonial state's project of spatial reordering can be found in the words of Major James Lind Sherwill, the revenue surveyor of Dinajpur. In 1863, he observed that

Map 6.6 Detail from the Revenue Survey of India's "Map of the District of Bhagulpoor," 1852 CE

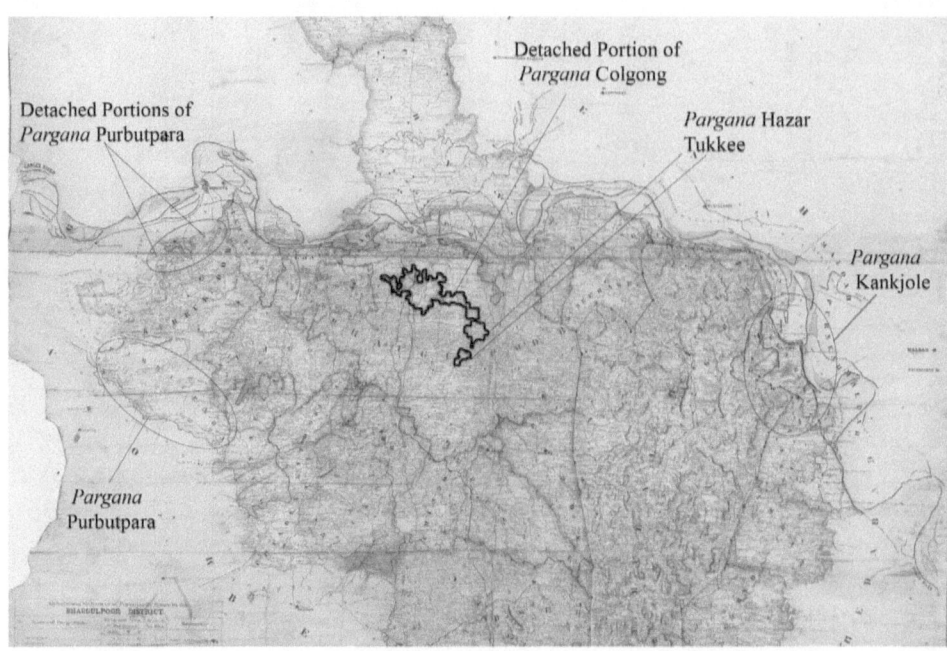

Surveyed by Capt. W. S. Sherwill and Mr J. J. Pemberton. 116.5 × 86 cm, north at the top, scale = four miles to one inch. The district covered nearly 7,803 sq. miles (approximately 20,210 sq. km) as was divided into 40 *parganas* ranging in size from 0.3 to 700 sq. miles (0.7 to 1,813 sq. km). In the 'Alphabetical Statement of Purgunnah Areas' (not shown) *pargana* Huzar Tukee is described as having two detached portions (lying within *pargana* Bhagulpoor). A detached portion of *pargana* Colgong also lies within *pargana* Bhagulpoor, near Huzar Tukee. Note, the two detached sub-divisions (*tappas*) below the Ganges River, Lodweh and Simrown, that lay separate from the main part of the *pargana* of Purbutpara (the upper and lower circles, respectively) by the *pargana* of Kurruckpoor. The *pargana* of Kankjole, lying to the east and straddling the Kosi River, possessed five smaller *parganas* scattered throughout its body. These *parganas*, being insignificant in size, were not shown on the map, but details of their respective areas were included in the above-mentioned tables. Reproduced by permission of the British Library © British Library Board.
Source: Historical Map Collection, India Office Records, X/1041/1, British Library.

the area of the entire tract included in the Dinajpore survey and under consideration in this report, is [...] 4,586 miles square and is divided into 84 pergunnahs, the lands of which are so cut up and intermixed as to baffle all attempts of a Revenue surveyor to define their limits, or even assign them a locality on the maps, except a few of the Northern ones. In addition to these 84 pergunnahs, there are portions of 14 more, belonging to other Districts. For the convenience of surveying, the whole has been lumped into 38 convenient sized blocks. These have been defined on the professional maps by distinguishing colors, and named after the pergunnah of which each one is chiefly composed. Some of these blocks contain portions of as many as 25 pergunnahs.[77]

These maps, then, had an important objective – to enhance the "simplicity and intelligibleness" of the divisions that made up the space of the colonial state.[78] This formed

Map 6.7 Detail from a section of the Revenue Survey of India's "Map of the District of Purneah [Purnea]," 1851 CE

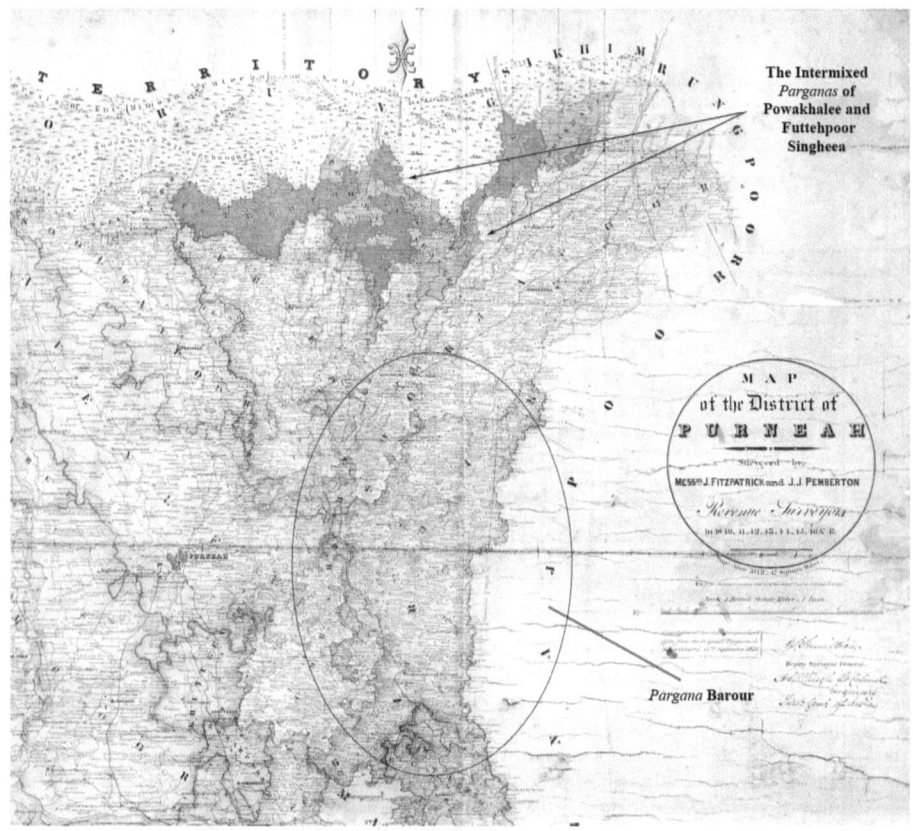

Surveyed by J. Fitzpatrick and J. J. Pemberton from 1840 to 1847. 97 × 92 cm, north at the top, scale = four miles to one inch. The district, which covered some 5,712 sq. miles (14,794 sq. km), was divided into 33 *parganas* whose names and acreages are listed in a table (not shown) on the map. A number of *parganas*, like Barour, Haveli, Hutundah, Kankjole and Kuttear, are listed as being "indicated in another" *pargana*. The *pargana* of Barour included lands belonging to *pargana* Soojainnuggur (from the neighboring district of Malda). However, these lands were not recorded in the area figures for Barour. Also note the excessive intermixing of the *parganas* of Powakhalee and Futtehpoor Singheea in the Himalayan foothills in the north, close to the frontier with Nepal and Sikkim. Reproduced by permission of the British Library © British Library Board. Source: Historical Map Collection, India Office Records, X/1058/1, Asia, Pacific & Africa Collections, British Library.

the most fundamental impulse behind the projects of territorial rearrangement initiated under the auspices of the colonial state. In attempting this, slowly but surely the British began to assemble a new geographical template for the state. The revised *pargana* divisions were a colonial invention. By the end of the nineteenth century the *thana* divisions had superceded the *parganas* in importance. Ultimately the *pargana* divisions ceased to even appear on district maps, and today they only remain in the minds of older inhabitants. The mapping of the *parganas*, the least known aspect of the Revenue Survey's activities in nineteenth-century India, was not driven by the purely pragmatic concerns of cadastral

Map 6.8 Detail from the Revenue Survey of India's "Map of the District of Rangpur including the independent state of Kooch Behar," 1861 CE

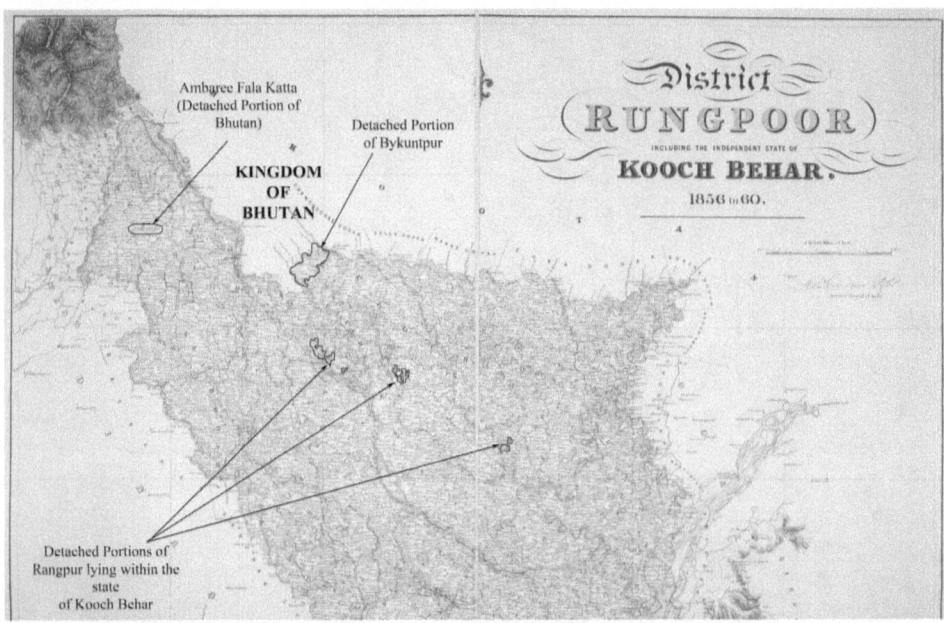

Surveyed by J. J. Pemberton from 1856–1860. 128 × 98 cm, north at the top, scale = four miles to one inch. Rangpur covered some 4,616 square miles divided into 13 *parganas*. In the top half of the map, patches of land (about 35 square miles) belonging to Rangpur lie scattered along the southern reaches of Kuch Bihar. Also note the detached portion of the *pargana* of Bykuntpur separated by a portion of territory belonging to the neighboring kingdom of Bhutan. The map also contains tabular statements of the areas of the Revenue Survey circuits or divisions of Rangpur district, as well as latitude, longitude and heights. Remarks in these statements note that "[i]n consequence of the great intermixture of Purgunnahs in this District, the areas of the separate or local fiscal Divisions could not be recorded, nor their exact limits shown on this scale. For such information the lithographed Maps published on the scale of 1 British Mile to the Inch must be consulted." Reproduced by permission of the British Library © British Library Board.
Source: Historical Map Collection, India Office Records, X/1298/1/1, Asia, Pacific & Africa Collections, British Library.

mapping and revenue administration. Rather, these surveys and *pargana* maps resolved the long-standing spatial anxiety experienced by colonial officials over the exact layout, boundaries and internal organization of these divisions – anxieties that had animated the territorial disputes that led to the Anglo–Gorkha War of 1814–16.

4. Reordering Territory: *Thanas*, Sub-divisions and Districts

One of the earliest observations on the spatial characteristics of the Company's districts came from Charles Bentley, the Collector of Chittagong. In 1772, Bentley was asked to give his opinion on the government's new policy of establishing farming contracts to collect revenue. In his comments, Bentley, without the aid of modern maps, noted that in the district under his charge not a single *chakla* or *pargana* "stood entire," making it difficult to determine the total resources of the district. Bentley tried to resolve this (unsuccessfully) by dividing Chittagong into nine new *compact* revenue zones, each called a *chakla*.[79] Bentley's experience suggests that such questions of spatiality lay at the heart of everyday governance and would surface time and again in official correspondence, finding expression in projects of territorial rearrangement. In 1786, on the advice of the Court of Directors in London, the Company created 35 new districts or "Collectorships."[80] In 1787, their number was reduced to 23 on the recommendations of John Shore, president of the Board of Revenue at Calcutta, who suggested that territorial divisions be reorganized with a view to preserving compactness and clear boundaries.[81] Again, in 1789, he would observe that a good idea of the revenues of the province of Bengal could be gained

> by assuming as a *ground-work* the present distribution of the country into collectorships, after such correction as it may admit, and by obtaining through the different collectors, an account of the distribution of the revenue upon pergunnahs and villages throughout their respective jurisdictions. To perform this, we must first determine the number of pergunnahs in each zamindarry, and prescribe a form of arrangement for them, which shall be established by law, imposing penalties for every unauthorized alteration. I do not by this mean to prevent a zemindar changing the subdivisions of a pergunnah, but to require only that the constituent subdivisions shall *always* stand under the same pergunnah, where they are originally placed, and that they shall *not* be transferred to any other. Thus, supposing a pergunnah to be portioned out into five or more terfs or kismuts, comprehending the *whole*, it shall stand in the accounts as *one* article only, comprising so many divisions.[82]

Further territorial rearrangements took place in 1792 when the Company's districts were divided into *thanas* or police jurisdictions of about 20 to 30 miles square in extent.[83] Considerations of economy, easy communication, revenue collection, internal security, administrative convenience and spatial compactness determined the location and layout of these new *thana* divisions. However, the reality was that these *thana* divisions remained patchy, irregular in shape and intermixed in many places, largely because they were constructed out of the older *pargana* divisions and their attendant villages. Commenting on the *thana* divisions of Gorakhpur district, contemporary surveyors like Francis Buchanan would observe that many *thanas* had highly irregular and dispersed bodies (see detached portions of *thana* nos. 2, 22 and 24 in Map 6.9). Buchanan-Hamilton's descriptions of these *thana* divisions are littered with spatialized descriptors such as scattered, detached, long narrow jurisdiction, compact, petty, centrical, ill arranged and so on. His description of the *thana* of Maghar (Gorakhpur district) exemplifies this when he observed that it had an "irregular straggling jurisdiction, exceedingly ill-arranged having nearly in its middle, or intermixed with it, the division of Bakhira, and containing two detached portions of Bangsi.".[84] He also noted that *thana*, *munsifi* and *tehsil* jurisdiction varied in size and did not always coincide (as in Gorakhpur), thereby making it harder to govern effectively.[85] For Buchanan-Hamilton, this situation was the product of "carelessness" and "confusion" and called for territorial resizing and compaction. He overlooked the complicity of the older *pargana* divisions and their villages in creating the discontinuous and patchy *thanas*.[86]

Map 6.9 Thana divisions of Gorakhpur district showing their detached portions and location of police posts in 1814 CE

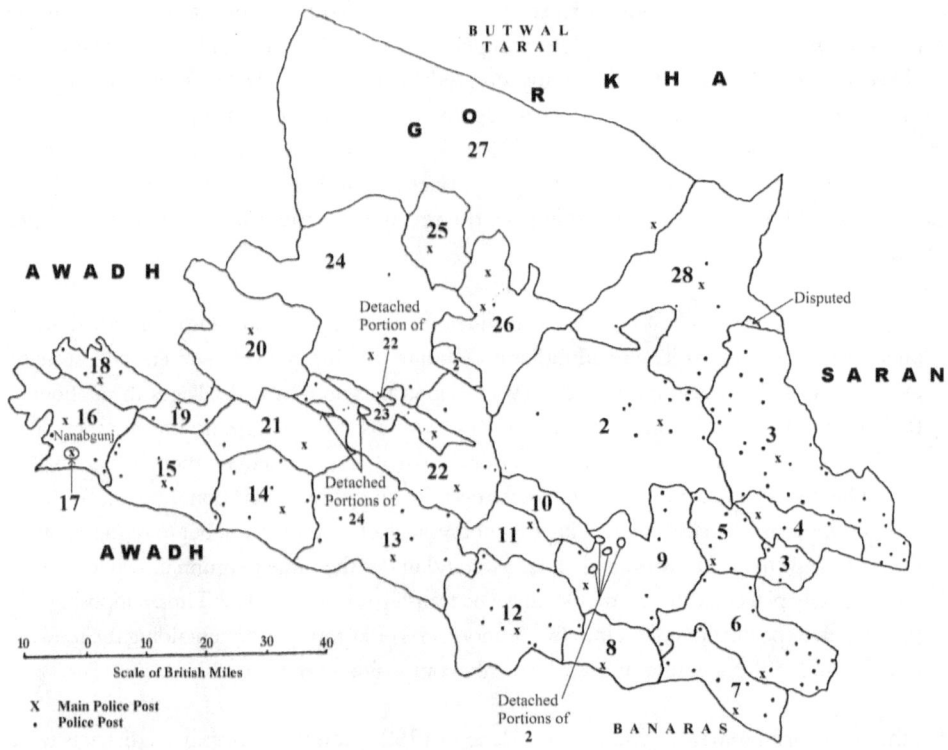

Mapwork by Bernardo A. Michael and Natalie Burack.
Source: This map has been adapted from Francis Buchanan-Hamilton's Map of the Northern Part of the District of Gorakhpur, Historical Maps, India Office Records, X\1020\2, Asia, Pacific & Africa Collections, British Library.

Buchanan-Hamilton's observations about the district of Purnea in Bihar reveal the situation on the ground and include a description of a local map of the *thana* of Dimiya. He noted that:

> The sub division into Thanahs [*thanas*] has been made with as little care as in Rongopur [Rangpur district, north Bengal]. Their jurisdictions are miserably intermixed, of very unequal sizes, and population and the residence of the officers has often without any apparent reason, been placed very far from a centrical position. In forming these jurisdictions the maps never seem to have been consulted and the guide seems to have been a report of some native (munshi [scribe] or amin [surveyor]) who knew nothing of the country. I saw a curious specimen of the ideas of such people in a plan of Thanah Dimiya, which was furnished from the public office and represented Dimiya as placed in the centre of a square district, with villages extending all around to nearly equal distances. Whereas the division is in reality somewhat semi-circular, with a projection at each angle, and Dimiya, until carried by the Kosi [river], stood exactly on its bank, which formed the boundary, and it was much nearer to the south angle than to the northern extremity.[87]

The indigenous map of *thana* Dimiya, to Buchanan-Hamilton's amusement, did not take into account either topographical accuracy and territorial contiguity or the exact location of villages and boundaries. In fact, its tabular construction suggests similarities with other indigenous maps discussed in Chapter 5 and also the Nepali maps lying in the Hodgson collection (see later in this chapter). In these maps, relationships between objects were not always yoked to a geographical template emptied of a human presence. Buchanan-Hamilton, on the other hand, sought to construct a bird's-eye view of the Company's territories that was perfectly consistent in its parts. Here, territory became visualized as "absolute space" or an empty geographical container made out of discrete locations on the earth that could be comprehended as a whole.[88]

As colonial rule progressed, its officials had to rearrange the intermixed bodies of *pargana* divisions in order to better align them with the new administrative divisions and sub-divisions being created. In 1793, a large number of territorial transfers were undertaken between various collectorships in Bihar and Bengal. Villages and *mahals*, either whole or in part, that lay detached from their parent *parganas* were transferred between various districts, so as to render the concerned districts more compact.[89] Later, in the early nineteenth century, when the Company state created new districts along with their *thana* sub-divisions in the Ceded and Conquered Districts in North India, it enacted regulations to ensure greater overlaps in the jurisdictions of these divisions. Thus Regulation 11 of 1833 directed that the revenue and police functions of the *tehsildar* (collector of revenue) should be made co-extensive with the jurisdictions of *thanas*. Again, when the Gorakhpur division was abolished in 1835 and its constituent districts integrated into the Banaras Division, the magistrate of Azamgarh commented on the lack of overlap between the *pargana* and *thana* divisions and the need to "adjust" the boundaries of the former. He reported to the commissioner of Ghazipur that "the great irregularity of the Pergunnah boundaries made this [the adjusting of *thana* jurisdictions] very perjudicial, but as the Pergunnah boundaries are now *adjusted* and *rounded* off, the objection ceases. The Thanah boundaries of course, correspond with the *new* Pergunnah boundaries."[90] The creation of intermediate administrative units between the district and *thanas* called sub-divisions, which took place after the 1840s, required further adjustments. For instance, the district of Champaran in Bihar was divided into two sub-divisions – Motihari and Bettiah, whose civil, criminal, revenue jurisdictions were rearranged and made coterminous by the 1870s.[91]

Munsifi (judicial divisions) also underwent similar changes and were gradually rearranged, rounded off and "adjusted" so that they would be coterminous with *thana* divisions;[92] villages under the criminal jurisdiction of one district and the fiscal jurisdiction of another were exchanged.[93] Conversely, *thanas* located in the fiscal and criminal jurisdiction of one district but in the civil jurisdiction of another were reshuffled. For instance, the *thana* of Raniganj straddled the civil jurisdiction of Birbhum district (in Bengal), the criminal jurisdiction of Bankura district (also in Bengal) and the revenue jurisdiction partly of Burdwan district and partly of Manbhoom [Manbhum] district. Such conflicts in jurisdiction resulted in people fighting cases in as many as three districts simultaneously (see Map 6.10).[94] The *thana* of Raniganj was subsequently rearranged.[95] By 1875 the colonial state was making serious efforts to render permanent the boundaries of these emerging districts. For example, every district contained estates which were

Map 6.10 Rearrangement of Thana boundaries in District Manbhoom [Manbhum], 1875 CE

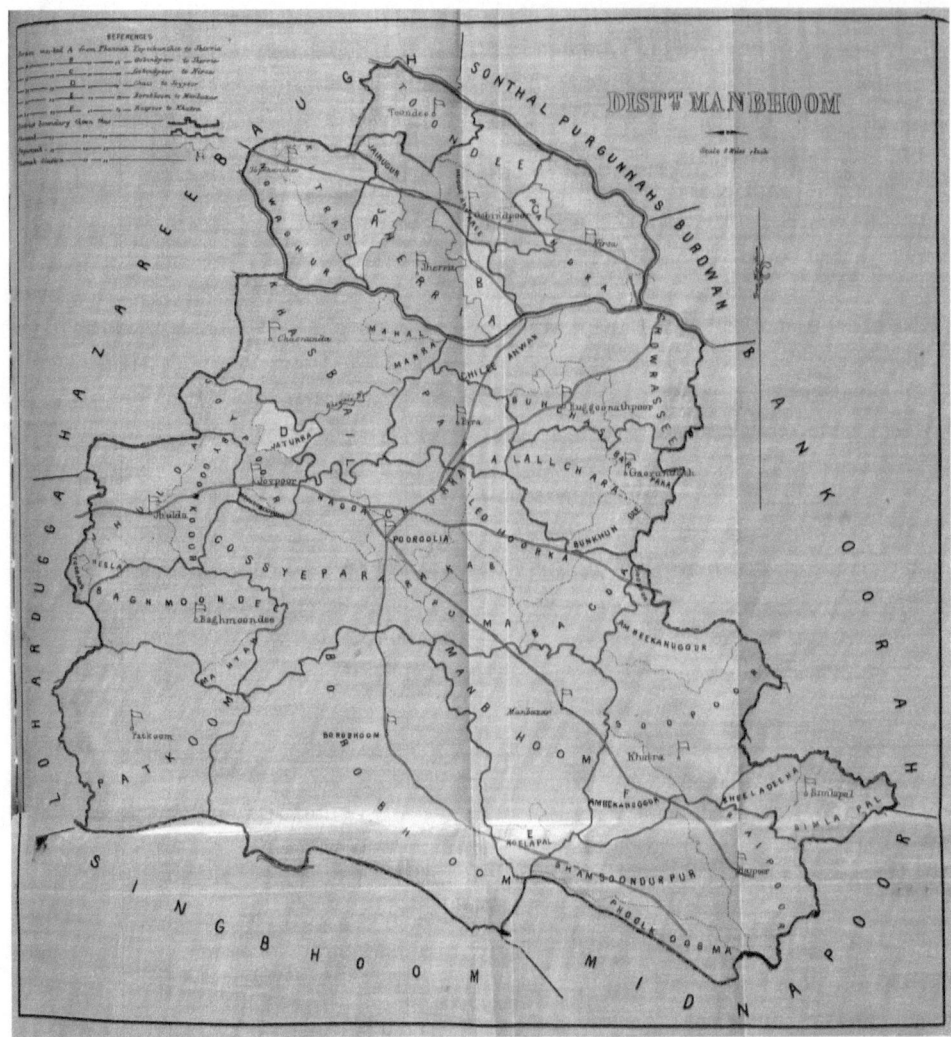

Map of District Manbhoom [Manbhum], 39 × 34 cm, scale = eight miles to one inch, north at top. Reproduced by permission of the British Library © British Library Board.
Source: Procs of the Lt. Governor of Bengal: Revenue Branch (Jurisdictions and Boundaries), Bengal Judicial Consultations P/242, March 1875, pp. 92–3, India Office Records, Asia, Pacific & Africa Collections, British Library.

placed on the revenue rolls of another district. Consequently, government ordered that the boundary of a district was to be a permanent one and distinct from the boundary of an estate paying revenue. From now onwards these boundaries of districts were made permanent and subject to change only under government fiat, as well as being delinked from the information on estates contained in the rent-rolls.[96] Over time the revenues of these estates would be redirected to the districts they were geographically located in and not the district they were identified as belonging to in the rent-rolls. In this manner, the policy of objectifying and compacting the colonial state's internal divisions through boundary demarcations and territorial exchanges would continue from the 1790s well into the twentieth century.[97] The process by which the structure of colonial territories was fashioned out of the older *pargana* divisions constitutes one of the great spatial settlements conducted by the British in South Asia – one that deserves more scholarly attention than given here.[98]

5. The Case of Gorkhali Territories

In the eighteenth and nineteenth centuries, Gorkha's territories also remained internally ill-defined with overlapping jurisdictions and shifting boundaries. The Gorkhali government was less anxious about creating territorially compact administrative divisions with linear boundaries and more concerned with the distribution of rights to administrative offices, revenue collection and the administration of justice. This, no doubt, must have found varied expressions across the kingdom, depending on distance from Kathmandu, the terrain and other local factors. The picture was further complicated by the fact that an individual could hold multiple administrative portfolios or a single office could be shared among two or more individuals. In 1794 AD, for example, the Gorkhali *vakil* Dinanath Upadhyaya may have held the two offices of *chaudhari* of *tappa* Rautahat, as well as the *subba* of Morang district.[99] Elsewhere, in 1802, the brothers Hastidal and Rudravir Shah shared the office of *subba* in Kumaon.[100] The administrative landscape was further peppered with jurisdictions created by rights to hold and cultivate land and collect revenue.[101] Often, this gave rise to all kinds of jurisdictional conflicts, and authorities in Kathmandu were forced to issue clarifications about the rights in question.[102] For instance, in 1811, disputes broke out between one Captain Chandra Bir Kunwar and the revenue collectors (*amils*) of *tappa* Sheoraj over whether the former's rent-free landholdings should be taxed. Authorities in Kathmandu ordered that a survey be conducted to separate the Captain's rent-free lands from revenue-yielding lands, and any remaining lands found not belonging to him were to be entered into the accounts of Palpa District (*upar gaon Palpa darai dinu*). All this was done without reference to preserving boundaries or territorial continuity.[103] The late Nepali historian Mahesh Chandra Regmi insisted that such jurisdictional complexity was a marked characteristic of Gorkhali administration in newly conquered areas like Kumaon, which "was based on what may be called the policy of overlapping jurisdictions. Various layers of administrative jurisdictions were created for the province and the region, but those jurisdictions although formally separate, *jutted* into one another in important fields."[104]

It might be worthwhile to point out that while the Gorkhali government made clear distinctions between different kinds of rights, no attempt was made to organize these rights around a clearly demarcated territorial structure of continuous districts and their sub-divisions. Gorkhali authorities were more concerned with the timely collection of revenue, the separation of tax yielding and rent-free lands and the administration of justice. In the Tarai what preoccupied them was the preservation of the agrarian entitlements that fell under their jurisdiction rather than the preservation of an abstract line that was divorced from these rights. The Gorkhali use of the term "*ambal/amval*" also suggests that they were more concerned with the exercise of specific rights and authority that translated on the ground into an array of dispersed obligations, claims, possessions and jurisdictions.[105] The kingdom's judicial system too was organized around jurisdictions that were territorially unclear and frequently overlapped.[106] Thus, in the Tarai areas, besides the customary village authorities, the civil and military officials like the *subba* and the *fauzdar* were also entitled to prosecute judicial cases.[107] However, more work needs to be done to understand the jurisdictional dynamics involving the collection of revenue and the maintenance of law and order within the Gorkhali kingdom.

Another term that finds frequent mention in Gorkhali records is "*dhungo*" (literally meaning "stone"), commonly used as a metaphor for kingdom. One of the earliest Gorkhali references to the term can be found in the Royal Letter of King Prithvinarayan Shah to Pandit Rajiv Lochan written in January 1746, in which he noted that it was appropriate ruling policy to uphold the common interests of both Gorkha and Kaski (*Gorkhako ra Kaskiko rekhjokh garnu dhungo ho*).[108] In some contexts, the term could also represent a strong state (*dhungo*) versus a weaker one (*tarul* or *yam*). Hence Prithvinarayan's famous observation that Gorkha was like a yam sandwiched between the powerful kingdoms of North India in the south and the Chinese to the north (*uparant yo raje dui dhungako tarul jasto rahe cha*).[109] Nepal's foremost historian of the Gorkhali state, the Mahesh Chandra Regmi, has commented that "the concept implied that the state was an entity that transcended the person of the ruler, and the allegiance to the state superceded personal loyalty to the ruler. The concept of *dhungo* found its practical application in the principle of territorial integrity, an essential attribute of the state in the modern sense of the term."[110] Given all the evidence emerging from the Anglo–Gorkha frontier, it is difficult to agree with Regmi's contention that the notion of *dhungo* emphasized the territorial features of the state in the "modern sense of the term." In general, the term *dhungo* represented service and loyalty to the state embodied in the person of the king rather than the territorial integrity of the state.

Gorkha's territories in the Tarai were divided into *pragannas*, *tappes* and *tarafs*, while in the hills they were divided into *thums*, *garkhas* and *thats*.[111] Since most of the revenue in the Tarai was collected on a contractual basis (*ijara*), there was little need for Kathmandu to maintain detailed accounts of every *mauza* or to discern the total area of a *pargana* (including both cultivated and uncultivated lands). With local officials having a greater say in recording information there was little consistency in the recording of territorial information. So while Rautahat is frequently referred to as a *tappe*, it also finds mention in the record as a *zilla* and even *praganna*.[112] It appears as a sub-division of the districts of Bara and was once included under the combined districts of Bara-Parsa and Bara-Parsa-Rautahat.[113] Rautahat was subdivided into *tarafs* which also find reference as *pragannas* (*praganna* Paroha, *zilla* Rautahat).[114] In another instance, and for reasons yet unclear, the *pargana* of Gadh Simraon was joined with the *pargana* of Mewa to form *pargana* Mewa Gadh Simraon.[115] There is also no unanimity regarding the number of *tarafs* (sub-divisions) the *tappe* of Rautahat was carved into. Gorkhali and East India Company records indicate that Rautahat possessed anywhere between seven and ten sub-divisions.[116] Over the nineteenth century, Rautahat witnessed changes in its internal divisions and in the twentieth century it is recorded as being divided into eight *thums*.[117]

As the Gorkhali state expanded in the eighteenth century, it incorporated lesser kingdoms directly through a policy of conquest or the bestowal of tributary status on some, like Mustang and Sallyan. This meant that they enjoyed a degree of autonomy in collecting taxes and administering justice. By the end of Rana rule (1951), these rights were gradually abolished, and all that remained of them were some minor judicial functions. Similarly, the Limbu and Rai tribal leaders in Eastern Nepal also enjoyed a certain degree of self-government during the Rana period (1846–1951). In keeping these kingdoms intact, the Gorkhalis also preserved the relations of *vassalage* that might have existed between them. This had implications for the organization of territory. For instance, in 1763, the Gorkhali king Prithvinarayan Shah gave the kingdom of Dang to Sallyan as a dowry for his daughter. Consequently, sometime during the reign of Gorkhali king Ran Bahadur Shah (1794–1806), Dang was attached to the kingdom of Sallyan.[118] Later, an attempt was made to attach the little kingdom of Chilli to Sallyan on the grounds that it was a vassal (*thapale*) of Dang. However, Chilli protested this move, and the proposed merger was abandoned when an inquiry revealed that Chilli had been rendered independent of the jurisdiction of Dang by the Gorkhali raja, Ran Bahadur Shah (1794–1806). Subsequently, in 1802, Chilli was separated from the jurisdiction of Salyan and Dang.[119] Spatially, Chilli became an autonomous space lying within Sallyani territory.[120] Again, when Gorkha incorporated the kingdom of Pyuthana in 1788, it preserved that kingdom's preexisting political ties with Dang and Sallyana. So, in 1809, Gorkha asked Pyuthana to continue remittances of revenue (*Pyuthana Danglai manitiro tiri ayako daidastur tari*) to Dang, as had been the practice in former times.[121] In granting revenue-collection rights in the area, Gorkha followed the usual custom. So, in 1827, one Tej Bahadur Shah, the tax collector of Sallyan, was appointed the raja of Phalabang (Dang). This gave him the right to collect revenue in Dang. In this fashion patches of Gorkhali territory continued to be constituted out of older relationships pertaining to service, authority, tribute and taxation. This must have prevented the creation of clear-cut territorial divisions of the type found in a modern state and is reminiscent of similar developments along the Anglo–Gorkha frontier. Though the Anglo–Gorkha boundary was formally demarcated after 1816, Gorkha internally remained a loose patchwork of administrative divisions and sub-divisions with entangled overlapping bodies and unclear boundaries.[122] In 1840, Brian Hodgson would observe: "The official divisions of the kingdom are vaguely designated, though well understood in *practice*."[123] Further research in this area might yield rich insights into the territorial basis of the Gorkhali state in the nineteenth century.

A number of territorial rearrangements were instituted within Gorkha during Rana rule (1846–1951).[124] During the prime ministership of Jang Bahadur Rana (1846–77), Gorkha's hill districts were clubbed into three groups called *gaundas*, each headed by a *gaunda* governor, while the Tarai districts were combined to form a single unit under a chief governor of the Tarai.[125] In 1895, Bir Shamsher, the Rana prime minister (1885–1901), reorganized district administration by dividing the hills into 23 *tehsils* and the Tarai areas into 12 *zillas*. These 12 *zillas* were organized into four circles. Each circle along with some *tehsils* was placed under the charge of a *bada hakim* (chief administrator). At the same time, the district boundaries were altered to produce 20 hill districts and 12 Tarai districts.¹²⁶ The older *thum*, *garkha* and *pargana* subdivisions were then placed within this new framework of districts. However, despite these developments there is no evidence to suggest that these details were worked out on the ground through cartographic surveys, which were only employed in the twentieth century.

Notwithstanding the absence of cartographic surveys, indigenous states, communities and individuals possessed their own mapmaking traditions. It is reported that among the various gifts sent by the Malla king of Bhaktapur to the Chinese court was a geographical map of India and Nepal (valley).¹²⁷ The Nepal valley was itself considered a sacred space demarcated by temples and inhabited by 5,600 gods and goddesses.¹²⁸ An eighteenth-century wall-hanging (*pauba*) from the Kathmandu valley depicting pilgrimage routes and an early twentieth century "ritual map" of Bhaktapur depicting the city as a *mandala* in a series of emboxed rhomboids, displaying the important shrines and sacred precincts in the city, provide further evidence of indigenous mapmaking traditions.¹²⁹

Another map, possibly made sometime after 1855, depicts the Central Asian region with the important rivers, mountains and towns and their distances from Kathmandu (see Map 6.11).¹³⁰ A number of route maps drawn by a Chinese high commissioner to Tibet (1794–99) named Song Yun have also been unearthed. It is unclear whether Song Yun, who took part in the Gorkha–China war of 1792, was inspired by some local cartographic tradition or indirectly influenced by the work of the Jesuits, who were already surveying and producing maps of the Qing Empire.¹³¹ While these maps provided general information on the location of urban settlements and routes, they were less concerned with topographical accuracy or displaying the territorial continuity and boundaries of the state.

However, it is uncertain when maps were systematically incorporated as tools of Gorkhali governance. Gorkhali officials were probably aware of the role of maps as far back as the eighteenth century. Francis Wilford, one of the first British students of Indian systems of geography and cosmography, observed in 1805 that one of the best indigenous "Hindu" maps he ever saw

> was one of the kingdom of Napal, presented to Mr. [Warren] Hastings [governor general, 1774–82]. It was about four feet long, and two and a half broad, of paste board, and the mountains raised about an inch above the surface, with trees painted all round. The roads were represented by a red line, and the rivers with a blue one. The various ranges were very distinct, with the narrow passes through them: in short, it wanted but a scale. The valley of Napal was accurately delineated: but toward the borders of the map, everything was crowed [*sic*], and in confusion.¹³²

Wilford was unimpressed by these maps and commented that these "works, whether historical or geographical, are most extravagant compositions, in which little regard indeed is paid to *truth* [...] Geographical truth is sacrificed to a symmetrical arrangement of countries, mountains, lakes, and rivers, with which they are highly delighted."¹³³ In another instance, the Gorkhali commander *budakaji* Amar Singh Thapa employed mapmakers to produce maps of Kangra on Gorkha's western front.¹³⁴

Map 6.11 A Nepali map of Central Asia, post-1855 CE (?)

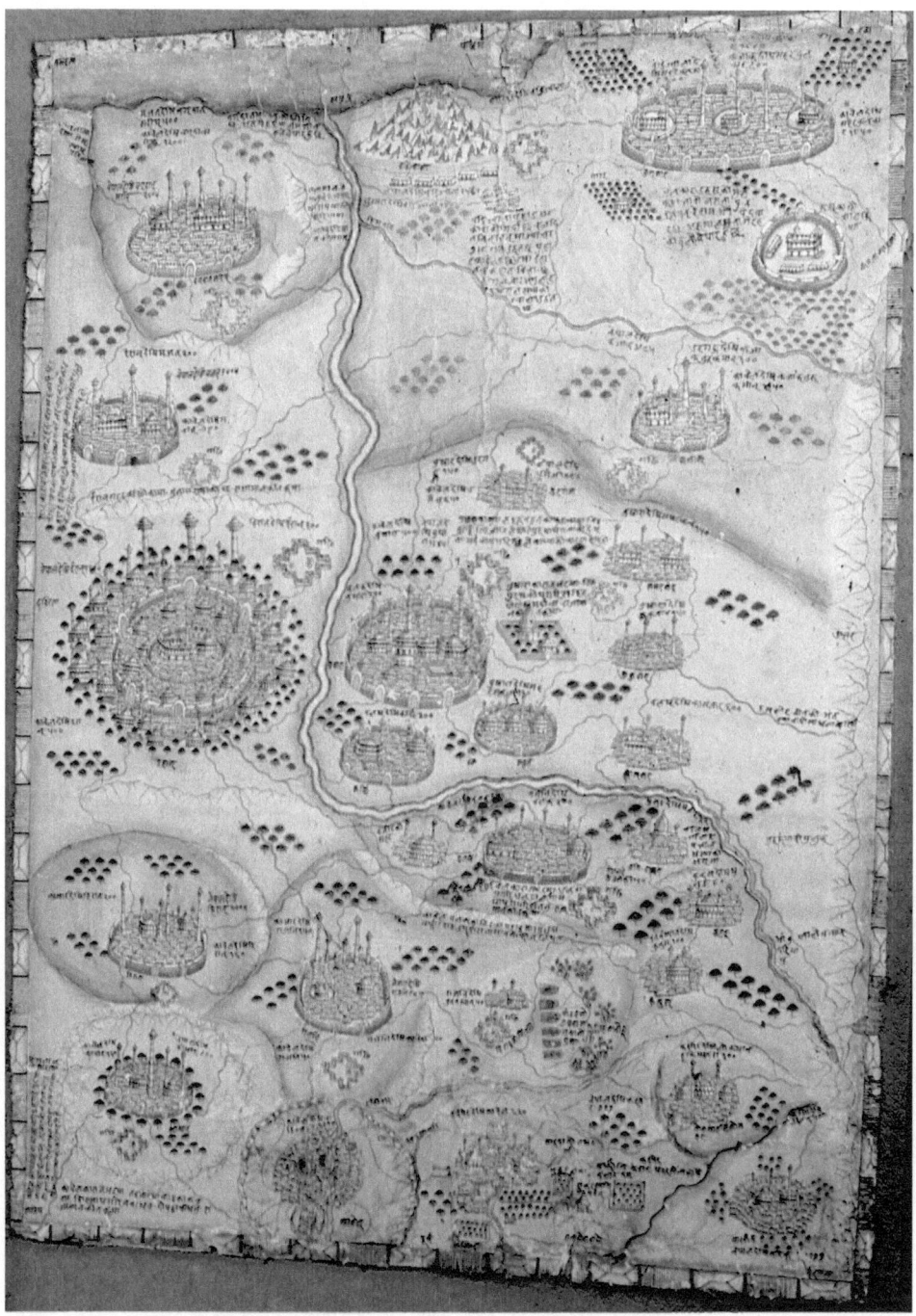

54 × 76 cm, Nepali, paper on cloth. The map shows rivers like the Amudarya, towns like Baghdad, Meshed, Herat, Kandahar and Kabul, and regions like Kashmir. Reproduced with permission of the Trustees of Columbia University.

Map 6.12 Map of Central Nepal in the Hodgson Collection, 1835–1840 CE

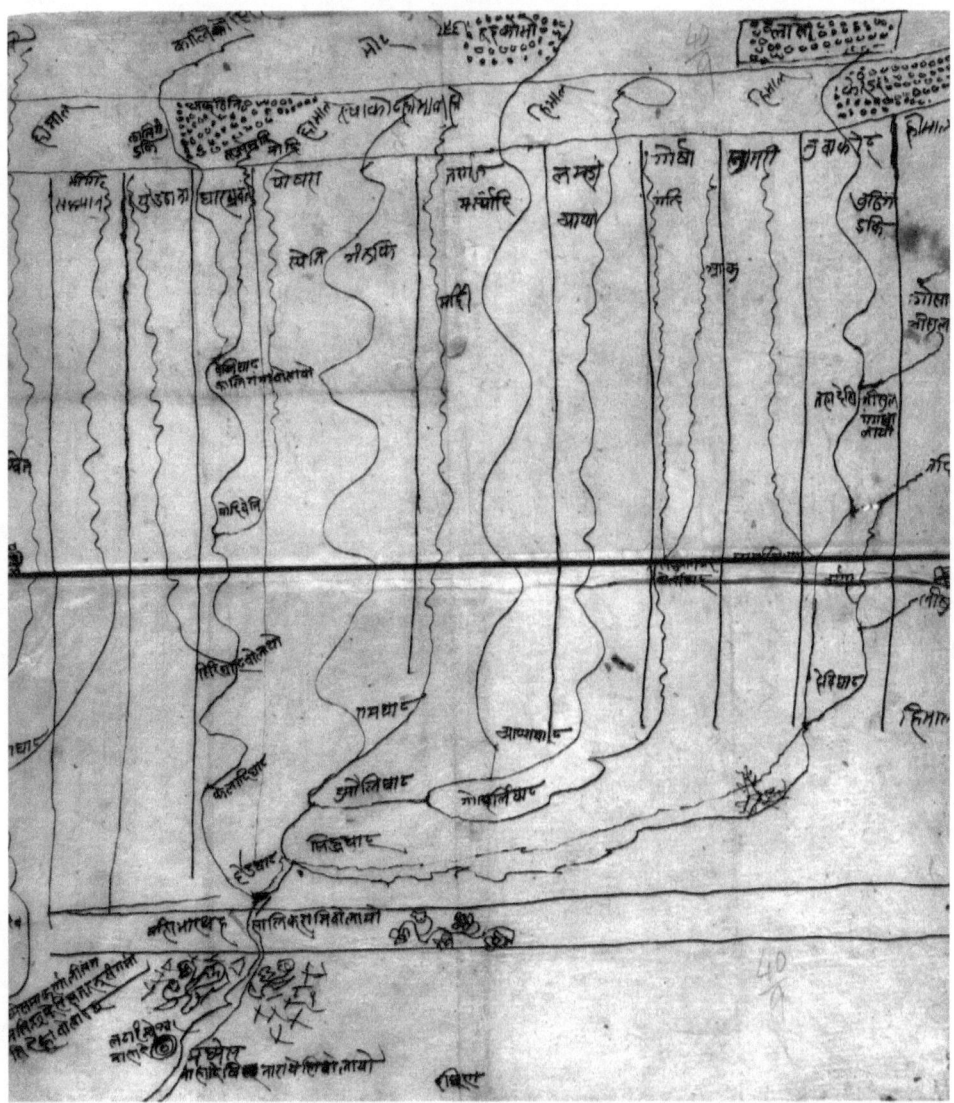

42 × 38 cm, ink on paper. Reproduced by permission of the British Library © British Library Board. Source: Hodgson Eur. Mss K474, vol. 56, folios 59–60, India Office Records, Asia, Pacific & Africa Collections, British Library.

The arrival of the British signaled a new intervention in the production of maps of Nepal. British surveyors like Francis Buchanan-Hamilton employed indigenous informants to produce maps of places he traveled through.[135] He observed that these maps were "very rude, and differ in several points; but they coincided in a great many more, so as to give considerable authority to their general structure; and, by a careful examination of the *whole*, many differences, apparently considerable, may be reconciled."[136] After the end

Map 6.13 Map of a portion of Western Nepal in the Hodgson Collection, 1830–1840 CE

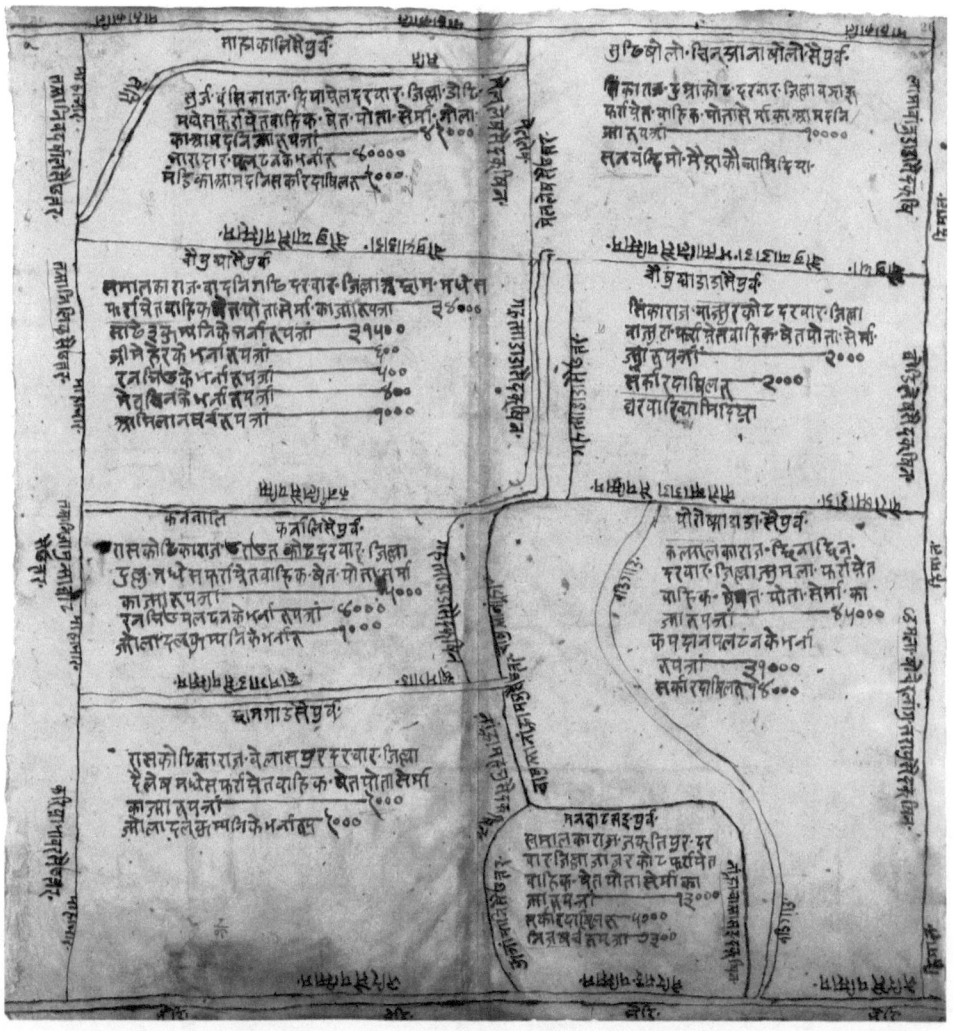

56 × 48 cm, ink on paper. Reproduced by permission of the British Library © British Library Board. Source: Hodgson Eur. Mss K474, vol. 59, folios 25–6, India Office Records, Asia, Pacific & Africa Collections, British Library.

of the Anglo–Gorkha War in 1816, Edward Gardner, who was the first British resident in Kathmandu (1816–29), noted that during the boundary demarcation proceedings the Gorkhalis used a sketch of the Tarai that they had composed. The inspiration for these Gorkhali maps, as well as their content and composition remain unidentified.[137]

A number of "Gorkhali" maps can be found in the manuscript materials lying in the Hodgson Collection, at the Oriental and India Office, London (see Maps 6.12 and 6.13).[138] The maps appear to be rough copies showing topographical features such as rivers and hills, riverain boundaries of administrative districts, names of their governors,

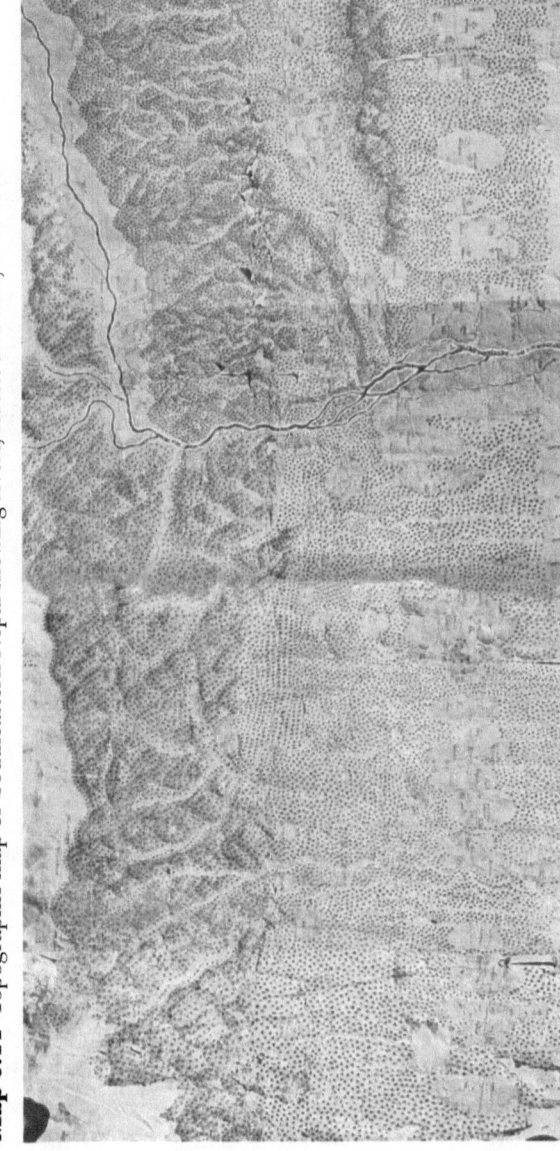

Map 6.14 Topographic map of Southeastern Nepal showing rivers, forests and hills, c. 1860 CE

84 × 495 cm. Ink on handmade Nepali paper with cloth backing. Reproduced with the permission of the family of Dr Harka Gurung.
Source: Harka Gurung, *Maps of Nepal* (Bankok: White Orchid Books, 1983), 10–11.

location of kingdoms, sources of revenue and the authorities to whom the revenue was to be remitted. The maps, such as "Sukhimko charkillako tapsil," represent a hybrid between a table displaying revenue accounts and a topographic map of the Sikkim region showing its location vis-à-vis its neighbors.[139] The indigenous informants who prepared these pictographic representations described them as abstracts (*terij*) or lists (*tapsil*), usually found in taxation documents.[140] There is no indication that these informants viewed these documents as maps (*naqsha*).[141] Finally, while no attempt was made to accurately represent the geographical layout or boundaries of Gorkhali districts, the desire to provide a graphical representation of territory might have emerged from Hodgson's own fascination for collecting information on the internal resources, divisions, distances and geographical features of the Gorkhali state.

In 1855, the Survey of India prepared a map of Nepal and its adjoining countries by compiling information from a number of sources including one referred to as "Jung Bahadoor's Nipal Sketch Map, in Deva Nagree characters received from Foreign Department and sent thereto by the Resident of Nipal (no scale)." Jang Bahadur's map is yet to be traced and many like it are probably lying in the archives of the Nepali Foreign Ministry.[142] In the Survey of India's map, the interior of Nepal is scantily marked, suggesting either that the kingdom's internal divisions were never accurately mapped in the nineteenth century or that the Gorkhalis were reluctant to divulge this information. Another notable example is a map of southeastern Nepal produced in 1860 CE (See Map 6.14). This hand-drawn map on Nepali paper shows a number of topographic features such as hills, forests, rivers, human settlements, religious sites and forts. The Nepali geographer Harka Gurung suggests that this map might have been prepared for military purposes.[143] A cursory examination of the map suggests some European influence in terms of its color scheme, and depiction of forests, hills and so on.

There is little information on the cartographic surveys conducted by Gorkhali authorities in the eighteenth and nineteenth centuries. Numerous cadastral surveys had been conducted by Gorkhali officials, with one of the earliest being the kingdom-wide survey of landholdings conducted by the Gorkhali regent Bahadur Shah (1785–94).[144] In the nineteenth century further surveys were conducted in 1827, 1847, 1854 and 1868.[145] The first attempt at deploying chain-based (*sarpat*) cadastral measurements was probably in the Kabhrepalanchok and Sindhupalchok revenue divisions in 1895, in Palpa district in 1896 and Achham in 1928.[146] In the Tarai the first cadastral surveys might have been conducted in 1909 AD.[147] In the end, it is unclear if any maps were produced out of these exercises. The first modern maps of Nepal were produced in the twentieth century. Between 1924 and 1927 the Survey of India, on the invitation of Prime Minister Chandra Shamsher, conducted reconnaissance surveys covering an area of about 55,000 square miles. The maps, drawn to a scale of four miles to an inch, were first published in 1928 and then again in 1934.[148] Systematic cadastral (*kittanapi*) surveys seem to have been employed much later, in the 1930s and 1940s, when trained officers of the Nepalese Army were employed for this purpose in the Kathmandu valley, and in select districts of the Tarai and the hills.[149] Surveyors were instructed to dispense with the intermixture of village lands, wherever possible, by consolidating such lands in consultation with landowners and cultivators.[150] The post-Rana Nepali government was increasingly aware of the importance of cadastral surveying for determining titles and boundaries, producing reliable agricultural statistics and developing equitable taxation policies.[151] In 1957 (2014 BS), a systematic cadastral survey of the country was initiated, which, in 1960, became a collaborative effort between the government and the United States Agency for International Development (USAID). Between 1958 and 1964, 2,141,986 acres of Nepali territory were surveyed.[152]

The country's ancient territorial divisions (such as *thums*, *pragannas*, *tappes*, *tarafs* and *garkhas*) remained unclear and ill-arranged, at least till very recently. In 1939, R. C. Malhotra, a deputy director of agriculture in the Western Tarai Circle, observed that the Tarai *parganas* of this Circle were "arbitrarily based without consideration of similarity in the amount of revenue, area, or the physical features of the landscape."[153] In time, territorial exchanges between districts were carried out in order to render them more consistent. One 1956 report observed that "here and there a few limbs of one district jutting out into another district have been added to the latter district, provided communication routes connected them. Such changes relate to the removal of Parvat *thum* from West No. 4 and its amalgamation with the newly formed district of Pokhara. Tibrikote *thum* of Jumla District has been transferred to Nepalganj. Three thums of Nausai, Satasi, and Athbazar have been transferred from Sallyan to Pyuthan. Nawalpur has been added to Bhairava as it is completely cut off from the East by the Gandak."[154]

Through much of the 1950s, the boundaries of districts were discernible only on the basis of information provided by local officials, while the sub-divisional boundaries remained largely undetermined. This is noted in Survey of India maps of Nepal prepared between 1953 and 1960.[155] Some of these maps, like the one on Dhading District, depict clear instances of a district possessing a detached piece of territory, reminiscent of a pattern visible in nineteenth-century British revenue maps. A close look at the map reveals that a portion of Dhading District lies detached from the main body of the district, separated by an intervening strip of territory from the district of Chitwan-Birganj (see Map 26). Similar instances of discontinuous districts can be found in Pradyumna Karan's map of the "*thum*" divisions of Nepal. For instance, the *pargana* of Beli in the district of Biratnagar is clearly shown as being comprised of two detached segments. The same applies to the sub-division of Palpa.[156] A closer look at some of the Tarai *parganas* in Karan's map reveals that a number of *parganas* straddled two districts. This gives us some idea of the former size of these divisions, suggesting that some of the *parganas* were larger than shown, and were presumably split and shared between districts in a series of territorial rearrangements.[157] Complete maps of Nepal's *pargana* and *thum* divisions are difficult to locate today and probably never existed, or at least were not the products of detailed cadastral surveys. In the 1940s a number of villages in the Far-Western Districts of Banke-Bardia and Mahalwara were surveyed under military supervision. The result was the production of a limited number of village maps. These maps reveal details of village lands, whether *asli* (original) or *dakhili* (dependent), intermixed or dispersed, along with topographical information and the *tappa* division they belonged to.[158]

The excavation of the ancient territorial divisions of Nepal came from an unexpected source – the Bureau of Census and Statistics (established in 1950). In 1958, when the

Map 6.15 Sketch of District West No. 1 (Dhading) showing detached segments, Nepal, 1957–1959 CE

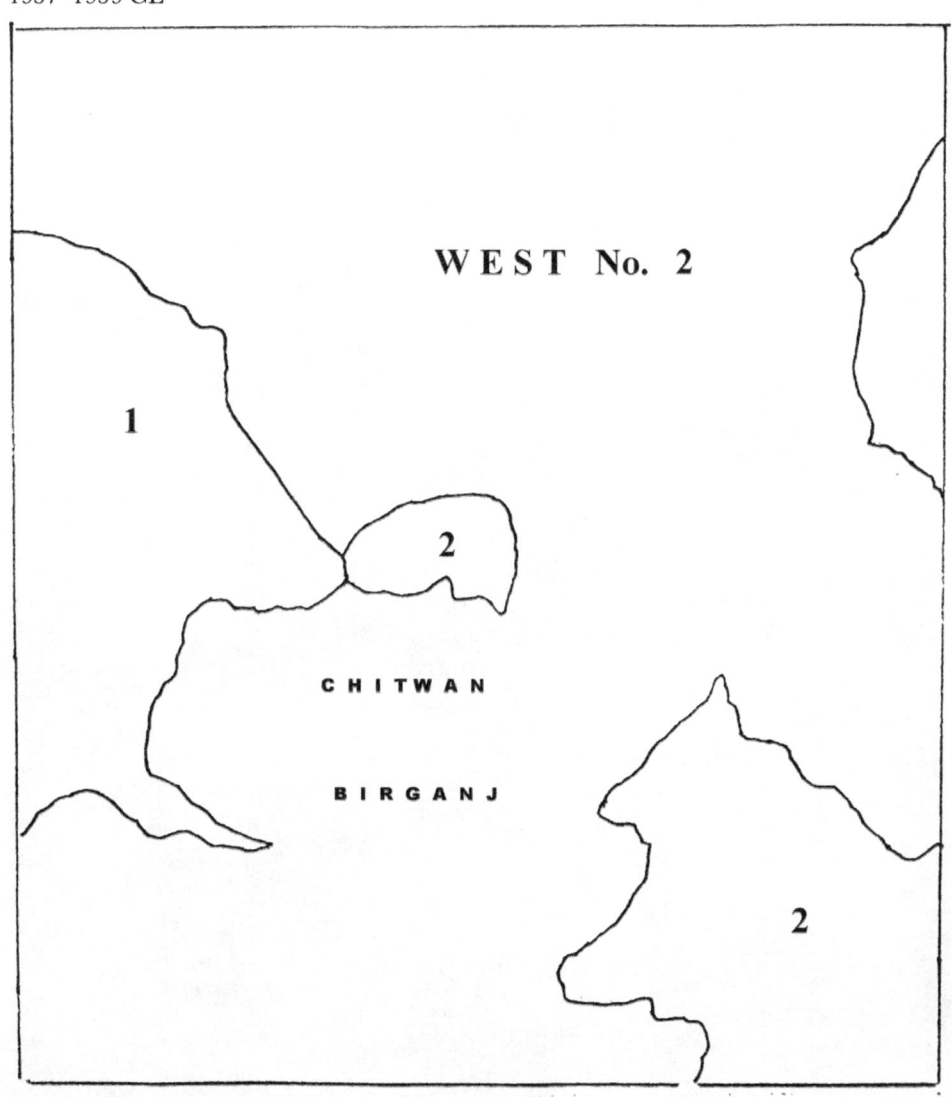

1. **District West No. 3 (Bandipur)**
2. **District West No. 1 (Dhading)**

Mapwork by Bernardo A. Michael
Source: Birganj West No. 1, West No. 2, and West No. 3 Districts, Survey of India Maps, 1957–58, Map 72 A/9, Kitta Napi Mahashaka, Survey Department, Kathmandu, Nepal.

Bureau was tasked with taking the kingdom's census, it found no reliable maps showing clearly demarcated districts and their sub-divisions. Consequently the Bureau took the available maps and inserted census districts, keeping natural features such as mountains and rivers as boundaries. Later, it deputed enumerators (*ganak*) into the countryside to investigate the matter in greater detail and align these boundaries on the basis of

Plate 6.2 The geo-body of Nepal displaying its non-overlapping and clearly defined divisions as depicted on Nepali notebooks

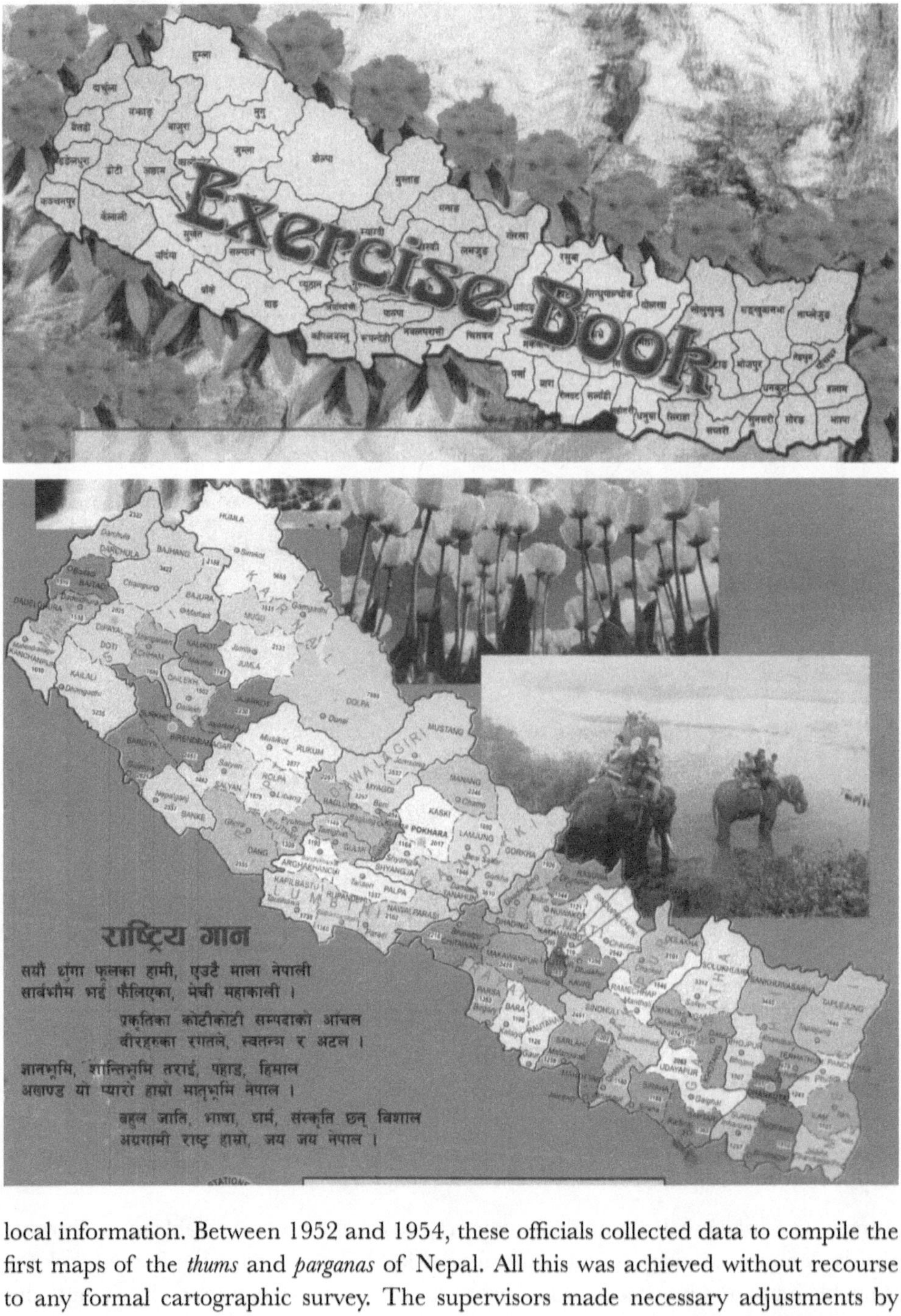

local information. Between 1952 and 1954, these officials collected data to compile the first maps of the *thums* and *parganas* of Nepal. All this was achieved without recourse to any formal cartographic survey. The supervisors made necessary adjustments by breaking up larger *thums* and *parganas* and joining smaller ones to create manageable census districts. The census districts were then organized into six larger divisions called

Plate 6.3 The geo-body of the Nepali nation as depicted on postage stamps, symbolizing the close connections between territory and Nepali nationhood despite its political transformation from a Hindu kingdom to a federal democratic republic in 2008 CE

*Pradesh.*¹⁵⁹ The only composite map of these ancient divisions based on this census data was collated by the geographer Pradyumna Karan in 1960.¹⁶⁰ Later, the country was divided into districts, sub-districts and blocks in descending order. In some cases, whole *thums* or *parganas* were combined to form compact blocks.¹⁶¹ District headquarters were designated on the basis of their central location and access to communication lines. Subsequent governments and administrative bodies used the maps produced by the census department to undertake administrative and territorial reorganizations in the country.¹⁶²

Throughout the twentieth century, a process of territorial rearrangement was initiated that ultimately produced the space of the modern nation-state of Nepal – occupying a definite portion of the Earth's surface and divided into non-overlapping divisions and sub-divisions. By the end of the twentieth century, the territory of Nepal had become a distinct geographic sign possessing a life of its own – a geo-body – signifying, among other things, citizenship, the state and a particular species of people(s), as can be discerned in plate 6.2 and 6.3. Such an understanding of the geo-body persisted even after the dissolution of the Shah dynasty in 2008 and the removal of its symbols from all public displays.

Today, Nepal's transition to a federal republic has raised new pressing questions about spatial restructuring concerning the creation of cohesive administrative divisions on lines of caste, ethnicity, language, development, and democracy.¹⁶³

6. Conclusion

Colonial rule saw the attempt to enforce many boundaries – racial, sexual, gender, class and territorial. The drawing of such boundaries formed one of the central tensions of empire. Following the conclusion of the Anglo–Gorkha War in 1816, the Company state made one of its earliest attempts to demarcate a timeless linear boundary that would separate its territories from another indigenous state. This and other efforts at territorial reordering and rearrangement instituted by the colonial state in North India became projects of legibility and simplification that sought to mark and bound space in new ways.[164] These projects of spatial reordering in South Asia were unlike those which unfolded in other parts of the world such as Australia. South Asian landscapes were not some *tabula rasa* for the Europeans to freely inscribe upon.[165] Rather, they were already inscripted with an indigenous territorial presence that could not be easily dismissed. The Company had to grapple with powerful cultures of governance whose territorial signature had to be modified using various military, administrative and cartographic means. In North India, the colonial revenue surveys of the nineteenth century took the first snapshot of the older *pargana* and *tappa* divisions the Company had inherited and subjected them to all sorts of pruning, grafting and reshuffling exercises that changed their contours forever. This also entailed a moment of forgetting where the historical forces at work in the constitution of indigenous territorial divisions such as the *pargana* would be hidden from view under the geographical scaffolding of modern maps. The colonial state's drive to create its own well-defined imperial space, capable of cartographic representation, dissolved the very fabric of the older *pargana* divisions, thereby transforming them into mere relics of the past. In 1903 the Report on the Administration of Bengal would define the term *pargana* thus:

> Parganas. For the purposes of revenue administration the country was divided by the Mogul government into parganas, each pargana comprising a certain number of villages with their lands. This arrangement still forms the basis of our own revenue system; but from want of compactness, as well as for other reasons, it has been found extremely inconvenient, and in Bengal it has fallen into such decay that in some districts the pargana boundaries can hardly be ascertained. Detached villages belonging to the same pargana may now be found all over the district, and in some cases in other districts altogether. Practically the pargana divisions of districts have died out, except for the purpose of land revenue payments, in favour of the simpler and more compact arrangements adopted for purposes of police.[166]

Over time, the geographical template of the colonial state was constructed out of the debris of these older *pargana* divisions. The colonial state, through its will to power, would create a new geographical scaffolding, propped up in maps and administrative routines that would hide from view these precolonial territorial divisions. This initiated a long process of forgetting that eventually consigned knowledge about these *pargana* and *thum* divisions to the memories of older folk – a mnemonic artifact that has outlived its worldly expressions.

Chapter 7

CONCLUSION

> Today [...] it is space more than time that hides consequences from us, the "making of geography" more than the "making of history" that provides the most revealing tactical and theoretical world. This is the insistent premise and promise of postmodern geographies.
>
> —Edward W. Soja[1]

In the eighteenth century modern states in Europe, the Americas and some parts of the "non-Western" world, embarked on a long and sometimes contentious process of demarcating their boundaries, both internal and international. An older spatial regime based on "jurisdictional sovereignty" gradually gave way to one based on the notion of "territorial sovereignty," and there are many nuances, aporias and variations in how this project unfolded and ultimately transformed the territorial structure of the state.[2] Throughout this process, surveying and mapmaking operations played an important role, initially in an uncoordinated fashion, in excavating the country's older territorial divisions as a prelude to their rearrangement. Within Great Britain, Christopher Saxton's sixteenth-century county maps made possible the assembling of a national map.[3] Even so, Great Britain's administrative geography continued to be characterized by an unwieldy agglomeration of as many as 15 different levels of local authority, involving civil, criminal and ecclesiastical jurisdictions. They included territorial divisions such as county, manor, parish, shire, township, hundred, rapes, tithes, wapentake and wards.[4] As was the case in precolonial South Asia, these British territorial divisions had been organized around an ensemble of entitlements concerning access to and control over rights to taxes, tithes, cultivable and waste lands, townships, forests, grasslands and water. Additionally, such entitlements were also expressions of a range of symbolic privileges and obligations pertaining to the preservation of lordship, honor, authority, service and local custom. The historical evolution of such resources and relationships of access and control left these territorial divisions with disjointed bodies, shifting boundaries and interpenetrating jurisdictions. Commenting on the county divisions, contemporary surveyors like Herman Moll would observe, in 1724, that these divisions possessed locations that were "so various and irregular that the frontiers of the adjacent counties by no means agree with one another."[5] Elsewhere, the shires of Midland regions possessed "frayed edges and detached portions of one county lying in another, a pattern which survived until being it was tidied up by the Counties (Detached Parts) Act of 1844," with one of the most complicated areas lying on the borders between Gloucestershire, Worcestershire and Warwickshire.[6] Yet another instance was the case of the parishes lying within the county of Durham, one of the first to have its boundaries surveyed by the Ordnance Survey. In 1871, the parish of Lancaster had lying within it four detached portions of Muggleswick Parish, within which there was a further portion of Lancaster Parish. Commenting on the spatial arrangement of the townships in these parishes, Sir Henry James, director-general of the Ordnance Survey noted: "I am utterly unable to describe in words the manner in which the detached portions are intermixed and can only refer to the 6-inch plans on which they are coloured."[7] James also noted that the parishes of Witton Gilbert, Ebchester and Chester-le-Street had three, thirteen and eight detached portions, respectively.[8] In its Progress Report of 1884, the Ordnance Survey noted that the "difficulty in dealing with the boundaries is greatly increased by the large number of detached portions…which sometimes exist, and which give rise to great complication."[9]

As England, Wales and Scotland developed closer ties in the modern period, attempts were made to articulate greater territorial coherence across the British Isles. The 1535 Act of Union with Wales imposed the English system of counties and hundreds on the country, and the Anglo–Scottish border was fixed in 1552.[10] Succeeding surveys, such as William Petty's Down Survey (seventeenth century) and Richard Griffith's Irish Townland surveys (nineteenth century), excavated the ancient townland, hundred and parish divisions of Ireland.[11] Between 1747 and 1755, Scotland was mapped and, in 1795, following the outbreak of war between England and France, the decision was taken to survey England and Wales.[12]

By 1800 these early efforts, driven by local patronage and initiative, had succeeded in mapping the entire British Isles (barring the highlands of Wales and Scotland) on a one-inch scale.[13] A triangulation-based Ordnance Survey was commenced in 1784 by Major General William Roy and finally completed for the entire British Isles in 1861.[14] The British government tried to regulate and consolidate boundaries through various legislations such as the Census Enumeration Abstracts (1831), Municipal Corporations Act (1835), the Boundary Commission (1837) the Inclosure Acts (1801 and 1845) and the Divided Parishes Acts (1876, 1879 and 1882).[15] This gave a push for the settlement of boundaries, allowing, for instance, Tithe Commissioners, empowered by the Tithe Commutation Act (1836), to make over 180 decisions determining parish and township boundaries.[16] Such enactments and activities were increasingly brought into sync with the systematic settlement of boundaries that was being undertaken by the Ordnance Survey following the passage of the Ordnance Survey Act of 1841.[17] This act empowered the Ordnance Survey to ascertain and mark the reputed boundaries of every "county, city, borough, town, parish, burghs royal, parliamentary burghs of regality and barony, extra-parochial and other places, districts and divisions in England, Scotland, Berwick-upon-Tweed and the Isle of Man."[18] Between 1841 and 1888 the Ordnance Survey embarked on a detailed survey and demarcation of Great Britain's "public" boundaries, in parallel with a topographical survey that would greatly assist ongoing efforts to impart a coherent territorial framework to the British nation. In 1882, the Divided Parishes Act undertook a major clearing of parish boundaries, whereby thousands of detached portions were included within the parish whose lands they were surrounded by.[19] In Scotland, the Local Government (Scotland) Act of 1889 rearranged counties and parishes to eliminate detachments in their bodies and sinuosities in their boundaries.[20] The spatial features and territorial histories of these ancient divisions are reminiscent of the historical pattern in South Asia, and ultimately the patchwork of territorial units that made up the British Isles was rearranged in the nineteenth century to create the geo-body of Great Britain.

The coincidence between British and colonial South-Asian experiences of territorial redrawing is illuminating, and merits further comment. It is possible to trace some of the lineages of the Company state's territorial vision to the context of Georgian England, with its military-fiscal state and associated rituals of rule, the institutions of parliamentary sovereignty, the growing coincidence between national identity and territory, the distinctions between public and private property, the natural rights of man and the rule of law.[21] In 1801, Adam Anderson, a prominent British historian of political economy in the latter half of the eighteenth century, captured the mood of this context when he noted that "public property excludes communion amongst nations; private property communion amongst persons. For, as particular persons, which they possess privately of other persons: so countries and territories, like greater manors, divided each from the other by limits and borders, are the public properties of nations, which they possess exclusively of one another."[22] But was such a notion neatly transferred and unpacked in South Asia by the English East India Company and its agents? There is no clear evidence of this in the documentary record pertaining to the Anglo–Gorkha territorial disputes. The British Empire at this time, and indeed until its very demise, despite the obsession to create clearly defined imperial spaces, remained an inchoate territorial entity over which colonial authority was exercised indirectly through indigenous elites who acted as intermediaries and clients. Such an expression of quasi-sovereignty jostled uneasily with colonial attempts to unify its territories by drawing boundaries and maps and imposing uniform law codes, bureaucratic routines, tax flows and tenurial rights. That is, enclaves, dispersed territories, straggling corridors of imperial control and shared sovereignty were as much an expression of empire as were the neat lines, order and rationality that have traditionally been viewed as its hallmarks.[23] The colonial state as a self-declared paramount power exercised indirect rule on the Indian subcontinent by sharing sovereignty with indigenous princely states who were allowed to retain their systems of rule with limited autonomy. This in some ways replicated the system of overlapping and non-coincident jurisdictions that had existed in precolonial India in general, and along the Anglo–Gorkha frontier in particular. Consequently, such an arrangement had spatial ramifications. Thus, in 1833, these princely states constituted slightly more than 41 percent – or two fifths – of the territory of the British Empire in India, many of them possessing "unadjusted" territories and boundaries. In western and central India many states, such as Baroda, ended with territories that were widely dispersed among British Indian provinces and other princely states. However, interstate boundaries were firmer where princely states abutted British Indian provinces, as in the case of Mysore and Hyderabad.[24] Such a state of territorial complexity would persist beyond India's independence in 1947 and only end with the redrawing of state boundaries on linguistic lines in the 1950s.[25] In the end, the story of the spatial redrawing of the colonial state needs to be understood against a wider background of the development of territorial sovereignty in Europe and the discontinuous and shared character of imperial rule at home and within the colony. This points to a more complicated and uneven story with possible counterflows that would decenter neat teleologies of an easy and innocent transfer of notions of territorial sovereignty from the metropole to the periphery. More research needs to be undertaken if we are to understand the distinct genealogies of these projects and the existence of any mutually informing connections, along with the mediation of local and regional forces that ultimately resulted in the creation of the dispersed geo-bodies of the British state and its colony in India.[26] Today these geo-bodies and their cartographic avatars are being subjected to growing pressures exerted by waves of globalization, expressed in the form of human migrations and the complex flows of capital in a media-saturated world. These forces are dissolving the imagined permanence of established political boundaries to remind us that despite the representation of modern states on maps, their spatial frames continue to be subject to flux, flows and movements involving individuals, groups, relationships and things.

Observers, indigenous and foreign, have long commented on the nature of precolonial political formations in Asia. Colonial observers commented frequently on the nature and workings of precolonial kingships, often characterizing them as unchanging and despotic.[27] More recently, scholars have developed numerous models to explain the basic features and dynamics of precolonial state systems in Asia. These state systems have been characterized in terms of loose coalitions of "little kingdoms" held together by the glue of symbols and royal performances.[28] Others like the historian Burton Stein have presented a view of the state in terms of hierarchical bundles of segments held together by royally sanctioned rituals that bound disparate agrarian communities to local and supralocal institutions and elites.[29] Some, like O.W. Wolters, Stanley Tambiah and Ronald Inden, have tried to depict the spatial substance of precolonial states in terms of pulsating *mandalas,* galactic polities and imperial formations.[30] The late anthropologist Richard Burghart added his voice to the conversation when he argued that the Gorkhali state was constituted by multiple and non-coinciding spaces produced by the tenurial and ritual authority of the king along with the kingdom's ethnoterritorial divisions.[31] Tambiah, Inden and Burghart offer sophisticated explanations of the shifting, overlapping and fluctuating nature of precolonial polities, taking into account the scalar, pragmatic, symbolic, ordered and disordered aspects of precolonial states. They avoid the cosmologically-driven, center-oriented and less supple orientations of the other models and display a greater sensitivity to the "multifaceted polyvalence," contestations and "disorderliness" that characterized such state formations.[32] However, barring Burghart, most of these models have little discussion of how a shifting structure of entitlements and privileges produced the pulsating territories of these kingdoms. This book has been less ambitious in its approach by focusing more narrowly on how cultures of governance along the Anglo–Gorkha frontier came to be shaped by struggles to gain access to and control over various kinds of agrarian entitlements and privileges that in turn informed the territorial disputes that led to the Anglo–Gorkha War of 1814–16. I have endeavored to weave an uneven and provisional narrative of territorial production as it emerged out of a specific historical context along a colonial frontier. Perhaps there is something to be learned from the Gorkhali ruler Prithvinarayan Shah's description of his kingdom in terms of a yam (*tarul*) sandwiched between the kingdoms (*dhungo*) of China in the north and India in the south.[33] Such a jostling hierarchy of yams and boulders, or weak and strong states, defined the interstate system along the Anglo–Gorkha frontier, and possibly elsewhere as well. This interstate system pulsated in sync with shifts within the hierarchies of entitlements to agrarian resources, causing their territories to intermix and overlap. Consequently, Chapters 2 to 4 focused more narrowly on connecting the dots between the shifting history of these agrarian entitlements and the production of territory rather than trying to construct a comprehensive gestalt model that would capture all the intricate workings and imaginings of the state. Thereafter, the latter half of the book stepped back to obtain a ring-side view of the nature of precolonial divisions in South Asia and the efforts made by the British to undertake territorial rearrangements in the nineteenth and twentieth centuries. The Gorkhali state, which escaped formal colonization by the British, would undertake similar measures, though much later, in the twentieth century.[34] Many of these rearrangements assumed the form of bureaucratic interventions within the daily routines of governance and have come to be perceived as innocent exercises in administrative reform and rationalization. They were certainly more than that. Clearly more work needs to be done to better understand how colonial spatial concerns were coded and then negotiated in administrative routines and policies concerning rural revenue-collection flows, the payment of tribute, rent-free tenures and waste lands. In the end, what these measures would have affirmed was the principle that states possessed distinct and discernible territorial frames that could be represented on modern maps.

Within South Asia, the territorial disputes that led to the Anglo–Gorkha War need to be placed within the context of a long-drawn spatial ground-clearing exercise initiated by the colonial state as it tried to discern the contours of the territories it had inherited. The British boundary investigations of 1813 and the boundary demarcation activities of 1816 to 1821 resulted in the delineation of the Anglo–Gorkha boundary. This represented an important signpost on that long road whereby the geographical frame of the colonial state was slowly put in place by its agents. The Anglo–Gorkha disputes also shed light on the nature and substance of precolonial territorial divisions such as *parganas* and *tappas*. Like territorial divisions throughout human history, they were constituted out of a patchwork of shifting agrarian environments and forms of knowledge and practices – concerning entitlements to material and symbolic resources – that jostled with the topophilic memories and experiences of its inhabitants. Consequently these territorial divisions were prone to much fluctuation as these environments, entitlements and lived experiences triangulated with the forces of culture, power and history to produce their discontinuous geographies. It was the political expression of these discontinuous geographies, inherited in the form of dispersed territories and unclear boundaries, that the Company state became anxious about. And it was only through systematic surveys and mapping that the colonial state was able to create an imaginary territorial envelope that would house this jostling collection of entitlements, memories, experiences and social relationships, and hide from view their spatial effects. This envelope would be determined through scientific surveys – represented on maps, affirmed in the colonial imagination and upheld ultimately through the threat of force. It would also be propped up in diverse administrative routines and procedures of everyday governance. Meanings and practices that transgressed the territorial boundaries of this envelope would be pruned, parsed or rearranged to produce a new geographical template for the state that would be unyoked from the social relations that had always produced territory. Such a geographical framework that was derived from modern cartography would hide from view the constant spatial entropy produced by the environment and human agency. This created a structural effect which in the words of Timothy Mitchell was the powerful "metaphysical effect of practices [of spatial organization, temporal arrangement, functional specification, supervision and surveillance] that make such structures appear to exist [independently of society]."[35] The same process unfolded for Gorkha, albeit with variations; by the nineteenth century, Gorkha had assumed a distinct territorial identity, in the colonial imagination at least, which did not escape the eye of indigenous South Asian observers. Shyamaldas, the court poet of *maharaja* Sajjan Singh of Mewar (1874–84) in Western India committed a section in his work the *Vir Vinod* (1890) to Nepal's geography (*nayapalka jugrafiya*). In this he noted, with great precision, that the kingdom was 512 miles long and 120 miles broad, lying encased between 80 degrees and 6 minutes to 88 degrees and 14 minutes east longitude; and 26 degrees and 25 minutes to 30 degrees and 17 minutes north latitude.[36] Thus, by the time of Shyamaldas' writing, this geographical scaffolding had been distilled for the Gorkhali state, and is one that has survived, almost unchanged, to this day. The manner in which this took place throughout much of South Asia constitutes one of the great silent spatial settlements initiated during the colonial period.

GLOSSARY

abad gulzar garnu	to populate land and bring to a flourishing state of cultivation
abadkars	squatters
abwabs	cesses, taxes, imposts and charges levied by *zamindars* and public officers
adalat	court of law
akbari	duty on the manufacture and sale of spirituous liquor, excise
amal	(lit. practice) collection of revenue, business, affairs, authority, government, being in charge of, possession; also term of office or assignment
amaldastak	a document giving possession of property; warrant or authority to collect rents on an estate
amalguzar	revenue collector
amanat	management of revenue collection directly by government departments or by an agency (for example, *jagirdars*) empowered by the government
amil / amali	revenue collector
amin	surveyor and record keeper, often deputed by authorities at the *sadr* to investigate local disputes and problems
amval / ambal	territory in Gorkhali official discourse; land occupied by force, land from which a state has acquired right to collect revenue; generally conveys the same meaning as the term *amal*, cited above
arsattas	monthly accounts of receipts and disbursements, especially in Rajasthan
arzi / arzee	petition
asami	cultivator; an individual name or entry in the record
aul	malaria
bada sahib	similar to the English governor-general in Gorkhali official discourse
bahata	unclaimed property
bahi	register
bakshi	supervisor of military contingents and postings of military commanders
bairani	uncultivated land
baise rajya	the 22 little kingdoms in the hills of far western Nepal
bamsavalis	chronicles

bandez	order
bandobast	settlement of revenue paid by a *zamindar*
bangar	hard clayey soil
bankar	right to collect duties on forest products
basta/poka	bundles of documents tied together and wrapped in cloth
begar	compulsory porterage services, usually unpaid
bekh buniyad birta	a category of land grants that was usually conferred on an inheritable basis
beth	compulsory agricultural labor, usually unpaid
bhala manis	respectable persons
bhardar	a member of Gorkha's ruling elite denoting top ranking posts such as *chautariya, kaji, sardar, khardar, karpardar* and *khanjanchi*
bigha	a measure of land varying in size across different parts of north India, but usually standardized at 3,025 yards
birtia	holder of a *birt* or maintenance grant awarded by a landholder
birta	tax free land grants made by the state to individuals, usually on an inheritable basis
bhit	fine, light sand and clay
bhumihar-brahman	Brahman lineages in north Bihar that had taken to the plough and military occupations
budakaji	elder *kaji*, distinct from *kaji* Amar Singh Thapa, the commander of Palpa and father of Prime Minister Bhim Sen Thapa
chak	detached fields of a village; in old revenue accounts, lands taken from the residents of a village and given to a stranger to cultivate. In the North-Western Provinces, it could also mean the sub-division of a *pargana* formed under clause 88 of the Settlement circular of 1839
chakbandi	determining the limits or boundaries of a detached piece of land, an estate or church
chakla	a large division of the country comprising a number of *parganas*
chakladar	collector of the revenue (*amil*) of a *chakla*
charai	dues charged for the right to graze cattle
chaudhari	a headman, usually of a village; a functionary appointed in each *pargana* for the purpose of collecting land taxes
chaudhrai	rights accruing to a *chaudhari*, which often included a grant of land in lieu of services performed
chautariya	a top ranking member of Gorkha's royal elite, usually of a ministerial rank and belonging to the royal family
chumawan	a levy collected on the occasion of the sacred thread investiture ceremony of the king or crown prince
cos	measure of distance approximating two measured miles
daroga	a manager, superintendent and, prior to 1861, the officer in charge of a police station in Bengal
darkhast	request, petition, representation, appeal

GLOSSARY

dasturs / dustoors	custom, usage, customary dues
dhadda	register, often containing land details
diara	lands thrown up or washed away due to riverain processes of alluvium or diluvium
dhitta	high ranking official in the Gorkhali executive or judicial hierarchy
dhungo	stone, a Gorkhali metaphor sometimes used to refer to a strong state in contradistinction to a weak one, signified in the term *tarul* or yam
diwan	head of the Revenue and Finance Departments, minister, chief officer of the State Revenue Ministry or Department
diwani	jurisdiction of the Mughal *diwan*; also refers to the right to collect the revenues of Bengal, Bihar and Orissa granted to the English East India Company by the Mughal Emperor in 1765
dowl, doul	an estimate or statement of the gross revenue demand levied from an estate or district
fakiranai	land grants made to members of religious sects
fasli	harvest or revenue year, which began on 10 September 1555 CE (era was instituted by Akbar); add 649 to the *fasli* for the *samvat* year or add 592–93 for the Gregorian equivalent
fauzdar	a Mughal officer in charge of prosecution within a district, an officer charged with the police jurisdiction of all criminal matters (such officers were employed by Gorkha in its *tarai* districts)
gadimubarak	levy imposed on occasion of royal coronation in Gorkha
garh / gadh	fortress
gumashta	agent, representative; an officer employed by *zamindars* to collect their rents, by bankers to receive money etc., and by merchants to carry on their affairs in other places
guthi	lands endowed by the state or individuals to temples, monasteries and other religious and philanthropic institutions, or for similar purposes
hakim	ruler, administrator, governor, superior administrative authority in a district
ijara	a revenue collection contract
ijaradar	revenue contractor, revenue farmer
ikrarnamah	an engagement; a written obligation, a deed of assent or acknowledgement in general
istimrari	a grant by which revenue is settled on a permanent basis
jagir	land assigned to government employees in lieu of cash salary
jagirdar	holder of a *jagir*
jalkar	right to collect cesses on fisheries or resources derived from water
jama	revenue assessed on taxable assets held by, for example, a cultivator or *zamindar*
jama-wasil-baki	an account showing collections and balances of revenue

kausi toskhana	Gorkhali central treasury
kabuliyat	written agreement, especially signifying assent or acceptance
kaji	a senior member of Gorkha's elite, higher in rank than a *sardar* and in charge of civil and military affairs
kalabanjar	uncultivated forest lands that, if cleared, are capable of high agricultural yields
kamtalasi mauza	a *mauza* on which taxes are assessed on concessional rates
kaptan	captain
Kausi Tosakhana	State Treasury
kham/ khas	revenue collected directly by the government from cultivators without the intervention of any intermediaries; lands held by *zamindars* and cultivated by themselves for their own benefit
khamid/ hakim	master, ruler, superior lord
kharij	to strike off, to remove, to cancel, excluded, separated from, extraneous to, external
khasra	a statement showing details of rights in land
khillat	robes of honor conferred on a dependent
khudkasht	one who cultivates land in the village of his residence; one who organizes cultivation by himself
khuwa	lands assessed on a cash basis to government functionaries
killadar	official in charge of a fort
kotwal	chief officer of the police in a city or town
kusa birta	*birta* grants made to Brahmins with religious motives (sometimes also called *sankalp birta*)
lakhiraj	rent-free grants (in 1801 there were at least 8 categories in Bihar – aima, altamgah, madad-i-maash, jagir, bishnuprit, brahmottar, sur shekan and *nankar*)
madesh	the plains as referred to in hill discourse
mahal	a source of taxation derived from a particular class of things or persons
mahant	religious superior, chief priest
mahfizkhana	record room
malguzar	revenue payer, land holder, landlord, a manager of cultivation and village matters, a tenant, a subject
malikana	proprietary right; annual or monthly allowance paid to a *zamindar* by the person who occupies his lands
mal wajib	right, proper or necessary revenue; fair assessment of revenue due
mauza/ mouza	village; a village as the primary unit of land-revenue administration in the Tarai; a revenue subdivision constituted by a group of villages in some hill districts and Kathmandu valley
milkiyat	possession, property, a proprietary right
mofussil	area away from the capital or headquarters
moglan	the Indo-Gangetic plains of North India as referred to in hill discourse

mokkaddams	village headman
mokam	camp
mokarrari	a grant by which a proprietors tenure is held at a fixed and permanent rate of revenue
muquaddam	chief, leader, headman of a village or caste
naib	deputy
nankar	right to lands enjoyed by *chaudharis, quanungos* and *mokaddams* in north India as their emoluments; allowance paid to *zamindar* out of the revenue collection or by allotment of tax-exempt land for services rendered in collecting land revenue
nawab	ruler of a province, honorific title
pahikasht	one who cultivates land in a village other than the one in which he is residing
pargana/praganna	a fiscal sub-division in north India which could be further sub-divided into *tappas* and *tarafs* (in Gorkha's Eastern Tarai, they comprised a number of villages or *mauzas*)
parwana	order, letter from a person in power to a dependant, warrant or letter of authorization
patta	title deed to land
patwari	a village functionary who assists the *zamindar* with the maintenance of tax records and accounts, village accountant
peshkash	offering, tribute, often in money, or "presents" offered in lieu of appointment
poka/basta	a bundle of documents wrapped in cloth
phikdar	inheritable *birta* grants made to reward individuals drawn from castes below Brahmins castes
pota	a tax on certain categories of *birta* lands
qazi	judge
quanungo/quanungoye	a record keeper locatable at various levels of the Mughal government
quanungoi	rights enjoyed by persons holding the office of *quanungo*, which often includes a grant of land
quazi	judge, a notary with minor local administrative, judicial and religious authority
raikar	land on which taxes are collected and appropriated directly or through intermediaries who are under the direct control of the state
raqba	the measured extent of lands (especially those paying revenue)
rukka	prohibitory order
rusums	customary fees
ryots/raiyat	cultivators
sadr	center, capital, headquarters
sair	tax, duty levied on personal property, land customs, excise and other duties

salami	a complimentary present, the first receipt of an appointment usually tendered to the person through whom it was obtained; a gratuity or offering on receiving a lease or settling for the revenue or on receiving a favor real or implied; a fee or fine levied annually on the holders of rent-free tenures as a quit rent applied adjectively to tenures so held; a special levy paid by *jagirdars, talukdars*, temple functionaries on their appointment or reconfirmation
sanad	official decree, royal ordinance
sankalp birta	A religious grant, usually rent-free, made to a Brahman
sarbasta	a method of summary assessment
sardar	a high ranking civil and military officer
sarkar	tract of territory under Mughal rule corresponding to a district or division under British rule, usually, but not always, sub-divided into *parganas* and *tappas* in descending order
sarpat	chain-based surveying
sawal	royal regulations in Gorkha
sawar	mounted soldier, rider, horseman
sera	crown lands
shiqdar	officer appointed to collect revenue from a tract of country
shujra	a roughly made *khasra* map
suba	province; viceroy under Mughal government
subba	chief provincial administrator usually in charge of a district in Gorkha
surathhal	a representation or report of the facts and circumstances of a transaction
syahamohar	historical documents belonging to the Sen Rajas and bearing a black seal
tahsil	subdivision of a district or an estate under the charge of a *tahsildar*. In British administration, intermediate in size between district or *pargana*
taluq/taluk/taluqa	a proprietary right signifying a holding, often, but not always, within a *tappa* and known by the holder's name, not the name of the largest village; dependence upon or connection; a collection of villages formed into an estate; generally signifying the sense of land or area over which any kind of right is exercised
taluqdar	a person enjoying the rights to a *taluqa*
tappa/tappe	a small tract or division of country, smaller than a *pargana* but usually comprising one or more villages
tapsil	list
taraf/tarf	a fiscal sub-division belonging to a *pargana* or *tappa* and including several villages
tarai	the stretch of plain land running from east to west across the foothills of the Himalayas (once thickly forested, today much of this land has been cleared for agriculture

Tehsildar	officer responsible for collection of revenue from a *tehsil* division
terij	abstracts, usually pertaining to accounts
thana	police post/station
thanadar	police officer in charge of a *thana*
thapale	vassal
thek	a generic term used to denote various categories of contractual systems for collection of taxes
thekbandi	a contractual system of settlement with local functionaries for the collection of homestead taxes in the central hill regions
thums	territorial divisions in Nepal's hills
tola	the suburbs of a town or village, a part of a town inhabited by persons belonging to a particular community or caste, a supplementary hamlet or huts outlying from the chief village; uncultivated ground
vakil	authorized public pleader, envoy, representative, advocate
vamsavali	chronicle
wairan	desolate, depopulated, waste; a village under the headman of a different village
zamindar	a landlord, a person entitled to collect revenue from land
zilla	district

NOTES

Chapter 1. Statemaking, Cultures of Governance and the Anglo–Gorkha War of 1814–1816

1 Cited in Young, *The African Colonial State in Comparative Perspective*, 13.
2 Massey, *For Space*, 9.
3 Mann, *The Sources of Social Power: A History of Power from the Beginning to AD 1760*, 4.
4 A brief sampling of the works on the nature of the state could include the following: Jessop, *State Theory: Putting the Capitalist State in its Place*; Migdal, *Strong Societies and Weak States: State–Society Relations and State Capabilities in the Third World*; Skocpol, Evans and Rueschemeyer, eds, *Bringing the State Back In*; Claessen and Skalnik, eds, *The Study of the State*; For works on the need to blur distinctions between categories such as state and society in order to capture interactive flows see Abrams, "Notes on the difficulty of studying the state," 58–89; Migdal, *State in Society: Studying how States and Societies Transform and Constitute One Another*; Timothy Mitchell, "The Limits of the State: Beyond Statist Approaches and their Critics," 77–96; Joel Migdal, Atul Kohli and Vivienne Shue, eds, *State Power and Social Forces: Domination and Transformation in the Third World*; Vivienne Shue, *The Reach of the State: Sketches of the Chinese Body Politic*. I also found Marilyn Strathern's *Reproducing the Future: Essays on Anthropology, Kinship and the New Reproductive Technologies* particularly useful. See especially ch. 2: "Parts and Wholes: Refiguring Relationships," 90–116.
5 I owe a debt of gratitude to K. Sivaramakrishnan, who has consistently argued for writing nuanced and dense accounts of statemaking. See Sivaramakrishnan, *Modern Forests: Statemaking and Environmental Change in Colonial Eastern India*.
6 The corpus of writings on "subaltern" history and culture is too vast to cite here. For a broad selection of such works see Chakrabarty, *Provincializing Europe: Postcolonial Thought and Historical Difference*; Chatterjee, *The Nation and its Fragments: Colonial and Postcolonial Histories*; Guha, *Elementary Aspects of Peasant Insurgency in Colonial Bengal*; Spivak and Guha, eds, *Selected Subaltern Studies*. A useful introduction to the subject can be found in Ludden, ed., *Reading Subaltern Studies: Critical History, Contested Meaning and the Globalization of South Asia*.
   Samples that signal the rich variety of writings on South Asian states and statemaking can be found in the following: Cohn, *An Anthropologist Among the Historians and Other Essays*, *Colonialism and its Forms of Knowledge*; Kulke, ed., *The State in India, 1000–1700*; Habib, *The Agrarian System of Mughal India*; Stein, *Peasant State and Society in Medieval South India*; Sivaramakrishnan, *Modern Forests: Statemaking and Environmental Change in Colonial Eastern India*; Alam and Subrahmanyam, eds, *The Mughal State, 1526–1750*; Sutton, *Other Landscapes: Colonialism and the Predicament of Authority in Nineteenth-Century South India*.
7 Source materials for the study of Nepali history can be found in government departments such as the Army (*jangi adda*), Central Treasury (*kausi tosakhana*), Department of Land Revenue (*Lagat Phant & Kumari Chowk*), Foreign Ministry (*parrashtra mantralaya*), chronicles (*bamsavalis*) and private collections. Numerous works by European travelers and colonial administrators, cited throughout this book, added to this corpus of works.
8 While the literature is too vast to cite here, a brief but representative sampling of both Nepali and English works should suffice. Immediately noticeable is the work of *Samsodhan Mandal* historians

with their mouthpiece journal *Purnima*. This collective was founded by Nayaraj Pant and his students, including his sons Maheshraj and Dineshraj Pant, along with the late Dhanabajra Bajracharya and Shankarman Rajbamshi. See Pant, "The Ups and Downs of an Intellectual Pursuit: Towards a History of the Historical Journal *Purnima*." See also Acharya, *Nepalko Samkshipta Vrittanta*; Bajracharya, *Bahadur Shah: The Regent of Nepal, 1785–1794*; Gyawali, *Amar Singh Thapa*; Narharinath, ed., *Itihasprakashmasandhipatrasangraha*; Nepali, *General Bhimsen Thapa ra tatkalin Nepal*; Regmi, *Modern Nepal* (vols 1 and 2); Stiller, *The Rise of the House of Gorkha: A Study in the Unification of Nepal, 1768–1816*; Vaidya, *Jayaprakash Malla: The Brave King of Kantipur, 1736–1767*.

9   Within nationalist historiography, the "unification" refers to a foundational moment in the eighteenth century, when Prithvinarayan Shah, ruler of the hill kingdom of Gorkha, inaugurated a phase of territorial expansion that resulted in the creation of modern Nepal. By 1814, Gorkha's territories stretched from the Tista River in the east to the Sutlej River in the west, and from Tibet in the north to the frontiers of the English East India Company in the south.

10 Regmi's published corpus is too vast to cite here, but see Regmi, *Land Tenure and Taxation in Nepal*; *The State and Economic Surplus: Production, Trade and Resource Mobilisation in the Early 19th Century*; and *Kings and Political Leaders of the Gorkhali Empire, 1768–1814*; Mention must also be made of the Regmi Research Collection (RRC) and the Regmi Research Series (*RRS*). The former is made up of over 90 volumes of transcripts from the *Lagat Phant* (Ministry of Land Revenue) records, while the latter consists of selected English translations from these volumes which were then published over a twenty year period (1969–89). The entire RRC has been microfilmed by the Nepal–German Manuscript Preservation Project and can be accessed at the National Archives of Nepal, Kathmandu, while the *RRS* can be found online at http://www.digitalhimalaya.com/collections/journals/regmi/

11 Regmi's own work on Gorkhali expansion into Kumaon is striking for taking a critical stance on the process of unification and on the unpopular nature of Gorkhali imperialism in that region. See Regmi, *Imperial Gorkha: An Account of Gorkhali Rule in Kumaon, 1791–1815*. See also Pradhan, *The Gorkha Conquests: The Process and Consequences of the Unification of Nepal with Particular Reference to Eastern Nepal*.

Elsewhere, a small number of scholars (mostly anthropologists from outside Nepal) have written on the state, statemaking, nationalism, ethnic identity and caste. Here of particular relevance is the work of Richard Burghart. See for example, Burghart, *The Conditions of Listening: Essays on Religion, History and Politics in South Asia*. See also Boullier, "The Nepalese State and Gorakhnathi Yogis: The Case of the former Kingdoms of Dang Valley: 18th–19th centuries," 29–52; DesChene, *Relics of Empire: A Cultural History of the Gurkhas, 1816–1987*; Guneratne, *Many Tongues, One People: The Making of Tharu Identity in Nepal*; Hofer, *The Caste Hierarchy and the State: A Study of the Muluki Ain of 1854*; Levine, "Caste, State and Ethnic Boundaries in Nepal," 88; Gellner, Pfaff-Czarnecka and Whelpton, eds, *Nationalism and Ethnicity in a Hindu Kingdom: The Politics of Culture in Contemporary Nepal*; Whelpton, *Kings, Soldiers, and Priests: Nepalese Politics and the Rise of Jang Bahadur Rana, 1830–1857*.

12 This point has already found timely expression in some of the writings of the Nepali historian Pratyoush Onta. See Onta, "Rich Possibilities: Notes on Social History in Nepal," 1–43 (see p. 1). See also "Creating a Brave Nepali Nation in British India: The Rhetoric of *Jati* Improvement, Rediscovery of Bhanubhakta and the Writing of *Bir* History," 37–76; DesChene and Onta, "Writing and Reading About Nepal," 1–4; Adhikari, *A Brief Survey of Nepali Historiography*; Chhetri, *A Brief Analysis of History Writing in Nepal*; Mehra, "Nepal in Some Recent Studies: An Overview," 95–107; Vaidya, "The Historiography of Nepal: An Analytical Approach," 89–101.

13 Again, the literature on cultural histories of statemaking is too vast to cite here. For an introduction to the theoretical and regional issues at stake see: Steinmetz, ed., *State/Culture: State-Formation after the Cultural Turn*; Ashforth, *The Politics of Official Discourse in Twentieth-Century South Africa*; Day, *Fluid Iron: State Formation in Southeast Asia*; Dirks, *The Hollow Crown: The*

Ethnohistory of a Little Kingdom; Duara, *Culture, Power and the State: Rural North China, 1900–1942*; Geertz, *Negara: Theater State in Nineteenth Century Bali*; Joseph and Nugent, eds, *Everyday Forms of State Formation: Revolution and Negotiation of Rule in Modern Mexico*; Corrigan and Sayer, *The Great Arch: English State Formation as Cultural Revolution*; Shue, *The Reach of the State*.

14 For a sampling of the literature on structured human agency, process and meaning making based approaches to culture see Bourdieu, *An Outline of A Theory of Practice*; Dening, *Islands & Beaches: Discourse on a Silent Land, Marquesas 1774–1880*; Giddens, *The Constitution of Society: An Introduction to the Theory of Structuration*; Sahlins, *Islands of History*; Comaroff and Comaroff, *Ethnography and the Historical Imagination*; Clifford Geertz, *The Interpretation of Culture*; Moore, "Explaining the present: Theoretical dilemmas in Processual Ethnography," 727–35 and "The Ethnography of the Present and the analysis of Process," 362–76; Ortner, *Anthropology and Social Theory: Culture, Power, and the Acting Subject*.

15 For works that affirm the nuanced interweaving of culture, power and history see Cohn, *An Anthropologist Among the Historians, and Colonialism and Its Forms of Knowledge*; Ohnuki-Tierney, ed., *Culture Through Time: Anthropological Approaches*; Dirks, Eley and Ortner, eds, *Culture/Power/History: A Reader in Contemporary Social Theory*. For the historian's perspective see Bonnell and Hunt, eds, *Beyond the Cultural Turn: New Directions in the Study of Society and Culture*; Tsing, *Friction: An Ethnography of Global Connection*.

16 See Kirby, *Boundless Worlds: An Anthropological Approach to Movement*.

17 Sack, *Human Territoriality: Its Theory and Practice*, 216.

18 Historian Frank Perlin calls this highly ingrained institutional infrastructure of knowledge and practices an "invisible city" that underlies South Asian political orders. See Perlin, "The Precolonial Indian State in History and Epistemology: A Reconstruction of Societal Formation in the Western Deccan from the 15th to the early 19th centuries," 275–302, and "State Formation Reconsidered," 415–480.

19 The Marxist geographer Henri Lefebvre affirms this point about the crucial role played by spatiality in determining social relations. He notes that "Social relations, which are concrete abstractions, have no real existence, save in and through space. *Their underpinning is spatial.*" See Lefebvre, *The Production of Space*, 404 (emphasis in the original).

20 Again, the literature is too vast to cite here, but see, for instance, Baden-Powell, *Administration of Land Revenue and Tenure in British India*; Moreland, *The Agrarian System of Moslem India*; Habib, *The Agrarian System of Mughal India*; Stein, *Peasant State and Society in Medieval South India*; Guha, *The Agrarian Economy of the Bombay Deccan, 1818–1941*; Ludden, *An Agrarian History of South Asia*. More recent writings have tried to rethink the study of agrarian life on new lines by emphasizing innovative work that is interdisciplinary, nuanced, collaborative and revisionist. See, for instance, Agrawal and Sivaramakrishnan, eds, *Agrarian Environments: Resources, Representations, and Rule in India*; Scott and Bhatt, eds, *Agrarian Studies: Synthetic Work at the Cutting Edge*; Pandian, *Crooked Stalks: Cultivating Virtue in South India*.

21 I have benefited immensely from the rich and diverse literature on property rights. A sampling of this would include: Berry, "Social Institutions and Access to Resources," 41–55; Blakie and Brookfield, *Land Degradation and Society*; Ribot and Peluso, "A Theory of Access," 153–81; Peluso, "Fruit Trees and Family Trees in an Anthropogenic Forest: Ethics of Access, Property Zones, and Environmental Change in Indonesia," 10–547; Rose, *Property and Persuasion: Essays on the History, Theory and Rhetoric of Ownership*. See also Bisson, ed., *Cultures of Power: Lordship, Status, and Process in Twelfth-Century Europe*; Herring, "Resurrecting the Commons: Collective Action and Ecology," 64–7; Chakravarty-Kaul, *Common Lands and Customary Law*; Peluso, *Rich Forests, Poor People: Resource Control and Resistance in Java*; Rangan, "Property vs. Control: The State and Forest Management in the Indian Himalaya,"; Richards, ed., *Land, Property, and the Environment*; Sturgeon, *Border Landscapes: The Politics of Akha Land Use in China and Thailand*. I am grateful to George Varughese for sharing his insights in these matters and alerting me to the relevant literature. For work that recenters the importance of regions see Agrawal and Sivaramakrishnan, *Regional Modernities: The Cultural Politics of Development in India*.

22 Territory is the politically determined appropriation, inhabitation, demarcation and representation of land. A fuller presentation of this view can be found in Gottmann, *The Significance of Territory*. See also Akerman, "The Structuring of Political Territory in Early Printed Atlases," 138–54, and Barrow, *Making History, Drawing Territory: British Mapping in India, c. 1756–1905*, 13–14.

23 The reference here, of course, is to the work of Edward Soja. See Soja, *Postmodern Geographies: The Reassertion of Space in Contemporary Social Thought*. But see also the monumental work of Lefebvre, *The Production of Space* (trans. by Richard Nice). Lefebvre's notion of space being produced through human action is nicely reiterated by Michel de Certeau's notion of "spatial practice" – of space being produced through its active occupation by people and not being an ontological pre-given. See Certeau, *The Practice of Everyday Life*. A representative though not exhaustive sampling of related works on space across disciplines in the humanities and social sciences is as follows: Bachelard, *The Poetics of Space*; Cosgrove, *Social Formation and Symbolic Landscape*; Gregory and Urry, eds, *Social Relations and Spatial Structures*; Gregory, *Geographical Imaginations*; Hubbard, Kitchin, Bartley, Low and Lawrence-Zuniga, eds, *The Anthropology of Space and Place: Locating Culture*; Hubbard, Kitchin, Bartley and Fuller, eds, *Thinking Geographically: Space, Theory and Contemporary Human Geography*; Lorimer, "Cultural geography: the busyness of being 'more-than representational,'" 83–94; Sparke, *In the Space of Theory: Postfoundational Geographies of the Nation-State*; May and Thrift, eds, *Timespace: Geographies of Temporality*; Thrift, "Space: The Fundamental Stuff of Human Geography," 95–107. For gendered understandings of space see Moore, *Space, Text and Gender: An Anthropological Study of the Marakwet of Kenya*; Rose, *Feminism and Geography: The Limits of Geographical Knowledge*; Massey, *For Space*; and Whitmore, *Hybrid Geographies: Natures, Cultures, Spaces*. For an alternate vision of Australian explorer narratives as spatial history see Carter, *The Road to Botany Bay*.

24 For a critique of such a notion of space see Smith and Katz, "Grounding Metaphor: Towards a Spatialized Politics," 67–83.

25 For more on the distinctions between space and place see Entrikin, *The Betweeness of Place*; Merrifield, "Space and Place: A Lefebvrian reconciliation," *Transactions of the Institute of British Geographers*, 516–31. See also Gidwani and Sivaramakrishnan, "Circular Migration and the Spaces of Cultural Assertion," 186–213.

26 The older approaches of understanding the world in terms of bounded geographical units that are defined by distinct civilizational and cultural traits are now giving way to newer understandings based on processes of interaction and movement involving trade, nomadism, travel, diasporas, colonization, dynamic borderlands and the like. While the literature is too vast to cite in full here, see Appadurai, *Modernity at Large: Cultural Dimensions of Globalization*; Lewis and Wigen, *The Myth of Continents: A Critique of Metageography*; Onta, "Institutional Geography and the Future of Academic History on Nepal," 25; and van Schendel, "Geographies of Knowing, geographies of ignorance: jumping scale in Southeast Asia," 647–68.

27 Explorations of territorial themes can be found in the following: Siu and David Faure, eds, *Down to Earth: The Territorial Bond in Southern China*; Giri and Kar, eds, *Thinking Territory: Some Reflections*; Hannah, *Governmentality and the Mastery of Territory in Nineteenth-Century America*; Johnston, "Territoriality and the State," 213–25; and Peluso and Vandergeest, "Territorialization and State Power in Thailand," 385–426. For works on the geography of state power see: Anderson, *Imagined Communities: Reflections on the Origins and Spread of Nationalism*, 163–85; Kierstead, *The Geography of Power in Medieval Japan*; Samaddar, ed., *Space, Territory and the State: New Readings in International Politics*; and Sivaramakrishnan, *Modern Forests*.

28 Winichakul, *Siam Mapped: The History of the Geo-Body of a Nation*.

29 In making this claim I build on the insights of James C. Scott, but also deviate in significant ways. Scott makes an analytic distinction between "state spaces" and "non-state spaces." The former signified the presence of political elites and the settled agrarian orders they attempted to establish, while the latter typically represented populations and elites that pursued more mobile subsistence strategies to create spaces that resisted state power. While Scott's distinction is a

useful one, it does not seem to have been very pronounced along the Anglo–Gorkha frontier, where actors from across this divide came together under highly inclusive circumstances to pursue or resist statemaking projects. See Scott, *Seeing Like a State: How Certain Schemes to Improve the Human Condition have Failed* (especially 186–7). Scott's arguments have been further developed in his *The Art of Not Being Governed: An Anarchist History of Upland Southeast Asia*.

30 Some scholars have characterized these dynamic and intransigent spaces that blunt state power as "zones of anomaly" and "fugitive landscapes." See Sivaramakrishnan, "British Imperium and Forested Zones of Anomaly in Bengal, 1767–1833," 243–82, and Craib, *Cartographic Mexico: A History of State Fixations and Fugitive Landscapes*; For recent work on boundaries and borderlands see Ellis, *Tudor Frontiers and Noble Power: The Making of the British State*; Sahlins, *Boundaries: The Making of France and Spain in the Pyrenees*; Sparke, "Triangulating the borderless world: geographies of power in the Indonesia–Malaysia–Singapore Growth Triangle," 485–98; Tooker, "Putting the Mandala in its Place: A Practice-Based Approach to the Spatialization of Power on the Southeast Asian 'Periphery' – the Case of the Akha," 323–58; van Schendel, *The Bengal Borderland: Beyond State and Nation in South Asia*; and Baud and van Schendel, "Towards a Comparative History of Borderlands," 211–42.

31 I define power both as the ability of persons, groups, institutions and forms of knowledge to impose their will over others. Resistance often signals the existence of relations of domination, resistance and subaltern agency. See Abu-Lughod, "The Romance of Resistance: Tracing Transformations of Power through Bedouin Women," 41–55; Campillo, "On War: The Space of Knowledge, Knowledge of Space," 277–99; Driver, "Power, Spaces and the Body: A Critical Assessment of Foucault's Discipline and Punish," 425–47; Foucault, *Discipline and Punish: The Birth of the Prison*; Mann, *The Sources of Social Power*, volume 1; and Wolf, "Facing Power – Old Insights, New Questions," 586–96.

32 In making these assertions, I have drawn from the work of Sally Falk Moore. See Moore, "Epilogue: Uncertainties in Situations, Indeterminacies in Culture," 234–35. See also Rosaldo, *Culture and Truth: The Remaking of Social Analysis*, 91–108.

33 Cited in Edney, *Mapping an Empire: The Geographical Construction of British India, 1765–1843*, 119. The emphasis is mine.

34 Scholars have explored such themes from a variety of perspectives. For a sampling, see: Arnold, *Colonizing the Body: State Medicine and Epidemic Disease in Nineteenth Century India*; Comaroff, *Body of Power, Spirit of Resistance: The Culture and History of a South African People*; McClintock, *Imperial Leather: Race, Gender, and Sexuality in the Colonial Contest*; Dirks, ed., *Colonialism and Cultures*; Guha, *A Rule of Property for Bengal: An Essay on the Idea of Permanent Settlement*; Philip, *Civilizing Natures: Race, Resources, and Modernity in Colonial South India*; and Singha, *A Despotism of Law: Crime and Justice in Early Colonial India*.

35 See Edney, "Putting 'Cartography' into the History of Cartography: Arthur H. Robinson, David Woodward, and the Creation of a Discipline," 14–29. Harley called for a theoretically sophisticated and ethically informed exercise of cartographic history that excavates the hidden agendas, aporias, silences and hierarchies inherent in cartographic exercises by contextualizing their production within time and space and relations of power. See Harley, "Deconstructing the Map," 109–48. For an overview of Harley's work see. Edney, "J. B. Harley (1932–91): Questioning Maps, Questioning Cartography, Questioning Cartographers," 175–8. For a critical engagement with Harley's work see Belyea, "Images of Power: Derrida/Foucault/Harley," 1–9. Harley's work has recently been collected and edited in a book by Paul Laxton and J.H. Andrews, titled *The New Nature of Maps: Essays in the History of Cartography*.

36 Critical cartographies can be found in the following: The *History of Cartography* series from the University of Chicago Press; Akerman and Karrow, eds, *Maps: Finding Our Place in the World*; Burnett, *Masters of All they Surveyed: Exploration, Geography, and a British Eldorado*; Conley, *The Self-Made Map: Cartographic Writing in Early Modern France*; Craib, *Cartographic Mexico*; King, *Mapping Reality: An Exploration of Cultural Cartographies*; and Safier, *Measuring the New World: Enlightenment Science and South America*. The relationship between mapping and non-Western cultures has been explored in the following: Mundy, *The Mapping of New Spain: Indigenous Cartography and the Maps of the Relaciones*

Geograficas; Rundstrom, "The Role of Ethics, Mapping, and the Meaning of Place in Relations Between Indians and Whites in the United States," 21–8; and Bourguet, Licoppe and Sibum, *Instruments, Travel, and Science: Itineraries of Precision from the Seventeenth to the Twentieth Centuries.*

37 See Edney's classic study of the Survey of India in *Mapping an Empire: The Geographical Construction of British India, 1765–1843*; and Mann, "Mapping the Country: European Geography and the Cartographical Construction of India, 1760–1790," 25–46; Waller, *The Pundits: British Exploration of Tibet and Central Asia*. See also Barrow, *Making History, Drawing Territory* and *Surveying and Mapping in Colonial Sri Lanka*; Sumathi Ramaswamy, *Beyond Appearances: Visual Practices and Ideologies in Modern India*, and "Maps and Mother Goddesses in Modern India," 97–114. Ajantha Subramanian's recent work is one of the few that expressly examines the question of spatiality and contested claims to rights. See Subramanian, *Shorelines: Space and Rights in South India*; and Tickell, "Negotiating the Landscape: Travel, Transaction, and the Mapping of Colonial India," 18–30.

38 See Raj, *Relocating Modern Science: Circulation and the Construction of Knowledge in South Asia and Europe, 1650–1900*; and Chester, *Borders and Conflict in South Asia: The Radcliffe Boundary Commission and the Partition of Punjab.*

39 The theoretical concerns of critical cartography can be found in the following: Woodward, "'Theory' and the History of Cartography" and "The 'Two Cultures' of Map History – Scientific and Humanistic Traditions," in *Plantejaments I objectius d'una historia universal de la cartgrafia (Approaches and Challenges in a Worldwide History of Cartography)*, Woodward, Delano-Smith, Yee, eds, 31–48 and 49–68; Martin Dodge, Rob Kitchin, and Chris Perkins, eds, *Rethinking Maps: New Frontiers in Cartographic Theory*; Edney, Jacob and Delano-Smith, "Theoretical Aspects of the History of Cartography: A Discussion of Concepts, Approaches and New Directions," 185–205; Edney, "Cartography without 'Progress' Reinterpreting the Nature and Historical Development of Mapmaking," 54–68. I am grateful to Matthew H. Edney for sharing his views on these matters at many times and places.

40 For a recent work that tries to rewrite the study of space by undertaking a close and critical reading of the social history of cartography and mapmaking, see Pickles, *A History of Spaces: Cartographic Reason, Mapping and the Geo-Coded World.*

41 But see Biggs, "Putting the State on the Map: Cartography, Territory, and European State Formation," 374–405.

42 This statement acknowledges the reminder of geographer Neil Smith that the rediscovery and rewriting of the imperial past should be done "in explicit connection with a sense of the lived geographies of empire." See Smith, "Geography, Empire, and Social Theory," 491–500. The quotation is from page 491.

43 Letter from John Adam, Secretary to Government, to Major-General David Ochterlony, FS Procs, 2 December 1815, no. 4, NAI. The emphasis is mine.

44 The term "principle of limitation" was coined by the Nepali historian Ludwig F. Stiller. See. Stiller, "The Principle of Limitation," 4–21.

45 Ibid., 6.

46 More details about these disputes can be found in the exchange of letters between Col. David Ochterlony, Gorkhali *budakaji* Amar Singh Thapa and Secretary John Adam in April–May 1813, FP Procs, 15 May 1813, nos. 36, 37, 38 and 39, NAI. See also the correspondence between Ochterlony and Government at Calcutta, FP Procs, 19 October 1813, nos. 34, 35, 36, 36A and 37, NAI.

47 The extent to which such projects were driven by agendas of administrative convenience in the colonies or were a result of the influence of cartographic traditions in the British Isles remains unclear.

48 Cited in Shireen Moosvi, *The Economy*, 44, f. 9.

49 Kieghly noticed that the accounts of his district were organized around *asli* (original) villages and not around the *pargana* divisions they belonged to. This created an unwieldy corpus of accounts, collection agents and disputes. See *Proceedings of the Comptrolling Committee of Revenue at Patna*, 1773, vol. 7, p. 193, BSA.

50 The Amini Commission was headed by English East India Company officers who deputed *amins* (surveyors) to collect these records. The complete report of the Amini Commission can be found in. Ramsbotham, *Studies in the Land Revenue History of Bengal, 1769–87*. See especially p. 80.
51 Ibid., 123.
52 Robert Travers makes the insightful point that the failure of the Amini Commission in North India might have been connected to the ongoing political debates in Britain about the right of the state to undertake detailed tax surveys. Warren Hasting's own detractors like Philip Francis would argue that such state sponsored surveys were deemed to be oppressive for local property holders. Travers, however, does not explore the question of territorial legibility and simplification that the Amini Commission was unable to address, despite the collection of a vast corpus of documents. See Travers, "'The Real Value of the Lands': The Nawabs, the British and the Land Tax in Eighteenth-Century Bengal," 517–58.
53 Instructions to Archibald Montgomerie, Collector of Saran, from BOR, January 1789, Letters Received Register, 1788–1789, Saran Collectorate Records, BSA.
54 Amended Code of Regulations for the Decennial Settlement for Bengal and Bihar, September 1791, in Procs. of the BOR, 23 September 1791, no. 17, WBSA.
55 Government to Board of Commissioners, 12 August 1815, Regulations of 1815, Section 4, Pre-Mutiny Records, Letters Received from the Government to BOR, 1810–1816, UPSA.
56 Extracts from the Proceedings of the Committee of Records, 6 August 1820, Pre-Mutiny Records, Letters Received from the Government to BOR, January–August 1820, UPSA.
57 Circular Orders by the Sudder Board of Revenue, North West Provinces Addressed to Commissioners of Revenue on Records and Registration (1840), Section 4, Commissioners Records, 263. In the Appendix the Commissioners' Divisions of the North-Western Provinces were listed along with their sub-divisions. For example, the Banaras Division had 6 districts – Gorakhpur, Azamghar, Jaunpur, Mirzapur, Benaras and Ghazipur.
58 Ibid., Section 5, Arrangement of Collectors Records and Distribution of Business, 267.
59 My understanding of a territorial archive is adapted from Thomas Richards' work on the imperial archive. See Richards, *The Imperial Archive: Knowledge and the Fantasy of Empire*, 6. Richards' characterization of the "archive" bears a strong resemblance to a panoptic conception of space. The construction of the archive was predicated on two moves: first, the world was divided into little pieces of facts; second, the facts were organized into coherent, whole bodies of knowledge. See Richards, *The Imperial Archive*, 6–7.
60 Such a claim merits further investigation and by no means suggests that European powers had an unchallenged monopoly over such territorial visions when compared to indigenous Asian regimes. The case of the Qing rulers of China using the Jesuits to map the kingdom in the eighteenth century is already well known, as is the case of modern Siam. See Hostetler, "Qing Connections to the Early Modern World: Ethnography and Cartography in Eighteenth-Century China," 623–62; and Winichakul, *Siam Mapped*.
61 On the idea of governmentality more specifically, see Foucault, "Governmentality"; Gordon, ed., *Power/Knowledge: Selected Interviews and Other Writings, 1972–1977*. For relevant work on governmentality and space see Hannah, *Governmentality and the Mastery of Territory in Nineteenth-Century America*.
62 Such an attempt to complicate the simplistic and linear narratives of cartographic history derives inspiration from the notion of multiple and bifurcating histories that coexist, as proposed by Prasenjit Duara. See Duara, *Rescuing History from the Nation: Questioning Narratives of Modern China*. See especially chapters 1 and 2: "Linear History and the Nation-state" and "Bifurcating Histories of China and India," 17–82.
63 Gorkha in its expansionist phase has also been referred to as "Greater Nepal," which prior to the Anglo–Gorkha War stretched from the Tista River in the east to Sutlej River in the west, with Tibet to its north and the provinces of Bihar, Gorakhpur and Awadh in the south. Nationalist historians of Nepal understand the creation of "Greater Nepal" as the outcome of a "glorious" phase of "unification" that was consummated in the creation of the Nepali

nation-state. However, I steer away from such representations to argue that the period between 1744 and 1814 witnessed not the unification of Nepal, but the expansion of Gorkha, through its systematic incorporation of neighboring kingdoms.

64 The Tarai refers to the then-thickly forested plains that stretched across the foothills of the Himalaya. In contemporary records, both English and Gorkhali, this region is often referred to as the '*tarriani*'.

65 On a conservative estimate, between 1765–1814 there were probably more than 200 villages that were disputed at various times along this frontier, which in 1814 stretched from the Sutlej River in the west to the Tista in the east.

66 Contemporary accounts of the war can be found in *Papers Respecting the Nepaul War*, vols 1 and 2, and *Military Sketches of the Goorkha War*. Military accounts of the war can be found in Pemble, *The Invasion of Nepal: John Company at War*; Khanduri, *A Rediscovered History of the Gorkhas*; Rana, *The Anglo–Gorkha War 1814–1816*; and Shaha, *Modern Nepal: A Political History, 1769–1955, Volume 1: 1769–1885*. The diplomatic perspective is represented in the work of Chaudhuri, *Anglo–Nepalese Relations*; Mojumdar, *Anglo–Nepalese Relations in the Nineteenth Century*; Sanwal, *Nepal and the East India Company*; and Sharma, "The Economic Theme in Nepali Foreign Policy: An Historical Analysis up to the End of the Anglo–Gorkha War."

67 Nepali historians have tended to view the war from a nationalistic perspective – see for instance Pant, "1871–72 ko Nepal Angrez Yuddhama Nepal le Harnema Euta Thulo Karan," 47–58; Regmi, *Modern Nepal, Vol. II, Expansion: Climax and All*, especially p. 291; Shaha, *Modern Nepal: A Political History, 1769–1955*; and Stiller, *The Rise of the House of Gorkha*, 240–47. One writer recently argued (rather unconvincingly) that the Treaty of Sugauli, which was signed at two different times (2 December 1815 and 4 March 1816), was unconstitutional due to the dubious role of Gorkhali negotiators, the duplicity of the British and the discrepancies between the two treaties. See Thapa, *Sugauli Sandhi ke ho?*

68 See Stiller, *The Rise of the House of Gorkha*, 240–47, "The Principle of Limitation" and *The Silent Cry*, 216–227.

69 See DesChene, "Relics of Empire: A Cultural History of the Gurkhas, 1815–1987," PhD diss., Stanford University (1991), 25–33 (especially 30).

70 Diagnostic events do not provide a neat index that catalogs or mirrors unchanging social and symbolic structures. See Moore, "Explaining the Present: Theoretical Dilemmas in Processual Anthropology," 727–36 (especially 729–30 and 735).

71 Such a view has been echoed by a number of recent studies, sometimes called "the new military history," which veer away from traditionalist accounts of war to include a wider range of variables such as culture, race, gender, class, society and space. See Chambers, "The New Military History: Myth and Reality," 395–406. For such studies from South Asia see Alavi, *The Sepoys and the Company: Tradition and Transition in North India, 1770–1830*; Caplan, *Warrior Gentlemen: 'Gurkhas' in the Western Imagination*; and Kolff, *Naukar, Rajput, Sepoy: The Ethnohistory of the Military Labour Market of Hindustan, 1450–1850*. For a consideration of war as a diagnostic event see Clayton, "The Creation of Imperial Space in the Pacific Northwest," 327–50.

Chapter 2. The Agrarian Environment and the Production of Space on the Anglo–Gorkha Frontier

1 I have found useful introductions to these issues in Arnold, *The Problem of Nature: Environment, Culture and European Expansion*; Bailes, ed., *Environmental History*; Cronon, *Changes in the Land: Indians, Colonists, and the Ecology of New England*; Crosby, *Germs, Seeds and Animals: Studies in Ecological History*; Kumar et al., eds, *Expanding Frontiers in South Asian and World History: Essays in Honour of John F. Richards, Special Issue of Modern Asian Studies*; Guha, *Environmentalism: A Global History*; Hughes, ed., *The Face of the Earth: Environment and World History*, 9–12; and Worster, ed., *The Ends of the Earth: Perspectives on Modern Environmental History*, 3–23, 277–309.

2 Environmental histories emerging from South Asia would include the following: Arnold and Guha, eds, *Nature, Culture, Imperialism: Essays on the Environmental History of South Asia*; Guha and Gadgil, *This Fissured Land*; Rangarajan and Sivaramakrishnan eds, *India's Environmental History: Colonialism, Modernity, and the Nation*; Richards, ed., *Land, Property, and the Environment*; Grove, Damodaran, and Sangwan, eds, *Nature and the Orient: Essays on the Environmental History of South and Southeast Asia*; Singh, *Natural Premises: Ecology and Peasant Life in the Western Himalaya, 1800–1950*; and Sivaramakrishnan, *Modern Forests: Statemaking and Environmental Change in Colonial Eastern India* and "Nationalisms and the Writing of Environmental Histories."
3 For similar work see Peluso, "Whose Woods are These? Counter-Mapping Forest Territories in Kalimantan, Indonesia," 383–406; Vandergeest and Peluso, "Territorialization and State Power in Thailand"; and Sletto, "We Drew What We Imagined."
4 My use of the term "frontier" is less in the sense of a peripheral zone, distant from the activity of a "centre," and more in terms of a matrix of rich social interactions and development. While the literature on frontier and borderland studies is too numerous to cite here, see the following for a sampling: Turner, *The Significance of the Frontier in American History*; Kopytoff, *The African Frontier: The Reproduction of Traditional African Societies*. See also the special issue on frontiers in *JWH* 4 (1993); Anderson, *Frontiers: Territory and State Formation in the Modern World*; Diener and Hagen, eds, *Borderlines and Borderlands: Political Oddities at the Edge of the Edge of the Nation-State*; Richards, *The Unending Frontier: An Environmental History of the Early Modern World*; Baud and van Schendel, "Towards a Comparative History of Borderlands," 211–42; and Tagliacozzo, *Secret Trades, Porous Borders: Smuggling and States Along a Southeast Asian Frontier, 1865–1915*.
5 My use of the term "agrarian environments" borrows from the recent work of K. Sivaramakrishnan and A. Agrawal who argue that agrarian environments are constituted by a field of social interactions in predominantly agrarian contexts. See Agrawal and Sivaramakrishnan, eds, *Agrarian Environments: Resources, Representations, and Rule in India*. See also Scott and Bhatt, eds, *Agrarian Studies: Synthetic Work at the Cutting Edge*. For more on the constitutive role of agrarian territories in South Asia's history see Ludden, *An Agrarian History of South Asia*, 41–3.
6 For a recent collection of articles on Tarai history, culture, society and economy see *Himalaya, the Journal of the Association for Nepal and Himalayan Studies*, vol. 29, nos. 1 and 2.
7 The Tarriani was also sometimes referred to as "Ketoni." See Buchanan-Hamilton, *An Account of the Kingdom of Nepaul*, 62, 101–17.
8 In present-day Nepal the Tarai is almost 900 km long, comprising 15 percent of the total land area. See Guneratne, *Many Tongues, One People: The Making of Tharu Identity in Nepal*, 21.
9 See Stevenson-Moore, *Final Report on the Survey and Settlement Operations in the Champaran District, 1892–1899*, 3. For more details about the numerous *tappas* of *pargana* Majhowa see Map 3.1 in Chapter 3. By 1814, the former *pargana* of Simraon (*praganna* Gadh Simraon in Gorkhali records) had broken into its constituent *tappas* – Rautahat and Nannor, with the former under Gorkhali possession and the latter within the Company's territories.
10 According to the treaty of November 1801, Awadh ceded the Company the territories of Gorakhpur, Rohilkhand and the Doab (the tract of land lying between the Ganges and Yamuna rivers), in lieu of arrears in payments for the maintenance of British troops. The Company divided the Ceded Provinces into seven *zillas* (districts) – Moradabad, Bareilly, Etawah, Farrukhabad, Kanpur, Allahabad and Gorakhpur, each with a judge, magistrate and collector to oversee legal and other administrative duties. See Letters Received by Collector (12 May 1802–25, June 1803), GCR, basta 1, vol. 1, *RSA*.
11 For a summary of the administrative changes the district underwent see Prakash, ed., *Uttar Pradesh District Gazetteers: Gorakhpur*, 1–3.
12 The Palpali raja, Prithvipal Sen, was executed in 1806 as part of a planned campaign of retributions unleashed by Bhim Sen Thapa following the assassination of the former raja of Gorkha, Ran Bahadur Shah. For details surrounding Rana Bahadur's assassination see Regmi, *Modern Nepal*, 162–74, and letter of Gribana Juddha Bikram Shah, raja of Gorkha, to Ran Bhim Shah, 1806, in Yogi Naraharinatha, *Ithihasaprakashma Sandhipatrasamgraha*, 410–11.

13 Such a melding of overlapping regimes constituting a frontier can be discerned in other times and places. I am referring in particular to Richard Eaton's account of the rapid and creative adaptation of Islam on the Bengal frontier between the thirteenth to the eighteenth centuries. See Eaton, *The Rise of Islam on the Bengal Frontier, 1204–1760*.
14 Stevenson-Moore, *Final Report*, 6.
15 For more details on this see Sharma, *Land-use Survey in Tarai Tract: A Study of Eastern Uttar Pradesh*; and Singh, *The Terai Region in U P: A Study in Human Geography*. Further details about the soil types of Gorakhpur can be found in Mufti Ghulam Hazrat's account of the history of Gorakhpur. See "History of Gorakhpur," compiled by Huzrut (law officer) and Ameen, 1810, *Islamic Oriental Manuscript*, IO 4540, 23–25, OIOC/BL.
16 Francis Buchanan-Hamilton, during his surveys of the region in the first decade of the nineteenth century, observed that the *pargana* of Ratanpur Bansi, had as many as 87 marshy lakes, the largest covering 400 acres, while one-tenth of the district remained flooded during the rains. See Buchanan-Hamilton, *The Gorakhpur Report*, vol. 1, 315, Eur. Mss D91, IOR, APAC, BL (hereafter referred to as *The Gorakhpur Report*). Also cited in Bhargava, *State, Society and Ecology: Gorakhpur in Transition, 1750–1830*, 26.
17 See "General Statement of the Resources of the Teraiee and Forests," 2 April 1815, KRR, microfilm IOR2, IOR 5/1/2, part 2, 363, NAN.
18 See Lt. Pickersgill's description of the plains of Binayakpur, FP Procs, 29 October 1813, no. 41, NAI. See also "Commercial and Other Routes from Nepal to the Plains," Eur. Mss Hodgson 3, folio 69–70, BL, APAC, IOR.
19 See Fraser, "Memorandum regarding the present state of the forests of Gorakhpur and Tarai and future benefits that might be derived from their proper management," 13 May 1814, Letters Received Register, GCR, basta 3, vol. 18, *RSA*.
20 "General Statement of the Resources of the Teraiee and Forests," in letter from Paris Bradshaw, political agent in Nepal to John Adam, secretary to government, 2 April 1815, KRR, microfilm IOR2, IOR5/1/2, part 2, 363, NAN.
21 See Kirkpatrick, *An Account of the Kingdom of Nepaul*, 17–18. See also Oldfield, *Sketches from Nepal*, 305.
22 See Kirkpatrick, *An Account*, 18; Buchanan, *An Account of the District of Purnea in 1809–10*, 415. Oldfield notes that in 1834 the pasturage tax amounted to one-twentieth of the total revenues of the Gorkha's Tarai. Cited in Arjun Guneratne, *Many Tongues, One People*, 29.
23 See deposition of Tharu leader Bikha Chaudhari, in Series of Letters and Papers, with Persian secretary John Monckton's report on them relating to the Nepal–British Border Disputes in Champaran, FP, Procs 4 March 1814, Consl. 53–65, 195–434, NAI (hereafter referred to as the *Monckton Report*).
24 See T. Ahmuty, Coll. of Gorakhpur to J. Fombelle, secretary to government in the department of the Ceded Provinces, 27 April 1804, FP Consl., 7 June 1804, no. 60, NAI.
25 Lt. Col. Paris Bradshaw, political agent to Nepal, to John Adam, secretary to government, 2 April 1815, KRR, microfilm reel no. IOR 2, IOR 5/1/2, part 2, 354–61, NAN. For details about the population composition of the Eastern Tarai see "Report on the population on the Tarai on the frontier of Champaran" by Lt. Col. Paris Bradshaw, political agent to Nepal, to John Adam, secretary to government, 2 April 1815, KRR, microfilm reel no. IOR 2, IOR 5/1/2, part 2, 362, NAN. For details on the social composition of the agricultural population of Champaran, see Stevenson-Moore, *Final Report*, 17.
26 See Choudhary, *History of Muslim Rule in Tirhut (1206–1765)*, 173–227. Some details on the Banturs can be found in Inglis, *Tent Life in Tigerland: Sport and Work on the Nepaul Frontier*. Some information on the Bhars can be gleaned from Fraser's "Memorandum" (1814), cited above.
27 Stevenson-Moore, *Final Report*, 13. These figures are in all probability inaccurate. In 1872, following the first regular census operations, Champaran District recorded a population of over 14 lakhs (ibid., 14). In 1847, one conservative estimate put the number at 421,197. See Wyatt, *Statistics of the District of Sarun consisting of Sircars Sarun and Chumparun*, 2. In the final analysis, it might be fair to conclude that between 1765 and 1814 the district saw, if

nothing else, a gradual increase in population as more and more land was brought under the plough.
28 See Records of the Controlling Committee of Revenue at Patna, 1772, vol. 5, 255, WBSA. The famine of 1770 may have reduced the population of Bengal (inclusive of Bihar) by anywhere between one-third to one-fifth. It has been estimated that during this famine between 35 and 50 percent of the agricultural population died, and the population levels may have taken 15 years to recover. Along with this, more than one-third of the cultivated land remained "deserted." See Marshall, *Bengal: The British Bridgehead*, 18; and Bose, *Peasant Labour and Colonial Capital: Rural Bengal since 1770*, 8–38. See also Mookerji, *Indian Land System: Ancient, Medieval and Modern*, 86; and McLane, *Land and Local Kingship in Eighteenth-Century Bengal*, 194–207.
29 Sinha, *From Decline to Destruction: Agriculture in Bihar during Early British Rule, 1765–1813*, 8, 11. Again, there were probably some variations in this process of agrarian expansion; agricultural growth might have been greater and more sustained in south Champaran (rather than the heavily-forested north) with its soil composed of fine, light sand and clay (*bhit*).
30 Stevenson-Moore, *Final Report*, 101. In addition to cultivation there were other reasons for people to move into and out of the area, such as banditry, asceticism and political refuge.
31 The Banjaras, who could be both Muslim and Hindu, were active as merchants, mercenaries and bandits. In 1790 the raja of Bansi ousted them from his territories. See Nevill, *Gorakhpur: A Gazetteer*, vol. 31 of *District Gazetteer of the United Provinces of Agra and Awadh*, 173–92; and Bhargava, *State, Society*, 141–2.
32 The term "gosain" is a broad, generic one, that by the early nineteenth century came to encompass various mendicant groups and orders operating in the Gangetic plains and beyond into "Nepal." Strictly speaking, *gosains* were Shaivite monks. For details see Pinch, *Peasants and Monks in British India*, 24, 43–4. Gorkhali rulers reconfirmed older grants such as those made by the kings of Makwanpur to various ascetic groups. See, for example, "The prohibitionary order (rukka) of King Girbaba Juddha Bikram Shah of sale or mortgage of land endowed as fakiranai [land grants made to members of religious sects] in taraf Paroha, tappa Rautahat to mahant Tej Giri, Marga Sudi 11, 1863 (1806 CE) [1863 BS]," RRC 5: 109–10, NAN.
33 For close examination of the activities of these groups on the Champaran–Tarriani frontier, see Burghart, "The History of Janakpurdham: A Study of Asceticism and the Hindu Polity," chapters 6 and 7.
34 Land Grant from King Ran Bahadur Shah to Abbot Pritam Das of Hanuman Nagar monastery (1781), and Land Grant from King Girbana Juddha Bikram Shah to Abbot Amar Giri of Ram Chandra monastery (1807), cited in Richard Burghart, "The History of Janakpurdham," 191–2.
35 In the eighteenth century, the Gosains, in addition to their military, religious and agricultural prowess, were also active in inter-regional trade circuits that connected the Kathmandu valley to the Gangetic plains. They were also active in financing the struggles between the kings of Kathmandu and Gorkha in the eighteenth century. See Regmi, *Modern Nepal: Rise and Growth in the Eighteenth Century*, 117–21. See also Cohn, "The Role of the Gosains in the Economy of Eighteenth and Nineteenth-Century Upper India," 175–82.
36 See Document 21 in Krauskopf, Panjiar and Shrestha, eds, *The Kings of Nepal and the Tharu of the Tarai: The Panjiar Collection of Fifty Royal Documents from 1726–1971* or Shrestha, ed., *Nepalka Rajaharu tatha Taraika Tharu*. See also documents 18 and 20 for information on shortages of labor along the Anglo–Gorkha frontier. The Panjiar Collection remains one of the best collections of primary documents for understanding the relationship between Tharu elites and Gorkhali authorities in managing the agrarian resources of Gorkha's Tarai lands.
37 A *sardar* was a high ranking civil and military official below the rank of *kaji*. See "Royal order to *sardar* Gaj Singh Khatri," *RRS* 16 (May 1984): 78, and "Sardar Gaj Singh Khatri ordered to issue *pattas* to tenants procured from India for settlement of waste lands in Morung, 1810 CE [1867 BS]," RRC 39: 230. Similar orders were given to Gosain Baburiya Das regarding reclamation of lands in Saptari. See ibid., 78–9; and "Land Tax assessment rates in Mahottari;

arrangements for reclamation of waste lands by tenants from India, 1793 CE [1850 BS]," RRC 36: 26; and "Tenants emigrated to India invited back to Morung; assurance of resolution of grievances by *subba* Anup Singh Adhikari and Dhokal Khawas, 1813 CE [1870 BS]," RRC 39: 561. See also the "Royal order granting *chaudharis* of Chitwan the authority to invite settlers from India to reclaim waste lands, 1818 CE [1875 BS]," RRC 42: 321.
38 Authorities in Kathmandu issued warnings of severe punishment to such landholders. However, it seems unlikely that such threats were actually carried out. See RRC 5: 537, no. 181, NAN.
39 See Huzrut, *History of Gorakhpur*, 1810, 26, in *Islamic Oriental Manuscript* IO 4540, 23–5, OIOC/BL; and Bhargava, *State, Society and Ecology*, 26. Francis Buchanan-Hamilton noted that, in Gorakhpur, tenants had a tendency to desert when asked for full rent. See Buchanan-Hamilton, *The Gorakhpur Report*, vol. 2, 60–64.
40 See translation of *sanad* (royal decree) from raja Girbana Juddha Bikram Shah of Gorkha to raja Shakti Prachand Shah of Gulmi, Boards Collections, F/4/185, 234–36, BL, APAC, IOR. See also A. Ross, Collector of Gorakhpur to BOR, 2 April 1804, Procs of the Sadar, BOR, Fort William, 17 April 1804, no. 4, UPSA; and petition (*arzi*) from Shakti Prachand Shah, the raja of Gulmi, 14 March 1804, Boards Collections, F/4/185, 226–32, BL, APAC, IOR.
41 See RRC 5:20–22, NAN. The historical documents in the Panjiar Collection provide further evidence of cultivators abandoning their lands when faced with political turmoil in the Butwal–Nawalparsi area between 1804 and 1828. See Krauskopf, Panjiar and Shrestha, eds, *The Kings of Nepal and the Tharu of the Tarai*, documents 37–41.
42 See Burghart, *The History of Janakpurdham: A study of Asceticism and the Hindu Polity*, 188–219.
43 See Panjiar, "Birtabal Tharu," 25–7.
44 See Bhargava, *State, Society and Ecology*, 83. On the Gorakhpur–Butwal frontier this seems to have been a recurring feature and the possibility of obtaining labor was an attractive proposition to all parties involved in taxing cultivation. In fact, earlier, in 1804, when the Butwal raja had complained of just such a loss of manpower, the British Collector of Gorakhpur was given specific instructions to encourage the settlement of emigrants from "Nepaul." See J. Fombelle, Secretary to Government in Ceded Provinces, 1 November 1804, Fort William, BOR, Procs, 13 November 1804, no. 5, UPSA.
45 Bhargava, *State, Society and Ecology*, 83.
46 The trend of agricultural labor to move from India to Nepal seems to have persisted well into the nineteenth century, despite the demarcation of a clear boundary between the two states. In this case, it was the attractive terms offered by the Rana regime and the oppressive conditions prevailing in Champaran that induced this migratory trend. See Mishra, *Agrarian Problems of Permanent Settlement: A Case Study of Champaran*, 60, 131, 268. Also cited in *RRS* 12, no. 4 (April 1980), 60–61. Such practices, I have been told, persist into the present. I am grateful to Abhay Mohan Jha, a friend and lawyer at Bettiah (present-day Champaran district), for providing me with this information.
47 There were approximately 14 *malguzari* and eight rent-free tenures after 1792, which fell to 11 *malguzari* tenures in 1811. See Scott, acting magst. of Gorakhpur to G. Dowdeswell, secretary to government in judicial department, 19 November 1811, FP Consl. 17 January 1812, no. 46, NAI. I might add that the information that collectors like David Scott gathered was invariably refracted through the interested lenses of local officials. Local accountants such as *quanungoes* and *patwaris* often colluded with other agents in concealing information in an effort to deprive the state of its share of revenues. In this sense, these hidden transcripts can never be fully unearthed in a historical investigation such as this one. Our access to that agrarian world will always be obstructed by this opacity inherent in the Company records.
48 D. Scott, acting magst. to G. Dowdeswell, secretary to government, 19 November 1811, in "Letters issued to Magst.," GCR, basta 25, vol. 164, 100–106, RSA. See also, FP Consl. 17 January 1812, no. 46, NAI. For more information on lands lying in commons in the northern reaches of *pargana* Bansi and the *taluqa* of Matka see reports and observations submitted by Paris Bradshaw on the negotiations and correspondence with the Nepaulese commissioners, April–May 1813, FP Procs, 18 June 1813, nos. 18–24, NAI.

49 Standing opposed to this category was the *khudkasht* cultivator, or one who cultivated lands in the village of his residence. For details see Hasan, *Some Thoughts on Agrarian Relations in Mughal India*, 19; and Chandra, "Some Aspects of Indian Village Society in Northern India During the 18th Century: The Position and Role of the *khud-kasht* and *pahi-kasht*," 51–64. Yasin's glossary notes that a *pahikasht* cultivator was a *raiyat* (cultivator) resident in one *mauza* belonging to a *zamindar*, but cultivating land belonging to a different *zamindar*. See Mahmud, *An Eighteenth Century Agrarian Manual: Yasin's Dastur-i-Malguzari*, 137. Bhargava clarifies that the *pahikasht* "were such cultivators who cultivated lands in villages, not belonging to the same *zamindari*, tribal or clan settlements as their own." See Bhargava, *State, Society*, 160; "Perception and Classification of the Rights of the Social Classes: Gorakhpur and the East India Company in the late Eighteenth Century and Early Nineteenth Century," 234; and "Landed Property Rights in Transition: A Note on Cultivators and Agricultural Labourers in Gorakhpur in the late Eighteenth and Nineteenth Centuries," 244–53 (especially 250).
50 "Estimates of the proportion of different classes of society employed in agriculture in the Northern Part of this District of Gorakhpur," Table no. 3, in Buchanan-Hamilton's "An Account of the Northern Part of the District of Gorakhpur," Eur. Mss G 22–3, BL, APAC, IOR (hereafter "An Account of the Northern Part of the District of Gorakhpur").
51 Bhargava, *State, Society and Ecology*, 31–2.
52 Bayly, *Rulers, Townsmen, and Bazaars: North Indian Society in an Age of British Expansion, 1770–1870*, 39.
53 Bhargava, *State, Society*, 31–2. Most *pahikashts* were also *khudkasht* cultivators as well, the latter often working as *pahikashts* in fields other than their own in order to supplement their income. See, Bhargava, *State, Society*, 159–68.
54 K. Sivaramakrishnan uses the term "agroforest" to stress this point about the mutual interconnections between grasslands, forests, and farms. See Sivaramakrishnan, "Transition Zones: Changing Landscapes and Local Authority in Southwest Bengal, 1880s–1920s." For a historical account of commons that captures the role of political power while sidestepping neat overgeneralizations within the discourses of environmental history see Guha, "Claims on the Commons: Political Power and Natural Resources in Pre-Colonial India." For an analysis of the colonial state's use of such classificatory categories see Burton Stein, "Idiom and Ideology in Early Nineteenth-Century South India," in *Rural India*, Rob, ed., 23–58. See also Bhattacharya, "Introduction" (Special issue on Forests, Fields, and Pastures), 165–71.
55 The recent work of Vinay Gidwani has examined the ideological freight of liberalism that was borne in the use of the term "waste" as the British proceeded with the "civilizing" of India. See Gidwani, *Capital Interrupted: Agrarian Development and the Politics of Work in India*, 18–31.
56 Colonial writers like W. W. Hunter had noted that the area under waste lands seems to have been enormous and virtually unknown at the time of the Permanent Settlement. Cited in Gidwani, *Capital Interrupted*, 21.
57 Cited in Stevenson-Moore, *Final Report*, 29.
58 The little kingdom of Ramnagar lay on the northern frontier of Champaran. In 1814 it was administered by the former rulers of the hill kingdom of Tanahu, lying to the north, which had been incorporated into the Gorkhali Empire in the late eighteenth century. For details see Adhikari, *Tanahu Rajyako Itihas*.
59 For details see Hunter, ed., *A Statistical Account of Bengal*, vol. 13, "Tirhut and Champaran"; Wyatt, *Statistics of the Districts of Sarun, Consisting of Sircars Sarun and Chumparun*; Kirkpatrick, *An Account of the Kingdom of Nepaul*, 18. Patterns of long-distance cattle grazing were often regulated by local customary arrangements, with the cattle grazer paying a grazing tax (*charai*) that was assessed on each animal. For instance, along the Champaran–Tarriani frontier, Ahir leaders like Bassun Raut were known to have collected such grazing taxes. See Paris Bradshaw, political agent to Nepaul to J. R. Eliot, magst. of Saran, 19 March 1815, in KRR, microfilm reel number IOR 2, IOR 5/1/2, Part 2, 346–50, NAN.
60 There are numerous instances of forest land being granted to encourage cultivation. See for instance "jagir grant to chopdar [royal attendant/mace bearer] Hidaram of mauza Idarwa in

pargana Sidhmas, *zilla* Parsa, 1793 CE [1850 BS]," *RRS* 21 (October 1989): 139; "10 year *ijara* grant to Subuddhi of 2 villages in *pargana* Simraon, *tappa* Rautahat, *taraf* Paroha, 1799 CE [1856 BS]," RRC 19: 35–6; "*kusa birta* grant of village to Pandit Hira Jha in *pargana* Mahottari, *zilla* Mahottari, 1800 CE [1857 BS]," *Kausi Tosakhana Collection, lal mohar* no. 60, NAN; "*Kusa-birta-bitalab* grants of 3 *mauzas* to Bal Bhadra Pandit, Motiraj Bhatta, and Brajlal in *parganas* Matiban, Naurangiya, and Bariyarpar respectively, 1805 CE [1862 BS]," *RRS* 24, no. 10 (October 1989): 149; "*sarb anka bitalab kusa birta* grant to *gosain* Hund Giri in *taraf* Sir, *pargana* Mahottari, *zilla* Mahottari, 1809 CE [1866 BS]," Lagat Phant, Poka 33, nos. 3357 and 168, Kathamandu; and "Reclaimed waste lands granted for cultivation to Hatbir Thapa and Jogram Newar under *adhiya* [crop-sharing] tenure in Dhurunchu, 1813 CE, [1870 BS]," RRC 41: 202.

61 See for instance "*Bikh Buniyad* grant to Bikha Chaudhari in *pargana* Cherbant, 1798 CE [1855 BS]," RRC 24: 684; "*Bekh Buniyad* grant to Bikha Chaudhari in appreciation of settling waste lands in *pargana* Dostiyan, district Bara, 1814 CE [1871 BS]," RRC 41: 552 (it was critical for Gorkhali elites, in their efforts to increase the revenues of the state, to co-opt Tharu leaders like Bikha Chaudhari, as they were able to mobilize their followers to achieve such ends); "*Ijara* for reclamation of waste lands granted to Ratan Chaudhari, in *pargana* Naurangiya, district (*zilla*) Parsa, 1815 CE [1872 BS]," RRC 42: 110; "*Bekh Buniyad* grant of waste lands to Ratan Choudhari in *pargana* Sidhmas, *zilla* Bara-Parsa, 1815 CE [1872 BS]," RRC 42: 109; and "*Bekh Buniyad* land grant on waste lands to Ranjit Choudhary in *pargana* Sidhmas, *zilla* Parsa for service rendered during the battle of Parsagarhi, 1814 CE [1871 BS]," RRC 41: 504. See also the excellent collection of royal documents in Krauskopf, Panjiar and Shrestha, eds, *The Kings of Nepal*.

62 Letter from Paris Bradshaw, political agent to Nepaul, to J. R. Eliot, magst. of Saran, 2 April 1815, in KRR, microfilm reel no. IOR 2, IOR 5/1/2, Part 2, 354–61, NAN. It might be appropriate to reiterate that *pargana* Simraon was made up of two *tappas*, Nannor and Rautahat. In this observation, Bradshaw is probably referring to *tappa* Nannor. Rautahat as a newly acquired territory was granted to Gorkha by the British in 1783. In the period of 1783–1814 the Gorkhalis strengthened their presence by conferring a large number of land grants in *tappa* Rautahat.

63 This can be seen in a notation made in the margins of a letter by a Company official (possibly John Adam, the secretary to government), who observed, "I should rather imagine that though the lands may have been considered to be his [the Bettiah raja, Bir Kishor Singh's] *de jure*, it was not actually his *de facto* and that the jumma [*jama*] of the 22 villages was not included in the settlement of his estate concluded in the year 1799." The *jama* was the expected revenue yield. See J. R. Eliot, magst. of Saran to John Adam, secretary to government, 5 January 1816, FS Consl. 3 February 1816, Consultation no. 21. NAI. It is possible that the year in this margin notation should actually read "1789" and not "1799," as it was in 1789 that the East India Company entered into a decennial – ten-year – settlement with the *zamindars* of Champaran. With the introduction of the Permanent Settlement in the Provinces of Bengal, Bihar and Orissa in 1793, the terms of this decennial settlement were fixed in perpetuity.

64 In the 1890s the district of Champaran possessed approximately 12 percent of old fallow land, or land that had after initial cultivation been under fallow for many years. These lands ultimately became common lands that were utilized for grazing purposes by pastoral castes such as the Goalas. For details see Stevenson-Moore, *Final Report*, 106.

65 Huzrut, *History of Gorakhpur*, 26.

66 See J. Routledge to Henry Wellesley, lt. governor and president of the board of commissioners for the Ceded Districts, 14 January 1802, Letters Issued Register, GCR, basta 16, vol. 112, RSA.

67 Buchanan-Hamilton, *The Gorakhpur Report*, vol. 1, 315.

68 Buchanan-Hamilton, *The Gorakhpur Report*, vol. 1, 324 and vol. 1, part 2, 8.

69 This information has been gleaned from the following sources: Alexander Ross, Coll. to BOR, 15 May 1805, Letters Issued Register, GCR, basta 16, vol. 4, RSA (in his estimate, Ross claimed that this figure applied to the entire district of Gorakhpur. Even if this figure might have been an exaggeration, it probably reflected the condition of the northern *tappas* of Gorakhpur

district, such as Dholiya Bandar); and "General Statistical Table about the Northern Part of the District of Gorakhpur," Table no. 1, Statistics of Gorakhpur, in Buchanan-Hamilton's "An Account of the Northern Part of the District of Gorakhpur." See also J. Carter, Coll. of Gorakhpur to H. Newnham, secretary, Board of Commissioners, 28 January 1819, Letters Issued Register, GCR, basta 17, vol. 122, 133–42, RSA; and Montgomery Martin, *The History, Antiquities, Topography, and Statistics of Eastern India*, Appendix, 10. Sarabjit Singh also claimed the title of Meer Bahar, or owner of all the water rights in the *pargana*. The same raja gave one Jurawan Chaudhari the *akbari* rights over the two *tappas* of Dhebrua and Khajahani in return for the hospitality he offered during the raja's hunting expedition. See *Report on Settlement of Gorakhpur: Basti District*, 61 and 73.

70 See Letter of M. Ricketts, Coll. of Gorakhpur, to J. Adam, secretary to government, 18 March 1818, Letters Issued Register, GCR, basta 17, vol. 122, 244–50, RSA.

71 Board of Commissioners to vice-president-in-council, Fort William, 11 September 1809, Letters Received Register, GCR, basta 2, vol. 11, RSA. Raja Sarabjit Singh of Bansi enjoyed as many as 78 villages in *nankar*. Raja Prithvipat Singh of Amorha enjoyed a *nankar* grant worth Rs 18,000 – originally granted to his grandfather raja Zalim Singh by *nawab* Shujauddaulah. Such *nankar* grants had varied histories too. While raja Zalim Singh's grant was reconfirmed by the *chakladar*, it was resumed during the *amilship* of Maj. Hannay (1777–80) when the said raja was expelled The *nankar* grant was later renewed in 1786. See A. Ross, Coll. to BOR, 15 May 1805, Letters Issued Register, GCR, basta 16, vol. 4, *RSA*; and translation of proceedings in "Cutchery of Gorakhpur, April 1807", Letters Issued Register, GCR, basta 16, vol. 116, 527–42, *RSA*.

72 When issuing such *jangalbari pattas* the Company imposed certain conditions. The *pattas* were to record the quantity of land granted, the names of the villages, and the *tappas* to which they belonged. The holder of the *patta* was expected to bring at least one-third of the land into cultivation, failing which the grant was resumed. If, on the other hand, he met all these stipulations he was deemed to be the proprietor of the land. See Board of Commissioners to vice-president-in-council, Fort William, 11 September 1809, Letters Received Register, GCR, basta 2, vol. 11, *RSA*.

73 For an insightful discussion of the need for human labor experienced by pre-modern Southeast Asian regimes see Scott, *The Art of Not Being Governed: An Anarchist History of Upland Southeast Asia*, 64–97.

74 In the eighteenth century, similar processes seem to have been unfolding elsewhere on other sections of the Company's frontier with Gorkha. For evidence from the Purnea frontier see Mishra, "Agrarian Economy of Purnea in the eighteenth century," 183–9.

75 Cited in Pemble, *The Invasion of Nepal: John Company At War*, 38.

Chapter 3. The Champaran–Tarriani Frontier

1 John Crawfurd, *Description of India, 1822–23*. IOR/Eur. Mss D457a and 457b, IOR, APAC, BL. The quote is from D 457a, pp. 177–8. The emphasis is mine.

2 The district of Champaran lies in the North Indian state of Bihar. Bounded on the west by the Gandak River and on the east by the Bagmati River, in 1814, it probably composed an area of over 3,000 square miles. At the time of the Anglo–Gorkha War in 1814, it was divided into four *parganas* – Majhowa (the largest), Mehsi, Babra and Simraon (see Stevenson-Moore, *Final Report on the Survey and Settlement Operations in the Champaran District, 1892–1899*, 3). Each *pargana* was further subdivided into *tappas*. The *pargana* of (Gadh) Simraon was made up of two *tappas* – Rautahat and Nannor, the former lying in Gorkhali territory while the latter lay in Champaran. For details see Map 3.1 and 3.2. Gorkha's Eastern Tarai was divided into a number of districts, namely Parsa, Bara, Rautahat, Mahottari, Saptari, Sarlahi and Morang. Each district was further subdivided, rather haphazardly, into a number of *parganas, tappas, tarafs*, which were in turn further divided into *mouzas* or villages.

152   STATEMAKING AND TERRITORY IN SOUTH ASIA

3 Such districts were often placed under the charge of a civil administrator/governor called a *subba* who was to oversee the activities of a number of local officials placed in charge of law and order (*fauzdar*) and revenue collection (*chaudhari, quanungoye, patwari* and *bicharis*). High-ranking military officials such as *sardars* and *kajis* could also be stationed along with their troops in various districts, and especially in those lying along the frontiers of the state. For further details see Kirkpatrick, *An Account of the Kingdom of Nepaul*, 197–203; Buchanan-Hamilton, *An Account of the Kingdom of Nepal*, 101–17; Regmi, *Kings and Political Leaders*; Stiller, *The Rise of the House of Gorkha*, 251–77; and Vaidya, *Prithvinarayan Shah, the Founder of Modern Nepal*, 213–52.

4 For instance, in 1809 several employees of the Army magazine in Kathmandu held *birta* lands in *taraf* Barhagama in *tappa* Rautahat. See list (*tapsil*) of employees of the magazine possessing lands in the Tarai, Poka 33, serial no. 3357, 1809 CE [1866 BS], *Lagat Phant*, Kathmandu. The powerful Pandit brothers, Sri Krishen and Ranganath, along with Gorkhali *vakil* Dinanath Upadhyaya, held various kinds of grants in the *tappa* of Rautahat. Ranganath Pandit possessed a *jagir* on the banks of the Bagmati River along the eastern border of the *tappa* (cited in FP Procs, 15 April 1814, no. 60, p. 272, NAI). Dinanath Upadhyaya, who once held the office of *chaudhuri* in *tappa* Rautahat, enjoyed a *nankar* grant of two villages in lieu of a cash salary. See *Kumari Chowk Goshwara Tahabil Records*, Poka 9, 1794 CE [1851 BS], *Lagat Phant*, Kathmandu. In 1798, *subba* Gaj Singh (Khatri?) was granted the *taraf* of Pachrauta, *tappa* Rautahat on a tax-farming basis (*ijara*). Cited in RRC 24: 692. Around the time of the outbreak of the Anglo–Gorkha War in 1814, the Gorkhali Prime Minister, Bhim Sen Thapa, himself held an *ijara* grant in *pargana* Sidhmas in the district of Parsa, while one Gosain Laxman Giri was given a five-year contract to collect revenue (*ijara*) in Rautahat. For details about this land grant to Bhim Sen Thapa see RRC 41: 611. Laxman Giri was appointed *subba* (the civil officer in charge of a "district") and authorized to make all of the collections in *tappa* Rautahat. From subsequent events we learn that Laxman Giri would play a critical role in the border disputes leading to the war in 1814. See "Five year *ijara* for *tappa* Rautahat granted to *gosain* Laxman Giri," RRC 40: 54. Further details can be found in the work of Mahesh C. Regmi. See for instance Regmi, *The State and Economic Surplus*; *Readings in Nepali Economic History*; *Land Tenure and Taxation in Nepal*; and *A Study in Nepali Economic History, 1768–1846*.

5 The Company had set up a number of offices and councils for overseeing the assessment and collection of revenue, which had met with limited success. With limited information about the actual resources of its territories, the Company had no choice but to enter into annual, biennial, quinquennial or decennial settlements with powerful landholders. For further details see Reginald-Hand, *Early English Administration of Bihar, 1781–1785*; Misra, *The Central Administration of the East India Company*; Stevenson-Moore, *Final Report on the Survey and Settlement Operations in Champaran District, 1892–1899*, 20–40; and Raye, *The Annals of the Early English Settlements in Bihar*.

6 Details about these settlements can be found in Stevenson-Moore, *Final Report*, 29–30. See also "Letter from Archibald Montgomerie, Collector of Saran district to the Board of Revenue dated 23 July, 1789" in BOR Procs, 3–10 August 1789, BSA; "J. Lumsden, Collector of Saran district to Governor-General in Council dated 9 May 1793," in BOR Procs, 13 May–22 May 1793, BSA; "J. Lumsden to Governor-General in Council, letter dated 25 July 1793," in BOR Procs, 9 August 1793, BSA.

7 Cited in Misra, *The Central Administration*, 128–9.

8 Numerous examples of how local initiative combined with the incapacity of Company administrators to blunt the implementation of the Permanent Settlement can be found in the following: "Letter of J. Lumsden, Collector of Saran to BOR, May 1793," "Letters Sent to BOR, 13 February 1793–95 July 1793," *District Record Room*, Chapra, Saran District, North Bihar. See also Stevenson-Moore, *Final Report*, 30–31. Further details of similar transactions in Bihar can be found in the following: "Letter from John Lumsden, Coll. Saran to Governor-General-in-Council, 9 May 1793," BOR Procs, 13–22 May 1793, BSA; "J. Lumsden to BOR 25 July 1793," BOR Procs, 9 August 1793, BSA; "J. Lumsden to BOR, 9 May 1793," BOR

Procs, 22 May, 1793, BSA; "J. Lumsden to BOR, 23 May 1793," BOR Procs, 13–22 May 1793, BSA; Bengal Draft Dispatches, Board of Control Records (BOCR), F/3/7 no. 18, 28 March 1795, paras 57 and 58, p. 413, OIOC/BL.

9   The English copies of the *dowl* (statement of the gross revenue to be collected from an estate) and *amaldastak* (warrant to collect revenue from an estate) recording the revenue engagements of Bir Kishor Singh, the raja of Bettiah at the time of the Deccennial Settlement (1791), clearly show that the *dowl* specified only the *parganas*, while the *amaldastak* specified the *parganas* and their constituent *tappas*. At this time no list of villages was provided nor were any measurements of land, boundary demarcations or surveys undertaken. See bundle of papers relating to legal case 'Maharaja of Bettiah versus the Government,' 1868, unmarked basta, Bettiah Raj Mahfizkhana (BRM), Bettiah; "Letter from C. H. Lushington, spl. deputy coll., Shahabad, Saran and Patna to E. C. Ravenshaw, Commissioner of Revenue, Patna Division, dated 16 May 1839," unmarked basta, BRM, Bettiah, West Champaran. Village lists were provided three years later, but the Company lacked the resources to verify their exact location, extent or resources.

10 While studies on the Permanent Settlement are too numerous to cite here, see Guha, *A Rule of Property for Bengal: An Essay on the Idea of Permanent Settlement*; Mishra, *Agrarian Problems of Permanent Settlement: A Case Study of Champaran*; and Islam, *The Permanent Settlement in Bengal: A Study of its Operation*.

11 Under the *amanat* system the district administrator (*subba*) was paid a salary to compensate him for his services – mainly the collection of revenue and its transmission to Kathmandu. Details about the *ijara* and *amanat* systems can be found in Regmi, *A Study in Nepali Economic History, 1768–1846*, 80–84, 124–41.

12 See "Benudhar Jaisi and Mahadev Upadhyaya instructed to inquire into details of Revenue Administration under Makwani Raja for *zillas* Parsa, Bara, Rautahat, Saptari and Mahottari, 1793 CE [1850 BS]," RRC 5: 246. These officials were ordered to collect all the details about the previous engagements of revenue collectors from the offices of the headmen (*chaudharis*) and accountants (*kanungoyes*) and bring them to Kathmandu. Again, in 1805 CE Bandhu Khawas was deputed to Bara, Parsa, Rautahat, Saptari and Mahottari to conduct a *parganawar* survey, examining revenue records, the quality of land, and so on (see RRC 5: 498); "Jetha Budha Benudhar Jaisi and other persons deputed to Mahottari to scrutinize *birta* land grants, 1797 CE [1854 BS]," RRC 25: 494; and "Royal order regarding survey of *jagir, bekh buniyad, phikdar* and *nankar* lands in Saptari-Mahottari, 1813 CE [1870 BS]," RRC 41: 435.

13 See for instance, "Waste lands granted as *nankar* to Dhaul Chaudhari in Saptari, 1793 CE [1850 BS]," RRC 25: 245; "Confirmation of *ijara* grant made to *subba* Gaj Singh Khatri for reclamation of *kalabanjar* lands in Bara, Parsa and Rautahat, 1797 CE [1854 BS]," RRC 25: 619; "Allocation of revenues to finance the reclamation of waste lands in Bara and Parsa from *ijara* revenues of these districts, 1800 CE [1857 BS]," RRC 23: 516; "Ijara for the reclamation of waste lands granted to mahant Ganesh Giri in Simraongarh, 1810 CE [1867 BS]," RRC 39: 119; "*Ijara* grant to *subba* Jalim Singh for reclamation of waste lands in *pargana* Sidhmas, *zilla* Bara-Parsa, 1810 CE [1867 BS]," RRC 39: 178; "Order regarding authorization of Kaji Balnarsingh Kunwar to make arrangements for reclamation of waste lands, n.d.," RRC 38: 592; "*Mokarrari* grant on reclaimed waste lands to *gosain* Shankar Giri in *pargana* Sidhmas, *zilla* Bara-Parsa, 1807 CE [1864 BS]," RRC 41: 152; "Seven year *ijara* to Lal Das for reclamation and settlement of *mauza* Rudauli, *pargana* Koradi, *zilla* Mahottari, 1810 CE [1867 BS]," *RRS* 16 (May 1984): 79; "Ten year *ijara* grant to Ramadhan Das and Bhitan Khan, *mauza* Mahanouri, *pargana* Maljhamuna, *zilla* Saptari, 1810 CE [1867 BS]," *RRS* 16 (May 1984): 79–80; "Nine year *ijara* for reclamation and settlement granted to Baburiya Das in *mauza* Chapki, *pargana* Jagadar-Sudhpur, zilla Saptari, 1810 CE [1867 BS]," *RRS* 16 (May 1984): 78–9; "Royal order to *Sardar* Gaj Singh Khatri to reclaim and settle *kalabanjar* lands in Morung, 1810 CE [1867 BS]," *RRS* 16 (May 1984): 78; "*Subedar* Jayant Khatri ordered to reclaim lands east of the Kamala river, which do not fall under the jurisdiction of the *subba\ijaradar* of Morung, 1810 [1867 BS]," *RRS* 16 (May 1984): 76–7.

14 Regmi estimates that between 1768 and 1814 these high ranking court officials (*bhardars*) amounted to a total of 102 men. Of these, 14 belonged to the Shah family and 70 to Chhetri families (further sub-divided into Khas and Brahmin families). See Regmi, *Kings and Leaders of the Gorkhali Empire, 1768–1814*, 36–48. "Five year *ijara* for revenues of Bara-Parsa granted to *chautariya* Dal Mardan Shah," *RRS* 20 (January, 1988): 1; "Tenancy rights granted to Dinanath Padhya and others in Khunjam, 1809 CE [1866 BS]," RRC 38: 663; "*Ijara* grant of *kalabanjar* lands to General Bhimsen Thapa, in *pargana* Sidhmas, *zilla* Bara-Parsa, 1814 CE [1871 BS]," RRC 41: 611; and "Allocation of revenues of Bara-Parsa-Rautahat to pay prescribed amount to *guru* Gajraj Mishra, 1815 CE [1872 BS]," RRC 42: 128; and "*Mokarrai* grant to *taksari* [superintendent of the mint] Chandrashekhar Upadhyaya in Mahottari, 1818 CE [1875 BS]," RRC 42: 361. Details about Ranganath Pandit's lands can be found in FP Procs, 15 April 1814, no. 60, 272, NAI. The land in question must have been in either *tappa* Rautahat or the neighboring district of Sarlahi. In any case, there were allegations that he was deeply involved in the disputes that emerged over the 22 villages between Gorkha and the Company. See "Deposition by Ram Bux Singh, former *amin* of the Tarai," in FP Procs, 22 April 1814, no. 59, 215–18, NAI. In 1806 CE, Ranganath Pandit was also appointed *danadhyaksha* (chief) of ritual gifts. See *RRS* 21 (April 1989): 46.

15 "Order replacing Dinanath Upadhayaya and Vrajvilas Upadhyaya, the joint *ijaradars* of Vijaypur (Morung) by *subba* Zorawar Khawas, 1795 CE [1852 BS]," *RRS* 20 (September 1989): 121–2. See *RRS* 20 (September 1988): 121–2. Between 1796 and 1799 CE he also held contracts to collect revenues from both Saptari-Mahottari and Morang. See "Order to Dinanath Upadhyaya, *ijaradar* of Saptari-Mahottari to make disbursements from the *ijara* revenues of Saptari as payment to the four *munshis* of the Governor-General (*bada saheb*) at Calcutta for having composed an eulogy after the Royal coronation 1799 CE," *RRS* 21 (November 1989): 157; In 1795 CE he also held a three-year *ijara* grant to lands east of the Adwara (?)River and west of the Koshi River, in *zilla* Saptari-Mahottari, RRC 40: 450. See "*Ijara* grant to Dinanath Upadhyaya of the revenues of Saptari-Mahottari, 1796," Poka 9, Bahi 8, no. 136, Lagat Phant, Kathmandu.

16 Observe "*Ijara* grant for revenue collection in Rautahat granted to Ran Mardan Khawas, 1805 CE [1862 BS]," RRC 19: 309; "Five year *ijara* grant to Laxman Giri who is also appointed *subba* for *tappa* Rautahat, 1809 CE [1866 BS]," RRC 40: 54; "Introduction of *amanat* system [of revenue collection by salaried officials] in Saptari-Mahottari and *sardar* Bal Bhanjan Pande appointed *amanat* authority, 1812 CE [1869 BS]," RRC 39: 500; "Chandrabir Thapa authorized to collect revenues in Bara-Parsa under *amanat* arrangements, 1813 CE [1870 BS]," RRC 14: 471; "Saptari-Mahottari granted on *ijara* basis to *sardar* Bal Bhanjan Pande who replaces Achal Thapa, 1814 CE [1871 BS]," RRC 41: 418.

17 See translation of a letter from *budakaji* (elder kaji) Amar Singh Thapa to the raja of Gorkha, 12 April 1815, FS Procs, 16 May 1815, no. 61, NAI.

18 Regmi, *A Study of Nepali Economic History*, 131. Brahmanand Padhya and Mahima Khawas were warned against further exactions. But like in numerous instances elsewhere, little came of this. For further examples from Gorkha's Eastern Tarai, see "Orders promulgated regarding the suspension of payment of revenues from Bara-Parsa following quarrels between the *ijaradar*, Dal Mardan Shah and the *quanungoyes* and *chaudharis* of these districts 1786 CE [1843 BS]," *RRS* 18 (March 1986): 1; and "Prohibition to *darogas* [superintendent] of the Elephant offices to extract *begar* (unpaid porterage service) labor in Bara-Parsa and Rautahat districts, 1793 CE [1850 BS]," RRC 36: 1; "Jagirdars and *birtawars* of Bara and Saptari are warned against attracting peasants from India, and replacing local revenue paying peasantry on *kalabanjar* lands, 1805 CE [1862 BS]," RRC 5: 537, no. 181; "*Chaudharis* Modi Rai and Bhinak Rai replaced by Gauri Rai and others on complaints of tenants in Simraongarh, 1810 CE [1867 BS]," RRC 39: 211; "*Subba* Bal Bhanjan Pande prohibited to make unauthorized revenue collections in Hariharpur, Sarlahi district, given on *ijara* to Jagjit Dwars, 1810 CE [1867 BS]," RRC 41: 50; "*Chaudharis*, *mokkaddams* of Bara-Parsa ordered to refund amounts for which they

had got remissions on false grounds, 1810 CE [1867 BS]," RRC 39: 342; "*Subbas, fauzdars* and others prohibited from obtaining goods without payment of appropriate prices from traders coming from the Company's territories and going to Janakpur market, 1810 CE [1867 BS]," RRC 38: 665; "Modi Misra ordered to pay prescribed *pota* tax or give up *jagir* lands arbitrarily appropriated by him in Rautahat, 1810 CE [1867 BS]," RRC 39: 185; "*Kajis, sardars* and others of Vijaypur prohibited to make collections in lands reclaimed between Kosi and Trisota Rivers by Jayant Khatri, 1813 CE [1870 BS]," RRC 41: 302; "Jai Singh Khatri prohibited to grant *ijara* on lands assigned to elephant pens to Indians. Ordered to make *thekbandi* arrangements and to return unauthorized amounts collected from *bekh buniyad* and *khuwa* holdings, 1814 CE [1871 BS]," RRC 41: 552; "*Amalidars* [collectors] of *pargana* Dhanchhabar, *zilla* Siraha prohibited from collecting fees on timber and catechu procured from revenue lands. Such fees could only be collected in *birta* holdings, 1814 CE [1871 BS]," RRC 41: 576; "*Dhittas* of *sora mahal* in Mahottari forbidden to interfere in *mokarrari* grant made to Khelpati Das in *pargana* Kesraha, *zilla* Mahottari, 1814 CE [1871 BS]," RRC 41: 614; "*Sardar* Gaj Singh Khatri prohibited to put obstructions regarding collection of amounts in arrears in Morung, 1815 CE [1872 BS]," RRC 42: 94; "*Amali* of Makwanpur prohibited to collect unauthorized amounts from *ryots*, 1818 CE [1875 BS]," RRC 41: 647; "Complaint of Zalim Singh of *pargana* Pakari, Mahottari district that the *mahajani* [banking fees] amount due on *ijara* contract was forcibly collected by *subba* Jayafor, 1818 CE [1875 BS]," RRC 38: 529.

19 Between 1810 and 1815 he was reprimanded for unauthorized collections and exactions from *raikar* (state-owned), *jagir* and *birta* lands, local markets, and for the movement of commodities like cotton, *begar* (corvee labor) and taxes on saltpeter. See RRC 41: 11–12, 50, 55, 117, 160, 300, 481, 569.

20 Most of these took place between 1802 and 1813 in the Eastern Tarai and had to do with unauthorized collections from cultivators, defaulting on payment of revenue, and redirecting cultivators from revenue paying lands to lands that did not fall into the tax net of the state. Dashrath Khatri and Chandra Bir Thapa also defaulted or obstructed the payment of creditors who had helped finance the stay of former Gorkhali raja Ran Bahadur Shah in Banaras (1799–1804). For details about Dashrath Khatri see *RRS* 19 (July–August 1987): 95; *RRS* 19 (June 1987): 84; and RRC 36: 209. Details about Chandra Bir Thapa can be found in RRC 38: 723 and 42: 118. Parshuram Thapa's activities find mention in RRC 41: 178.

21 Regmi, *Kings and Political Leaders*, 58–9. See also Acharya, *Nepalko Samkshipta Vrittanta*, 123.

22 For data on declining revenue collection in the Eastern Tarai between 1791–1814, see Regmi, *A Study*, 132 and 137. (Figures are unavailable for some of the years.)

23 "Laxmi Narayan Pandit deputed to look into the complaints against *amils* and *subbas* of the Tarai, 1805 CE [1862 BS]," RRC 5: 569, no. 119; "*Subedar* Ramjit Bhandari deputed to investigate complaints of oppression in eastern Tarai, 1809 CE [1866 BS]," RRC 36: 255–65; "Order to *subba* Dashrath Khatri regarding complaints of *ryots* about exaction or unauthorized taxes, 1809 CE [1866 BS]," RRC 36: 209; "*Kaji* Bahadur Bhandari ordered to scrutinize *guthi* land endowments in the entire kingdom, 1810 CE [1867 BS]," RRC 39: 232; "Orders issued to Jayant Khatri to look into the complaints against local *fauzdars* in the Morang area who were obstructing the procurement of settlers from *moglan*, 1810 CE [1867 BS]," *RRS* 16 (May 1984): 76–7; "Royal priests, *chautariyas* and others with *birta* and other land holdings in Saptari-Mahottari warned that they should proportionately share water with *raikar* lands, 1810 CE" [1867 BS]," RRC 41: 58; "*Kaji* Bhaktawar Singh Basnayet empowered to check complaints lodged by *amils* and *ryots* in areas west of Bheri river, 1812 CE [1869 BS]," RRC 41: 192; "*Ijaradar* Jai Mangal Padhya (?) prohibited from collecting unauthorized amounts from tenants and *mokaddams* in *pargana* Mahottari, 1812 CE [1869 BS]," RRC 41: 177; "Army personnel prohibited from oppressing people in Rautahat by getting forcibly goods at cheap prices and by impressing *begar* labor, 1812 CE [1869 BS]," RRC 41: 108.

24 It is useful to remember that when *ijaras* were granted, the *ijaradar* was responsible not only for the collection of revenue, but also for matters pertaining to defense, entertainment of

foreign dignitaries and the administration of justice. Since the administration of justice was an additional and often substantial source of income (through the collection of judicial fines), *ijaradars* were understandably reluctant to part with them. Regmi, *A Study*, 133–4.

25 For instance in Morang district, Gaj Singh Khatri, Dashrath Khatri and Sri Krishna Padhya were joint *subbas* in 1802 CE, and Shakti Ballabh and Siddhi Karna Padhya were joint *amanat* collecting authorities in 1816 CE. Earlier, Shakti Ballabh himself was *subba* for both districts of Bara and Parsa in 1802 CE, while Bala Bhanjan Pande was *subba* for the three districts of Bara, Parsa and Rautahat in 1810 CE. My information is drawn from a number of sources, including the writings of Mahesh Chadra Regmi, the RRC, and records from the Lagat Phant (the Department of Land Revenue, Government of Nepal).

26 An important depository of sources for the study of the Bettiah raj can be found in the Raj's *mahfizkhana* (record room) in Bettiah, west Champaran, Bihar, where a huge collection of records pertaining to the raj's revenue and legal history can be found. These await scholarly scrutiny. An official account of the raj was published in 1936–37 under the authorship of Rai Bahadur M. L. Basu, titled *A Consecutive Account of the Bettiah Raj* (1936) and published by the Bettiah Raj Press. Despite strenuous efforts, I have failed to trace a single copy of this rare work. I am grateful to Shri Badshah Chaubey, the officer-in-charge of the Regional Archives in Bettiah for providing me with a copy of the notes he had transcribed from said book. I will refer to it in the appropriate places as the "Chaubey Notes." Scattered references to the Bettiah Raj may be found in the following: Choudhary, *History of Muslim Rule in Tirhut (1206–1765 CE)*, vol. 82, 178–80, 208 and 226; Singh, *History of Tirhut: From the Earliest Times to the end of the Nineteenth Century*, 206–10; Harindra Prasad, "Bettiah Rajvamsha ka Samkshipta Itihas," *Julm ka Pratikar, Champaran Visheshanka*; and *Brief History About Bettiah Estate*, 8. I am grateful to Shri Banaras Babu, former farm manager of the Bettiah estate, for providing me with this copy. A nine-page typescript titled *Bettiah Raj ka Itihas* (n.d.), has been prepared by Shri Revati Kant Dwivedi, one of the descendents of the *rajguru* of the Bettiah raj. I am grateful to Jose K. John SJ for sharing a copy of this document with me.

27 For details see Prasad, "Bettiah Rajvamsha ka Samkshipta Itihas," 44; and Dwivedi, *"Bettiah raj ka Itihas,"* 1–4. Legal expressions of these disputes that extend well into the twentieth century can be found in law digests such as *Calcutta Weekly Notes, Moore's India Appeals* and the *All India Register*. I am grateful to Dr Krishnanandan Singh, a descendant of the raj and currently Advocate of the Patna High Court for sharing this information with me.

28 In 1729 *nawab* of Bengal, Alivardi Khan, sent an expedition that subdued the Bettiah raja Dhrub Singh for his intransigence. In 1759, one Major Caillaud and Miran, the son of *nawab* Mir Jafar Khan, subdued Bettiah. These expeditions were followed by a British one in 1766, led by Sir Robert Barker. See Singh, *History of Tirhut*, 206–10.

29 Shitab Rai had been the former *diwan* of the province of Bihar. Bir Kishor was unable to provide any evidence of the receipt of this *malikana* in the past by Shitab Rai. Company officials annulled Bir Kishor's claims, on the grounds that his father Jugal Kishor had forfeited any claims to Belwa, as he was at that time a refugee in Bundelkhand. See Chaubey Notes, 26–8.

30 See letter from the BOR to Archibald Montgomerie, Collector of Saran, 7 March 1792, Copies of Letters Received in the Revenue Department from 18 January 1792 to 25 January 1793, Saran Collectorate Records, BSA.

31 Information on the Tanahu raj can be gleaned from the following sources: Adhikari, *Tanahu Rajyako Itihas*; Pant, "Tanahuka Raja Trivikram Senka Dash Aprakashit Patra," 47–52; "Tanahu raja Kamaridat Senka Dui Aprakashit Patra," 10; "Tanahu raja Harkumardat Senka Satwota Aprakashit Patra" and "Tanahuka Gunanand Pantlai Lekhiyeko Char wota Aprakashit Patra," 1–3, 19–21, 25–6; Badshah Chaubey, "Ramnagar Raj (in Hindi)," 47–9; Sharma, *Chitwan Upatyakako Itihasik Rup Rekha*, 1–21 and appendices; Ghimire, "Tanahuko Rajnitik Itihas," 22–8; and Upadhyaya, *Nepalko Itihas*. This work has a section devoted to the Ramnagar raj, that portion of the Tanahu raj which lay in the plains of Champaran, and to which the Tanahu rajas retired following the incorporation of Tanahu's hill territories into the Gorkhali Empire in 1782. The

Ramnagar estate was made of the *tappas* of Jamauli, Ramgir and half of Chigwan. Most of these works tend to be repetitive, and draw heavily on the earlier work of Ambika Prasad Upadhyaya.

32 See Buchanan-Hamilton, *An Account of the Kingdom of Nepal*, 131; Ghimire, *Palpa Rajyako Itihos*, 37; and Adhikari, *Tanahu Rajyako*, 25. Tanahu's Digvijayasen (1673–1694 CE) initially obtained possession of eleven *tappas* from the Mughal emperor Aurangzeb. Later, under the rule of Kamrajdat Sen (1694–1749 CE), Tanahu's claim to 15 *tappas* was recognized by the Mughal emperor Farrukhsiyar. See Adhikari, *Tanahu Rajyako*, 13 and 34.

33 See Proceedings of the Governor-General of Bengal in Council, 28 September 1781, Consl. nos. 1–3, WBSA.

34 See, the petition of Dharindar Upadhyaya *vakil* to Har Kumar Dat Sen to Governor General, 9 January 1793, *CPC* 10, no. 1078.

35 It appears that the other half of Chigwan lay in the hills lying north of Champaran and possibly outside the province of Bihar, and therefore outside the bounds of their authority. An ethnography of such disputes cannot take at face-value any of the claims being made by the contestants. For instance, the mention of the fact that half of *tappa* Chigwan lay outside Champaran across its northern hills was a claim made by Harkumar Dat Sen, the raja of Tanahu. See letter from D. Vanderhayden, special commissioner (investigating revenue arrangements in Champaran) to Bihar to Board of Revenue, October 4, 1793, no. 20–32, in BOR Procs, 1–11 October 1793, WBSA.

36 Ibid.

37 See "Letters from Ran Bahadur Shah and Dinanath Upadhyaya," in *CPC* 8, no. 5 and 6.

38 See "Memorial of Dinanath Upadhyaya," in Proceedings of the Governor-General of Bengal in Council, 28 September 1781, Consl. no. 2, WBSA.

39 Adhikari, *Tanahu rajyako Itihas*, 68. It is unclear from whom the Bettiah raja wrested control of these *tappas*. Between 1793 and 1804 Harkumar Dat Sen would file cases against the Bettiah raja, Bir Kishor Singh, in the civil courts, pleading that these 12½ *tappas* be restored to him. But his rights over these 12½ *tappas* would not be recognized by the Company's courts. See Chaubey Notes, 24–6.

40 For details see "Petition of Bir Kishor Singh, raja of Bettiah dated 30 December 1796," in Judicial (Criminal) Proceedings 13 January 1797, nos. 15–16, WBSA. See also letter of Lt. Henry Carter to Charles Boddam, judge and magistrate of Saran, dated 18 January 1797, in Letters Received Register, 24 June 1797 to 27 December 1798, Saran Collectorate Records, BSA. For the Palpali perspective see ibid.; and letter of Lt. Carter to Major Coningham, commanding officer at Burragaon, 5 January 1797, in op. cit. British timber agents found it difficult to cut timber in the area due to this dispute. See letter from Stephen Cowgill to Charles Boddam, judge and magst. of Saran, dated 12 September 1797, in op. cit.

41 Gorkhali records refer to "Tauter" as "Thathar." See "Madhesh tirako sandhi vigraha," in Naraharinath, *Itihasprakashmasandhipatrasamgraha*, 7–10.

42 Information pertaining to Makwanpur and its Tarai possessions, though highly dispersed, is available in the Regmi Research Collection (RRC). Some details can be obtained from the following sources: Buchanan-Hamilton, *An Account of the Kingdom of Nepal*, 130 and 160–62; Amatya, "Makwanpurka Kehi Puratatvik Upalabdhi," 34–54; Koirala, "Senvamshi Rajaharuko Itihasik Paricharcha ra Purvi Pahadki Kehi Brahman Vamsha," 16–24; Panjiar, "Birtabal Tharu," 25–7; and a number of documents in Krauskopf, Panjiar and Shrestha, eds, *The Kings of Nepal*.

43 The Nawabs of Bengal and the East India Company sent military expeditions in 1763 and 1767. Led by generals Gurgin Khan and one Captain Kinloch respectively, both expeditions were repelled by Gorkhali forces. Captain Kinloch, however, remained in the Tarai districts of Bara, Parsa and Rautahat for over three years. See D. R. Regmi, *Modern Nepal*, vol. 1, 161–6; Raj, *Expedition to the Nepal Valley: The Journal of Captain Kinloch Related to the Nepal Expedition August 26 – October 17, 1767*; "An Account of the Origins, Progress and Termination of Captain Kinloch's Expedition to Napaul, 1767," Memorandum Containing Minutes and Dispatches

by Governor-Generals, Item 1, Foreign Miscellaneous, no. 8, NAI. This second account also mentions the fact that the raja of Gorkha had claimed the *zamindari* of Bettiah as belonging to his family, though under what circumstances remains unclear.

44 D. R. Regmi notes that the Tauter *parganas* were Sarlahi and Rautahat, but gives no evidence. See Regmi, *Modern Nepal*, vol. 1, 195. For more scattered information on the Tauter *parganas* see the following: Letter of J. Kieghly, Collector of Tirhut to the CCRP, 14 February 1772, in Proceedings of the Comptrolling Council of Revenue at Patna (CCRP) Procs, vol. 3, 79, WBSA; Qeyamuddin Ahmad, "Early Anglo-Nepalese Relations with Particular Reference to the Principality of the Raja of Makwanpur," 17–26; Kumar Pradhan, *The Gorkha Conquests*, 72, 77 and 83; and Regmi, *Modern Nepal*, 183, 186, 193, 195, 197 and 249–50. Gorkhali records refer to *pargana* Tauter as "*praganna* Thathar."

45 See "Diwan Raja Shitab Roy's Account of Pergunnah Tauter Belonging to Sirkar Tirhut of Bihar Province," 30 July 1771, CCRP, vol. 1, 1 January 1771 to 30 July 1771, WBSA.

46 Ajay Skaria provides evidence of similar tendencies in the Dang highlands, which the British ultimately resolved through the deployment of boundary surveys and demarcation in the nineteenth century. See Skaria, *Hybrid Histories: Forests, Frontiers, and Wildness in Western India*, 165–75.

47 Simraon was an old *pargana* that was the site of the ancient fortress of Simraongarh. It also finds mention in the sixteenth-century work of Abul Fazl, the *Ain-i-Akbari*. See Jarrett, *Ain-i-Akbari of Abul Fazl-i-Allami*, vol. 2 (Calcutta, 1949), 167. The name "Simraon" might have been derived from the Bhojpuri word "*simr*" which stands for the *simal* tree (*Bombax malabaricum*) found in the area. See Koirala, "Senvamshi Rajaharuko Itihasik Paricharcha ra Purvi Pahadka Kehi Brahman Vamsha," 22. See also, Miscellaneous Extracts from Dr Buchanan's Travels, Eur. Mss D639, 19–26, IOR, APAC, BL. *Pargana* Simraon may have disintegrated into its two constituent *tappas* in the eighteenth century. See deposition of Girdhari Lal *quanungo* of *pargana* Simraon, witness no. 5, Table 10, Appendix 2, in Michael, "Separating the Yam from the Boulder," 544. While Company records use the term "*pargana* Simraon," Gorkhali records mention "*praganna* Gadh Simraon." For convenience I will use "*pargana*" instead of "*praganna*."

48 The original grant was instituted to reward Ali Quli Khan's services. As the *amil* of Tirhut, he had assisted the raja of Makwanpur when he was attacked by one Kanak Singh, the *diwan* of _____(illegible). At this time Hem Karna Sen had also sought assistance from Dhrub Singh, the raja of Bettiah, who refused his request. Ali Quli Khan raised 20,000 men and rendered valuable assistance to Hem Karna Sen. Hem Karna then came down to Bara and conferred this grant to Ali Quli Khan. See Procs of the Governor-General-in-Council in Bengal (PGGCB), 28 September 1781, Consl. 1–3, WBSA.

49 PGGCB, 28 September 1781, Consl. 2, WBSA. The tenor of the grant clearly suggests that Hem Karna Sen's grant was free from revenue obligations and inheritable – a *bekh birta* grant.

50 Bir Kishor would continue to claim this *tappa* until his death in 1816, 33 years after it had been formally handed over to Gorkha by the East India Company. See Bir Kishor Singh's *arzi* to Lt. Colonel Paris Bradshaw of 24 August 1816 in FS Procs, August 24 1816, no. 18, NAI.

51 Series of letters and papers with Persian secretary John Monckton's report on them relating to the Anglo–Gorkha border disputes in Champaran, in FP Procs, 4 March 1814, Consl. 53–65, 195–434, NAI. Hereafter, these papers will be referred to as the "Monckton Report." See also, Report of Jonathan Duncan, Preparer of Reports in the Revenue Department, dated 6 October 1783, in PGGCB (Revenue Department), 11 November 1783, no. 55, 2350–63, WBSA. Hereafter, these papers will be referred to as the "Duncan Report." Witnesses produced by the Bettiah raja Bir Kishor Singh to stake his claim to the proprietorship of Rautahat would assert that the Beg was a dependent *jagirdar* of his (Bir Kishor's) father, raja Jugal Kishor, who ultimately dismissed the Beg. See testimonies of Sheikh Ziauddin and Har Lal Singh, witnesses nos. 9 and 12, Monckton Report.

52 The circumstances under which Jugal Kishor obtained Rautahat remain unclear.

53 These *parwanas* were issued by Mir Jafar, *nawab* of Bengal in 1765. Mir Jafar's *parwana* also addressed Jugal Kishor Singh, the Bettiah raja, asking him to reinstate Ali Quli Khan's family.

The other *parwanas* were issued by one Saif-ul-mulk-Saif-ud-daula-Saiyid Najibat Ali Khan Bahadur Shehamat Jang (probably the son of Mir Jafar and *nawab* of Bengal from 1766–1770) in 1765, *maharaja* Shitab Rai, *diwan* at Patna, in 1770, and Edward Golding, English Supervisor at Saran, in 1770. *Tappa* Rautahat was detached from the *suba* of Bihar in 1765 and the *taraf* Pachrauta was separated the following year, in 1766. See the *Duncan Report*; the *Monckton Report*; PGGCB, 28 September 1781, Consl. 1–3, WBSA; PGGCB, 1781 Press List Index, vol. 9, 6 March–18 December 1781, 111–12, WBSA.

54 See "List of the villages in the Tuppeh of Nunnour, Purgunnah Simraon, Surcar Chumparun as taken from a document under the seal of Cazee Noorulhuk, 1173 Fuslee, being 48 years old," in Paris Bradshaw, political agent on the Nepal frontier, FP Procs, 25 March 1814, 625–31, NAI. Bradshaw gives the names of only nine villages, leaving the tenth one unknown.

55 The actual date is uncertain, but in 1813 *kaji* Randip Singh and *sardar* Parshuram Thapa noted that following Makwanpur's conquest by Gorkha in 1762, Mirza Abdulla Beg the *"jagirdar"* of Rautahat got his *jagir* confirmed by authorities at Kathmandu. See Monckton Papers, 272–4.

56 Deposition of Tharu leader Bikha Chaudhari, witness no. 1, Monckton Report, 1814. Bikha interestingly notes that between 1766–70 Gorkhali officials like *subba* Shivanand Upadhyaya and *fauzdar* Prajapat Updhyaya collected revenue from these parts. Mirza Abdulla Beg is referred to as the *jagirdar* (and not *birtadar*) of Rautahat from 1770–82.

57 See Deposition of Sheikh Ziauddin, *malguzar* of Mahsoonda – witness produced by the Bettiah raja Bir Kishor Singh in the Monckton Report, 1814. Sheikh Ziauddin would assert that Dinanath Upadhyaya had bribed one Mohammad Hashim the *mokhtar* (agent) of Mirza Abdulla Beg with a promise of five villages. While this statement is difficult to ascertain, such practices were frequently pursued when making fiscal arrangements.

58 The Gorkhali state was never a unified entity, including its ruling elite in Kathmandu. There is evidence to suggest that there were at least two competing factions in Kathmandu jockeying for control during this period, their spokesmen being Dinanath Upadhyaya and one Bhavnanni Shah (an agent of Regent Bahadur Shah, and a brother of Prithvinarayan Shah). In the 1780s, the three main issues that needed to be resolved with the East India Company were Gorkha's claims over the dependent *tappas* of the Fort of Someshwar, the disputed status of *tappa* Rautahat and *taraf* Pachuauta, and the surrender of the Makwani Prince living in the Company's territories. See letter from raja Ran Bahadur Shah to Bahadur Shah, January 1782, Historical Letters, Kausi Tosakhana Collection, no. 91, NAN; and letter from Ran Bahadur Shah to Bahadur Shah, March 1783, Historical Letters, Kausi Tosakhana Collection, no. 86, NAN.

59 See John Young, acting magistrate of Saran district, to W. Leycester, magistrate of Saran; and Leycester to N. B. Edmonstone, and Edmonstone to Leycester, in FP Procs, 4 September 1812, nos. 50, 51 and 52, NAI.

60 Deposition of Tharu leader Bikha Chaudhari, witness no. 1, Monckton Report, 1814.

61 For details see PGGCB (Revenue Department), Procs, 3 June, 1783, nos. 1–7, WBSA.

62 See letter of raja Ran Bahadur Shah to Bahadur Shah, March 1783, Historical Letters, Kausi Tosakhana Collection, no. 85, NAN. That the retention of Rautahat was an issue of honor for the Gorkhalis is apparent from the statements of the English explorer George Foxcroft, who traveled through the area in 1783. Foxcroft observed that Rautahat had assumed great significance for the "Nepaulians," and their loss of it might have been a great blow to Gorkha's territorial rights by way of conquest. See letter of George Foxcroft to Warren Hastings, governor general of Bengal, 13 May 1783, PGGCB (Revenue Department), 3 June 1783, no. 1, WBSA. I have not come across any further evidence that might clarify this issue.

63 See PGGCB (Revenue Department) Procs, 3 June 1783, nos. 1–7, WBSA.

64 To give weight to their claim, a Gorkhali *vakil* Dinanath Upadhyaya was sent on a mission to Calcutta. The *vakil* met Warren Hastings at Patna and promised him Gorkhali assistance in his ongoing efforts to quell a major rebellion by raja Chait Singh of Banaras. This seems to have created a favorable impression on Hastings, if the Gorkhali version of this encounter is to be believed. See *PRNW* 2: 371.

65 PGGCB (Revenue Department), 11 November 1783, no. 56, WBSA (emphasis added).
66 What became of Mirza Abdulla Beg is not known. In 1801, Girbana Juddha Bikram Shah, the raja of Gorkha, is recorded as having given instructions to Beghuwa Khawas and Damodar Jaisi (who were probably officers based in the Saptari-Mahottari area) to present an elephant as a gift to one Mirza Abdulla Beg. It is unclear if this Mirza Abdulla Beg was the former "*jagirdar*" of Rautahat. See RRC 24: 127.
67 Laxman Giri was appointed *subba* in 1809, after he was awarded a five-year *ijara* for *tappa* Rautahat (see "Ijara granted to Laxman Giri for revenue collection in Rautahat, 1809 CE [1866 BS], RRC 40: 54–58). In 1811 he was ordered to check disturbances in *tappa* Rautahat involving the followers of the raja of Bettiah (see "*subba* Laxman Giri deputed to Rautahat to check disturbances, Baisakh 6, 1868, 1811 CE [1868 BS]," RRC 40: 194). A few days later he was also asked to take over the *mauzas* of Dumriya and Padari (?) in *tappa* Rautahat and *tappa* Cherbanta in *zilla* Bara (see "*gosain* Laxman Giri authorized to collect revenue in Dumriya and elsewhere in Rautahat, Baisakh 11, 1868, 1811 CE [1868 BS]," RRC 40: 221). He then built a fort at the village of Kewyya and initiated a number of armed attacks on the villages belonging to the Bettiah raja. He was killed on 19 June 1811 by the Bettiah raja's followers, who decapitated his body and sent the head to Bettiah (see Monckton Report). The death of Laxman Giri then resulted in a Gorkhali investigation of the affair. This was led by *sardar* Ranjang Bania, *subba* Bal Bhanjan Pande, *guru* Ranganath Pandit, *kaji* Ranoddip Singh and *sardar* Parsuram Thapa. See deposition of Durga Chaudhari, Gorkhali witness no. 6, Monckton Report.
68 See "Report on the inquiry into the disputes between the Nepaulese and the raja of Bettiah concerning the lands on the frontier of Zillah Sarun in the dominions of the Honourable Company," in FS Procs, 26 March 1813, Consl. no. 36, NAI; letter of John Young to Henry Douglas, in Extracts from Procs of Government, 9 and 16 July, 13 August, 26 November and 31 December, FS Consl. 13 March 1812, no. 41, NAI (hereafter the "Young Report"); and series of dispatches between Lt Col. Paris Bradshaw, the government at Calcutta and the Gorkhali border commissioners, in FP Procs, 25 March 1814, nos. 25–34, 547–635, NAI (hereafter the "Bradshaw Report"). Details about the Monckton report can be found in endnote 51.
69 In 1803, one Mahadev Upadhyaya was deputed to the "*parganas*" of Rautahat, Bara and Sarlahi – term used is "*bara sarlahipar*"? – to investigate the dispute over 20 villages with *moglan*. He was instructed to examine the old boundary. See "Orders to Mahadev Upadhyaya to investigate border dispute with *moglan*, 1803 CE [1860 BS]," RRC 5: 421, no. 900; "*sardar* Gaj Singh Khatri deputed to resolve border dispute in village of Jasmanpur, 1810 CE [1867 BS]," *RRSRRS* vol. 16, no. 6 (1984): 81; "subbas and other officials of Bara-Parsa and Rautahat directed to provide necessary help to Ramjit Bhandari and Mir Munshi Raza Khan in settling Border Disputes, 1810 CE [1867 BS]," RRC 39: 165; and "*sardar* Gaj Singh Khatri ordered to proceed to Vijaypur after resolving border disputes in Jasmatpur, 1811 CE [1868 BS]," RRC 41: 41. In 1817, after the war, *sardar* Balabhanjan Pande and others were directed to demarcate the India–Nepal boundary. He was assisted in this task by Ranganath Pandit and his brother Sri Krishan Pandit. See RRC 36: 394.
70 For fuller details see, for instance, Table 12, Appendix 2, "The twenty-two villages on the interface of *tappas* Rautahat and Nannor, *pargana* (Gadh) Simraon," in Michael, *Separating the Yam from the Boulder: Statemaking, Space, and the Causes of the Anglo–Gorkha War of 1814–1816*.
71 In the neighboring district of Tirhut, 63 villages were subject to a dispute between the two states. See Report of C. I. Sealy, magst. of Tirhut, to John Adam, secretary to government at Fort William, FS Consl. 16 August 1814, no. 20, NAI.
72 See Paris Bradshaw to J. Adam in FP Procs, 25 March 1814, Consl. no. 33, 618–33, NAI.
73 More details about these disputes as well as statements of witnesses can be found in Michael, *Separating the Yam from the Boulder*, 536–48.
74 The collecting agents were: Gorkhali officials (1766–70; 1782–85), Mirza Abdulla Beg (1770–82), and Bir Kishor Singh and the raja of Bettiah (1790 onwards). The dates are as given by Bikha Chaudhari, and even though they might be speculative, they do clearly indicate that between

1743 and 1814, the collection of revenue on the Champaran–Tarriani frontier was never resolved in favor of one party for any length of time. See Michael, *Separating the Yam from the Boulder,* 544.
75 See Bassun Raut's deposition, witness no. 4, Table 10, Appendix 2, op. cit.
76 In theory, *nankar* grants could be resumed by the granting authority on the abolition of the office or the dismissal of the office-holder. And since the Gorkhalis had assumed the territorial rights of Makwanpur by virtue of conquest, they had the right to do this. This resumption was undertaken even after Shivnath Singh's *nankar* tenure had been confirmed by the local *ijaradar*, Dal Mardan Shah, in 1786. For more details see *RRS* 20 (1988): 1.
77 See the Young and Monckton Reports.
78 See letter of J. Lumsden, Coll. of Saran to Governor-General in Council, 9 May 1793, BOR Procs, 13 May to 22 May 1793, BSA.
79 Bounra and Bounree lay in *tappa* Bulthur, *pargana* Majhowa, *sarkar* Champaran, while Tehoki, Jaimangalpur and Boodgaon lay in *pargana* Naurangiya, in the Gorkhali district of Parsa. The Bounra-Bounree vs. Tehoki village disputes revolved around the right to control certain *pynes* (water channels). The village of Ghewra lay along the boundary of *tappa* Rautahat and Nannor and was originally given on an *ijara* contract by the Gorkhali raja to Gosain Hait Giri in 1799. For details see "Evidence provided by Hait Giri, former zamindar of Ghewra," 6 July 1814, in FP Procs, 26 July 1814, nos. 69–70, 508–18, NAI. See also Dispatch from P. Bradshaw to J. Adam, 6 July 1814, KRR, microfilm reel IOR 2, Part 2, 35–8, NAN.
80 In fact, so frequent were these territorial disputes that Bikha Chaudhary, a Tharu magnate, noted that Gorkhali *subbas* spent most of their time in the Tarai, settling border disputes. Most of this took place during the winter months of the year (October–March) when the Tarai was relatively malaria free. See deposition of Bikha Chaudhari, witness no. 1, Monckton Report.

Chapter 4. The Gorakhpur–Butwal Frontier

1 See translation of a letter from the raja of Gorkha to the governor-general, FS Procs, 16 August 1814, no. 16, NAI.
2 In 1803, the Company acquired further territories around Delhi following the defeat of the Marathas. Together, these districts were referred to as the Ceded and Conquered districts. For more details see Chapter 2, endnote 10.
3 Useful accounts of Awadh's emergence from Mughal dominion to regional autonomy and eventual decline during the colonial period can be found in the following works: Alam, *The Crisis of Empire in Mughal North India*; Barnett, *North India Between Empires: Awadh, the Mughals, and the British, 1720–1801*; Fisher, *A Clash of Cultures*; Mann, *British Rule on Indian Soil: North India in the First Half of the Nineteenth Century*, 22–53; and Pemble, *The Raj, The Indian Mutiny, and the Kingdom of Oudh, 1801–1859*. For studies on early British rule in the Ceded and Conquered Districts see Brodkin, "British India and the Abuses of Power: Rohilkhand Under Early Company Rule," 129–56; Gupta, *Agrarian Relations and Early British Rule in India: A Case Study of Ceded and Conquered Provinces (Uttar Pradesh) 1801–1833*; and Rosselli, "Theory and Practice in North India," 134–63.
4 Cited in Mann, "A Permanent Settlement for the Ceded and Conquered Provinces: Revenue Administration in North India," 260.
5 See letter from John Routledge, Collector of Gorakhpur to Charles Boddam, Collector of Saran, 5 March 1803, Letters Issued Register, GCR, basta 16, vol. 2, RSA.
6 See letter from A. Ross, acting Coll. to Graeme Mercer, secretary to affairs of Ceded Provinces, 30 April 1803, in Letters Issued Register, GCR, basta 16, vol. 2, RSA. Under *kham* management, the Company issued *nagadi pattas* (registration deeds confirming revenue engagement and its payment in cash) directly to the cultivators, while the Palpali raja was given an allowance (*malikana*) of Rps 4000. See translation of proceedings of April 1817, Gorakhpur Collectorate, Letters Issued Register, GCR, basta 17, vol. 122, RSA. Further details about these proceedings can also be found in the letter of Thomas Balfour, Coll. of Gorakhpur to BOR, 20 April 1807, Letters Issued Register, GCR, basta 16, vol. 116, 522–3, RSA.

7   See letter from Capt. W. Knox to governor-general, FS Consl., 30 June 1802, no. 4, NAI. I am not sure what became of this request. The *nawab* of Awadh too tried to secure the Company's assistance in clearing these arrears. See "Extract from the Proceedings of the Secret Department," 23 October 1806, Letters Received from BOR, GCR, basta 1, vol. 7, RSA. See also letter of BOR to A. Ross, Coll. of Gorakhpur, 20 August 1804, Letters Received Register (10 September 1804–2 April 1805), GCR, basta 1, vol. 4, RSA.
8   Sometime in 1804, *kaji* Amar Singh Thapa, the father of Gorkhali prime minister Bhim Sen Thapa, was given charge of the newly occupied Palpali territories. It is generally held that the Palpali raja was executed as part of a planned campaign of retributions unleashed by Gorkha's prime minister Bhim Sen Thapa following the assassination of the former raja, Ran Bahadur Shah, in 1806. For details surrounding Ran Bahadur's assassination, see Regmi, *Modern Nepal*, 2:162–74. See also letter of Gribana Juddha Bikram Shah, raja of Gorkha, to Ran Bhim Shah, 1806, in Naraharinatha, *Ithihasaprakashma Sandhipatrasamgraha*, 410–11.
9   *Kaji* Amar Singh Thapa was the father of Gorkhali prime minister Bhim Sen Thapa.
10 See Bishnu Prasad Ghimire, *Palpa Rajyako Itihas*, 59, 60, 235 and 249; and "Order authorizing Ram Chander Tiwari to reclaim waste lands in Palhi, 1811 CE [1868 BS]," RRC 41: 36. One Mahadev Upadhyaya was appointed as *subba* in the Butwal Tarai while former Palpali officials like Maniraj Bhaju and Shiv Buksh were appointed *fauzdar* and custom master at Butwal. See Boards Collections, F/4/185, vol. 2, 326, IOR, APAC, BL; and translation of a letter from Amar Singh Thapa to Roy Bhawani Sahye, the *daroga* [in-charge] of police in *pargana* Tilpur-Binayakpur, 10 July, 1804, Boards Collections, F/4/185, 477–80, IOR, APAC, BL. Some Palpali documents can be found in Krauskopf, Panjiar, and Shrestha, eds, *The Kings of Nepal and the Tharu of the Tarai*. See especially documents 37, 38, 44 and 45.
11 There exists a considerable body of literature that has examined the role of Hindu temples in the political life of kingdoms and communities. See "Chapter 9: Temples and Society," in Dirks, *The Hollow Crown*; Appadurai and Breckenridge, "The South Indian Temple: Authority, Honor and Redistribution,"187–211; and Stein, *South Indian Temples: An Analytic Reconsideration*, 61–2.
12 According to these terms, for the first three years no tax was levied. The lands were to be measured in the fourth year of their cultivation, and the government's share of the produce was gradually raised until it was fixed in the fifth year. The Tharu *muquaddams* (headmen) were allowed to keep one-third of the *jama* (total revenue dues) as their *muquaddami* right. See petition from *sarkari quanungos*, no date, in letter from acting Collector, A. N. Forde, to H. Newnham, secretary to the Board of Commissioners, 16 May 1816, Letters Issued Register, GCR, basta 17, vol. 121, 203–19, RSA.
13 Cited in Buchanan-Hamilton, *An Account of the Kingdom of Nepal*, 179.
14 See D. Scott, acting magst. to G. Dowdeswell, 16 January 1812, in Letters Issued by Magst., GCR, basta 25, vol. 164, 149–51, RSA.
15 See Buchanan-Hamilton, The Gorakhpur Report, vol. 1, ch. 4, 98–243, Eur. Mss D91, IOR, APAC, BL (hereafter The Gorakhpur Report). The "Trookia" Muslims cultivated most of the lands lying to the north of *pargana* Bansi. See Meena Bhargava, *State, Society and Ecology, 1750–1830*, 124–8.
16 See "History of Gorakhpur," compiled by Mufti Ghulam Hazrat, law officer and Sudder Ameen, 1810. Islamic Oriental Manuscript, I.O. 4540, 27–8, OIOC/BL. While Huzrut refers to those who have no sharers in the property as Absolute Proprietors, I will discuss them under the name of "rajas" in the paragraphs that follow.
17 See Thomas Balfour, Coll. to BOR, 30 April 1807, BOR Procs, Fort William, 19 May 1807, no. 21 and enclosures, UPSA.
18 The term "*taluq*" literally signifies dependence on or connection with something – here a proprietary right enjoyed by an individual. Khwaja Yasin's eighteenth-century glossary notes that a *taluq* could not be comprised of any units larger than villages. Yasin also notes that people who secured land through imperial *sanad* were called *zamindars*, whereas those who purchased it, or got it through usurpation, were called *taluqdars*. In the eighteenth century they

constituted a growing body of influential landholders in Awadh. For details about Khwaja Yasin's eighteenth-century glossary, see Mahmud, *An Eighteenth Century Manual: Yasin's Dastur-i-Malguzari*, no. 121, 160–61. For a discussion of the origins of the *taluqdari* system see Metcalf, *Land, Landlords and the British Raj: Northern India in the Nineteenth Century*, 3–43; Jafri, "Origins and Growth of *Taa'alluqadari* Tenures in Awadh," 73–82; and also Rizvi, "Srinet Zamindars of Sarkar Gorakhpur under the Mughals," 35–41.

19 For details see Bhargava, *State, Society*, 128–37. Where such rights and privileges had been conferred not by the *nawabs* of Awadh (who Company officials recognized as the only sovereign authority in Awadh) but by local officials, such entitlements were then declared to be illegal and void. See Bhargava, *State, Society*, 140.

20 Mufti Ghulam Hazrat noted the presence of as many as six types of *birtias*. Cited in Huzrut, *History of Gorakhpur*, 27–8.

21 For example, in 1810, raja Sarabjit Singh of Bansi made a number of *jiwan birt* grants to his illegitimate sons in the northern *tappas* of Khajahani and Dhebrua (*pargana* Ratanpur Bansi) along the Gorakhpur–Butwal frontier (cited in Bhargava, *State, Society*, 143). A *jiwan birt* was given as an *appanage* – an allowance usually granted to younger members of the grantor's family in perpetuity.

22 For more details on the *birtias* see Michael, *Separating the Yam from the Boulder*, Appendix 3; Bhargava, *State, Society*, 144–7, and "Perception," 215–37. See also *Report on Settlement of Gorakhpur: Basti District*, vol. 1, 53–4.

23 Cited in Martin, Coll. Gorakhpur to R. M. Tilghman, BOR Patna, 21 October 1822, GDR, basta 8, vol. 63, 175–99, RSA; and petition from *sarkari quanungoes*, n.d., ibid., 203–19.

24 The *maafidars* enjoyed absolute rights over the produce of their lands, including the proceeds of bazaars. The *nawabs* also relinquished one-quarter of the *sair* (custom) and other *zamindari* dues including *jalkar* and *bankar* (cesses on water and forest produce, respectively) in favor of the grantee. Cited in Bhargava, *State and Society*, 181–2.

25 The *nawabs* of Awadh had come to the early realization that they could not afford to alienate this powerful class of landed interests, and therefore made every attempt to co-opt them into the framework of the kingdom as allies. For rich details about the role of rent-free landholders in Awadhi statemaking see Alam, *The Crisis of Empire*; Bhargava, *State, Society*, 177–83; and Bhargava, "Madad-i-mash and Maafi Grants in Gorakhpur During the late Eighteenth and early Nineteenth Century," PIHC, Session 52, 338–44.

26 See Alam, *The Crisis of Empire*, 22–34, 313.

27 Bhargava, *State and Society*, 182. Over time, the Company would take steps to initiate large-scale resumption of rent-free lands, with the largest resumptions taking place in Gorakhpur by 1840. For details see Metcalfe, *Land and Landlord*, 68–71.

28 While the Company's records contain detailed information, they are subject to error given the scant information its officials possessed about the lands lying along this frontier. Thus, the conclusions that can be drawn are only indicative of broad trends rather than disaggregating specific aspects of these trends.

29 Michael, *Separating the Yam from the Boulder*, Appendix 3, Table 19.

30 The Palpali rulers during this period were Mahadat Sen (1782–93) and his son Prithvipal Sen (1793–1806 AD).

31 I have gathered this information from the following sources: "Statement of the Assets of Bootwul in Year 1212 *fasli* (1804 CE)," Letters Issued Register, GCR, basta 16, vol. 4, 17 July 1805, 158–62, RSA; "Statement exhibiting the resources in the year 1212 *fasli* (1804 CE) of each of the three divisions comprising the pargana of Binayakpur," Letters Issued Register, GCR, basta 16, vol. 4, October 1805, 294–96, RSA; and "Reports and Observations of the Company's Political Agent on the Gorkha frontier," Lt. Col. Paris Bradshaw, following his meetings with Gorkhali commissioners, April–May 1813, FP Procs, 18 June 1813, nos. 18–24, NAI. For more specific details on these matters see Michael, *Separating the Yam from the Boulder*, Appendix 3, Table 20, 552. See also Tables 19 and 21–3.

32 See A. Ross, acting Collector of Gorakhpur to BOR, 16 September 1805, Letters Issued Register, GCR, basta 16, volume 4, 245, para. 6, RSA.
33 See A. Ross, Coll. of Gorakhpur to Board of Commissioners, 17 July 1805, in Procs of Board of Commissioners of Ceded and Conquered Provinces, 31 July 1810, no. 31a, UPSA; G. Dowdeswell, secretary to government to Board of Commissioners, Ceded and Conquered Provinces, 30 October 1810, Letters Received from Government to Board of Commissioners, 1810–16, Procs of the Board of Commissioners (Pre-Mutiny Series), UPSA.
34 See "Memorial Relative to the District of Gorakhpur," by P. Warden Grant, surveyor and joint commissioner on the frontier, March 10 1821, GDR, basta 2, vol. 15, 66–113. RSA.
35 See "Translation of Proceedings of April 1817", Gorakhpur Collectorate, Letters Issued Register, GCR, basta 17, vol. 122, RSA.
36 See Encroachments of the Nepaulese, Boards Collections, F/4/422, no. 10381, 293–382 (see especially 378), IOR, APAC, BL.
37 This did not always work, as Gorkhali commanders in these areas wielded considerable autonomy in deciding such cases. In some instances, Gorkhali governors, *bhardars* and military commanders in Kumaon were known to grant land (often waste) under different tenures, independent of Kathmandu's authority, to various individuals in lieu of some service. See Lt. Gen. Sir David Ochterlony to John Adam, secretary to government, 7 February 1816, FS Consl., 17 February 1816, no. 1, NAI.
38 This is clear from the arguments of Gorkhali commissioners like Gaj Singh Khatri and the depositions of Gorkhali witnesses in the 1813 Anglo–Gorkha border investigations. See "Reports and Observations made by Paris Bradshaw the Company's Agent to the Anglo–Gorkha frontier," April–May 1813, FP Procs, 18 June 1813, nos. 18–24, NAI. Gaj Singh Khatri would clarify that the Gorkhali raja was claiming the *maafi* lands in "right of his feudal superiority." See Encroachments of the Nepaulese, Boards Collections, F/4/422, no. 10381, 293–382, IOR, APAC, BL. The quotation is from p. 298. Unfortunately, it is unclear as to when and by what act such a "feudal" authority was constituted, as this would enable us to better understand the *locus standi* of the Gorkhali commissioner's claim.
39 This argument seems very reminiscent of the arguments made a mere thirty years ago by Mirza Abdulla Beg when he sought to lay claim to the *tappa* of Rautahat (see Chapter 3). It might be recalled that, in that instance, the Gorkhalis had rejected the Beg's claims in 1783. However, in 1814, in a curious reversal, they argued on lines very similar to the Beg's in order to justify their claims to the lands of the Butwal Tarai.
40 Ibid. While the Gorkhalis admitted that the Palpali raja had received his lands from the *nawab* of Awadh, they were also claiming to be new overlords of Palpa. This probably took place sometime in 1787. See Encroachments of the Nepaulese, Boards Collections, F/4/422, no. 10381, 293–382, IOR, APAC, BL.

The Gorkhalis obtained the services of one Ram Nawaz, a former *quanungo* of *parganas* Tilpur and Binayakpur, to confirm these claims. In return, the Gorkhali commander at Palpa, Amar Singh Thapa requested Kathmandu to give Ram Nawaz some land on *jagir* terms. Later, Ram Nawaz would represent Gorkha's claims in the boundary investigations of 1813. See T. Balfour, Coll. of Gorakhpur to, BOR, 20 April 1807, Letters Issued Register, GCR, basta 16, vol. 116, 522–3, RSA. See *Shahkalin Chittipatra*, 6; and Michael, *Separating the Yam*, Table 29, Appendix 4, nos. 6 and 7, 569–70.
41 Cited in Alam, *The Crisis of Empire*, 213.
42 Within Gorakhpur, and after 1815, the Company attempted to remedy the situation by converting local functionaries such as the *patwari* and *quanungo* into state employees. However, this measure failed to eliminate the problem of maintaining reliable records. Bhargava, *State, Society,* 174–7.
43 Buchanan-Hamilton, The Gorakhpur Report, vol. 2, 79–81.
44 In the first two decades of the nineteenth century Company officials never knew the exact number of villages within their respective jurisdictions – waste or otherwise. Such kinds of information would emerge only after the first revenue surveys were conducted in the 1830s. These surveys would reveal the extent to which local cultures of governance had succeeded in

evading the tax claims of the state. In one instance, as many as 520 villages in the *pargana* of Hasanpur Maghar had been concealed from the eyes of the Company. See Hooper, *Final Report of the Settlement of the Basti District*, 46.

45 See, Memorial Relative to the District of Gorakhpur, by Lt. P. W. Grant, surveyor and joint commissioner on the frontier, March 10 1821, GDR, basta 2, vol. 15, 66–113, RSA.

46 See letter from Board of Commissioners to vice-president-in-council, Fort William 11 September 1809, GCR, basta 2, vol. 11, Letters Received Register, RSA. See also, R. M. Bird to J. Armstrong, Coll. of Gorakhpur, 18 June 1829, GCR, basta 6, vol. 43, 21–2, RSA.

47 See "Letters Received by Collector" (12 May 1802 – 25 June 1803), GCR, basta 1, vol. 1, letter no.31, RSA. Meena Bhargava feels that it was only by 1835 that the Company recognized their rights. In 1835, *birt* tenures were declared to be independent and transferable, and the *birtias* were considered to be proprietors of the village held by them. Settlements since 1835 were made with the *birtias* independent of their *zamindar* and *taluqdar* patrons. This must have seriously reconfigured tenurial relationships in Gorakhpur, because it would have reduced the authority, honor and status of the *zamindars* while elevating the status of the *birtias*, rendering them (theoretically at least) independent of the influence of the *zamindars*. See, Bhargava, *State, Society*, 148; "Perception", 228–31. How such older relations were reconfigured might have been determined loyalties towards the Company at the time of the outbreak of the revolt of 1857.

48 See letter from J. Carter, acting Coll., to Board of Commissioners, 22 January 1819, Letters Issued Register, GCR, basta17, vol. 122, 144–8, RSA. Pahalwan Singh was an illegitimate son of Sarabjit Singh, the raja of Bansi. The latter had granted these villages as a *jiwan birt* grant to Pahalwan Singh. Pahalwan Singh had then granted these villages to revenue collection officials (*chaudharis*) of Dhebrua in return for their services. See Bhargava, *State, Society*, 143.

49 The quotes belong to David Scott, acting magistrate of Gorakhpur. See letter from David Scott to M. H. Turnbull, registrar to the court of the Nizamat Adalat, Fort William, 11 March 1812, Letters Issued Register, GCR, basta 17, vol. 120, RSA.

50 Buchanan-Hamilton, The Gorakhpur Report, vol. 1, part 2, 10–11.

51 See report of W. Scott, resident at Lucknow, to governor-general's office, FS Consl., December 1800, no. 43, NAI. A copy of the Bettiah raja's petition to the Coll. of Gorakhpur was sent to Lal Ran Bahadur Sen, the brother of Palpali raja Prithvipal Sen. See letter from John Routledge, Coll. of Gorakhpur, to Charles Boddam, Coll. of Saran, 5 March 1803, Letters Issued Register, GCR, basta 16, vol. 2, RSA.

52 It appears that Moorid Beiji Sing's father was once in the employment of the raja of Butwal, where he was given the three villages for his support. When the Butwal rajas removed his father from his office, they also resumed these three villages. This was opposed by Moorid Beiji Sing[h], who even used force to obtain the restitution of these three villages. However, Survir Sen succeeded in killing Moorid Beiji Sing[h], and as a result the Satasi–Butwal raj feud intensified. See report of W. Scott, resident at Lucknow, to governor-general's office, FS Consl. December 1800, no. 43, NAI.

53 "Order regarding new villages settled by kaptan Chandra Bir Kunwar on bekh buniyad lands in Sheoraj, 1812 CE [1869 BS]," RRC 40:341.

54 Buchanan-Hamilton, The Gorakhpur Report, vol. 1, part 2, 10–11.

55 At the end of 1802, one Lt. Smyth was sent to survey the Gorakhpur area, including the *zamindari* of Butwal. See Letters Received by Collector (12 May 1802 – 25 June 1803), GCR, basta 1, vol. 1, letter no.31, RSA. In July 1804 unsuccessful efforts were made to determine the boundaries of the Butwal *zamindari* and its constituent *mahals* from the *kabuliyats* made by Lal Ran Bahadur Sen. See J. Ahmuty, magst. to A. Ross, acting Coll., 3 July 1804, Miscellaneous Revenue Letters Received, basta 12, vol. 89. 63, RSA.

56 *Jagera* lands were those lands whose income had not been alienated to agents like rajas, *kipat*, *birta* and *jagir* holders. That is, their income went directly into the central treasury (*kausi tosakhana*). See Regmi, *The State and Economic Surplus*, 135–7, 140.

57 For a general history of the Palpali raj see Bishnu Prasad Ghimire, *Palpa Rajyako Itihas*, parts 1 and 2; Buchanan-Hamilton, The Gorakhpur Report, vol. 1, 166–8; and R. C. Majumdar, "An Account of the Sena Kings of Nepal." For a genealogy of these kings see Rajvamshi, *Sena Vamsavali*.
58 See. Nevill, *Gorakhpur: A Gazetteer: A District Gazetteer of the United provinces of Agra and Awadh*, 179. Under Mukund Sen I, the Palpali kingdom reached its greatest extent, controlling the Tarai areas as far east as Morung. See Regmi, *Modern Nepal*, 60.
59 Buchanan-Hamilton, The Gorakhpur Report, Appendix, vol. 3, 29.
60 For details see Nevill, *Gorakhpur*, 180; Buchanan-Hamilton, *An Account of the Kingdom of Nepal*, 170–72. See also Buchanan-Hamilton, The Gorakhpur Report, vol. 1, 331–3.
61 Half of this was paid in cash and the other half in kind (such as musk, Tibetan cowtails, birds, animals and so on). One of Mahadat's sons, the lame Samar Bahadur, was even conferred the title "Nadir Shah" by the *nawab* of Awadh. Buchanan-Hamilton, The Gorakhpur Report, vol. 2, 143; Buchanan-Hamilton, *An Account of the Kingdom of Nepal*, 173. See also "An account of the several powers bordering on ours and the Viziers Dominions," Add Mss 29210, 89–95 (especially 90), Western Manuscripts, BL, Foreign Secret Proceedings, Consultation 43, December 1800, NAI.
62 Regmi, *Modern Nepal*, 1:314.
63 It is said that the Gorkhali ruler Prithvinarayan Shah deputed one *vakil* named Vaikuntha Upadhyaya to Awadh to meet the *nawab* Shujauddaulah in 1774, possibly to explore the merger of Palpa with Gorkha. See "Prithvinaryan Shah to *yogi* Bhagvanthanatha, 1774 AD" in Yogi Naraharinatha, *Ithihasprakashma*, 6–7. See also Tulasi Ram Vaidya, *Prithvinarayan Shah: The Founder of Modern Nepal*, 204.
64 Buchanan-Hamilton, The Gorakhpur Report, vol. 3, 32–3; Regmi, *Modern Nepal*, vol. 1, 313. See also Dinesh Raj Pant, "Sri Panch Ran Bahadur Shahka Nauwota Aprakashit Lal Mohar," 37–9; Ghimire, *Palpa Rajyako*, part 1, 96.
65 See "Translate of the Instructions to (the Gorkhali *vakil*) Chandrashekhar Upadhyaya prior to his departure to Calcutta," FS Procs, 6 June 1815, no. 78, NAI. See also Dinesh Raj Pant, "Ashrit Rajyaupar Bahadur Shahle Liyeko Niti," 51–5.
66 See, Buchanan-Hamilton, *An Account of the Kingdom of Nepal*, 173; and Mahesh Raj Pant, "Palpa's Relations with Awadh," *RRS* 5 (1973): 1–6. A Nepali version of this article can also be found – see Pant, "Palpa Rajyako Nepal Adhirajya ra Avadhsangha Sambandha," 1–8.
67 See Pant, "Ashrit Rajyaupar," 52.
68 See W. Scott to Governor-General Lord Wellesley, December 1800, FS Consl. 30 December 1800, no. 39, NAI.
69 Reports and observations of Major Paris Bradshaw on the negotiations and correspondence with the Gorkhali commissioners, April–May 1813, FP Procs, 18 June 1813, nos. 18–24, NAI.
70 See, Capt. W. Knox to secretary to government, FS Consl. 30 June 1802, nos. 48 and 49, NAI.
71 Prithvipal Sen was executed on the orders of the new prime minister Bhim Sen Thapa as part of his campaign of retributions following the assassination of the former Gorkhali king Ran Bahadur Shah in 1806. The Palpali heir to Prithvipal Sen was the young Ratan Sen, and he and his successors continued to live in Gorakhpur, unable to recover their kingdom. Under the British rule they do not seem to have prospered, and therefore it is not surprising to discover that when the Revolt of 1857 broke out, they participated on the side of the rebels – and lost everything when the British defeated them.
72 In July 1804, *kajis* Amar Singh Thapa and Dalabhanjan Pande informed the Company's *daroga* (in-charge) of police in the *parganas* of Tilpur and Binayakpur that they had received orders from the raja of Gorkha to take over the Butwal lowlands and honor Palpa's former obligations. One Mahadev Upadhyaya, the *subba* of the Butwal Tarai, was also deputed as *vakil* to Gorakhpur. See translation of a letter from *kajis* Amar Singh Thapa and Dalabhanjan Pande to Roy Bhawani Sahye, 10 July 1804, Boards Collections F/4/185, 477–80; and translation of a letter from *kajis* Amar Singh Thapa and Dalabhanjan Pande to Roy Bhawani Shaye, 26 July

1804, Boards Collections F/4/185, 535–39, IOR, APAC, BL. See also letter from *kajis* Amar Singh Thapa and Dalabhanjan Pande to the magistrate of Gorakhpur, received 2 September 1804, Boards Collections, F/4/185, vol. 2, 87–90, IOR, APAC, BL.
73 See letter from J. Adam, secretary to government, to Lt. Col. Paris Bradshaw, the Company's agent on the Anglo–Gorkha frontier, 13 January 1813, FP Procs, 15 January 1813, no. 46, NAI. It might be noted that the raja of Gorkha was not only claiming the Tarai territories of Palpa, but also those belonging to the hill kingdoms of Pyuthana, Argha, Khanchi and Gulmi as well.
74 See translation of a letter from the raja of Gorkha to the Governor-General, FS Procs, 16 August 1814, no. 16, NAI.
75 The Company had had not always held this position. At least until 1804, the Company had been willing to admit the Palpali kingdoms claims to lands lying within the district Gorakhpur. See Letter from John Fombelle, Secretary to Government in the Department of Ceded Provinces to BOR, 5 April 1804, Procs of Sadr BOR, Fort William, 10 April 1804, no. 25, UPSA. However, after the Anglo–Gorkha War ended in 1816 the Company would disallow such cross border territorial claims by other states.
76 The term *"dhungo"* is a metaphor for the state, which finds frequent reference in Gorkhali documents. My use of the terms "yams" and "boulders" draws inspiration from the Gorkhali raja Prithvinarayan Shah's statement comparing Nepal to a yam wedged between two boulders – India and China (*"uparant yo raje dui dhungako tarul jasto rahe cha"*). Cited in Naraharinatha and Acharya, eds, *Rashtrapita Shri Panch Badamaharaja Prithvinarayan Shah Dev ko Dibya Upadesh*, 15.
77 Metcalf, *Land, Landlords*, 24.
78 See "Statement regarding the resources in the year 1212 *fasli* (1804 AD) of each of the three divisions comprising the *pargana* of Binayakpur." Letters Issued Register, GCR, basta 16, vol. 4, October 1805, 294–6, RSA.
79 In the petition (*arzi*) from the Lal Ran Bahadur Sen, *diwan* of the Butwal raja, to Company officials Matka was described as as a *tappa*. See Extract from the Report of John Routledge, Coll. of Gorakhpur on the settlement of Butwal, 14 December 1802, in Letters Issued Register, GCR, basta 16, vol. 2, December 1802 – February 1804, RSA. Alexander Ross, acting Coll. of Gorakhpur, noted that Matka was comprised of 18 *tappas*. See A. Ross to BOR, 10 March 1804, Letters Issued Register, GCR, basta 16, vol. 3, RSA.
80 While the raja of Gulmi claimed that Matka was made up of 19 *tappas*, the Palpa raja asserted that the number was 18. See List of Tuppehs of Purgana Mutka, Received 14 March 1804, in Claim of the Nepaul Government to possess the Zamindarry of Butaul, Boards Collections, F/4/185, IOR, APAC, BL.
81 The raja of Gulmi further claimed that his family had held this *taluqa* for ten generations. See translation of an *arzi* from Shakti Prachand Shah, the minor raja of Gulmi, 17 January 1804, Boards Collections, F/4/185, 46–50, IOR, APAC, BL.
82 See translation of the deposition of Semnarayan, *quanungo* of Bansi, on 24 April 1804, Boards Collection, F/4/185, 256–60, IOR, APAC, BL.
83 See testimony of Kanak Niddhi Tiwari, *vakil* of the Palpa Raja, in A. Ross, Coll. of Gorakhpur, to BOR (with enclosures) 9 June 1804, Letters Issued Register, GCR, basta 16, vol. 3, 100–23, RSA. There is also a translation of a letter from Gorkhali *kaji* Amar Singh Thapa to Col. Ochterlony, 1807, confirming this in *PRNW* 1: 19.
84 The Palpali ruler, Mahadat Sen, met *nawab* Asafuddaulah – both exchanged turbans and the latter was conferred the title of "Brother." For details of this see "Questions put to Bandhu Khadka (?) *vakil* of the raja of Gulmi," in magistrates' Procs, of the Faujdari Court, Zilla Gorakhpur, 7 March 1804, Boards Collections, F/4/185, 207–20, IOR, APAC, BL.
85 Cited in *RRS* 3 (April 1971): 79.
86 Ibid. The Gulmi raja's sister Rajrajeshwari Devi was the eldest wife of the Gorkhali raja Ran Bahadur Shah. In 1799, she had accompanied Ran Bahadur to Benaras but later returned to Kathmandu in 1802 to assume the reins of government as the Regent. For details see Regmi, *Modern Nepal*, vol. 2, chapters 1–4.

87 The grant was made by raja Girbana Juddha Bikram Shah, the infant king of Gorkha, on 26 Bhadau 1860 BS (August–September 1803 CE). See translation of *sanad* from raja Girbana Juddha Bikram Shah of Gorkha to raja Shakti Prachand Shah of Gulmi, Boards Collections, F/4/185, 234–36, IOR, APAC, BL. The grant stated that the Tarai belonging to Baldyang *garhi* (fort) has always belonged to Gulmi and it is today being taken from Palpa to be restored to Gulmi. Cited in Rajaram Subedi, *Gulmiko Aitihasik Jhalak*, 127. See also A. Ross, Coll. of Gorakhpur to BOR, 2 April 1804, Procs of the Sadar BOR, Fort William, 17 April 1804, no. 4, UPSA; and petition (*arzi*) from Shakti Prachand Shah, the raja of Gulmi, 14 March 1804, Boards Collections, F/4/185, 226–32, IOR, APAC, BL.

88 See "Translation of an arzi from Lal Ran Bahadur Sen, brother of Prithvipal Sen, the raja of Butwal to the Gorakhpur Collector," in J. Fombelle to BOR, January 1804, Letters Received Register (30 June 1803–17 February 1804), GCR, basta 1, vol. 2, RSA; and Rajaram Subedi, *Gulmiko Itihasik Jhalak*, 57–8. For more details about the Gulmi–Butwal–Gorkha nexus see the following: J. Ahmuty, magst. of Gorakhpur, to J. Fombelle, secretary to government in the Department of the Ceded Provinces, 5 April 1804, Procs. of the Sadr BOR, Fort William, 10 April 1804, no. 25, UPSA; and translation of an *arzi* from Shitab Rai, *vakil* of Lal Ran Bahadur Sen, manager for Prithvipal Sen, the raja of Nepal, 26 December 1803, both in "Claim of the Nepaul Government to possess the zamindarry of Butwal," Boards Collections, F/4/185, 36–8, IOR, APAC, BL.

89 At least this is what the Palpali raja claimed. See translation of an *arzi* from Shakti Prachand Shah, raja of Gulmi, 25 May 1804, Boards Collections, F/4/185, 191–6, IOR, APAC, BL.

90 See BOR to A. Ross, Coll. of Gorakhpur, 20 August 1804, Letters Received Register (10 August 1804–2 April 1805), GCR, basta 1, vol. 4, RSA.

91 The Company also rejected an offer made in 1806 by Gorkhali military commander Amar Singh Thapa to farm the Butwal *zamindari*. Company officials felt there was no security and that the revenue engaged for with the Gorkhalis would never be realized. See N. B. Edmonstone, Secretary to Government, to J. Ahmuty, Coll. of Gorakhpur, 29 December 1806, Procs BOR for Ceded and Conquered Provinces, 31 July 1810, no. 31a, UPSA.

92 For a brief history of the Pyuthana kingdom, see Giri, *Pyuthana Rajyako Itihasik Jhalak*.

93 Regmi, *Modern Nepal*, vol. 1, 324; and Giri, *Pyuthana Rajyako*, 20.

94 Mahesh C. Regmi also mentions that tax assessments in Sheoraj, Banke and Bardia were based on "ox-team units," or the *halbandi* system. In 1800, in the *tappa* of Sheoraj, an assessment of Rs 5½ per plough was levied during the second year after any land had been brought under cultivation. This was raised to Rs 17 during the third and subsequent years. See Regmi, *A Study*, 81; and *The State and Economic Surplus: Production, Trade and Resource Mobilization in Early 19th Century Nepal*, 140. For information on the Ox-team mode of assessment, see Siddiqui, *Agrarian Change in a North Indian State: Uttar Pradesh, 1819–33*, 55–6.

95 The officials were Jasoghar Pant, Dashrath Tiyari and Dalel Singh. See Giri, *Pyuthana Rajyako*, 49.

96 Regmi, *Modern Nepal*, vol. 1, 11.

97 See Letter of Kirtibam of Parbat to Governor-General Warren Hastings, 15 February 1782, *CPC* vol. 5, no. 378.

98 See *CPC* vol. 9, no. 653; *CPC* vol. 9, no. 1737.

99 See "Governor-General-in-Council's Political Letter to the Court of Directors, 4 August 1791," paragraphs 68–79, in *Fort William India-House Correspondence, 1787–1791*, vol. 16, 397.

100 For details see Boards Collections F/4/422, no. 10381, p. 426, IOR, APAC, BL; BOR to A. Ross, Coll. of Gorakhpur, 20 August 1804, Letters Received Register (10 August 1804–2 April 1805), GCR, basta 1, vol. 4, RSA. The outstanding balances due from Sheoraj rose from Rs 2,656 in 1801–2 to Rs 7,650 in 1803. For details on the above see the following: A. Ross, Coll. of Gorakhpur, to BOR (with enclosures), 9 June 1804, Letters Issued Register, GCR, basta 16, vol. 3, 100–23, RSA; A. Ross, Coll. Gorakhpur, to BOR 8 November 1804, in Procs of the BOR, Fort William, 20 November 1804, no. 10, UPSA; and BOR to Coll. of Gorakhpur (extract from the Procs of the Secret Department), 23 October 1806, GCR, basta 1, vol. 7, RSA.

101 See for instance the following: "Order to local functionaries in Sheoraj regarding reclamation of waste lands, 1797 CE [1854 BS]," RRC 25: 346; "Jhungha Chaudhari, Mansukha Chaudhari and Santhokhi Chaudhari asked to make the *bandobast* for the *raiyat* to cultivate in '*pargana*' Sheoraj. Jhungha Chaudhari was also given the *kalabanjar mauza* of Maladeva (?) on a *jagir* basis, 1800 CE, [1857 BS]," RRC 24: 32; "Tax assessment rate applicable to the 4 *varnas* and 36 *jat* in '*pargana*' Sheoraj, *zilla* Pyuthana, 1800 CE [1857 BS]," RRC 24: 31; "Order regarding new villages settled by *kaptan* (captain) Chandra Bir Kunwar on *bekh buniyad* lands in Sheoraj, 1812 CE [1869 BS]," RRC 40: 341; "Chaudhari and Laskari Chaudhari are appointed *chaudharis* for the whole of Sheoraj. They were granted one *kalabanjar mauza* Shankarpur (?) in *praganna* Sheoraj as *jagir*, 1800 CE [1857 BS]," RRC 24: 32; "Birya Rokaya deputed to Sheoraj along with troops under his jurisdiction, 1797 CE [1854 BS]," RRC 25: 639; and "*Subedar* Parsu Ram transferred from Sheoraj to Gorkha to construct embankments on *sera* (crown) lands, 1797 CE [1854 BS]," RRC 25: 639.
102 *Chaudhrai* grant made to Jas Raj Chaudhari, from *pargana* Deokhori-Sheoraj, 1796 AD, poka 9, no. 8, serial no. 919, *Lagat Phant*, Kathmandu.
103 J. Ahmuty, Coll. of Gorakhpur, to N. B. Edmonstone, secretary to government, FS Consl. 16 January 1806, no. 106, para 2, NAI.
104 Alexander Ross, Coll. of Gorakhpur, to Charles Buller Secretary, BOR, 12 February 1805, in Letters Issued Register, GCR, basta 16, vol. 3, RSA; and ibid. in Proc BOR for Ceded and Conquered Provinces, Procs, 31 July 1810, no. 31a, UPSA.
105 Jurawan Chaudhari held 39 villages. The Gorkhali officials were *fauzdars* Maniraj Bhaju, Tarapeet Upadhyaya, *jemadar* (head constable) Lashkari Chaudhari and *mutsaddi* (writer) Shiv Baksh. At least two Rajput *zamindars*, Hanumant Singh and Pahalwan Singh, were also involved in these disputes. My information is derived from the following sources: J. Grant, Collector of Gorakhpur, to Board of Commissioners, 22 September 1811, Revenue Letters Issued Register, GCR, basta 17, vol. 18, RSA; D. Scott, acting magst. of Gorakhpur to G. Dowdeswell, Secretary to Government, 19 November 1811, Letters Issued Register, GCR, basta 25, vol. 164, 100–106, RSA; FP Consl. 17 January 1812, no. 46, NAI; and letter from J. Carter, acting Coll., to Board of Commissioners, 22 January 1819, Letters Issued Register, GCR, basta 17, vol. 122, 144–8, RSA.
106 The *fauzdar* was none other than Maniraj Bhaju. Maniraj, who also possessed certain villages in the Butwal Tarai on a *sir* tenure (those lands cultivated by a landholder or village zamindar directly or with hired labor). See "Translation of a report from Mirza Hussain Ali Beg, Tehsildar of pargana Tilpur," Benaiyakpur, 30 October 1814, cited in *PRNW* 1: 177.
107 D. Scott, acting magst. to George Dowdeswell, 16 January 1812, Letters Issued Register, GCR, basta 25, vol. 164, 149–51, RSA.
108 Some lands in Sheoraj were given to one Kunwar *sardar* (either Chandra Bir Kunwar or Bal Narsingh Kunwar, but more likely the former). See Ganapat Upadhyaya to Ujir Singh Thapa, Phalgun 9 (no year), in Shankarman Rajbamshi, ed., *Shahkalin Chittipatra Samgraha*, 79–85. Senior Gorkhali officials like Ranganath Pandit and Dalabhanjan Pande also held lands on or near the Gorakhpur–Butwal frontier. See translation of a letter from *budakaji* [elder *kaji*] Amar Singh Thapa to the raja of Gorkha, 12 April 1815, FS Procs, 16 May 1815, no. 61, NAI.
109 *Kaji* Amar Singh Thapa to Bhim Sen Thapa and Ran Dhwaj Thapa, April 1813, in Rajbamshi, *Shahkalin Chittipatra*, 6–8.
110 The actual term used is "*mamilat ma yeti yeti paisa diyako ho*" (ibid., 8). It probably means *muamalaat*, or pertaining to official affairs. The sense of the statement is probably that Sheoraj was included in the management of government affairs.
111 See *kaji* Amar Singh Thapa to *janral* [General] Bhim Sen Thapa, April 1813, *Bir Pustakalaya Itihasik Chittpatra Samgraha*, no. 400, NAN. During this time Gorkhali officials like Amar Singh Thapa had made unsuccessful attempts to obtain local records and even influence the course of the boundary investigations along Sheoraj. See the *kaji* Amar Singh Thapa to *janral* Bhim Sen Thapa and Ran Dhwaj Thapa, n.d. (probably 1813) *Bir Pustakalaya Itihasik Chittipatra Samgraha*, nos. 169 and 400, NAN.

112 See raja of Nepaul to governor-general, 4 May 1814 and 3 June 1814, in FS Consl. 23 June 1814, nos. 22 and 23, NAI.
113 See letter from the secretary of government to J. Ahmuty, judge and magistrate of Gorakhpur, 16 January 1806, FS Procs, 16 January 1806, no. 105, paragraphs 3 and 4, NAI.
114 After the Anglo–Gorkha War in 1816, a claim to the *tappa* of Sheoraj was put forward by one Soobah Lal Sahye, a relative of the raja of Pyuthana. His claims were denied after it was decided to return Sheoraj to the Gorkhalis. The Palpali royal family, headed by Rattan Sen and now residing in Gorakhpur, protested this handover. See petition of Soobah Lal Sahye, 9 January 1818, Letters Issued Register, GCR, basta 17, vol. 122, 189–90, RSA; and Boards Collections, F/4/550, no. 13378, 21, IOR, APAC, BL.
115 J. Fombelle, Secretary to Government to BOR, 5 April 1804, Procs, Of the BOR for the Ceded and Conqurered Provinces, 31 July 1810, no. 31b, UPSA.
116 Translation of the decision of the Amins deputed from Nepaul to Goolmee, received, in 1804, Boards Collections, F/4/185, 236–9, IOR, APAC, BL. However, the raja of Gulmi complained that the moment the *amins* departed, the Palpalis resumed their "oppressions," making forcible collections from the *tappas* of Bhatinpar, Bhandar and Majhar. See ibid., 226–32.
117 See "Reports and Observations submitted by Paris Bradshaw on the negotiations and correspondence with the Nepaulese Commissioners", April–May 1813, FP Procs, 18 June 1813, nos. 18–24, NAI. The petition of Suba Lal Sahye claiming the *tappa* of Sheoraj mentions that the *tappa* of Khajahani belonged to the districts of the Khanchi raj. See "Papers relating to the proposed grant of land to Soobah Lall Sahye," Boards Collections F/4/550, no. 13378, 21, IOR, APAC, BL.
118 In 1786, the Khanchi raja had granted a *guthi* (religious endowment) in *tappa* Khajhani, which was then attached to *pargana* Binayakpur. The rulers of Khanchi claimed the *tappas* of Khajahani, Chop and Gurhwa (?) in the Butwal Tarai. See RRC 4: 948–50.
119 See "Extract from John Routledge's Report on the Settlement of Butwal, 14 December 1802," in Letters Issued Register, December 1802 – February 1804, GCR, basta 16, vol. 2, RSA; and John Routledge to Lt. Governor-General and Board of Commissioners of the Ceded Districts, Boards Collections, F/4/185, 91–108, IOR, APAC, BL. For details pertaining to the *pargana* of Bansi see "Translation of Proceedings held in the Gorakhpur Kutcherry with other Reports," 25 July 1806 – 23 August 1806, Letters Issued Register, GCR, basta 16, vol. 116, 547–96, RSA.
120 See Buchanan-Hamilton, The Gorakhpur Report, vol. 2, 147–8. There is some confusion about the actual location of this *tappa*. Buchanan-Hamilton mentions that they were once separate *tappas* that had been combined by 1809. See Buchanan-Hamilton, The Gorakhpur Report, vol. 1, 324.

Chapter 5. The Disjointed Spaces of Precolonial Territorial Divisions

1 Perlin, "The Precolonial Indian State in History and Epistemology: A Reconstruction of Societal Formation in the Western Deccan from the 15th to the Early 19th Century," 290.
2 "A Memoir, Historical, Statistical and Military illustrative of a map of the Province of Bundelkhand including all the native states of that Province situated between the boundaries of the possessions of Daulat Row Scindia on the West and Baghelkhand on East," by Capt. J. Franklin, 1819–20, Memoirs of the Survey of India, SOIR, memoir no. 84, NAI.
3 Major Vans Agnew, *A Report on the Subah or Province of Chattisgarh Written in 1820 AD*, 45.
4 Mughal administrative divisions may have evolved from earlier divisions such as *vilayats*, *shiqs*, *iqtas*, and *khittas*. For more details see Siddiqi, "Evolution of the Vilayat, the Shiq and the Sarkar in Northern India," 10–32 (especially 19 and 26). A detailed account of the administrative divisions of the Mughal empire can be found in Abul Fazl's *Ain-i-Akbari*. See *Ain-i-Akbari*, trans. Jarrett, 219–420. During the reign of Emperor Shah Jahan (1638–58) a new division called the *chakla* was introduced, which was variously made up of *sarkars* or *parganas*. See Elliot, *Memoirs*, 1:80; Ahmad, "Meaning and Usage of Some Terms of Land Revenue Administration," 279; and Alam, *The Crisis of Empire*, 33, n40.

5 The term *"pargana"* may have been introduced into North India possibly as early as the fourteenth century. See Gordon and Richards, "Kinship and Pargana in Eighteenth Century Khandesh," 372. Elliot suggests that the term *pargana* means "tax paying land," and cites an inscription dated 1210 AD at Piplianagar in Bhopal as providing the earliest evidence of this division. See Elliot, *Memoirs on the History, Folklore and Distribution of Races of the North Western Provinces of India*, ed. Beames, vol. 1, 201–2.

6 For instance, in some parts of the northwest, a *tappa* could denote a tract that formed around one principal town or a large village and forming a sort of corporate body, although they were not identical in any other way. See. Grover, "'Raqba-Bandi' Documents of Akbar's Reign," 55–60. The term *tappa* – in the Gorakhpur area, at least – seems to have signified "a share or offshoot of some larger whole." See Alexander, *Statistical, Descriptive and Historical Account of the Gorakhpur District*, 278.

7 It is highly unlikely that these *dastur* were territorial units of some kind. See Habib, *The Agrarian System of Mughal India*, 2nd edition, 249, n57.

8 See Hasan, *Yasin's Glossary of Revenue Terms: Edition, English Translation, Annotation and Analysis*, 13. This has since been published as *An Eighteenth Century Agrarian Manual: Yasin's Dastur-i-Malguzari*.

9 See letter of J. Lumsden, Collector of Saran, to BOR, 20 April 1793, Letters sent to BOR Register, 13 February 1793–95 July 1793, District Record Room, Chapra, Saran District, Bihar.

10 For further details see Siddiqui, "The Classification of Villages under the Mughals," 72–83 and *Land Revenue Administration under the Mughal*, 9. See also Mahmud, *An Eighteenth Century Manual*, no. 121, 160–61.

11 They went by terms such as *"doabas"* (in Multan), *"visaya,"* *"mandals"* and *"desh"* (in Jodhpur), *"hobli"* and *"taraf"* (in parts of South India) and *"waziris,"* *"kothis,"* *"tikas,"* *"pathi"* and *"graons"* (in the Western Himalayas). For references to *doabas* see Moosvi, *The Economy of the Mughal Empire, c. 1595*, 14. References to Jodhpur's divisions can be found in Jagatvir Singh Agre, "Pargana Administration in Marwar under Maharaja Jaswant Singh (1638–1678 AD)." For *hobli* and other divisions in South India see Murton, "Key People in the Countryside: Decision-Makers in Interior Tamil Nadu in the Late Eighteenth Century," 157–80 (especially 165–6). Finally, for the western Himalayas see Singh, *Natural Premises: Ecology and Peasant Life in the Western Himalayas, 1800–1950*, 25–7 and 36.

12 Details pertaining to the Moreland-Saran debate can be found in Saran, *Provincial Government*, 70–71 and 81–101. Some like S. N. Sinha have accepted Moreland's position over Saran's views. See. Sinha, *The Subah of Allahabad under the Great Mughals*, 101–2.

13 For information on the *fauzdar* see the following: See Malik, "Problems of Fauzdari Jurisdiction in Baiswara," 211–5; Siddiqui, "The Fauzdar and Fauzdari under the Mughals," 22–35; Zilli, "Two Administrative Documents of Akbar's Reign," 367–73 (especially 368); Richards, *Document Forms for Official Orders of Appointment in the Mughal Empire*, 16, document nos. 218b and 220b; and Sinha, *Subah of Allahabad Under the Mughals*, 95–102. I am also grateful to Prof. Irfan Habib for sharing his views on the shifting boundaries of *fauzdari* jurisdictions in May 1998.

14 Gommans, "The Silent Frontier in Asia, c. CE 1100–1800," 1–24. The quotation is from p. 22.

15 Bayly calls this widespread tendency of eighteenth-century regimes to farm out revenue collection contracts the "commercialization of power." See Bayly, *Rulers, Townsmen, and Bazaars*, 460. For further details on the formation of districts in Awadh, and the joining of *ijara* and *fauzdari* rights, see Elliot, *Memoirs*, 2:108; Alam, *The Crisis of Empire*, 218, n45 and n48. Understanding the territorial implications of this "commercialization of power" merits further research.

16 See the following: Elliot, *Memoirs*; Ambashthya, *Beames' Contributions to the Political Geography of the Subahs of Awadh, Bihar, Bengal and Orissa in the Age of Akbar*; Blochmann, "Contributions to the Geography and History of Bengal," 209–44. See also Sarkar, *The India of Aurangzeb: Topographs, Statistics and Development Compared with the India of Akbar*, xlvii–xlviii; and Habib, *An Atlas of the*

Mughal Empire. Out of the 3,053 *mahals* recorded in the *Ain*, only 2,187 have been recorded in *An Atlas of the Mughal Empire*, leaving untraceable the remaining 866 *mahals* or *parganas* (*The Atlas*, xiv).

17 See Ambashthya, *Beames' Contributions*, 19–39. Beames examined a wide variety of sources to reconstruct the political geography of the Mughal Empire. These included *quanungo* papers, settlement reports and translations of the *Ain*, British gazetteers and the historical memories of the inhabitants.

18 In a number of these studies, *parganas* become the residence of dominant Rajput lineages while *tappas* become "secondary clan areas" For examples of such work see Kashi N. Singh, "The Territorial Basis of Medieval Town and Village Settlement in Eastern Uttar Pradesh, India," 203. See also the following: R. L. Singh and Ram Bali Singh, "Spatial Diffusion of Rajput Clan Settlements in a Part of Middle Ganga Valley"; R. L. Singh, "Evolution of Clan Territorial Units Through Land Occupance in the Middle Ganga Valley"; R. L. Singh and Rana P. B. Singh, "Some Approaches to the Morphogenesis of Indian Village," 128–46, 353–66 and 367–76, respectively; and Rana P. B. Singh, "Morphogenesis of the Cultural Landscape: The Case of the Saran Plain, India." For more recent work, see Fox, ed., *Realm and Region in Traditional India* and Sharma, "Social Configuration in the Three Parganas under British Rule," 81–6.

19 Gordon and Richards, "Kinship and Pargana in Eighteenth-Century Khandesh," 371–97. I thank Sanjay Subrahmanyam for directing my attention to this article.

20 Muzaffar Alam has already pointed this out for the case of Awadh in the seventeenth century. See Alam, *The Crisis of Empire*, 106–7.

21 See Grover, "Nature of the *Dehati-i-Taaluqa* (Zamindari Villages) and the Evolution of the *Taaluqdari* System During the Mughal Age," 258–89. The quotation is from p. 275.

22 Habib, *The Agrarian System*, 23n77 and n117.

23 Again, some instances of this would include attempts by local organizers of cultivation in 1790 to offer 8,500 *bighas* of Tarriani lands belonging to *tappa* Bulthur (in the northern reaches of *pargana* Majhowa) for cultivation to "hill people." See letter from Archibald Montgomerie, Collector of Saran, to BOR, 18 April 1790, in Procs BOR 19–30 April 1790, WBSA. In another instance, in April 1793, one Janki Ram and other merchants of Nepal had asked the Board of Revenue for permission to farm lands in pargana Batiya (Bettiah?). See *Bengal MS Records*, vol. 1, 1782–93, no. 394. For similar instances from Eastern Nepal see Joseph Dalton Hooker, *Himalayan Journals: Notes of a Naturalist in Bengal, the Sikkim and Nepal Himalayas, the Khasi Mountains*, 269–70.

24 See deposition of witness no. 6, Ram Newaz, former *quanungo* of *tappas* Netwar, Bhatipar, and Palee in Bernardo Michael, "Separating the Yam from the Boulder," Appendix 4, Table 29, 569.

25 The term "intermediate space" has been used by Chetan Singh to describe the "wastes" of the Western Himalayas, which lay somewhere between cultivated and forest lands. See Singh, *Natural Premises: Ecology and Peasant Life in the Western Himalayas, 1800–1950*, 92. So well established was this back-and-forth movement between cultivated and waste, that it persisted on the northern reaches of Gorakhpur till as late as 1880. See Alexander, *Statistical, Descriptive, and Historical Account of Gorakhpur District*, 338–9. For a study of land categories in the South see Murton, "Changing Land Categories in Interior Tamil Nadu, 1750–1850: Propositions and Implications for the Agricultural System," 31–40 (especially 37). See also Murton, "Towards a Deconstruction of Land Categories in the Late Eighteenth Century British Records in Southern India," 101–8. For a similar argument concerning broader colonial categories see Stein, "Idiom and Ideology in Early Nineteenth-Century South India," 23–58.

26 See Wink, *Land and Sovereignty in India: Agrarian Society and Politics under the Eighteenth Century Maratha Svarajya*, 27–8. See also 162. For Wink, the sovereignty of states in India was characterized by a combination of generalized taxation and institutionalized conflict best captured in the Arabic word "*fitna*" (sedition). Lack of space prevents a fuller discussion of Wink's work, which has

on the whole been well-received, though it came under strong criticism from Irfan Habib, the historian of Mughal India. Details of the Wink–Habib exchange can be found in the following: Habib, "Review of Land and Sovereignty in India: Agrarian Sovereignty under the Eighteenth Century Maratha Svarajya,"; Wink, "A Rejoinder to Irfan Habib," 363–67; and Habib, "Reply," 368–72. For more on agrarian territory see Ludden, *An Agrarian History of South Asia*, 41–3.

27 At same time, such a *zamindari* had all the hallmarks of an article of private property. It could be freely bought and sold. See Habib, *The Agrarian System*, 1st edition, 154, and 2nd edition, 200–202. Also Hasan, *Some Thoughts on Agrarian Relations in Mughal India*.

28 Such a conception of property rights in South Asia is not an entirely novel one. Colonial experts on question of property like B. H. Baden Powell had recognized the complex, multi-layered character of property rights in the South and their close interconnections with variables of political authority. See Baden Powell, *Land Systems in British India*.

29 See "Questions put to Bandhu Khadka (?) vakil of the raja of Gulmi," in magistrates procs of the Faujdari court, Zilla Gorakhpur, 7 March 1804, Boards Collections, F/4/185, 85–9, 207–20, IOR, APAC, BL. The emphasis is mine.

30 My information on these states is primarily drawn from the following sources. See "Settlements of the Districts of Joobul and Ootraj," in Bengal Political Letters 11 December 1816, no. 5, in Boards Collections F/4/570 no. 13993, 87, IOR, APAC, BL; FS Procs 30 March 1816, nos. 10, 11 and 16, NAI. In the Western Himalayas there were four large-sized kingdoms exercising varying degrees of authority over the nearly 26 petty principalities of the region. The four kingdoms were Basahar, Bilaspur, Hindur and Sirmur. The petty kingdoms were grouped into constellations of 12 and 14 petty kingdoms. Detailed information on the states of the region can be found in the "Statistical and Geographical Memoir of the Hill Countries by Lt. Ross," in FS Procs, 27 September 1815, no. 41, NAI.

31 The ruler of Jubal claimed that his state was attached to Sirmur through ties of *nalbandi*. "*Nalbandi*" refers to a contribution exacted from petty princes or peasantry under indigenous Islamic governments on the plea of keeping up cavalry of the state and which later was converted into a small tribute. See translation of a petition from Puran Chand Thakur of Jubal to Captain Birch at Nahan, 20 February 1816, Boards Collections F/4/570 no. 13993, 23–4, IOR, APAC, BL.

32 See letter of Capt. Birch, assistant to the governor-general's agent to C. T. Metcalf, 29 February 1816, in FS Procs 30 March 1816, no. 11, NAI.

33 Capt. Birch to C. T. Metcalf, 29 February 1816, Boards Collections F/4/570 no. 13993, 11–14, IOR, APAC, BL. The term "*mye*" can be easily translated in Hindi to mean any of the following: "in," "within" or "inside." See also the response by Charles Metcalfe, the British Resident at Delhi, in C. T. Metcalf, Resident at Delhi to J. Adam, secretary to government, 5 March 1816, FS Procs 30 March 1816, no. 10, paragraph 3, NAI.

34 My use of the term "total" signifies a phenomenon that is a composite of perceived dichotomies such as the symbolic and the material. For details see Tambiah, "The Galactic Polity in Southeast Asia.," 252–86.

35 See Elliott, *Chronicle of Oonao*, and cited in Habib, *The Agrarian System*, 2nd ed. 199. However, since Elliott saw these proprietary rights being held by powerful clans, he hastily concluded that *parganas* in Unnao were clan territories.

36 A useful glossary of these terms can be found in Carnegy, *Kachahri Technicalities or A Glossary of Terms Rural, Official and General*, 2nd edition.

37 For more on the subject of gifting and state formation in the little kingdom of Pudukkottai in South India see Dirks, *The Hollow Crown*. Two-thirds of the cultivated land in Pudukkottai was held on rent-free (*inam*) terms, with about 30 percent of these involving temples (*devasthanam*). Dirk's work is particularly interesting because it raises questions of spatiality at a time of colonial transformation that merit further exploration. Some tentative explorations of the questions of spatiality are explored, using maps, in an appendix at the end of the first edition of the book (407–34). Intriguingly, this appendix is left out of the second edition of the book (1993). The questions that remain unanswered are: were there distinctive spatial patterns to be observed in the

granting of these *inams*? How did colonial rule bring about changes in these spatial patterns, if it did? Did the establishment of a linear boundary for Pudukkottai impact upon the distribution of these grants? What were the connections between the distribution of these grants and ecology and political context?

38 Burghart, "Gift to the Gods: Power, Property and Ceremonial in Nepal," 259. The emphasis is mine.
39 Cited in Alam, "Eastern India in the Early Eighteenth Century Crisis: Some Evidence from Bihar," 43–72; Habib, *An Atlas*, 39.
40 Habib, *An Atlas*, 65. Thus, U. N. Day notes that between 1594 and 1695 the number of subdivisions in *suba* Bihar rose from 199 to 240 *mahals*, while in the *suba* of Awadh they rose from 133 to 197. See U. N. Day, *The Mughal Government, 1556–1707 AD*, 69.
41 See Habib, *An Atlas*, 29.
42 See Gupta, *Agrarian System of Eastern Rajasthan*, 13–14n33, 28, 29, 31 and 34. See also Bhadani, "Revenue Estimation and Realization in the Mughal Empire: A Case Study of Marwar," 69–81 (especially 73); and Peabody, "Kota Mahajagat, or the Great Universe of Kota: Sovereignty and Territory in 18th Century Rajasthan," 29–56 (especially 43).
43 Alexander Ross, Coll. of Gorakhpur, to Charles Buller, secretary, BOR, 12 February 1805, in Letters Issued Register, GCR, basta 16, vol. 3, RSA; and ibid. in Proc. BOR for Ceded and Conquered Provinces, Procs 31 July 1810, no. 31A, UPSA.
44 See letter from Ahmad Ali Khan, the Amil of Champaran, to the Patna Council, Procs 7 November 1774, Proceedings of the Provincial Council of Revenue at Patna, WBSA.
45 Richards, *The Mughal Empire*, xv.
46 Elliot, *Memoirs*, 121.
47 *CPC*, vol. 9, no. 662.
48 See, letter from D. Vanderhayden, special commissioner (investigating revenue arrangements in Champaran) to Bihar, to Board of Revenue, October 4, 1793, nos. 20–32, in Procs BOR, 1–11 October 1793, WBSA.
49 See Elliot, *Memoirs*, 120.
50 For disputes on the Tirhut–Sarlahi frontier see the following: translations of report of *tehsildar* Fazl Ali of Turki, and *kaifiyat* of Nadir Ali, *daroga* [in-charge] of *thana* Ruga, sent to Collector of Tirhut, 16 September 1801, FS Procs, 16 September 1801, no. 3, NAI; extracts of judicial department, no. 1831, containing letters from magistrate of Tirhut, C. I. Sealy, as well as Persian translation relating to these disputes, January–February 1813, FS Procs, 14 June 1813, no. 47, NAI; Report of C. I. Sealy, magistrate of Tirhut to John Adam, secretary to government, Fort William, FS Consl. 16 August 1814, no. 20, NAI.

Similarly, details of disputes along the Purnea–Morang frontier can be found in the following: letter from the governor-general, the Earl of Minto, to Raja Girbana Juddha Bikram, shah of Gorkha, 5 June 1809, FP Consl. 13 June 1809, no. 72, NAI; raja of Gorkha to the governor-general 25 April 1810, FP Consl. 15 May 1810, no. 35, NAI; raja of Gorkha to Mr. Lumsden, late vice-president, received 11 July 1810, FP Consl. 12 October 1810, no. 172, NAI; Gorkhali *sardar* Gaj Singh Khatri to Gorkhali *vakil*, received 1 November 1810, FP Consl. 7 December 1810, no. 73, NAI; raja of Gorkha to governor-general, received 12 January 1811, FP Consl. 19 April 1811, no. 46, NAI. See also *Stiller Typescript* 2:104–6.

Territorial disputes also arose on the Khairigarh section of the frontier in the west and the Chittagong section of the frontier in the northeast. Similar disputes could also be found all along the Company's frontier with the states of Awadh, Rampur, Bharatpur, Bhutan, Kutch-Bihar and Bykantpur. Numerous complicated disputes also arose in the territories of the rajas and *zamindars* lying west of the River Jamuna. See Memorandum of British Possessions West of Jamuna by C. T. Metcalf, Assistant to the Governor-General, 1805, Memoirs of the Survey of India, Memoir no. 19, SOIR, NAI.
51 Changes in the topography caused by shifts in the courses of rivers due to alluvium were known as *diara* disputes, and the colonial record in South Asia is littered with such cases.

52 During the 1820s, Robert Wroughton, a revenue surveyor employed by the Company, discovered that over 60 percent of the 124 villages he had surveyed in the *pargana* of Amorha (Gorakhpur) were involved in long-standing disputes over land, standing crops, forests, tanks, mango groves and so on. See survey of 124 villages in the parganas of Amora, district Gorakhpur, by Lt. Robert Wroughton, 1829, Historical Maps F 19/24, SOIR, NAI; "Boundary and Statistics of Several Villages of Uttar Pradesh with Village Plans by Lt. Robert Wroughton", 1822–23, Memoirs of the Survey of India, memoir no. 90, map no. 52, SOIR, NAI.

53 However, take for instance the dispute between the *fauzdar* Bidesh Raut and one Fakir Baksh over some villages in the *pargana* of Naurangiya and Sidhmasa in the district of Bara-Parsa in 1810 CE in RRC 40: 158. See also: "Dispute between Laxmidhar Pandit and Gaureshwar Aryal of Makwanpur" and "Dispute between Bir Bhadra Upadhyaya and the descendents of the Basnayet family," both in *RRS* 21 (May 1989): 69; "Complaint by cultivators of Vijaypur against the encroachments of the cultivators of Chainpur, 1805 CE [1862 BS]," RRC 5: 579; "Modi Misra ordered to pay prescribed *pota* tax or give up *jagir* lands arbitrarily appropriated by him in Rautahat, 1810 CE [1867 BS]," RRC 39: 185; "Complaint of Raut that the *birta* lands granted to Ishwari Datta Misra encroached on lands assigned for elephant pens in Mahottari, 1810 CE [1867 BS]," RRC 39: 240; "Complaint of tenant Kalu Pandit of Raginas that lands reclaimed by him were unjustly claimed by *hulaki* [porter] Nanda Ram, 1818 CE [1875 BS]," RRC 38: 512; "Madhav Timilsina reprimanded for false claim on land assigned to *hulaki* Ram Chandra Timilsina, 1818 CE [1875 BS]," RRC 38: 518; "Kuber Adhikari reprimanded for encroachment on lands assigned to *hulaki* Dev Datta Padhya, 1818 CE [1875 BS]," RRC 38: 520; "Complaint of tenant Harka Mani Gurung of Pangmi that Narayan Shahi was unjustly trying to appropriate his lands, 1818 CE [1875 BS]," RRC 38: 531.

54 Historian Robert Frykenberg used the term "inner logic" to characterize the consensus-building activities that took place between different social groups and the Company state as it expanded its influence on the subcontinent. In South India this took shape in the form of a "Silent Settlement" whereby the old privileges enjoyed by these elites (especially their rights to rent-free or *inam* lands) were preserved, provided they professed loyalty to the Company's authority. Frykenberg, however, does not incorporate variables of conflict or rule-negotiation within this "logic," as the work of Wink and evidence from the Anglo–Gorkha frontier suggests. See Frykenberg, "Company Circari in the Carnatic, c. 1799–1859: The Inner Logic of the Political Systems in India," 117–64.

55 Iqtidar Alam Khan has estimated that Mughal revenues did not account for even half the average *dastur* rates (crop rates), because of the large-scale defalcation of revenues mainly through the manipulation of revenue records by interested officials: Khan, "The Middle Classes in the Mughal Empire," Presidential Address, Medieval India Section of Indian History Congress, Aligarh 1975, cited in S. A. N. Rizvi, "The Mughal Empire and Bureaucracy," 455–95 (especially 489). See also Moosvi, "Aurangzeb's Farman to Rasikdas on Problems of Revenue Administration, 1665," 197–208, and Hasan's article, "The Mughal Fiscal System in Surat and the English East India Company," 711–18.

56 For a sampling see: "Royal Priests, *chautariyas* and others with *birta* and other landholdings warned (in Saptari-Mahottari) they should proportionately share irrigation water with *raikar* lands, 1811 CE [1868 BS]," RRC 41: 58; "Company personnel prohibited to oppress people in Rautahat by getting goods at cheaper prices forcibly and by impressing begar labor, 1812 CE [1869 BS]," RRC 41: 108; "Complaints by people of Dharma against Daulat Singh and Radhpati Singh (rank unspecified) for making unauthorized collections in excess of the prescribed *thekbandi* amount. Chautariya Bam Shah told to look into the complaints, 1813 CE [1870 BS]," RRC 41: 257; "*kajis, sardars* of Vijayapur prohibited from making collections from the lands reclaimed between the rivers Kosi and Trisota by Jayant Khatri, 1813 CE [1870 BS]," RRC 41: 302; "Jai Singh Khatri prohibited granting *ijara* on lands assigned to elephant pens to Indians. He is ordered to make *thekbandi* arrangements and to return all unauthorized collections from *bekh buniyad* and *khuwa* holdings, 1813 CE [1870 BS]," RRC 41: 552; "*Subba, fauzdars* and others prohibited from obtaining goods from Indian traders

coming to Janakpur market without payment of appropriate prices, 1811 CE [1868 BS]," RRC 38: 665; "House of Baijnath in Patan sold for collection of fine imposed on him for acceptance of bribe, 1810 CE [1868 BS]," RRC 39: 405; "Sahu Harkrishna Das appointed to collect revenues in Saptari-Mahottari district in view of the oppression by amils, 1802 CE [1859 BS]," RRC 5: 378; "Orders to Sahu Harkrishna Das not to collect salami on *nankar* lands of Saptari, 1804 CE [1861 BS]," RRC 5: 461; and "Orders to *fauzdar, chaudhari, qanungoyes* and *sairdar* to desist from encroaching on the lands of Bikha Chaudhari, 1809 CE [1866 BS]," RRC 40: 42.

57 For Gorkha see the following: "*Ijara* on cultivated lands granted to Pranpati Mishra in *pargana* Naurangiya (district Parsa), 1813 CE [1870 BS]," RRC 41: 153. Numerous *ijara* grants were given out in Gorkha's Eastern Tarai – see Chapter 3 for details. Jaskarna Khatri Bhattarai given right to collect *jalkar* tax all over the kingdom. In 1785, Tanahu, Lamjung, Kaski, Dhor, Nuwakot, etc., were also added to his sphere of collection (*RRS* 16 (June 1984): 93). See also "*Ijara* granted to Hanumant Singh for collecting of custom duties in Makwanpur, Naurangiya, Sidhmas, Chisapani, Hetauda and Parsa. He replaces Kulanand Jha, 1807 CE [1864 BS]," RRC 36: 419; "*Ijara* granted to *chaudharis* for collection of *mal, sair*, and other revenues in Mahottari 1780 CE, [1837 BS]," RRC 36: 472; and "*jogi mandali* revenues in entire kingdom assigned to Uttim Nath Jogi, 1811 CE [1868 BS]," RRC 41: 23.

58 For a sampling of records from Western India see Chandra and Gupta, "The Jaipur Paragana Records," 303–15; Gupta, *Agrarian System of Eastern Rajasthan*, 317–34; Gupta, "Khasra Documents in Rajasthan,"168–76; Gupta and Khan, *Mughal Documents: Taqsim (c. 1649–1800)*; and Sharma, "Some Aspects of the Land Revenue Records of Udaipur State: A Study of the Karan Mahal Revenue Records of the Rajasthan State Archives," 99–108. However, according to Satish Chandra and S. P. Gupta, such *pargana* records, as for example in Rajasthan, despite their detailed nature possess gaps which "do not permit the continuous study of any pargana." See Chandra and Gupta, "The Jaipur Paragana Records," 304. For Maratha records see Sharma and Dhot, "Marathi Records on the State Revenue in Gujarat during the Second Half of the Eighteenth Century," 83–98. For a detailed examination of eighteenth-century *zamindari* records from Bengal, see Taniguchi, "The Zamindar's Estate-Control on the Eve of the Permanent Settlement in Bengal (1793) – A Case-Study of a Middle-Size *Zamindari* in Northern Bengal," 1–41. For a broad historical treatment of information gathering and social communication in India see Bayly, *Empire and Information: Intelligence Gathering and Social Communication in India, 1780–1870*.

59 Such *raqbabandi* documents are available for many parts of the Mughal Empire, such as, for the year 1593, the *pargana* of Bhagalpur (*sarkar* Monghyr, *suba* Bihar). See Grover, "Raqba-Bandi Documents of Akbar's Reign," 55–60. Commenting on the spatial continuity of the *pargana* and its internal divisions (*tappas*), Grover, however, observes that there were no differences in the names of the *tappas* of this *pargana* between 1593 and 1771. This is indeed intriguing, given all the political jostling and fluctuations in fiscal arrangements in the *suba* of Bihar during the eighteenth century. Grover also does not wonder if the similarities in *tappa* lists of this period did not have anything to do with the attempts of Company officials to systematize the accounts of their districts by preserving the unity of the village and *tappa* lists (*fahrist-i-dehat-i-tappajat*). In any case, the continuous presence of a *tappa* or *pargana* in revenue documents does not necessarily mean that the *tappa* or *pargana* had existed unchanged on the ground. While name could be retained, the layout and territorial organization of such divisions usually varied over time.

60 Such dependence on producing lists rather than maps was also visible in Ottoman cadastral surveys. See Kark, "Mamluk and Ottoman Cadastral Surveys and Early Mapping of Landed Properties in Palestine," 46–70. Kark's basic argument is that the Ottomans never needed to develop maps for their cadastral surveys, because all the lands were state-owned. The state did not need the extra information provided by maps. While Kark attempts to set the historiographical balance right, it is hard to agree with her claim that state ownership of lands prevented their cadastral mapping. She also avoids discussion on a number of crucial fronts, such as: the structure of agrarian entitlements, internal political relationships within the Ottoman Empire, the nature and structure of property rights, tax claims, and the spatial organization of the empire's

administrative divisions. Examining these variables might provide clues as to why non-European states delayed in developing mapping technologies, compared to their development in the West.
61 See Fazl, *Ain-i-Akbari*, 186 and 167. Thus, what is at stake is the reliability of the data. Scholars like Habib and Moosvi treat the *Ain* as a mine of rich statistical data and have used it copiously to write their histories of Mughal India. Others like Khan and Trivedi, while reaffirming the usefulness of the *Ain*, feel its centralized data needs to be supplemented by and interpreted with the help of regional and local sources of information. In contrast, others like Sanjay Subrahmanyam prefer treating the *Ain* more along the lines of a manual of administration whose statistical data is suspect. In this, he echoes similar views expressed by Ashok Desai who, in the 1970s, had warned against unnecessary statistical processings of the *Ain*, as the conclusions arrived at would be unreliable. While locating the present study within these debates would be both unnecessary and beyond the competence of this writer, Desai's cautionary statements seem to be apt and still valid. For details see Desai, "Population and Standard of Living in Akbar's Time – A Second Look". See also Khan, "Agricultural Statistics of Mughal India: A Reconsideration," 121–46; Subrahmanyam, "Review of Shireen Moosvi's *The Economy of the Mughal Empire, c. 1595*, 103–7; and Trivedi, "Reappraisal of *A'in's* Area Statistics: A Note," 45–59 and "Estimating Forests, wastes and fields, *c.* 1600."
62 Habib, *The Agrarian System*, 1st edition, 4.
63 Moosvi, *The Economy*, 64n34. Moosvi also notes that Gorakhpur's area under cultivation grew over fifteen times from 1595–1909/10 (ibid., 50–51).
64 Shaukat Ullah Khan has suggested that Mughal revenue surveys were not merely conducted for revenue purposes, but were "extended to cover vast portions of uncultivated lands, presumably to assert the state's authority and control over the lands treated as cultivable and unreclaimable." See Khan, "Agricultural Statistics," 142. Such moves would have met with local resistance as landholders often used the pretext of possessing waste lands to conceal their cultivable lands or escape the tax obligations imposed by the state. Perhaps it might be safer to take Sanjay Subrahmanyam's line that the *arazi* was differently conceived in different regions or measured very poorly in some regions. See Subrahmanyam, "Review," 105.
65 See letter of J. Lumsden, Collector of Saran District to BOR, May 1793, in Letters Sent to BOR Register, 13 February –5 July 1793, District Record Room, Chapra, North Bihar. See also C. J. Stevenson-Moore, *Final Report on the Survey and Settlement Operations in the Champaran District, 1892–1899*, 30.
66 See Rizvi, "Srinet Zamindars of Sarkar Gorakhpur Under the Mughals," 35–41.
67 Elsewhere, in Rajasthan, the village of Bamanvas, which had 12 smaller villages attached to it, belonged to the *pargana* of Liwali. But for the purposes of revenue assessment it was temporarily attached to the *pargana* of Udehi. See Gupta and Khan, *Mughal Documents: Taqsim (c. 1649–1800)*, 6.
68 See *PRNW* 2: 680–700.
69 See, Elliot, *Memoirs*, 116.
70 Ibid., 69. See also Petition from the *sarkari quanungoes*, n.d., and enclosed in letter from Roger Martin, Coll. of Gorakhpur to R. M. Tilghman, BOR Patna, 21 October 1822, Tharu Colony 1815–29, GDR, basta 8, vol. 63, 175–99, RSA.
71 The dispute was waged in the law courts for 76 years (1790–1866), when ultimately 79 villages were granted to the raja of Ramnagar and the remaining 6 to the raja of Bettiah. See "Proceedings of the Privy Council on Appeal from the High Court of Judicature at Fort William in Bengal, Maharaja Rajendra Kishor Singh (defendant) Appelant; Maharaja Sahib Prahlad Sen (plaintiff) Respondent, 29 September 1866," papers relating to this in an unmarked basta, BRM, Bettiah.
72 See "List of Tuppehs of Purgana Mutka, Received 14 March 1804," in Claim of the Nepaul Government to possess the Zamindarry of Butaul, Boards Collections, F/4/185, IOR, APAC, BL. See also the *arzi* from Shakti Prachand Shah, the raja of Gulmi, 14 March 1804, Boards Collections, F/4/185, 226–32, IOR, APAC, BL.

73 See letter of J. Fombelle, secretary to government to BOR, 5 April 1804, Procs Of the BOR for the Ceded and Conquered Provinces, Procs 31 July 1810, no. 31B, UPSA.
74 For details about the terms of the Treaty of 1801, see C. U. Aitchison, *A Collection of Treaties, Engagements and Sanads Relating to India and Neighbouring Countries*, 130–33.
75 For Khairigarh see letter of A. Ross, Collector to BOR, 15 May 1805, Letters Issued Register, GCR, basta 16, vol. 4, RSA. The six *parganas* of Nawabgung were separated from Gorakhpur by lands belonging to the Bahu Begum, the mother of the former *nawab* Asaf-ud-daulah. See Letters Issued Register, GCR, basta 16, vol. 4, RSA; E. Alexander, *Statistical, Descriptive and Historical Account of the Gorakhpur District*, 275; and Bhargava, *State, Society*, 13.
76 *Chaudhrai* grant made to Jas Raj Chaudhari, from *pargana* Deokhori-Sheoraj, 1796 AD, poka 9, no. 8, no. 919, Lagat Phant, Kathmandu.
77 See "Proceedings of the Privy Council on Appeal from the High Court of Judicature at Fort William in Bengal, Maharaja Rajendra Kishor Singh (defendant) Appelant"; "Maharaja Sahib Prahlad Sen (plaintiff) Respondent," 29 September 1866, papers relating to this in an unmarked basta, BRM, Bettiah. Since the 1780s, the rajas of Bettiah had also been involved in long-standing land disputes with the Catholic priests of Bettiah. Details pertaining to this dispute can be found in the archives of the Nativity of Our Lady of the Blessed Virgin Mary, Bettiah, north Champaran. See letter of Holt Mackenzie, secretary to government, to judge and magistrate of Saran 12 March 1824; letter of commissioner of Saran forbidding the measurement of Bettiah church lands, ordered by the Collector of Saran, 7 June 1833; *kaifiyat* (history) of the case prepared by record keepers (*sheristadars*) of the Collectorate of Saran, 12 March 1833; draft of Rev. Joachim's memorial to the Sudder Board of Revenue, 11 April 1834, Bettiah Church Records, Bettiah.
78 For instances of this in Gorakhpur, Champaran, and Awadh see *Report on the Settlement of Gorakhpur, Basti District* (Allahabad, 1871), 2:28, paragraph 8; C. J. Stevenson-Moore, *Final Report on the Survey and Settlement Operations in Champaran District, 1892–1899*, 42; In Awadh in 1813, for instance, an examination of a large number of *sanads* (official deeds) granting pensions and issued by the *nawab* of Awadh were found to have been "forged." See letter from the Board of Commissioners to Lord Minto, governor-general, 4 August 1813, FP Procs, 15 October 1813, no. 51, NAI.
79 See Deposition of Ram Baksh Singh, FP Procs, 22 April 1814, no. 59, 215–18, NAI.
80 See FP Procs, 26 June 1814, no. 16, NAI.
81 The lack of standardized orthographic practices compounded the situation for the British, at least during the early years of colonial rule. So the hill kingdoms of Pyuthana, Malebhum, Kanchi and Argha became "Penthannee," "Mullaibum," "Konchailee" and "Urgallee," respectively. See letter from Captain Knox to secretary to government, Foreign Secret Consultations, 30 June 1802, Consultation no. 49, NAI. On a more humorous note, Siraj-ud-daulah became "Sir Roger Dowlah", Karachi became "Crotchy" and Allahabad became "Isle of Bats." Cited in Markham, *A Memoir on the Indian Surveys*, 384.
82 For a fine description of the varying histories and cultural traditions of forts, both as enshrined in written political texts and actual practice, see Gordon, *Marathas, Marauders, and State Formation in Eighteenth Century India*, 82–98.
83 Elliot, *Memoirs*, 101, 106, 110 and 125.
84 The details of the account that follows are taken from the following translations (by Mahesh C. Regmi) of Shiva Prasad Dabral's *Uttarakhand Ka Rajanaitika Tatha Sanskritika Itihas* (Garhwal, 2030 BS). "From Yamuna to Satluj," *RRS* 19, no. 4 (April 1987): 50–53; "Struggle for Kangra Fort (1)," *RRS* 19, no. 5 (May 1987): 63–9; "Struggle for Kangra Fort (2)," *RRS* 19, no. 6 (June 1987): 79–83.
85 The very appointment of these officers who were rivals of the *budakaji* suggests that Kathmandu was suspicious of Amar Singh Thapa's moves. Such statements reveal the existence of various factions that operated within the Gorkhali state and energized processes of statemaking, both prior to and after the war. See translation of a letter from Amar Singh Thapa to the raja of Gorkha, 12 April 1815, FS Procs, 16 May 1815, no. 61, NAI.

86 Amar Singh Thapa lost much face in these proceedings. The hill rulers and chieftains, who had once supported him, now deserted him. It was with this loss of face that he approached Col. David Ochterlony, the Company's officer in charge of the areas in the Punjab, in December 1813, and solicited his neutrality, so that he could retake Kangra Fort. For details about this meeting see Michael, "When Soldiers and Statesmen Meet: 'Ethnographic Moments' on the Frontiers of Empire," 80–94.
87 Ambashthya, *Beames' Contributions*, 19.
88 I am grateful to the late Professors Qeyamuddin Ahmad and the late R. S. Sharma for pointing this out to me. The role of modern maps in creating and consolidating such circuits of affect still remains to be explored. Such an emotional attachment to territorial spaces find echoes in the work of Yi-Fu Tuan and Gaston Bachelard - see Tuan, *Topophilia: A Study of Environmental Perception, Attitudes and Values*; and also Bachelard, *The Poetics of Space*.
89 Blochmann, "Contributions," 216.
90 See Elliot, *Memoirs*, 47–78. The quote is from page 57. These *chaurasis* usually, though not always, represented 84 villages or tanks. In some cases they may have referred to the distance measured (in *coses*). Elliot goes on to argue that above the *chaurasis* lay a larger division of 360 villages.
91 See Narain Singh Bhati, ed., *Mumhta Nainsi-ri Likhi Marwar-ra Parganan-ri Vigat*.
92 Cited in Wyatt, *Geographical and Statistical Memoir of the District of Tirhut* (Calcutta, 1854), 6–7. I am also grateful to the late Dr R. S. Sharma for sharing this information with me.
93 Alexander, *Statistical, Descriptive, and Historical Account of Gorakhpur District*, 278.
94 Hazrat, *History of Gorakhpur*, 1810 CE, I. O. 4540, IOR, APAC, BL. See also, E. Alexander, *Statistical, Descriptive, and Historical Account of Gorakhpur District*, 326.
95 Wyatt, *Geographical and Statistical Memoir*, 7.
96 Cited in Buchanan-Hamilton, *The Gorakhpur Report*, 2, 169, Eur Mss D 92, IOR, APAC, BL.
97 Alexander, *Statistical, Descriptive*, 443.
98 Cited in Ahmad, "Aspects of Historical Geography of Medieval Bihar," 119–37 (especially 132).
99 See letter of Capt. Birch, assistant to the governor-general's agent, to C. T. Metcalf, 29 February 1816, in FS Procs 30 March 1816, no. 11, NAI.
100 I am grateful to Shri Hari Shankar Pandey, library assistant at the National Library at Calcutta, for sharing this piece of information with me (16 January 1999).
101 See Burghart, "The Formation of the Concept of the Nation-State in Nepal," 101–26. See also "Gift to the Gods: Power, Property and Ceremonial in Nepal," 237–70 (especially 267–9); and Burghart, "The History of Janakpurdham: A Study of Asceticism and the Hindu Polity," 244–7.
102 Ethnosociology in the seventies and early eighties came to represent the attempts of a number of anthropologists and sociologists to capture authentic indigenous voices. Such an enterprise, needless to say, collapsed under the weight of its own premise – that it could ever locate authentic indigenous voices – and has few supporters today. For a sampling of the ethnosociological approach, see McKim Marriot, ed., *India Through Hindu Categories*. See also Burghart, "Hierarchical Models of the Hindu Social System," 519–36; and "For a Sociology of Indias: An Intercultural Approach to the Study of "Hindu Society," 275–99.

Chapter 6. Making States Legible: Maps, Surveys and Boundaries

1 Said, "Representing the Colonized: Anthropology's Interlocutors," 205–26. The quotation is from p. 218. Edward Said has consistently called for an exploration of the connections between geography and empire. See also Said, *Culture and Imperialism* and his classic *Orientalism*. For a sympathetic treatment of Said's "imaginative geographies," see Gregory, "Imaginative Geographies," 447–85.
2 Cohn and Dirks, "Beyond the Fringe: The Nation-State, Colonialism, and the Technologies of Power," 224–9. The quotation is from p. 224. The emphasis is mine.
3 Harley and Woodward, eds, *The History of Cartography*, 1:xvi. This broad definition seeks to be inclusive so as to give room to maps and mapmaking traditions that have stood outside the

established canon of European "scientific cartography." For examples of the remarkable and rich traditions of mapmaking among indigenous peoples, such as the Inuit and the Mixtec, see Rundstrom, "A Cultural Interpretation of Inuit Map Accuracy," 155–68; and Harley and Woodward, "An Alternative Route to Mapping History," 6–13.

4 Excellent examples of this can be found in the following: Gole, *Indian Maps and Plans: From Earliest Times to the Advent of European Surveys*, *India Within the Ganges*, and *Early Indian Maps*; Madan, *Indian Cartography: A Historical Perspective*; and Schwartzberg, "South Asian Cartography," 293–388.

5 An impressive attempt to map the empire can be found in Habib, *An Atlas of the Mughal Empire*, vi. Nevertheless, Habib's otherwise pioneering *Atlas*, remains a modern representation of the Mughal Empire as it depicts it in terms of linear boundaries and contiguous territories. There is little consideration of the jostling mosaic of territorial divisions and fuzzy boundaries that must have constituted the spatial reality on the ground. For more on cartography during this period see Habib "Cartography in Mughal India," 122–34.

6 In 1579, Saxton produced *An Atlas of England and Wales* containing 35 color maps. The *Atlas* was the first attempt to conduct a survey of the kingdom and its parts in a consistent format. Interestingly, when the English traveler and diplomat Sir Thomas Roe visited the Mughal court in the seventeenth century, he presented a copy of an atlas to the Mughal emperor Jahangir. Roe was surprised when the Emperor returned the atlas, explaining that no one in the Mughal court could find any usefulness for it. Noting this, Susan Gole has suggested that perhaps the courtiers "were not in the habit of seeing their land in a pictorial representation." See Gole, *India Within the Ganges*, 59.

7 See Phillimore, "Three Indian Maps," 111–14 (including three maps); Schwartzberg, "Geographical Mapping," in Harley and Woodward, eds, *History of Cartography*, vol. 2, no. 2, 405–8. This map is currently in the National Archives of India (F 97/10, 11).

8 The *parganas* or *mahals* mentioned in the *Ain* do not seem to match those on this map, suggesting changes in Mughal territorial organization in the eighteenth century. See *Ain-i-Akbari*, trans. Jarrett, 334–5.

9 A similar point is made by Christopher Bayly when he notes that indigenous maps were more schematic in their layout, showing information more along the lines of a genealogical tree, full of climatic, sociological and religious meanings. See Bayly, *Empire and Information*, 304–9.

10 Gentil's atlas consists of 21 color folios, each depicting one of the Mughal *subas*, along with its internal *sarkar* divisions clearly marked out. Each map is framed by pictures depicting scenes from the wildlife, history and culture of the province. Gentil's maps contain some errors: Champaran is shown as having three *parganas* – Madjora (Majhowa), Maessi (Mehsi) and Samroun ((Gadh) Simraon) – while *pargana* Bubra is omitted. See Gole, *Maps of Mughal India Drawn by Colonel Jean Baptiste Gentil, Agent for the French Government to the Court of Shuja-ud daula at Faizabad, in 1770*; and Archer, "Colonel Gentil's Atlas: An Early Series of Company Drawings," 41–5.

11 Gentil's maps have often been dismissed for their quality since they were based on literary sources rather than surveys. Schwartzberg calls atlases like Gentil's "hybrid" maps as they incorporate both European and indigenous styles – made at the behest of Europeans but executed by indigenous artists. See Schwartzberg, *The History of Cartography*, 427–9; Archer, "Colonel Gentil's Atlas," 43 and 45.

12 Details pertaining to this map can be found in Gogate and Arunachalam, "Area Maps in Maratha Cartography: A Study in Native Maps of Western India," 126–40; Gole, *Indian Within the Ganges*, 19–20 and 140–41; Phillimore, "Three Indian Maps," 113–14 and map 3; and Schwartzberg, *History of Cartography*, 423–5.

13 Gogate and Arunachalam, "Area Maps," 127 and 129–30, figure 1 and plate 7.

14 See Phillimore, "Three Indian Maps," 113–14.

15 See Gole, *Indian Maps and Plans*, 118–25. These 33 maps were prepared in the early nineteenth century to create an atlas of Kashmir.

16 See Gole, ibid., 91–3. The quotation is from page 92. See also Schwartzberg, *History of Cartography*, 435–6.

17 See Sahlins, *Boundaries: The Making of France and Spain in the Pyrenees*, 63. Such multiple jurisdictions can be found in other early European maps, such as a map tracing the lands belonging to Venice and Germany along the Aussa River, and prepared by the Office of the Border Commissioners in 1538. See Buisseret, *Monarchs, Ministers, and Maps*, 7.
18 Details about the Qing emperors employing the Jesuits to survey China in the eighteenth century and of Siam's cartographic projects can be found in the following: Hostetler, *Qing Colonial Enterprise: Ethnography and Cartography in Early Modern China*; and Winichakul, *Siam Mapped: The History of the Geo-Body of a Nation*. The notable early advances made by Arabic cartography, exploration and geographical knowledge, and their impact on Asia as early as the thirteenth century have been detailed in the work of historian Fuat Sezgin. See Sezgin, "The Precolumbian Discovery of the American Continent by Muslim Seafarers," *Geschichte des Arabischen Scrifttums* 13 (2006): 1.39. See also Hyunhee Park, *Mapping the Chinese and Islamic Worlds: Cross-Cultural Exchange in Pre-Modern Asia*.
19 Schwartzberg has suggested that since South Asian societies were traditionally more concerned with otherworldly cosmological ideas they had little incentive to map their physical world. See Schwartzberg in *History of Cartography*, 330. Such an idealistic view is not supported by evidence from the Anglo–Gorkha frontier.
20 See Embree, "Frontiers into Boundaries: From the Traditional to the Modern State," 259. See also Batten, "Frontiers and Boundaries of Pre-Modern Japan," 166–82; Febvre, "*Frontière*: The Word and the Concept," 208–18; Prescott, *Boundaries and Frontiers*; and Sahlins, *Boundaries*, 7.
21 H. M. Elliot, writing in the nineteenth century, noted that village boundaries in the North-Western Provinces were demarcated by placing some imperishable material (such as large stones, bones, tails of cows, bran, ash, potsherds, dried cowdung, bricks, tiles, charcoal, pebbles and even sand) within jars and burying them in the ground. See Elliot, *Memoirs*, 172–3.
22 Cited in Riccardi, "The Royal Edicts of King Rama Shah of Gorkha," 29–65 (especially 46–9). The boundaries of the *thum* division of Phirkep granted to Bahadur Shah, *subedar* of Jajarkot, in 1797 AD were fixed along rivers or marked by pillars. See *RRS* 21, 108.
23 Cited in "Nepal, Sikkim and the East India Company, 1793" *RRS* 3 (December 1971/2028 BS): 278–9.
24 See "Administrative Regulations for Areas between the Kanka and Mahakali Rivers," 1863 BS (1806 AD), Historical Documents, no. 117, *sawal* 29, Kausi Tosakhana Collection, NAN.
25 There are numerous instances of Gorkhali officials being deputed to conduct similar investigations of its interstate boundaries: see "Orders to Mahadev Upadhyaya to investigate border dispute with moglana [India], 1803 CE [1860 BS]," RRC 5: 421; "*Sardar* Gaj Singh deputed to resolve border dispute in village of Jasmanpur, 1810 CE [1867 BS]," *RRS* 16: 81; "*Subbas* and other officials of Bara-Parsa and Rautahat directed to provide necessary help to Ramjit Bhandari and Mir Munshi Raza Khan in settling border disputes [with India], 1810 CE [1867 BS]," RRC 39: 165; "Ram Bux Singh deputed to inspect Nepal–India borders, 1810 CE [1867 BS]," *RRS* 4, 46; "*Gurujyu* [Ranganath Pandit] authorized to demarcate Nepal–India border with *amil* from India, in Butwal and elsewhere, 1813 CE [1870 BS]," RRC 39: 557; "*Sardar* Balabhanjan Pande and other directed to demarcate India–Nepal border, 1817 CE [1874 BS]," RRC 36: 394–397; "Similar orders to *kaji* Prasad Singh Basnayet and others, 1817 CE [1874 BS]," RRC 36: 398–399.
26 In Purnea, along the Anglo–Gorkha frontier, the local custom of placing bamboo markers was followed in order to separate the English border *pargana* of Dhappar from the Gorkhali district of Saptari. See translation of letter from Gorkhali boundary commissioner Gaj Singh Khatri to Gorkhali *vakil*, received 1 November 1810, FP 7 December 1810, no. 73, NAI. Within the Himalayas, stone pillars and rivers formed the boundaries of many kingdoms. See, for instance, Ramble and Vinding, "The Bem-Chag Village Record and the Early History of Mustang District," 5–46; and Naraharinath, *Itihasprakasmasandhipartasamgraha*, 11–12, 55.
27 Such *diara* disputes persist right down to this day. For instance, district collectors in the Champaran District (Bihar state) routinely meet with their counterparts in Nepal to resolve

such boundary disputes. I am grateful to Abhay Mohan Jha, a friend and longtime resident at Bettiah, for providing me with this information.

28 See Sahlins, *Boundaries*, 28. It might be worthwhile to note that a similar situation existed on France's eastern frontier. There too was a multiplicity of overlapping and discontinuous jurisdictions that produced "anomalies" in the organization of territory. However, the territories on the eastern frontier were mapped and rearranged much faster than those existing on the west (the Franco–Spanish boundary in the Pyrenees), where a number of enclaves still exist. For details about the organization and representation of territory on France's eastern frontier see Buisseret, "The Cartographic Definition of France's Eastern Boundary in the Early Seventeenth Century," 72–80.

29 This was probably one Lt. Col. James Salmond. See Lt. Col. James Salmond (?) to chairman, Court of Directors, 7 April 1818, Political and Secret Department Records (Miscellaneous), L/P&S/19/8, Collection of Miscellaneous Letters, letter no. 8, IOR, APAC, BL. The emphasis is mine.

30 The notion of "imperial space" is Edney's. See Edney, *Mapping an Empire*, 333.

31 "Instructions from the governor-general-in-council to Lt. Col. Paris Bradshaw," FS Consl. 9 December 1815, no. 2, NAI.

32 See the following letters for details of these negotiations: J. Adam, secretary to government to E. Gardner, Resident at Kathmandu, 4 May 1816, FS Procs, 4 May 1816, no. 70, NAI; FS Procs, 24 August, 1816, nos. 8–12, NAI. See also letter from E. Gardner to J. Adam, 14 July, 1816, FS Procs, 3 August 1816, no. 12, NAI and E. Gardner to J. Adam, 2 August 1816, FS Procs, 24 August 1816, no. 10, NAI.

33 Correspondence concerning this can be found in the following letters: from the raja of Gorkha to E. Gardner, 2 October 1816, KRR R/5/37, 73–4, IOR, APAC, BL; Raja to *chautara* Bam Shah, 2 October 1816, KRR R/5/37, 77–9, IOR, APAC, BL; and Gorkhali raja to Bam Shah, in Lal Mohar Collection, no. 555, NAN.

34 Instructions from J. Adam, secretary to government to W. F. Clarke, acting magistrate of Saran, 17 December 1816, "Napal Correspondence," vol. 1, Saran Collectorate Records, BSA. See also J. Adam, secretary to government to E. Gardner, Resident at Kathmandu, 4 May 1816, FS Procs, 4 May 1816, no. 70, NAI; Clarke was appointed border commissioner on the Champaran–Tarriani frontier. The Gorkhali side was represented by *chautara* Pran Shah, Bir Kishor Pande, *kaji* Bahadur Bhandari, *kaji* Nur Singh Thapa and *taksari* Chandrashekhar Upadhyaya. The two British surveyors who would conduct the survey and prepare the maps were Lieutenants John Peter Boileau and Joshua Pickersgill. Boundary superintendents were appointed along the Anglo–Gorkha frontier to oversee demarcation proceedings. For instance, in 1820, on the Gorakhpur–Butwal frontier it was Capt. Stoneham, while Major Barre Latter was appointed boundary superintendent on the Rangpur frontier. See KRR (on microfilm) reel no. 4, IOR, APAC, BL. R/5/8 and 10, pp. 89 and 60, respectively, NAN.

35 The areas west of Gorakhpur, the Gorakhpur–Butwal, Champaran–Tarriani, and Tirhut–Saptari–Mahottari sections of the Anglo–Gorkha frontier were demarcated in 1817. The delimitation proceedings were accepted by Gorkhali prime minister Bhim Sen Thapa in July 1817. In 1819–20 the Anglo–Gorkha boundary was actually demarcated on the ground while the Gorkha–Sikkim boundary was fixed in 1821. Information sourced from: Hasrat, *History of Nepal: As Told by its Own Chroniclers and Contemporaries*, 191; and Shaha, *Modern Nepal*, 148–9.

36 See Stiller, *The Silent Cry: The People of Nepal, 1816–1839* (Kathmandu, 1976), 218–27. Stiller believes that it was during the latter half of 1816 that the Gorkhali prime minister Bhim Sen Thapa realized the critical importance of linear boundaries to the British in defining the edges of their territories. See also Stiller, *A Typescript of Microfilms Preserved in the Tribhuvan University Library from Documents in the Archives of India (The Stiller Typescript)*, vol. 2; and DesChene, *Relics of Empire*, 29n34.

37 See letter from *kaji* Prasad Singh Basnayet, Ganapat Upadhyaya and others to Ujir Singh Thapa (n.d.), Bir Pustakalaya Historical Letters, no. 253, NAN.

38 For instance, the Gorkhali *taraf* of Pachrauta (*tappa* of Rautahat) was divided in two, with the northern half going to Gorkha and the southern half going to one Ram Bux Singh, a loyal supporter. See "Napal Correspondence."
39 See letter from E. Gardner, Resident at Kathmandu, to W. F. Clarke, acting magistrate and boundary commissioner on the Champaran–Tarriani frontier, 21 and 22 March 1817, in "Napal Correspondence."
40 See letter from E. Gardner to J. Adam, 13 October 1817, KRR R/5/37, 143–54, IOR, APAC, BL.
41 For instance, Tej Pratap Sen, the raja of Ramnagar was given a remission in his revenue dues. This remission was given in lieu of the lands he had forfeited to the Gorkhalis. See E. Gardner to J. Adam, 13 October 1816, KRR R/5/37, 101–3, IOR, APAC, BL; and "Napal Correspondence." In another instance, one Jurawan Chaudhari, a Tharu *zamindar* on the Gorakhpur frontier was fined Rs 300 for erecting an irrigation channel (*kulo*) on the boundary, and also for cultivating land which lay in Gorkhali territory without informing the Company. However, Jurawan was allowed to harvest his standing crop in Gorkhali lands, on the condition that he paid Rs 9 to the Gorkhali commissioners. See letter from Ganapat Upadhyaya to Ujir Singh Thapa (n.d.), in *Shahkalin Aitihasik Chittpatra Samgraha*, 79–85; and letter from Roger Martin to E. Gardner, 14 January 1817, KRR R/5/66, 149–53, IOR, APAC, BL.
42 Such descriptions of boundaries can be found in the following: "Description of the boundary of the zilla Madura between the Shivaganga country of Ramnad," 1800, Historical Memoirs, no. 9, SOIR, NAI; "Description of the Cunneevaudy Zamindaree Dindigul" (n.d.) Historical Memoirs, no. 121, SOIR, NAI; and "Description of the boundaries of Dindigul," (n.d.) Historical Memoirs, no. 122, SOIR, NAI.
43 Information on various colonial boundary disputes can be found as follows: disputes pertaining to the modern Nepal–Champaran boundary are recorded in the 54 files of the "Search Series: Nepal Champaran Boundary," files 1–54, BSA; for boundary disputes in the United Provinces see "List 18: Political Dept," file 60, box 103, 1912, UPSA; "List 18: Political Dept," file 99, box 119, 1916, UPSA; and "List 18 A: Dept. Political Block," file 756, box 28, Nepal–Kheri District, 1892, UPSA. For boundary disputes between Jhansi District and Orchha state, which culminate in the exchange of territory, see "List 19: Political Department," file 49, box 148, 1909, UPSA. For disputes on the Rampur–Nainital district boundary, see "List 18 A: Dept. Political Block," file 789, box 29, 1894, UPSA. For Bharatpur State vs. Agra District, see "List 19: Political Department. Boundary dispute between Bharatpur State and Agra District," file 243, box 245, 1921, UPSA. For disputes that arose between various petty kingdoms and the colonial forest department in Tehri–Garhwal, see "List 18: Political Department, 1901–1936," file 33, box 84, Boundary disputes between Tehri Garhwal and Adjoining states, 1904, UPSA; "List 56A: Department-Revenue, Forest Block," "A" series, file 52, box 9, 1885, UPSA; and "List 14(i): Dept Revenue, 1904–1921," file 780, 1914, UPSA.
44 Such affirmations and sentiments of loyalty can be found in the letters from the Ramnagar raja to the Gorkha raja in the Foreign Ministry Historical Letters Collection, NAN. See also letters of Tej Pratap Sen to Bhim Sen Thapa (1825 and 1826), and *subba* Bhawani Dutt Thapa (1827), and the letter from Queen Amar Rajya Laxmi to Bhim Sen Thapa (1833), all cited in S. M. Adhikari, *Tanahu Rajyako Itihasik Jhalak*, letter nos. 40–43, pp. 114–17. In these letters, the Ramnagar raja asserted that while he was a *zamindar* of the Company, his kingdom was fully dependent on Gorkha for its continued survival. What came out of these declarations is yet unclear.
45 See *parwana* of Ramnagar Queen Laxmi Kumari Devi granting Kashi Gurau Tharu the right to collect taxes in *tappa* Chitwan, in S. M. Adhikari, *Tanahu Rajyako Itihasik Jhalak*, no. 44, 118. In 1807 this Kashi Gurau had received some lands in *nankar* in *pargana* Belod (Chitwan district) from the Gorkhali raja, Girbana Juddha Bikram Shah. See Devi Prasad Sharma, *Chitwan Upatyakako Aitihasik Ruprekha* (Bharatpur, 1985), Appendix 1.

46 During my eight-year stay in far-western Nepal (1987–94), I resided in a small town, close to the Indian border. I learned that, in the first half of the twentieth century, a raja on the Indian side of the border gave a rent-free grant of over 100 acres of barren lands to a Nepali *zamindar*. The Nepali *zamindar* cultivated these lands lying in India and enjoyed its proceeds till 1947, when India gained independence. Thereafter, the Nepali *zamindar* found it increasingly difficult to farm these lands, and was eventually forced to relinquish these lands to "Indians," who were increasingly reluctant to uphold the rights of a foreign (Nepali) landlord. I am grateful to Karna Bahadur Thapa for sharing this information with me.

47 In 1803, these villages were originally granted as dowry to the Ramnagar raja's son for marrying the daughter of the former Gorkhali raja Ran Bahadur Shah. The Gorkhalis claimed that since the queen had now died, these villages were due for resumption. See Adhikari, *Tanahu Rajyako Itihasik Jhalak*, 70. See also Giri, *Pyuthana Rajyako Itihasik Jhalak*, 20 and 76.

48 Cited in Burghart, "The Creation of the Concept," 116.

49 For details see Skaria, *Hybrid Histories*, 165–75.

50 "*Naqsha*" is the Arabic equivalent for "map." "Naqsha Compass" was the term used by the inhabitants of Basti District – in 1833 – when the first revenue-survey maps were published by the Company. The term came to signify the maps drawn with the help of the compass and I use it generically to signify the maps produced by the colonial state in India in order to suggest that they were not just European creations but also the products of local agency as well. See Hooper, *Final Report on the Settlement of Basti District*.

51 For a sampling of the vast literature on this subject see: Frangsmyr, Heilbron, and Rider, eds, *The Quantifying Spirit of the 18th Century*; Petitjean, Jami and Moulin, eds, *Science and Empires: Historical Studies About Scientific Development and European Expansion*; and Poovey, *A History of the Modern Fact: Problems of Knowledge in the Sciences of Wealth and Society*.

52 See Pratt, *Imperial Eyes: Travel Writing and Transculturation*. See especially chapter 2 titled "Science, Planetary Consciousness, Interiors." See also Driver, *Geography Militant: Cultures of Exploration and Empire*; Driver and Rose, eds, *Nature and Science: Essays in the History of Geographical Knowledge*; Godlewska, *Geography Unbound: French Geographic Science from Cassini to Humboldt*; Gregory, *Geographical Imaginations*; and Raj, *Relocating Modern Science: Circulation and the Construction of Knowledge in South Asia and Europe, 1650–1900*.

53 Cited in Nicholls, *Outlines of Indian Geography for the use of Schools and Colleges in India*, 5. The emphasis is mine.

54 Richard Helgerson's work reveals that this process of mapping was rent with social and ideological tensions. See Helgerson, "Nation or Estate? Ideological Conflict in the Early Modern Mapping of England," 68–74 (especially 68–9). See also Helgerson, *Forms of Nationhood: The Elizabethan Writing of England*.

55 This issue is explored in greater detail in Akerman, "The Structuring of Political Territory in Early Printed Atlases," 138–54. See also Buisseret, *Monarchs, Ministers and Maps: The Emergence of Cartography as a Tool of Government in Early Modern Europe*. For a richly illustrated history of modern mapmaking in India see Manosi Lahiri, *Mapping India*.

56 The term "map-mindedness," is Edney's. See Edney, "British Military Education, Mapmaking, and Military 'Map-mindedness' in the Later Enlightenment," 14–20. Edney argues that, by the turn of the nineteenth century, "map mindedness" – a dependence on the map as a tool for conceptualizing the world – had become widespread in the British military establishment.

57 Rennell himself confessed that he never possessed accurate information on the boundaries of provinces and their districts. See Phillimore, *Historical Records of the Survey of India*, vol. 1, 33–4. See also Rennell, *Memoir of a Map of Hindustan*, and his "A Map of the Kingdom of Bengal," 10 September 1768, Historical Map, IOR\1018, IOR, APAC, BL. This map has all the internal districts of the province of Bengal clearly marked out, with distinctive color-coded boundaries. For more information on Rennell see Phillimore, *Historical Records*, vol. 1, 22–36, and Cook, "Major James Rennel and A Bengal Atlas (1780 and 1781)," 4–42.

58 This point has been made by Barrow, *Making History, Drawing Territory: British Mapping in India, 1756–1905*, 36–59.
59 For details see Phillimore, *Historical Records* (4 vols); Edney, *Mapping an Empire*; and Kalpagam, "Cartography in Colonial India," *Economic and Political Weekly* 87–98.
60 For details about the GTS see Edney, *Mapping an Empire*. Another important project that would seek to do the same by building on the work of the GTS was the Atlas of India project (1827–1905).
61 This serves as a reminder that the Company state's cartographic projects did not unfold in any neat, sequential fashion. Such a call for a non-teleological account of cartography's history has been made by Matthew Edney. See Edney, "Cartography without 'Progress': Reinterpreting the Nature and Historical Development of Mapping," 54–68.
62 Hamilton, *A Geographical, Statistical, and Historical Description of Hindostan and the Adjacent Countries*, vii. The emphasis is mine.
63 Earlier, in 1764, the Company's official historian, Robert Orme, had experienced the same difficulty when writing his history of India and had asked his friend Robert Clive to make him a map of Bengal, "in which not only the *outlines* of the provinces, but also the different *subdivisions* of Burdwan, Beerboom, etc., may be justly marked". The emphasis is mine. Cited in Phillimore, *Historical Records*, vol. 1, 22.
64 Cited in Phillimore, *Historical Records*, vol. 1, 242. I use the term "cartographic anxiety" to indicate the anxiety experienced by Company officials as they struggled to discern the layout, internal organization and boundaries of their territories. For more on cartographic anxiety see Gregory, *Geographical Imaginations*, 70–205; and Krishna, "Cartographic Anxiety: Mapping the Body Politic in India," 193–214.
65 Information on the Revenue Surveys is obtainable from a number of sources: the "Historical Records of the Survey of India," which are stored in the National Archives of India (New Delhi), contain both maps and correspondence pertaining to the activities of the Survey of India from the eighteenth century onwards. Maps from the revenue surveys can also be found in the map collections of the British Library (London), the National Archives of India, the National Library (Calcutta), and various regional and local archives spread throughout India. For the history of the Survey of India in general, Phillimore's magisterial work – *Historical Records of the Survey of India* – still remains unmatched in its ambition and chronological spread. The literature on the British revenue surveys of India is limited. See Dossal, "Knowledge for power: the significance of the Bombay Revenue Survey, 1811–1827," 227–43; and for a fuller, but by no means comprehensive, treatment of the revenue surveys, see Michael, "Making Territory Visible: The Revenue Surveys of Colonial South Asia," 78–95. Finally, a broad introduction to cadastral surveying can be found in Kain and Baigent, *The Cadastral Map in the Service of the State: A History of Property Mapping*.
66 Regulation 7 flowed out of the recommendations made by Holt Mackenzie, secretary to government in the Territorial Department in his famous minute of 1 July 1819. Mackenzie recommended that systematic survey was the only way by which the Company would acquire accurate knowledge of its territories, their resources and the potential for development and taxation. See extract of this regulation in "Miscellaneous Revenue Letters Received by Collector of Gorakhpur," GCR, basta 12, vol. 92, 139–68, RSA. See also Holt Mackenzie's "Observations on Execution of Revenue Surveys," 25 August 1821 GDR, basta 2, vol. 15, 27–54, RSA.
67 For details about these regulations see Misra, *The Central Administration of the East India Company*, 214–18. However, Regulation 9 sought to introduce economy and rapidity in surveying by asking that only village boundaries and sites be delineated, along with rough outlines of roads and rivers. However, this hasty surveying and lack of coordination with the Great Trigonometrical Survey (GTS) resulted in maps of questionable accuracy (many topographic surveys often preceded the GTS, when they should have followed it).
68 Further details about the progress, technicalities, local adaptations and alignments with the Great Trigonometrical Survey can be found in the various volumes of Phillimore's *Historical*

Records of the Survey of India; and Michael, "Making Territory Visible." See also Smyth and Thuillier, comps, *A Manual of Surveying for India Detailing the Mode of Operations on the Revenue Surveys in Bengal and the North-Western Provinces*. Various survey-related documents including circulars, orders, and correspondence can be found in the "Historical Records of the Survey of India," lying in the National Archives of India, Delhi or the British Library in London. See for instance, *Return to an Order of the House of Commons, dated 22 July 1853 for a Selection of Papers Illustrative of the Character and Results of the Revenue Survey and Assessment which has been Introduced in the North-West Provinces of Bengal Presidency, Since the year 1833*.

69 See these additional maps: "Map of the Rampoor Jagir," Historical Maps, IOR/X/1503, IOR, APAC, BL; See the northern part of the district of Shahjahanpur, in "Map of District Shahjahanpur," 1842, by Capt. J. Abbot and Lt G. Fraser, Historical Maps, IOR/X/1481, IOR, APAC, BL; Alex Wyatt's "Map of Districts of Saran and Champaran," 1848, *Historical Maps*, IOR/X/1163/27, IOR, APAC, BL; "Map of Pargana Erinch and Bainda Bazar," by R. Mathison, 1839–40, Historical Map Collection, Map no. 5. National Library, Calcutta; "A Map of Sikkim and Eastern Nepal," by J. D. Hooker, 1852, Historical Map, IOR/X/1288/2, IOR, APAC, BL; and "Map of the District of Tirhut," by Alex Wyatt, Revenue Surveyor, 1846, Historical Maps, IOR/X/1168/1–25, IOR, APAC, BL.

70 The late Professor Qeyamuddin Ahmad of Patna University was one of the earliest scholars to comment on the historical value of these maps. I am grateful to Prof. Ahmad for granting me access to his collection of rare photographs of *pargana* maps of Bihar. I was unable to locate the originals of these hand-drawn *pargana* maps, which are probably lying somewhere in the Survey Office at Patna. See Ahmad, "Pargana Maps and Village Survey Records: A Note on an Unnoticed Source Material for the History of Bihar," 588–94. See also Madan, "Field-Books and Memoirs: Untapped Source for Historical Research."

71 The emphasis is mine. This resolution also deplored changing the "old established ancient divisions of a country as it broke up old relations and tended to form new ones." See Resolution of the Revenue Board, North West Provinces, 30 October 1837. BOR See also Map Shelf Series, serial no. 86, misl no. 86, box 14, para 3, Vernacular Maps, General Questions, UPSA.

72 This is clear on an examination of the map of Tirhut district by Alex Wyatt in his *Geographical and Statistical Memoir of the District of Tirhoot*. Wyatt vividly describes the broken geographies of the *parganas* of Tirhut, but does not include these in his map of the district. Rather, the *parganas* appear whole and compact.

73 However, the presence of detached lands was carefully noted in the tables that accompanied *pargana* maps. I am grateful to the late Prof. Qeyamuddin Ahmad for initially alerting me to these details and for his stimulating discussions on the same.

74 A comparison of maps from a single district over a period of time clearly confirms this trend. Later maps depict districts with more compact bodies and with fewer detachments and intermixture of lands. See for example the maps of districts of Kuch Behar state, 1868–70, 1872, Historical Maps, IOR/X/1277/1, IOR, APAC, BL and District Saran, Historical Maps, IOR/X/1162/1, IOR, APAC, BL.

75 For evidence of this, compare the following maps of Purnea between 1871–1903 from the Map Collection, India Survey, box 132, BL (all based on the revenue survey of Messrs J. Fitzpatrick and J. J. Pemberton, 1840–47): District Purnea, 1871. 35.75 × 22.25 in., 18 sheets, lithographed on cloth, 1 inch = 1 mile; District Purnea, 1879, 30.125 × 27.87 in., lithograph on cloth, 1 inch = 4 miles; and District Purnea, 1903, lithograph on cloth, 31.75 × 28.25 in., 1 inch = 4 miles.

76 The territorialization of the colonial state's power and its representation on maps provided a spatial foundation that underwrote many colonial projects. For instance, the introduction of the rule of law could only take maximum effect once the Company's territories were properly demarcated. Such a view adds an oft-ignored spatial dimension to otherwise excellent studies on the rule of law or the creation of a documentary archive in colonial South Asia. See Singha, *A Despotism of Law*; and Saumarez-Smith, *Rule by Records: Land Registration and village custom in early British Panjab*.

77 Major J. L. Sherwill, *A Geographical and Statistical Report of the District of Dinajpore District*, 1–2.

78 These words are those of H. L. Thuillier, the deputy surveyor general. See letter of H. L. Thuillier to William Muir, secretary to government of the North-West Provinces, 11 November 1854, BOR Map Shelf Series, serial no. 86, misl no. 86, box 14, Vernacular Maps, General Questions, UPSA. In order to simplify these maps, color codes were established to distinguish *parganas* and *tehsils*.
79 Cited in Serajuddin, *The Revenue Administration of the East India Company in Chittagong, 1761–1785*, 60–61. See also pages 58–76.
80 The Collectorships would have a minimum rent-roll of 5 lakh rupees each. See Misra, *The Central Administration*, 156–7; Mookerji, *Indian Land System: Ancient, Medieval and Modern*, 74–5.
81 For details, see Sir John Shore's minute of 13 March 1787, cited in Firminger, ed., *The Fifth Report from the Select Committee on the House of Commons on the Affairs of the East India Company*, 734–6.
82 Minutes of Sir John Shore, dated 18 June 1789, regarding the permanent settlement of the land in the Bengal Provinces, cited in Firminger, *The Fifth Report*, 1–145. The quotation is from p. 100. The emphasis is mine.
83 The emergence of the *thana* as a territorial sub-division can be traced back to 1782 and the governor-generalship of Warren Hastings. See Chakrabarti, "The Origin of Subdivisions in Bengal," 36–64 (especially 37–8). It appears that *thanas* as police divisions were formally introduced by Lord Cornwallis through Regulation 22 of 1793. See Hirst, *Notes on the Revenue Surveys of Bengal, Bihar, Orissa and Assam*, 5n2.
84 Buchanan-Hamilton, "The Gorakhpur Report," vol. 1, 297, Eur. Mss D 91, IOR, APAC, BL (hereafter "The Gorakhpur Report"). Similar descriptions can be found in Buchanan-Hamilton's accounts of the districts of Bihar – see his *An Account of the District of Purnea in 1809–10*; and *An Account of the Districts of Bihar and Patna in 1811 and 1812*. In all these and the other districts that Buchanan surveyed, he noted that the *thana* divisions were "miserably intermixed and discordant" – see his *Journal of Francis Buchanan (*Patna–Gaya Report), 3–4. An examination of his maps of the Gorakhpur district clearly shows the various *thana* divisions – detachments and all. See his "Map of the Northern Part of the District of Gorakhpur," Historical Maps, X\1020\2, IOR, APAC, BL. See also "Map of the District of Ronggopur," Historical Maps, X\1020\3, IOR, APAC, BL; Plan of the District of Purnea 1809–10, Historical Maps X\1020\6, IOR, APAC, BL.
85 Buchanan-Hamilton, "The Gorakhpur Report," 1:10–11.
86 However, on the Anglo–Bhutan border the commissioner of Kuch Bihar noted that the boundaries of the districts of the Doars were "badly defined owing to their being the boundaries of the so called pergunnahs which we found in existence when we took possession of the country." See letter from W. J. Herschel, commissioner, Cooch Behar Division to secretary to the government of Bengal (Revenue Department), P/242 Bengal Judicial Consultations, 22 July 1874, 5, IOR, APAC, BL. For similar observations about the *thana* divisions of Rangpur district, see Thomas Sisson to W.B. Bayley, acting secretary to the government, Judicial Department, 4 January 1815, Historical Records of the Survey of India, SGO 6, PP. 133–6, NAI.
87 Buchanan-Hamilton, *An Account of the District of Purnea in 1809–10*, 4. Hamilton was an alert observer of such performances, and his comments on local maps are most interesting. In another instance, he commented on the efforts of a Burmese informant to construct, in Hamilton's view, a "horribly distorted map" of a province. See Hamilton, "An Account of a Map of the Country North from Ava,"76. Cited in Gole, *Indian Maps and Plans*, 37.
88 Neil Smith and Cindi Katz define "absolute space" as "our naively assumed sense of space as emptiness." See Smith and Katz, "Grounding Metaphor: Towards A Spatialized Politics," 67–83. The quotation is from p. 75.
89 See Procs of BOR, 15 May 1793, BSA; Procs of BOR 16 August 1793, BSA; Printed Index to the Procs of the BOR, 1793, WBSA. In Bengal, such exchanges took place, for example, between the districts of Dacca, Mymensingh, Tipperah, Murshidabad, Dinajpur, Bhagalpur and many others.

90 Letter of magistrate of Azamghar to the commissioner, Ghazipur, 8 November 1835, GDR, basta 27, vol. 57, RSA. The emphasis is mine. In 1829, Gorakhpur was made a division comprising the additional districts of Azamgarh and Ghazipur. In 1835, the Gorakhpur division was abolished only to be revived in 1853.

91 In the nineteenth century, Champaran district underwent a number of territorial rearrangements. For instance, the *pargana* of Babra was transferred from Champaran to Tirhut. In 1837 a Magistrate was stationed for the first time at Motihari (in Champaran). In 1852, Bettiah was made a subdivision under Motihari, and in 1866 the latter became a separate collectorate. See Hunter, *A Statistical Account of Bengal*, vols 8, 9, 18 and 220.

92 For example, in 1874, in the Gaya district of Bihar, the *munsifi* of Aurangabad was made coterminous with that of the sub-division of Aurangabad. This was achieved by adding the *thana* of neighboring Daudnagar to Aurangabad *munsifi*. In this manner the civil and executive jurisdictions were made to coincide. See P/242, Bengal Judicial Consultations, Procs of the Revenue Branch, Jurisdictions and Boundaries, 1–131, IOR, APAC, BL. See especially 12–14.

93 For example, 15 villages belonging to the Collector's rent-roll of Gaya (in province of Bihar) and under the criminal jurisdiction of the neighboring Hazaribagh district (Chotta Nagpur region) were transferred from Gaya to Hazaribagh, so that the civil and executive jurisdictions overlapped. Ibid., 45–6.

94 The Bengal Judicial Consultations are full of such instances, running into hundreds of pages. See Procs of the Lt. Governor of Bengal (Revenue Department), March 1875, 155–60, P/242 Bengal Judicial Consultations, IOR, APAC, BL.

95 In another instance, the *thana* of Mirserai (in Bengal) had its executive, fiscal and police jurisdictions spread over different districts. Its criminal jurisdiction was vested in the sub-divisional officer of Fenny, and the judge of Noakholly district, but its civil jurisdiction lay with the *munsif* of Dewangunj. Later, all these jurisdictions were made coincident and the *thana* of Mirserai was included within the Fenny sub-division of District Noakholly (in Bengal). See P/910, Bengal Judicial Consultations, Procs of July 1877, p. 77, IOR, APAC, BL.

96 P/242 Bengal Judicial Consultations, Revenue Department: Branch Jurisdictions and Boundaries, July 1875, 47–53, IOR, APAC, BL.

97 See the following series in the *Bengal Judicial Consultations*, Judicial (1887–1905) especially P/5408–5410 and Revenue (1874–1886 and 1906–1936) especially P/242, P/236, P/910, P/1319, P/1641, P/1836, P/2024, P/2238, P/2487, OIOC, APAC, BL.

98 Other variables that informed these exercises in territorial rearrangement include: accessibility to roads; central location of police posts and other offices; presence of "wild," "criminal" and other "undesirable" elements within the precincts of the district; population density; workload; number of staff; topography; and frontier location. Descriptive accounts of the administrative experiments of the Company during the late eighteenth century and early nineteenth century can be found in: Dhar, *The Administrative System of the East India Company in Bengal, 1714–1786* (2 vols) (Calcutta, 1964); Misra, *The Central Administration of the East India Company, 1773–1834* (Manchester, 1959); Misra, *The Judicial Administration of the East India Company in Bengal, 1765–1782* (Delhi, 1961); and Patra, *The Administration of Justice Under the East-India Company in Bengal, Bihar and Orissa* (London, 1962). However, none of these works discuss the crucial role played by spatial concerns in the reorganization of the administrative geography of the Company state. Animesh Chakrabarti's piece on "The Origins of Subdivisions in Bengal," however, views the whole episode from the perspective of government policy and administrative rationalizing and not in terms of a *longue durée* view of ongoing spatial transformation. The constitutive role of *pargana* divisions in the formation of modern divisions is also completely overlooked.

99 See "Dinanath Upadhyaya informed of his replacement as *chaudhari* by Bhakhat and others in Simraongarh, Ashwin 1851 BS [1794 AD]," RRC 24: 403; and "Dinanath Upadhyaya replaced as *subba* of Morung by Zorawar Khawas, Marga 1851 BS [1795 AD]," RRC 24: 511.

100 Cited in Regmi, *Imperial Gorkha: An Account of Gorkhali Rule in Kumaon, 1791–1815*, 51.

NOTES 189

101 Jurisidictional themes crop up in the following Gorkhali documents: "Subedar Jayant Khatri granted authority to promote settlement on virgin lands (*kalabanjar*), east of the Kamala river, which do not fall under the jurisdiction of the suba-ijaradar of Morang, 1810 CE [1867 BS]," in *RRS* 16 (May 1984): 76–7; "Raghav Singh (Khadka?) authorized to collect *sair* [custom] duties in Jaleswar and *jalkar* [water tax] duties in Bhadwa, 1810 CE, [1867 BS]," RRC 39: 207; "Dhananjay Padhya (a clerk of *kaji* Amar Singh Thapa) authorized to collect revenues under the *amanat* system in areas assigned to the royal prince in Sallyan, 1810 CE [1867 BS]," RRC 39: 313 and 317; and "Narjit and Thakur Singh Newar granted the *ijara* [contract] of *namak mahal* [salt collections] in Saptari-Mahottari, Bara-Parsa, Rautahat and Chitwan." The local *subbas*, Achal Thapa and Dashrath Khatri, who till then were in charge of making such collections, were informed of their supersession by these two new *ijaradars*. See also RRC 36: 122–3; and "Judicial authority granted to Baraha Dal and Devi Dal companies over *jagir* lands assigned to them, 1816 CE [1873 BS]," RRC 28: 129.

102 Again, consider the following. In 1810, Umanidhi Pant and Jayanta Khatri were deputed *dhittas* (judicial officers) to Morang, to investigate complaints of oppression by revenue collectors. They were specifically instructed not to interfere in revenue-collection matters. See Adalat Regulations, 1805 AD, in "Ran Bahadur Shah's Expenses in Banaras," *RRS* 19 (July–August 1987): 94. In another instance, when *subba* Dashrath Khatri was granted the right to collect revenues (*amanat*) from the districts of Bara-Parsa, Morang, Rautahat, and Saptari-Mahottari, he was specifically instructed to refrain from making collections from lands which had been restored through royal orders, or included in the revenue-collection contracts issued to other parties. See "Subba Dashrath Khatri and Subba Gaj Simha Khatri," *RRS* 19 (June 1987): 84–5.

103 See "Order regarding new villages settled by Capt. Chandra Bir Kunwar on Bekh Buniyad lands in Sheoraj, 1812 CE, [1869 B.S.]," RRC 40: 341. For more instances of this see Royal Letter of Girbana Juddha Bikram Shah to the Shepherds of Jhiri, Cited in Dinesh Raj Pant, "B.S. 1832 dekhi B.S. 1858 sammako Nepalko Itihasma Naya Prakash Parne Kehi Patraharu," *Purnima* 17 (2021): 50–51. See also "Order regarding dispute [over *sair* rights] between Fauzdar Bidesh Raut and Fakir Baksh in Bara-Parsa, 1810 CE, [1867 B.S.]," RRC: 40: 158.

104 Regmi, *Imperial Gorkha*, 60, and personal communication. The emphasis is mine.

105 The Gorkhali term "*ambal/amval*" was derived from the Persian "*amal*" and signified a jurisdiction created through the exercise of some right to office, revenue-collection or tenure. Various, and almost similar, definitions can be found in the following: Moosvi, "Aurangzeb's *Farman* to Rasikdas on Problems of Revenue Administration, 1665," in *Medieval India 1: Researches in the History of India, 1200–1750*, 207; Irfan Habib, *The Agrarian System of Mughal India*, 1st edition, 213n67; Gupta, *The Agrarian System in Eastern Rajasthan*, 139; Jafri, *Awadh: From Mughal to Colonial Rule*, 64; Wilson, *A Glossary of Judicial and Revenue Terms* (1850; Reprint, Delhi, 1968). Nepali historians broadly concur with this definition and Mahesh Chandra Regmi defines *amval* as signifying territory (personal communication), while Dinesh Raj Pant defines it as meaning territory that is held under the authority of a ruling power (personal communication). See Pant, "B.S. 1832–58, Sammako Nepalko Itihasma Naya Prakash Parne Kehi Patraharu," 27–51 (especially 28).

106 My information is derived from the following: Stiller, "Hodgson on Justice," *RRS* 16 (September–October 1984): 139–40 and *RRS* 17 (January–February 1985); "Supplement to the papers on the Judicial system of Nepal", Hodgson Collection, Mss Eur. Hodgson 12, ff. 16–20, IOR, APAC, BL; "Judicial System of Nepal: Additional Queries and their Answers", Hodgson Collection, Mss Eur. Hodgson 12, ff. 28–45, IOR, APAC, BL. For an overview see Tulasi Ram Vaidya and Tri Ratna Manandhar, *Crime and Punishment in Nepal: A Historical Perspective*.

107 Appeals against the *fauzdar*'s decisions went to the *subba*, then to the Kumari Chowk at Kathmandu (for revenue cases), and finally to superior courts like the "Kot Sing" (*koti ling*) and Inta Chapli (at Kathmandu) in civil and criminal matters, respectively. See Mss Eur. Hodgson

12, ff. 16–20. See also B. H. Hodgson, "On the Administration of Justice in Nepal," *Asicatick Researches* vol. 20 (1836): 94–134

108 Cited in Dhanabajra Bajracharya and Gyanmani Nepal, eds, *Aitihasik Chittpatrasangraha*, 19–20. In the 26th edict of the Gorkhali raja Rama Shah (1603–36) we hear that those who violated the king's rules were to be punished by touching the stone (*dhungo*) representative of Sri Laxminarayan. The use of the term in this sense, suggests that that the metaphor *dhungo* might have possibly entailed a sacred notion of kingship. Cited in Theodore Riccardi Jr, "The Royal Edicts of King Rama Shah of Gorkha," 29–65 (especially 64). Further references to the term *dhunga* can be found in D. R. Pant, "B.S. 1832–1858," 30; and "Royal Administrative Regulations for the Regions west of the Tista and east of the Mahakali, 1806 CE" *Abhilekh* 10 (2049 BS), Regulation (*sawal*) no. 8, 13–18.

109 Cited in Naraharinatha and Acharya, eds, *Rashtrapita Shri Panch Badamaharaja Prithvinarayan Shah Dev ko Dibya Upadesh*, 15.

110 See Regmi, "Preliminary Notes on the Nature of the Gorkhali State and Administration," *RRS* 10 (November 1978): 171–4. The quotation is from p. 173. See also Regmi, *Kings and Political Leaders of the Gorkhali Empire, 1768–1814*, 15.

111 Gorkhali documents record *parganas* as *pragannas* and *tappas* as *tappe*. Elsewhere, the Kirati kingdoms in the eastern territories of Gorkha had been traditionally divided into *thums*. Each *thum* had five elders (*panch*) who administered it. See H. N. Aggarwal, *The Administrative System of Nepal: From Tradition to Modernity*, 1. In Garhwal, we hear of *fauzdari* (military police) jurisdictions being divided into *thats* or *garkhas* – a system that was adopted by the Gorkhalis when they conquered these areas. See Siva Prasad Dabral, "Gorkhali Administration in Garhwal," 16. Elsewhere, the Mustang region was divided into six tax-paying sectors (*tshogs*). See Ramble, "Civic Authority and Agrarian Management in Southern Mustang," 114.

112 See "Jagir Grant to Kokil Khawas, 1793 CE [1850 BS]," RRC 24: 244; and "Five year *ijara* grant to Laxmi Mahajan, 1799 CE [1856 BS]," RRC 24: 18. However, most of the records I have examined refer to Rautahat as a *tappe*.

113 See "*Ijara* grant to Kulchandra Sahu for land reclamation for Rautahat, 1806 CE [1863 BS]," RRC 5: 166; "Orders to *subba* Indra Singh to release Rs 4001 from the *ijara* of *zilla* Bara-Parsa-Rautahat, 1796 CE [1853 BS]," Poka 8, bahi 8, no. 133, Lagat Phant, Kathmandu.

114 See "*Mokarrari* grant to *mahant* Badri Bas, 1792 CE [1849 BS]," RRC 5: 206. The *mokarrari* grant worth Rs 125 is recorded as lands belonging to the village of Baluwa, *pargana* Paroha, *zilla* Rautahat (not *taraf* Paroha, *tappa* Rautahat).

115 See *lal mohar* of *maharani* Raj Rajeshwari Devi conferring *patta* on Bhairo Ram, 1858 BS (1801 CE), in Shankarman Rajbamshi, ed., *Puratatva Patra Sangraha*, 37. Such mutations occur frequently in the revenue record such as in the case of *pargana* Jhamuna, which split to become the sometimes conjoined *parganas* of Raijhamuna and Maljhamuna. See "*Kus birta* grant by raja Hemkarna Sen of Makwanpur of the *mauza* of Vetahi (?) in *pargana* Jhamuna to Bhuwan Jha Jaisi, 1738 BC [1795 BS]," RRC 5: 199; and "Orders to Sahu Harikrishna Das not to collect *salami* on *nankar* lands of *chaudharis* of *pargana* Raijhamuna-Maljhamuna, in Saptari district, 1804 CE [1861 BS]," RRC 5: 461.

116 See proceedings of the governor-general of Bengal in council, 28 September 1781, Consultation nos. 1–3, WBSA; series of letters and papers with Persian secretary John Monckton's report on them relating to the Anglo–Gorkha border disputes in Champaran, in FP, Procs 4 March 1814, Consl. 53–65, pp. 195–434, NAI (The Monckton Report); and various records from the Lagat Phant between the years 1790–1813.

117 These are recorded in the map prepared by the geographer Pradyumna P. Karan. See enclosed map titled "Nepal: Administrative Units," in Karan, *Nepal: A Physical and Cultural Geography*. The *tappa* of Rautahat saw further changes sometime after the mid-nineteenth century, when three new sub-divisions were created – Chand West, Chand East, and Ratahati Kachad. The *taraf* of Pachrauta was transferred to the district of Bara and for sometime was attached to the *pargana*

of Gadh Simraon. Later these two *parganas* were detached to form separate *parganas* of Gadh Simraon, and Pachrauta. They appear as such in Karan's map. See also Regmi, "Districts and Pargannas of the Eastern Tarai Region," *RRS* 17 (January–February 1985): 22–4.
118 See Bouillier, "The Nepalese State and Gorakhnathi Yogis: The Case of the Former Kingdoms of Dang Valley: 18th–19th Centuries," 36–7. See also *RRS* 21 (December 1989): 172; and RRC 5: 418–19.
119 For details see *RRS* 21 (December 1989): 172.
120 This becomes apparent on an examination of the map of the kingdom of Dang in Bouillier's article (30). In this map, Chilli appears surrounded by the combined territories of Sallyan and Dang. In 1809, the kingdom of Sallyan was itself incorporated into the Gorkhali Empire following a confrontation between Gorkhali prime minister Bhim Sen Thapa and the Sallyani raja.
121 See Gitu Giri, *Pyuthana Rajyako Aitihasik Jhala*, 106–7, 110–11, letter nos. 19 and 29. Such engagements were not uncommon. See Bouillier, *The Nepalese State and the Gorakhnathi Yogis*, 36–7.
122 While Gorkha's southern boundary with British India was demarcated in 1816, its northern boundary remained undefined till recently. It was only in 1979 that Chinese and Nepali teams conducted joint surveys of their common borders and demarcated the boundary line. See Gurung, *Maps of Nepal*, 3.
123 Hodgson Collection, Eur Mss. Hodgson 4, folio 104, IOR, APAC, BL. The emphasis is mine. See also Hodgson, *Selections from the Records of the Government of Bengal*, 224. Details about Nepal's administrative districts can be found in the following: Kirkpatrick, *An Account of the Kingdom of Nepaul*, 42; Hamilton, *An Account*, 150–62; Hodgson, "Sketch of the Kingdom of Nepal, 1834," Hodgson Collection, Eur. Mss Hodgson 3, folios 209–264, IOR, APAC, BL; "Jamabandi of Nepal Tarai in 1897 B.S. or 1840 AD," Hodgson Collection, Mss Eur. Hodgson 14, folios 76–8, 88 IOR, APAC, BL; Hodgson Collection, Eur. Mss Hodgson 60, folio 78, IOR, APAC, BL; Hodgson, "On the Administration of Justice in Nepal," 94–134; and Anon., *Provinces of Nepal* (n.p., 1858?). This last book can be found in the Shish Mahal Library belonging to the rajas of Bettiah in Champaran.
124 The Ranas were the powerful prime ministers who dominated Gorkhali/Nepali politics between 1846–1951, leaving the king a mere figurehead.
125 Sever, *Nepal Under the Ranas*, 209–10. The headquarters of the Eastern *gaunda* was at Dhankuta, the Central *gaunda* at Palpa, and the Western *gaunda* at Doti.
126 Sever, *Nepal Under the Ranas*, 213 and 260. The four-Tarai circles were centered at Hanumannagar, Birganj, Taulihawa and Nepalgunj. Sever does not cite the source of this information, and nor does he inform us about how such alterations were put into effect on the ground.
127 See Gurung, *Maps of Nepal: Inventory and Evaluation*, 7n98.
128 See Buchanan-Hamilton, *An Account of The Kingdom of Nepal*, 192.
129 See Kolver, "A Ritual Map of Nepal," 68–80; Schwartzberg, *History of Cartography*, vol. 2, 455–7. Schwartzberg also cites evidence of another undated Nepali map of Kathmandu in the shape of a sword and showing the various quarters (*tols*) of the city. Ibid., vol. 2, part 2, 455. See also the following works on the ritual ordering of urban spaces in the Nepal valley: Gutschow and Kolver, *Ordered Space Concepts and Functions in a Town of Nepal*; Gutschow, "Functions of Squares in Bhaktapur" and "Ritual as a Mediator of Space in Kathmandu, Nepal," both in *South Asia: 30th International Congress of Human Sciences in Asia and North Africa* (Mexico, 1982); Gutschow and Michaels, eds, *The Heritage of the Kathmandu Valley: Proceedings of an International Conference in Lubeck, June 1985*; and Slusser, *Nepal Mandala*, 2 vols. For a similar argument on a grander scale, see Levy, *Mesocosm: Hinduism and the Organization of a Traditional Newar City in Nepal*.
130 See Gole, *Indian Maps and Plans*, 68; and "A Nepali Map of Central Asia," 81–9.
131 These maps showing the trading routes and military marches of the Chinese Army can be found in Boulnois, "Chinese Maps and Prints on the Tibet–Gorkha War of 1788–92," 84–112.

The Jesuits conducted a survey of China from which they produced a map in 1717. Impressed by the mapmaking efforts of the Jesuits, the Qing emperor ordered a number of his officials to undertake exploratory surveys in Tibet to draw maps of that region. Cited in Phillimore, *Historical Records*, 70. See also Hostetler, "Qing Connections to the Early Modern World: Ethnography and Cartography in Eighteenth-Century China," 623–62 (especially 651–8).

132 Wilford, "An Essay on the Sacred Isles in the West, with Other Essays Connected with That Work," 245–375, cited in Schwartzberg, "South Asian Cartography", in Harley and Woodward, eds, *History of Cartography*, vol.2, no.2, 293–388. See p.326. Schwartzburg suggests that Wilford's is the "first unambiguous Western reference to Nepali cartography". See Schwartzberg, "Geographical Mapping," 430.

133 Cited in Schwartzberg, 430. The emphasis is mine.

134 See Dabral, "From the Yamuna to the Sutlej," 51. In 1807 one Kesav Gurung was paid Rs 325 for this purpose. See also Gurung, *Maps of Nepal*, 9; and Yogi Naraharinath, *Ithihasprakashma Sandhipatrasamrgaha*, 92.

135 Hamilton's Nepali assistants were a number of Brahmans, such as Hariballabh, Sadhu Ram Upadhyaya, Prati Nidhi and Kanak Nidhi Tiwari, the former Palpali *diwan* Samar Bahadur Sen and one Kamal Lochan. For further details see Hamilton, *An Account of the Kingdom*, 1–5. Today, these maps can be found in the India Office Map Collections of the British Library and in the Foreign Ministry Archives at Kathmandu. Unfortunately, the latter archive is currently closed to the public.

136 Hamilton, *An Account of the Kingdom of Nepal*, 1–5. The emphasis is mine. The quote is from p. 3. Once again, Hamilton's choice of metaphors is interesting. Hamilton's vision of the Gorkhali state was an Icarian one that saw the presentation of the kingdom as a whole in a manner that was internally consistent and coherent.

137 Letter from Edward Gardner, Resident at Kathmandu, to John Adam, secretary to government, 31 July 1816, in Boards Collections F/4/550, no. 13376, 83–111(especially 83), IOR, APAC, BL.

138 Hodgson held various posts, including that of the British Resident at Kathmandu (1820–44). Hodgson was responsible for amassing a collection of materials covering the history, culture, ethnology and other miscellaneous topics pertaining to Nepal. The maps can be found in the following volumes and pages of the Hodgson Collection, 3: f. 103; 7: ff. 32, 197–215; 55: f. 106; 56: ff. 59–60; 59: ff. 15–16, 25–37, 38–40, 41–8, 49–50, 81–90 and 91–2; and 73: f. 111, 117 and 142. See also Schwartzberg, "Geographical Mapping", 474–5.

139 See "Sukhimko charkillako tapsil," (1830 CE) 45 × 50 cm, ink on Nepali paper, Hodgson Collection, Eur. Mss K474, vol. 59, ff. 15–16.

140 This echoes Susan Gole's view that the route maps in eighteenth-century writings like the *Chahar Gulshan* were "little more than tables abstracted from the text of itineraries." See Gole, *Indian Maps and Plans*, 91–3. The quotation is from page 92. See also Schwartzberg, "Geographical Mapping", 435–6.

141 The term Hodgson's indigenous informants used was "*kagaz*" or "paper/document." See Hodgson Eur. Mss K474, vol. 59, f. 24, 35.

142 See "Preliminary Sketch of Nipal and the Countries Adjoining to the South, West, and East" (1855 CE), 69 × 126 cm, color ink on paper, scale = 16 miles to one inch. IOR/X/2996/1, APAC, BL. A further note adds that the position of Humla, information regarding the military posts, and the subdivisions of the country were supplied by Major G. Ramsay, the then-Resident at Nepal. But a note at the top by Andrew Waugh, the surveyor general of India, suggests that the map has been compiled by discordant materials and that Nepal has not been surveyed. The note also adds that the northern boundaries seem incorrect. The maps shows Baise and Chaubise kingdoms, the Barapak Zemindaree (the Mustang Area), the districts of Morung, Mihteree (sic), Subteree and the *sal* forests of the Bhabar. In the west the Naya Muluk territories (which were returned to Nepal after the revolt of 1857) lie clearly in Awadh and the Anglo–Gorkha boundary extends right up to the foothills or the Chure range. Trigonometrical points are noted.

143 See Gurung, *Maps of Nepal*, 9. The map, which measures 84cm × 495cm, is presently stored in the National Museum of Nepal.
144 Interestingly, the Gorkhali Regent, Bahadur Shah's (1785–94) downfall was reputedly caused by his "sin" of "finding out the secrets of the earth" (read: survey) on the advice of "evil minded ministers." See Dhanabajra Bajracharya and Gyanmani Nepal, eds, *Aitihasik Patra Sangraha*, part 1 (Kathmandu, 2012 BS), 78. References to these surveys have been made at various places in Chapters 3, 5 and 6.
145 Regmi, *Land Tenure and Taxation in Nepal*, 153–5. Gorkhali documents also make references to a caste of Newari land measurers called "Dangol" who were deployed in these surveys. For instance, see "Administrative Regulations for Areas between the Kanka and Mahakali Rivers," (1863 BS/1806 CE), Kausi Tosakhana Collection, Historical Document no. 117, *sawal* 29, NAN. This regulation instructs officials to investigate cases of land encroachment through survey by Dangols and confiscation of such lands.
146 Regmi, *Land Tenure and Taxation in Nepal*, 15–35.
147 Ibid., 156.
148 See *Survey of India: General Report, 1926–1927*, 92–5. See also "Nepal" (three sheets), scale = 96 miles to one inch, Calcutta, Survey of India, 1934 (second edition). Cited in Gurung, *Maps of Nepal* (Bankok, 1983), 33n4.
149 The only secondary source I have come across that studies these early Nepali cadastral maps has no discussion of the issues being covered here. See Muller, "Interpretation of Cadastral Maps and Land Registers – Examples from the Kathmandu Valley and Gorkha," 141–58.
150 See *Naapi Dorko Sawal*, issued in 2003 BS (1948CE) that I found in an unmarked *basta* of the Kumari Chowk records in the National Archives of Nepal.
151 "Government of Nepal, Draft five-year Plan, A Synopsis" (n.d.), 30, in Regmi, *Land Tenure and Taxation*, 69.
152 In some instances, lands held under traditional *kipat* tenure in eastern Nepal were subjected to modern cadastral surveys only as recently as 1994. See Forbes, "The Boundary Keepers: The Poetry and Politics of Land in Northeastern Nepal," 3, 296–8.
153 The hill *parganas* on the other hand seem to have been based on their hilly topography and natural products. Malhotra also adds that, generally speaking, the soil and soil structure was common within a *pargana*, suggesting that soil characteristics might have played a role in the constitution of these Tarai *parganas*. See Malhotra, *Agricultural Investigations of Morung District (terai), Kingdom of Nepal*, 16.
154 *Report on the Re-Organization of District Administration in Nepal*, 52.
155 See District maps of Nepal, Survey of India, 1953–1960, stored at the Kitta Napi Mahashakha, Baneshwor, in Kathmandu. These maps were made to a scale of one inch to a mile. Today these maps can be found in a *basta* lying at the Cadastral Survey Office in Kathmandu.
156 See map titled "Nepal: Administrative Units," in Karan, *Nepal: A Cultural and Physical Geography*. *Pargana* Beli is numbered "2" under the district of Biratnagar, while the sub-division of Palpa is numbered "1," under the district of Palpa.
157 Another instance of this would be the *tappa* of Rautahat. Many of the older subdivisions of this *tappa* cannot be located in Karan's map. Under what circumstances these subdivisions were dissolved is, as yet, unclear.
158 The examples referred to above have been drawn from maps of the Tarai *tappas* of Far Western Nepal (2003 BS or 1946–7). Today, these survey maps of Bardia district (in Far Western Nepal) lie in the newly created Central Archive Office of the Survey Department, Baneshwor, Kathmandu.
159 For details see *Nepalko Naksa (thum/pragannama vibhajit janganna jillaharu), Interim Report of the Census of Nepal* and *Census of Population Nepal 1952/54 A.D.* See also Raimajhi, "Nepalko Janganako parampara," and "Nepalko vibhinna ganana," in *Nepalko Janganna*, vol. 1, part 1, 6–8 and 9–21; and Adhikari, "Jangannaka Vibhin Ekai," in *Nepalko Janganna*, 2–4. See also Adhikari, "Yas Jangannama Apnayeka Tarika Tatha Karya Vidhi," in *Nepalko Janganna*,

22–8. I am also grateful to Shri Thir Bahadur Raimajhi and Shri Nara Kanta Adhikari, who superintended these operations, for sharing their experiences with me in summer 2005.
160 These *pargana* and *thum* maps probably lay in the various district survey offices (*napi vibhag*). I have found only two published versions of these *pargana* and *thum* maps, one in *Nepalko Naksa* (cited in the previous endnote) and in Karan's *Nepal: A Cultural and Physical Geography* (especially p. 8). However, a Government of India's publication on the Gurkhas contains 24 maps of Western Nepal including *thum* divisions. See *Gurkhas*, 2 vols.
161 *Report on the Re-Organization of District Administration in Nepal*, 56. For instance, Keshraha block (district Bara), which was constituted by amalgamating the Tarai *parganas* of Keshraha, Totni and Cherwant. And the block of Gad Simraon was composed of the *parganas* of Gad Simraon, Dostiya, while the block of Jataha comprised the *parganas* of Jataha, Chand Parwa, Rathatti and Matiban (ibid., v).
162 However, discontinuous administrative divisions still exist in Nepal. For instance, there are Village Development Committee (VDC) divisions in the Tarai and hills that possess discontinuous bodies. The reasons behind this are unclear, and it is possible that the older underlying *pargana* and *thum* divisions might have something to do with this. I am grateful to Mr Damodar Wagle of the Survey Dept for sharing this information with me. More research is needed to understand the spatial history of these discontinuous administrative divisions.
163 For details see Pitamber Sharma, *Unravelling the Mosaic: Spatial Aspects of Ethnicity in Nepal* and Pitamber Sharma, Narendra Khanal, and Subhash Chaudhary Tharu, *Towards a Federal Nepal: An Assessment of Proposed Models*.
164 My use of the terms "projects of legibility" and "simplification" is adapted from the recent work of James C. Scott, *Seeing like a State: How Certain Schemes to Improve the Human Condition have Failed*.
165 Such a case has been argued for the colonial naming of Australian landscapes. See Carter, *The Road to Botany Bay: An Essay in Spatial History*.
166 Cited in *Report on the Administration of Bengal, 1901–1902* (Calcutta, 1903), paragraph 256, pp. 133–4. I am grateful to the late Prof. Qeyamuddin Ahmad for pointing out this citation. The province of Bengal on the whole seems to have witnessed the early death of the *pargana* system owing to the extremely diffuse and fractured nature of the *parganas* there. Why this happened in Bengal, and why other areas varied in their experiences of *pargana* formation and dissolution is a question that merits further research. It might be suggested that such research would advance the call for the reinsertion of space in the study of history, a call that has constituted the main pivot around which this study has revolved.

Conclusion

1 Soja, *Postmodern Geographies: The Reassertion of Space in Critical Social Theory*, 1.
2 See Sahlins, *Boundaries: The Making of France and Spain in the Pyrenees*, 21. This project remained incomplete as some interstate boundaries remained peppered with a patchy mosaic of around 250 exclaves. See also Catudal, *The Exclave Problem of Western Europe*, ix,19–20. Today, nearly three-quarters of these are located in a small corner of Asia between India and Bangladesh, while 41 have survived in Europe, especially along the Franco–Spanish border. For recent work on the Indo–Bangladesh enclaves see van Schendel, "Stateless in South Asia: the making of the India–Bangladesh enclaves," 115–17. A cadastral survey was also undertaken in France by Napoleon in 1807. See "Appendix to the Report," in *Reports from Committees: Eleven Volumes (Session 6 February–7 August 1862)*, vol. 6, 1–19 (especially 2).
3 See Morgan, "The Cartographic Image of 'The Country' in Early Modern England," 129–54.
4 For details see Fletcher, "The Ordnance Survey's Nineteenth Century Boundary Survey: Context, Characteristics and Impact," 131–46. For details about the different levels of local authority see p. 140, figure 6. The county system was put into place by the 12th century and between it and smaller divisions – such as the vill or tithing – lay intermediate divisions such

as the hundred, wapentake and ward. See Winchester's *Discovering Parish Boundaries*, 69–70. Winchester's book contains valuable information on the spatial substance and boundaries of Great Britain's ancient divisions.
5 Moll, *A New Description of England and Wales*, iii.
6 See Winchester's *Discovering*, 69. See figure 23 on p. 77 showing the knotted boundaries of these three counties. W.L.D. Ravenhill makes the same observations about the hundred divisions of Devon county. Ravenhill, "Introduction," in *Benjamin Donn: A Map of the County of Devon, 1765*, 17–18.
7 Fletcher, 132. In 1855, out of the 360 townships in the Yorkshire region, 66 had anywhere from one to fifty detached parts. Access to natural resources, climatic factors, tenure, lordship and settlement histories were factors that contributed to the creation of detached parts and sometimes jurisdictional disputes. For details see Jean LePatourel, Long and Pickles, eds, *Yorkshire Boundaries*, 19–20 and 75–84.
8 Fletcher, 143n9.
9 Ibid., 142.
10 See Winchester's *Discovering*, 42 and 87.
11 For details see Reilly, *Richard Griffith and His Valuations of Ireland: With an Inventory of the Books of the General Valuation of Rateable Property in Ireland*. From the sixteenth century a growing number of surveyors and mapmakers produced a large number of estates, county and other local maps. The number of maps produced grew from 42 between 1546 and 1602 to 160 between 1784 and 1850, while the number of surveyors grew from 235 to nearly 7900, respectively. See Bendall, *Dictionary of Land Surveyors and Local Map-Makers of Great Britain and Ireland, 1530–1850*, 2nd edition, vol. 1, p. 5.
12 Bendall, *Dictionary of Land Surveyors*, 51 and 53.
13 See Harley, "The Re-Mapping of England, 1750–1800," 56.
14 See "Report from the Select Committee on the Cadastral Survey; with the Proceedings of the Committee and Appendix," in *Reports from Committees: Eleven Volumes (Session 6 February–7 August 1862)*, vol. vi, iv.
15 See Winchester's *Discovering*, 42.
16 Ibid., 46.
17 See Fletcher, 131–4; J. H. Andrews, *A Paper Landscape: The Ordnance Survey in Nineteenth Century Ireland*; Booth, *Public Boundaries and Ordnance Survey, 1840–1980*; Davey, "The Ordnance and the Ordnance Survey," 181–7; and Seymour, *A History of the Ordnance Survey*.
18 Fletcher, 135–6.
19 Winchester, *Discovering*, 33.
20 Ibid., 86.
21 The growth of the military-fiscal state in Great Britain has been covered by John Brewer, *The Sinews of Power: War, Money and the English State, 1688–1788*. It would be worth considering the role played by spatiality in the creation of the apparatus of the fiscal-military, a missing piece in Brewer's argument.
22 Cited in Sen, *Distant Sovereignty: National Imperialism and the Origins of British India*, 21.
23 For detailed explorations of this theme see Benton, *A Search for Sovereignty: Law and Geography in European Empire, 1400–1900*; Sen, *Distant Sovereignty*; and Stoler, "On Degrees of Imperial Sovereignty," 125–46. For a timely study of the English East India Company set against the evolving backdrop of the transition from early-modern to modern forms of state, sovereignty and political power see Stern, *The Company-State: Corporate Sovereignty and the Early Modern Foundations of the British Empire in India*.
24 Ramusack, *The Indian Princes and their States*, 52–3 and 208.
25 Post-independent India's states were redrawn on linguistic lines following the passing of the States Reorganization Act in 1956. This process of the linguistic redrawing of state boundaries in India merits further scholarly study that has yet to be undertaken.
26 For works that emphasize the incoherence and ambivalence of imperial projects through the exploration of such connections and contexts see Bhabha, "Of Mimicry and Man: The

Ambivalence of Colonial Discourse,"125–33; Cooper and Stoler, eds, *Tensions of Empire: Colonial Cultures in a Bourgeois World*; and Travers, "'The Real Value of the Lands': The Nawabs, the British and the Land Tax in the Eighteenth-Century Bengal," 517–58.

27 The list of such works is too large to be cited here, but would include the South Asian writings of men like Buckler, Kirkpatrick, Buchanan-Hamilton, Moreland, Tod and many others.

28 The term "little kingdoms" is Bernard Cohn's. See Cohn, "Political Systems in Eighteenth Century India: The Benaras Region," in *An Athropologist Among the Historians and Other Essays*, 483–99. It was the anthropologist Clifford Geertz who classified states in Southeast Asia as power-laden sites of performance in his *Negara: The Theater State in Nineteenth Century Bali*.

29 The historian of South India, Burton Stein, developed the idea of the "segmentary state" from the anthropological work of Aidan Southall among the Neur in Africa. Stein understood these states as being made up of ritually bound and hierarchically arranged social segments including peasant communities, landed magnates and royal families. See Stein, *Peasant State and Society in Medieval South India*. He later modified his stance on the segmentary state following criticisms that it focused too much on the ritual aspects of the state. See Stein, "The Segmentary State: Interim Reflections," 217–38.

30 O. W. Wolters and Stanley Tambaiah described the territorially shifting design of Southeast Asian states in terms of *mandalas* and "galactic polities." See Wolters, *History, Culture and Region in Southeast Asia*; and Tambiah, "The Galactic Polity in Southeast Asia," in *Culture, Thought and Social Action*, 252–86. More recently, Tambiah's galactic model has been extended to the study of South Asian states – see Tambiah, "What did Bernier actually say? Profiling the Mughal Empire," *CIS* (n.s.) vol. 32 (1998), 360–86; and Peabody, "Kota Majajagat, or the Great Universe of Kota: Sovereignty and Territory in 18th Century Rajasthan," 29–56. The historian Ronald Inden described precolonial imperial formations in terms of a complex shifting and overlapping interstate system operating on multiple scales. See his *Imagining India*.

31 This has already been discussed in the concluding section of Chapter 5. See Burghart, "The Creation of the Concept of the Nation-State in Nepal," 101–26.

32 For more recent work calling for the development of open-ended models of the state in Asia see Talbot, *Precolonial India in Practice: Society, Region, and Identity in Medieval Andhra* and Tooker, "Putting The Mandala in Its Place: A Practice-based Approach to the Spatialization of Power on the Southeast Asian 'Periphery' – The Case of the Akha," 323–58.

33 The Gorkhali ruler stated in his *Dibya Upadesh* that *"uparant yo raje dui dhungako tarul jasto rahe cha."* Cited in Naraharinatha and Acharya, eds, *Rashtrapita Shri Panch Badamaharaja Prithvinarayan Shah Dev ko Dibya Upadesh*, 15.

34 Throughout the colonial period Gorkha retained its independence, with the British exercising some indirect control over its foreign affairs and defense, mostly through the office of the British Resident stationed in Kathmandu. Following the Treaty of Friendship with the British in 1923, Gorkha became a sovereign independent state that was increasingly known as Nepal.

35 Mitchell, "The Limits of the State: Beyond Statist Approaches and their Critics," 77–96. The quotation is from p. 94.

36 Cited in Riccardi Jr, "An Account of Nepal from the Vir Vinod of Shymaldas," 199–286.

ARCHIVAL SOURCES

A. INDIA

Bihar State Archives, Patna (BSA)

Saran Collectorate Records, 1779–1820
Champaran Collectorate Records, 1837–48
Proceedings of Provincial Council of Revenue, Patna, various volumes
Board of Revenue, various volumes
Patna Commissioners Records, 1811–18
Search Cases Series: Notes on the Survey of Nepal–Champaran Boundaries

District Record Room, (DRM) Chapra, Saran District

Saran Collectorate Records, 1790–1815

Bettiah Raj Mahfizkhana (BRM), Bettiah, Champaran District

Various records, including translations of petitions and proceedings of court cases involving boundary disputes, surveying methods, dowls and village notes.

Bettiah Church Records (BCR), Church of the Nativity of Our Lady of the Blessed Virgin Mary, Bettiah, Champaran District

Correspondence and land deeds, 1833–34

Private Collections

Private Collection of British Pargana Maps of Subah Bihar (1840s), in custody of the late Prof. Qeyamuddin Ahmad, Patna University.

National Archives of India (NAI)

Foreign Secret, 1799–1819
Foreign Political
Survey of India
  Historical Maps
  Map Record and Issue Office (MRIO)
  Memoirs
Foreign Miscellaneous

Uttar Pradesh State Archives, Lucknow (UPSA)

Proceedings, Board of Revenue, Fort William, 1803–7
Proceedings, Board of Revenue, North West Provinces, 1807–22
Board of Revenue Pre-Mutiny Records (list 3)
Board of Revenue, Miscellaneous Shelf, Map Shelf Series (list 19I)
Kumaon Commissionary Records, 1814–36
  Miscellaneous letters received, 1814–15
  Political letters received, 1815–36
Various files from Political, Forests and Revenue Departments, North West Provinces, 1820–1938, dealing with disputes on issues such as political boundaries, adjustment of district boundaries, forest boundaries and customary rights, village boundaries, cadastral surveys and settlement operations.

Regional State Archives, Allahabad (RSA)

Gorakhpur Collectorate Records, 1802–35
Gorakhpur Commissioners Records, 1807–42
Banaras Residents Records, 1798–1801

Regional Archives, Dehra Dun (RADD)

Pre-Mutiny Records, Pauri-Garhwal Collectorate, 1814–42
Pre-Mutiny Records, Dehra Dun, 1816–25

West Bengal State Archives (WBSA)

Board of Revenue,
  Printed Indexes and select Proceedings, 1790–1800
  Registers, etc., relating to Land Revenue
Miscelleneous Records (Revenue Department)
Judicial (Criminal), 1794–1807
Proceedings of the Controlling Committee of Revenue at Patna, 1770–73
Proceedings of the Provincial Council of Revenue at Patna, 1774–80
Proceedings of the Governor General in Council in Bengal (Revenue Department), 1781–83

National Library

Historical Map Collection
Rare Book Collection

B. NEPAL

Lagat Phant (Dept of Revenue, HMG, Nepal), Dilli Bazaar, Kathmandu (LP)

An assorted number of *pokas/bastas*, *panjikas* (abbreviated lists), and *bahis* (registers), dealing with *lal mohar* grants, *bandhki patras* (mortgage deeds) and *rukkas* (prohibitionary orders)

National Archives of Nepal, Ramshah Path, Kathmandu (NAN)

Kumari Chowk Goswara Tahabil (KCGT)
  1980 BS survey records, regulations and treaties
Historical Letters, Bir Library Collection
Historical Letters and Lal Mohars, Kausi Tosakhana Collection
Historical Letters (index only), Foreign Ministry Collection
The Regmi Research Collection (RRC)
Microfilm Collection of India Office Records (includes Kathmandu Residency Records)

Survey Department, Ministry of Land Reform and Management, Baneshwor, Kathamandu

Cadastral Maps of Bardia District, showing the old revenue divisions, 2003 BS/1946 AD
Nepal Map Series, based on the Survey of India surveys of Nepal, 1954–58 AD

Tribhuwan University, Kirtipur, Kathmandu

The Stiller Typescript
Singha Collection
Nepal Collection

Nepal Research Center, New Baneshwor, Kathmandu

Index to the Regmi Research Collection

C. ENGLAND

British Library, St Pancras, London (BL)

Oriental and India Office Collections (OIOC)
  Bengal Proceedings and Consultations
  Board of Control Records
  Minutes
  Home Correspondence
  Draft Despatches
  Boards Collections
  Kathmandu Residency Records, 1792–1818 (KRR)
  European Manuscripts (Eur. Mss)
  Historical Maps
  Home Miscellaneous
  Departmental Records, Political and Secret, Miscellaneous Series (L/P&S/19)
  Official Publication Series
  Political and Secret Department Records
Manuscripts –
  Additional Manuscripts (Add. Mss)

BIBLIOGRAPHY

Nepali

Acharya, Baburam. *Nepalko Samkshipta Vrittanta*. Kathmandu: Jore Ganesh Press 1965 (2022 BS).
Adhikari, Narkant. "Jangannaka Vibhin Ekai" and "Yas Jangannama Apnayeka Tarika Tatha Karya Vidhi." In *Nepalko Janganna*, vol. 1, part 1. 2–4 and 22–8. Kathmandu: Department of Statistics, 1958 (2015 BS).
Adhikari, Surya Mani. *Tanahu Rajyako Itihasik Jhalak*. Chitwan: Chandraprabha Prakashan 1998 (2055 BS).
Amatya, Saphalya. "Makwanpurka kehi Puratatvik Uplabdhi." *Ancient Nepal* 14 (1971): 34–54.
Bajracharya, Dhanabajra, and Gyanmani Nepal. *Aitihasik Patrasangraha*, part 1. Kathmandu: Sanskrit Parishad 1955 (2012 BS).
Ghimire, Bishnu P. *Palpa Rajyako Itihos*. Chitwan: Padma Ghimre 1988 (2045 BS).
———. *Palparajyako Itihas*, part 2. Narayangadh, Chitwan: Chitwan Study Center 1999 (2056 BS).
Ghimire, Sriram. "Tanahuko Rajnitik Itihas." *Ancient Nepal* 113 (1989): 22–8.
Giri, Gitu. *Pyuthana Rajyako Itihasik Jhalak*. Pyuthana: Jilla Vikas Samiti 1995 (2052 BS).
Gyawali, Surya Vikram. *Amar Singh Thapa*. Darjeeling: Ratnakar Press 1951 (2008 BS).
Koirala, Kulchandra. "Senvamshi Rajaharuko Itihasik Paricharcha ra Purvi Pahadka Kehi Brahman Vamsha." *Ancient Nepal* 105 (1988): 16–24.
Narharinath, Yogi. *Itihasa Prakasha*. Kathmandu: Itihasa Prakasha Mandal 1955 (2012 BS).
———. *Itihasaprakashma Sandhipatrasamgraha*. Dang: Narharinath 1966 (2023 BS).
Narharinath, Yogi, and Baburam Acharya, eds. *Rashtrapita Shri Panch Badamaharaja Prithvi Narayan Shah Dev ko Dibya Upadesh*. Kathmandu: Prithvi Jayanti Samaroh Samiti (2010 BS).
Nepali, Chittaranjan. *General Bhimsen Thapa ra tatkalin Nepal*. Kathmandu: Jorganesh Press 1957 (2014 BS).
Nepalko Naksa (thum/pragannama vibhajit janganna jillaharu), Interim Report of the Census of Nepal and Census of Population Nepal 1952/54 A.D. Kathmandu: Department of Statistics 1958 (2015 BS).
Panjiar, Tej Narayan. "Birtabal Tharu." *Ancient Nepal* 135 (1993): 25–7.
Pant, Dinesh Raj. "Sri Panch Ran Bahadur Shahko Nauwota Aprakashit Lal Mohar." *Purnima* 58, no. 15 (2) (2040 BS): 30–44.
———. "Aprkashit bara wota aitihasik patra." *Purnima* 21, no. 6 (1) (2030 BS): 49–70.
———. "Ashrit Rajyaupar Bahadur Shahle Liyeko Niti." *Purnima* 6, no. 2 (2) (2022 BS): 51–5.
———. "B.S. 1832 dekhi B.S. 1858 sammako Nepalko itihasma prakash parne kehi patraharu." *Purnima* 17, no. 5 (1) (2029 BS): 27–51.
———. "Lahorema Nepali viraharu." *Purnima* 5, no. 2 (1) (2022 BS): 63–70.
———. "Padre Michael Angelole Bahun Nanilai lekheko aprakashit patra." *Purnima* 55, no. 14 (3) (2040 BS): 42–3.
———. "Rajkumar Bahadur Shahlai Padre Michael Angelole lekheko char wota aprakashit patra." *Purnima* 55, no. 14 (3) (2040 BS): 36–41.
———. "Royal Administrative Regulations for the Regions West of the Tista and East of the Mahakali, 1806 CE." *Abhilekh* 10 (2049 BS): 13–8.

———. "Shri Panch Pratapsingh Shah lai Padre Michael Angelole lekheko aprkashit patra." *Purnima* 55, no. 14 (3) (2040 BS): 34–5.
Pant, Mahesh Raj. "Tanahu Raja Harkumardat Senka Satwota Aprkashit Patra." *Purnima* 54, no. 14 (2) (2040 BS): 19–21.
———. "Tanahuka Gunanand Pantlai Lekhiyeko Char wota Aprkashit Patra." *Purnima* 54, no. 14 (2) (2040 BS): 25–6.
———. "Tanahu Raja Kamaridat Senka Dui Aprakashit Patra." *Purnima* 53, no. 14 (1) (2040 BS): 10.
———. "Nepal-Angrezyuddha shuru hunubhanda ek barshaaghadi Amarsimha Thapaka chora ra Ochterlonyka chorale miteri layethe." *Purnima* 9, no. 3 (1) (2033 BS): 48–64.
———. "Tanahuka Raja Trivikram Senka Das Aprkashit Patra." *Purnima* 52, no. 13 (4) (2039 BS): 47–52.
———. "Palpa Rajyako Nepal Adhirajya ra Avadhsangha Sambandha" *Purnima* 7, no.1 (2028 BS): 1–8.
———. "Nepalsang ladai khelnuaghi Angrezharule gupt bheshma gareko Nepal-Bhotbhraman," *Purnima* 26, year 7, no. 2 (2023 BS): 67–100.
———. "Nepal Angrez yuddha: Nepal Angrez yuddhako ghoshana nahundai Angrezle gareko yuddhako taiyari." *Purnima* 5, year 2, no. 1 (2022 BS): 54–62.
———. "1871–72 ko Nepal angrez yuddhama nepal le harnema euta thulo karan." *Purnima* 1, no. 1 (2021 BS): 47–58.
Pokhrel, Balkrishna, ed. *Panch Saya Barsha: Nepali Gadhsahityako Aithihasik Sanglo*. Lalitpur: Sahja Prakashan 2050 BS (1993 CE).
Raimajhi, Thir Bahadur. "Nepalko Janganako parampara" and "Nepalko vibhinna ganana." In *Nepalko Janganna*, vol. 1, part 1. 6–8 and 9–21. Kathmandu: Department of Statistics 1958 (2015 BS).
Rajbamshi, Shankarman. *Shahkalin Atihasik Chittipatra Sangraha*. 2 vols. Kathmandu: Bir Pustakalaya 2023 BS.
———. *Puratatva Patra Sangraha*, vol. 3. Kathmandu: Department of Archaeology and Culture 2018 BS.
Rajvamshi, Shankarman. *Sena Vamsavali*. Kathmandu: Bir Pustakalaya Publication 2020 BS.
Sharma, Devi Prasad. *Chitwan Upatyakako Itihasik Roop Rekha*. Bharatpur: Itihas Shikshan Samiti, Birendra Bahumukhi Campus 1985.
Shreshta, Shankar Kumar, ed. *Nepali Kanuni Shabdakosh*. Kathmandu: Pairavi Prakashan 2053 BS (1996 CE).
Shrestha, Tek Bahadur, ed. *Nepalka Rajaharu tatha Taraika*. Kathmandu: Center for Nepal and Asian Studies, Tribhuvan University 2000.
Subedi, Rajaram. *Baise Rajyako Itihas*. Chitwan: Chandraprabha Prakashan 1998.
———. *Gulmiko Itihasik Jhalak*. Gulmi: Kiran Pustakalaya 1998 (2055 BS).
Thapa, Shamsher Bahadur. *Sugauli Sandhi ke ho*. Kathmandu: Shamsher Bahadur Thapa 2048 BS
Tiwari, Ramji. *Aitihasik Patrasangraha*, part 2. Kathmandu: Sanskrit Parishad 1964.
Upadhyaya, Ambika Prasad. *Nepalko Itihas*. 1929. Reprint, Patna: Rajeshwori Udadhaya, 2004 BS (1947 CE).

Hindi/Marwari

Bettiah Raj ka Sankshipta Itihas. Bettiah: Manager, Bettiah Raj. Typewritten Manuscript, 6 pp., n.d.
Bhati, Narain Singh, ed. *Mumhta Nainsi-ri Likhi Marwar-ra Parganan-ri Vigat*. 3 vols. Jodhpur: Rajasthan Oriental Research Institute 1968–1974.
Chaubey, Badshah. "Ramnagar Raj," *Julm ka Pratikar, Champaran Visheshanka*. 47–49. 1984.
Dwivedi, Rewati Kant. "Bettiah raj ka Itihas." Typescript, 9, n.d.

Prasad, Harindra. "Bettiah Rajvamsha ka Samkshipta Itihas." *Julm ka Pratikar, Champaran Visheshanka*, (1948): 43–6.
Rizvi, Sayyad Nazmul Raza. *Attharavi Sadi ke Jamindar*. Delhi: Peoples Publishing House 1988.

English

Abrams, P. "Notes on the Difficulty of Studying the State." *JHS* 1, no. 1 (1988): 58–89.
Abu-Lughod, Lila. "The Romance of Resistance: Tracing Transformations of Power through Bedouin Women." *AE* 17, no. 1 (1990): 41–55.
Adhikari, Krishna Kanta. *Nepal Under Jang Bahadur Rana, 1847–1877*. Kathmandu: Sahayogi Press 1984.
———. *A Brief Survey of Nepali Historiography*. Kathmandu: Baku 1980.
Agnew, P. Vans. *A Report on the Subah or Province of Chattisgarh Written in 1820 A.D.* Nagpur: Government Press 1922.
Agre, Jagatvir Singh. "Pargana Administration in Marwar Under Maharaja Jaswant Singh (1638–1678 A.D.)." *PIHC*, 34th Session, Chandigarh 1973.
Ahmad, Qeyamuddin. "Pargana Maps and Village Survey Records: A Note on an Unnoticed Source-Material for the History of Bihar." In *Comprehensive History of Bihar*, vol. 2, part 2. 588–94. Patna: K. P. Jayaswal Institute 1988.
———. "Early Anglo-Nepalese Relations with Particular Reference to the Principality of Makwanpur." *PIHRC* 34, no. 2 (1958): 17–26.
———. "Meaning and Usage of Some Terms of Land Revenue Administration." In *Medieval India: A Miscellany*, vol. 2. 275–81. Bombay: Asia Publishing House 1972.
Aitchison, C. U. *A Collection of Treaties, Engagements and Sanads*, vols 1, 2 and 14. 1929. Reprint, Delhi: Mittal Publications 1983.
Akerman, James. "The Structuring of Political Territory in Early Printed Atlases." *Imago Mundi* 47 (1995): 138–54.
Akerman, James R. and Robert W. Karrow, eds. *Maps: Finding Our Place in the World*. Chicago: University of Chicago Press 2007.
Alam, Muzaffar. *The Crisis of Empire in Mughal North India: Awadh and Punjab, 1707–1748*. Delhi: Oxford University Press 1986.
———. "Eastern India in the Early Eighteenth Century Crisis: Some Evidence from Bihar." *IESHR* 28, no. 1 (1991): 43–71.
Alam, Muzaffar, and Sanjay Subrahmanyam, eds. *The Mughal State, 1526–1750*. Delhi: Oxford University Press 1998.
Alavi, Seema. *The Sepoys and the Company: Tradition and Transition in Northern India, 1770–1830*. Delhi: Oxford University Press 1995.
Alexander, E. *Statistical, Descriptive and Historical Account of the Gorakhpur District*. Edited by H. C. Conybeare and Edwin T. Atkinson. Allahabad: North West Provinces and Oudh Government 1880.
Ambashthya, B. P. *Beames' Contributions to the Political Geography of the Subahs of Awadh, Bihar, Bengal and Orissa in the Age of Akbar*. Patna: Janaki Prakashan 1976.
Anderson, Benedict. *Imagined Communities: Reflections on the Origins and Spread of Nationalism*. London: Verso 1991.
Anderson, Malcolm. *Frontiers: Territory and State Formation in the Modern World*. London: Polity Press 1996.
Anonymous. "*Brief History of the Bettiah Estate*." Typescript, 8, n.d.
Anonymous. *Military Sketches of the Goorkha War in India in the years 1814, 1815 and 1816*. London: Woodbridge, printed by J. Loder 1824.
Andrews, J.H. *A Paper Landscape: The Ordnance Survey in Nineteenth-Century Ireland*. Oxford: Clarendon Press 1975.

Appadurai, Arjun. *Modernity At Large: Cultural Dimensions of Globalization.* Minneapolis: University of Minnesota Press 1996.

———. "The South Indian Temple: Authority, Honor and Redistribution." *CIS* (n.s.) 10 (1976): 187–211.

Archer, Mildred. "Colonel Gentil's Atlas: An Early Series of Company Drawings." In *India Office Library and Records: Report for the 1978.* 41–45. London: Foreign and Commonwealth Office 1979.

Arnold, David. *Colonizing the Body: State Medicine and Epidemic Disease in Nineteenth Century India.* Berkeley: University of California Press 1993.

———. *The Problem of Nature: Environment, Culture and European Expansion.* Oxford: Blackwell 1996.

Arnold, David, and Ramachandra Guha, eds. *Nature, Culture, Imperialism: Essays on the Environmental History of South Asia.* Delhi: Oxford University Press 1995.

Ashforth, Adam. *The Politics of Official Discourse in Twentieth-Century South Africa.* New York: Oxford University Press 1990.

Bachelard, Gaston. *The Poetics of Space.* Boston: Beacon Press 1964.

Baden-Powell, B. H. *Administration of Land Revenue and Tenure in British India.* Delhi: Ess Ess Publications 1978.

Bailes, Kenneth E. *Environmental History.* Lanham: University Press of America 1985.

Bajracharya, Bhadra Ratna. *Bahadur Shah: The Regent of Nepal.* Delhi: Anmol Publications 1992.

Barnett, Richard B. *North India Between Empires: Awadh, the Mughals and the British, 1720–1801.* Berkeley: University of California Press 1980.

Barrow, Ian. *Making History, Drawing Territory: British Mapping in India, c. 1756–1905.* New Delhi: Oxford University Press 2003.

Batten, Bruce. "Frontiers and Boundaries of Pre-Modern Japan." *Journal of Historical Geography* 25, no. 2 (1999): 166–82.

Baud, Michiel and Willem Van Schendel. "Towards a Comparative History of Borderlands." *Journal of World History* 8, no. 2 (1997): 211–42.

Bayly, C.A. *Empire and Information.* Cambridge: Cambridge University Press 1996.

———. *Rulers, Townsmen and Bazaars: North Indian Society in the Age of British Expansion, 1770–1870.* Cambridge: Cambridge University Press 1982.

Belyea, Barbara. "Images of Power: Derrida/Foucault/Harley." *Cartographica* 29, no. 2 (1992): 1–9.

Bendall, Sarah. *Dictionary of Land Surveyors and Local Map-Makers of Great Britain and Ireland, 1530–1850.* 2nd ed. 2 vols. London: The British Library 1997.

Benton, Lauren. *A Search for Sovereignty: Law and Geography in European Empire, 1400–1900.* Cambridge: Cambridge University Press 2010.

Berry, Sara. "Social Institutions and Access to Resources." *Africa* 59, no. 1 (1989): 41–55.

Bhabha, Homi K. "Of Mimicry and Man: The Ambivalence of Colonial Discourse." *October* 28 (1984): 125–33.

Bhadani, B. L. "Revenue-Estimation and Realization in the Mughal Empire: A Case Study of Marwar." *Islamic Culture* 64, no. 1 (1990): 69–81.

Bhargava, Meena. *State, Society and Ecology: Gorakhpur in Transition, 1750–1830.* Delhi: Manohar 1999.

———. "Landed Property Rights in Transition: A Note on Cultivators and Agricultural Labourers in Gorakhpur in the Late 18th and 19th Centuries." *SIH* 12, no. 2 (1996): 244–53.

———. "Perception and Classification of the Rights of the Social Classes: Gorakhpur and the East India Company in the late Eighteenth Century and Early Nineteenth Century." *IESHR* 30, no. 2 (1993): 215–37.

"Madad-i-mash and maafi Grants in Gorakhpur During the late Eighteenth and early Nineteenth Century," *PIHC*, 52 Session (1992): 338–44.

Bhattacharya, Neeladri. "Introduction" (Special issue on Forests, Fields, and Pastures). *Studies in History* 14, no. 2 (1998): 165–71.

Biggs, Michael. "Putting the State on the Map: Cartography, Territory, and European State Formation." *Comparative Studies in Society and History* 4, no. 2 (1999): 374–405.

Bisson, Thomas, ed. *Cultures of Power: Lordship, Status, and Process in Twelfth-Century Europe.* Philadelphia: University of Philadelphia 1995.
Blakie, P. and H. Brookfield. *Land Degradation and Society.* London: Metheun 1987.
Blochmann, H. "Contributions to the Geography and History of Bengal." *JASB* 42 (1873): 209–44.
Bonnell, Victoria E. and Lynn Hunt, eds. *Beyond the Cultural Turn: New Directions in the Study of Society and Culture.* Berkeley: University of California Press 1999.
Booth, J.R.S. *Public Boundaries and Ordnance Survey, 1840–1980.* Southampton: Ordnance Survey 1980.
Bouillier, Veronique. "The Nepalese State and the Gorakhnathi Yogis: The Case of the Former Kingdoms of Dang Valley: 18–19th Centuries." *CNS* 20, no. 1 (1993): 29–52.
Boulnois, L. "Chinese Maps and Prints of the Tibet–Gorkha War of 1788–92." *Kailash* 15, no. 1–2 (1989): 84–112.
Bourdieu, Pierre. *An Outline of a Theory of Practice.* Cambridge: Cambridge University Press 1977.
Bourguet, Marie-Noelle, Christian Licoppe, and Heinz Otto Sibum. *Instruments, Travel, and Science: Itineraries of Precision from the Seventeenth to the Twentieth Centuries.* London: Routledge 2002.
Brewer, John. *The Sinews of Power: War, Money and the English State, 1688–1783.* New York: Alfred A. Knopf 1989.
Brodkin, E. I. "British India and the Abuses of Power: Rohilkhand under Early Company Rule." *IESHR* 10, no. 2 (1973): 129–56.
Buchanan-Hamilton, Francis. *An Account of the Kingdom of Nepal and of the Territories Annexed to this Dominion by the House of Gurkha.* Delhi: Manjushri 1971 (1819).
———. *An Account of the District of Purnea in 1809–10.* Patna: Bihar Orissa Research Society 1928.
———. *An Account of the District of Bihar and Patna in 1811 & 1812.* Patna: Bihar Orissa Research Society 1928.
———. *Journal of Francis Buchanan Kept during the Survey of the Districts of Patna and Gaya in 1811–1812.* Patna: Superintendent Government Printing Press 1925.
Buisseret, David, ed. *Monarchs, Ministers and Maps: The Emergence of Cartography as a Tool of Government in Early Modern Europe.* Chicago: University of Chicago 1992.
Burghart, Richard. *The Conditions of Listening: Essays on Religion, History and Politics in South Asia.* Edited by C. J. Fuller and Jonathan Spencer. Delhi: Oxford University Press 1996.
———. "Gift to the Gods: Power, Property and Ceremonial in Nepal." In *Rituals of Royalty: Power and Ceremony in Traditional Societies.* Edited by David Cannadine and S. Price. 237–70. Cambridge: Cambridge University Press 1987.
———. "The Formation of the Concept of the Nation-State in Nepal." *JAS* 44, no.1 (1984): 101–26.
———. "For a Sociology of Indias: An Intercultural Approach to the Study of 'Hindu Society'." *CIS* (n.s.) 17 (1983): 275–99.
———. "Hierarchical Models of the Hindu Social System." *Man* 13 (1978): 519–36.
———. "The History of Janakpurdham: A Study of Ascetism and the Hindu Polity." PhD diss., University of London 1978.
Burnett, D. Graham. *Masters of All They Surveyed: Exploration, Geography, and a British Eldorado.* Chicago: University of Chicago Press 2000.
Calendar of Persian Correspondence, vol. 9. Delhi: Imperial Record Department 1949.
Campillo, Antonio. "On War: The Space of Knowledge, and Knowledge of Space." In *Reconstructing Foucault: Essays in the Wake of the 80s.* Edited by Ricardo Miguel-Alfonso and Silvia Caporale-Bizzini. 277–99. Atlanta: Rodopoi 1994.
Carnegy, Patrick. *Kachahri Technicalities: Or A Glossary of Terms Rural, Official and General.* 2nd ed. Allahabad: Allahabad Mission Press 1877.
Caplan, Lionel. *Warrior Gentlemen: 'Gurkhas' in the Western Imagination.* New York: Berghahn Books 1995.

Carter, Paul. *The Road to Botany Bay*. London: Faber & Faber 1987.
Catudal, M. *The Exclave Problem of Western Europe*. Alabama: University of Alabama Press 1979.
Chakrabarti, Animesh. "The Origins of Subdivisions in Bengal." *Bengal Past and Present* 47, no. 1 (1978): 36–64.
Chakravarty-Kaul, Minoti. *Common Land and Customary Law: Institutional Change in North India over the Past Two Centuries*. Delhi: Oxford University Press 1996.
Chambers, John. W. "The New Military History: Myth and Reality." *Journal of Military History* 55, no. 3 (1991): 395–406.
Chandra, Satish, and S. P. Gupta. "The Jaipur Pargana Records." *IESHR* 3, no. 3 (1966): 303–15.
Chatterjee, Partha. *The Nation and its Fragments: Colonial and Postcolonial Histories*. Princeton: Princeton University Press 1993.
Chaudhuri, K. C. *Anglo–Nepalese Relations*. Calcutta: Firma K. L. Mukhopadyaya 1960.
Chhetri, D. B. *A Brief Analysis of History Writing in Nepal*. Kathmandu: Parbati Chhetri 1996.
Choudhary, Radhakrishna. *History of Muslim Rule in Tirhut*. Banaras: Chowkhamba Sanskrit Series Office 1970.
Circular Orders of the Sudder Board of Revenue, North West Provinces Addressed to Commissioners of Revenue on Records and Registration. Calcutta: Baptist Mission Press 1840.
Claessen, Henri J.M. and Peter Skalnik, eds. *The Study of the State*. The Hague: Mouton 1981.
Cohen, Ronald, and Elman Service, eds. *Origins of the State: The Anthropology of Political Evolution*. Philadelphia: Institute for the Study of Human Issues 1978.
Cohn, Bernard S. *An Anthropologist among the Historians and Other Essays*. Delhi: Oxford University Press 1987.
———. *Colonialism and Its Forms of Knowledge*. New Jersey: Princeton University Press 1996.
———. "The Role of the Gosains in the Economy of Eighteenth and Nineteenth-Century Upper India." *IESHR* 1, no. 4 (1963–4): 175–82.
Cohn, Bernard S. and Nicholas B. Dirks. "Beyond the Fringe: The Nation-State, Colonialism and the Technologies of Power." *JHS* 1, no. 2 (1987): 224–9.
Comaroff, Jean. *Body of Power, Spirit of Resistance: The Culture and History of a South African People*. Chicago: University of Chicago Press 1985.
———. *Ethnography and the Historical Imagination*. Boulder: Westview Press 1992.
Conley, Tom. *The Self-Made Map: Cartographic Writing in Early Modern France*. Minneapolis, Minn.: University of Minnesota 1996.
Cook, Andrew. "Major James Rennell and *A Bengal Atlas* (1780 and 1781)." In *India Office Library and Records: Report for the Year 1976*. London: India Office Library 1978.
Cooper, Frederick, and Laura Ann Stoler, eds. "Introduction." In *Tensions of Empire: Colonial Cultures in a Bourgeois World*. 1–58. Berkeley: University of California Press 1997.
Corrigan, Philip, and Derek Sayer. *The Great Arch: State Formation as Cultural Revolution*. London: Basil Blackwell 1985.
Cosgrove, Denis. *Social Formation and Symbolic Landscape*. Cambridge: Cambridge University Press 1984.
Craib, Raymond. *Cartographic Mexico: A History of State Fixations and Fugitive Landscapes*. Durham, NC: Duke University Press 2004.
Cronon, William. *Changes in the Land: Indians, Colonists and the Ecology of New England*. New York: Hill and Wang 1983.
Crosby, Alfred. *Germs, Seeds and Animals: Studies in Ecological History*. New York: M. E. Sharpe 1994.
Davey, A.B.T. "The Ordnance and the Ordnance Survey." *The Cartographic Journal* 28 (December 1991): 181–7.
Day, Tony. *Fluid Iron: State Formation in Southeast Asia*. Honolulu: University of Hawaii Press 2002.
Day, U. N. *The Mughal Government, 1556–1707 AD*. New Delhi: Munshiram Manoharlal 1970.
De Certeau, Michel. *The Practice of Everyday Life*. Berkeley: University of California Press 1988.
Dening, Greg. *Islands and Beaches: Discourse on a Silent Land, Marquesas 1774–1880*. Melbourne 1980.

DesChene, Mary K. F. "Relics of Empire: A Cultural History of the Gurkhas, 1816–1987." PhD diss., Stanford University 1991.
DesChene, Mary K. F. and Pratyoush Onta. "Writing and Reading about Nepal." *SINHAS* 2, no.1 (1997): 1–4.
Dhar, Niranjan. *The Administrative System of the East India Company in Bengal, 1714–1786*. 2 vols. Calcutta: Eureka Publishers 1964.
Dhar, T. N. and K. P. Srivastava. *Development of Archives in Pre-British India*. Lucknow: U. P. State Archives, n.d.
Diener, Alexander C. and Joshua Hagen, eds. *Borderlines and Borderlands: Political Oddities at the Edge of the Nation-State*. New York: Rowman & Littlefield 2010.
Directions for Revenue Officers of the North-Western Provinces of the Bengal Presidency. Calcutta: Baptist Mission Press 1850.
Dirks, Nicholas B. *The Hollow Crown: The Ethnohistory of a Little Kingdom*. Cambridge: Cambridge University Press 1987.
———. *The Hollow Crown: The Ethnohistory of a Little Kingdom*. Ann Arbor: University of Michigan Press 1993.
———. *Colonialism and Culture*. Ann Arbor: University of Michigan Press 1992.
Dodge, Martin, Rob Kitchin, and Chris Perkins, eds. *Rethinking Maps: New Frontiers in Cartographic Theory*. New York: Routledge, 2009.
Dirks, Nicholas B., Geoff Eley and Sherry B. Ortner, eds. *Culture/Power/History: A Reader in Contemporary Social Theory*. Princeton: Princeton University Press 1994.
Dossal, Miriam. "Knowledge for power: the significance of the Bombay Revenue Survey, 1811–1827." In *Ports and their Hinterlands (1700–1950)*. Edited by Indu Banga. 227–43. Bombay: Manohar Press 1992.
Driver, Felix. *Geography Militant: Cultures of Exploration and Empire*. Oxford: Blackwell Publishers 2001.
———. "Power, Space and the Body: A Critical Assessment of Foucault's 'Discipline and Punish'." *Environment and Politics D: Society and Space* 3, no. 4 (1985): 425–47.
Driver, Felix and Gillian Rose, eds. *Nature and Science: Essays in the History of Geographical Knowledge*. Historical Geography Research Series, no. 28. London: London Group of Historical Geographers.
Duara, Prasenjit. *Culture, Power and the State: Rural North China, 1900–1942*. Stanford: Stanford University Press 1988.
———. *Rescuing History from the Nation: Questioning Narratives of Modern China*. Chicago: University of Chicago Press 1995.
East India Company. *Fort William India House Correspondence and Other Contemporary Volumes Relating Thereto*, vol. 21. Manager of Publications 1985.
Eaton, Richard M. *The Rise of Islam on the Bengal Frontier, 1204–1760*. Berkeley: University of California Press 1993.
Edney, Matthew H. "Cartographic Narratives in the History of North America: Discussion." Discussion of papers presented by Raymond Craib, Martin Bruckner and Susan Schulten at the American Historical Association, Boston, 5 January 2001.
———. "British Military Education, Mapmaking, and Military 'Map-Mindedness' in the Later Enlightenment." *The Cartographic Journal* 31 (1994): 14–20.
———. "Cartography Without 'Progress': Reinterpreting the Nature and Historical Development of Mapmaking." *Cartographica* 30, nos. 2 and 3 (1993): 54–68.
———. "J. B. Harley (1932–1991): Questioning Maps, Questioning Cartography, Questioning Cartographers." *Cartography and Geographic Information Systems* 19, no. 3 (1992): 175–78.
———. *Mapping an Empire: The Geographical Construction of British India, 1765–1843*. Chicago: University of Chicago Press 1997.
———. "Putting 'Cartography' into the History of Cartography: Arthur H. Robinson, David Woodward, and the Creation of a Discipline." *Imago Mundi* 59, no. 2 (2007): 14–29.

Edney, Matthew H., Christian Jacob and Catherine Delano-Smith. "Theoretical Aspects of the History of Cartography: A Discussion of Concepts, Approaches and New Directions," *Imago Mundi*, vol. 48 (1996): 185–205.

Elliott, Charles. *Chronicle of Oonao: A District in Oudh*. Allhabad: Allahabad Mission Press 1862.

Elliott, H. M. *The History, Folklore and Culture of the Races of North-West Provinces of India*. 2 vols. Edited by John Beames. Delhi: Sumit Publications 1985. First published 1869 by Trubner, with title *Memoirs on the History, Folklore and Distribution of Races of the North Western Provinces of India*.

Ellis, Steven G. *Tudor Frontiers and Noble Power: The Making of the British State*. Oxford: Clarendon Press 1995.

Embree, Ainslie T. "Frontiers into Boundaries: From the Traditional to the Modern State." In *Realm and Region in Traditional India*. Edited by Richard G. Fox. 255–80. Delhi: Vikas 1977.

Entrikin, J. Nicholas. *The Betweenness of Place*. Baltimore: John Hopkins University Press 1991.

Fazl, Abul. *Ain-i-Akbari*. 3 vols. Translated by Col. H. S. Jarrett. Calcutta: Asiatic Society of Bengal 1949.

Febvre, Lucien. "Frontiere: The Word and the Concept." In *A New Kind of History: From the Writings of Febvre*. Edited by Peter Burke. Translated by K. Foka. 208–18. New York: Harper and Row 1973.

Firminger, Walter K., ed. *The Fifth Report From the Select Committee of the House of Commons on the Affairs of the East India Company, Dated 28th July, 1812*. Calcutta: R. Cambray and Company 1917.

Fisher, Michael. *A Clash of Cultures: Awadh, the British, and the Mughals*. Delhi: Oxford: University Press 1987.

Fletcher, David. "The Ordnance Survey's Nineteenth Century Boundary Survey: Context, Characteristics and Impact." *Imago Mundi* 51 (1999): 131–46.

Forbes, Ann Ambrecht. "The Boundary Keepers: The Poetry and Politics of Land in Northeastern Nepal." PhD diss., Harvard University, 1995.

Foucault, Michel. "Governmentality." In *The Foucault Effect: Studies in Governmentality*. Edited by Graham Burchell, Colin Gordon and Peter Miller. Chicago: University of Chicago Press 1991.

———. *Discipline and Punish: The Birth of the Prison*. New York: Vintage 1979.

Fox, Richard G., ed. *Realm and Region in Traditional India*. New Delhi: Vikas 1977.

Frykenberg, Robert. "'Company Sircari' in the Carnatic, c. 1799–1859: The Inner Logic of Political Systems in India." In *Realm and Region in Traditional India*. Edited by Richard G. Fox. 117–64. Delhi: Vikas 1977.

Geertz, Clifford. *Negara: Theater State in Nineteenth-Century Bali*. Princeton, New Jersey: Princeton University Press 1980.

Gellner, D. N., J. Pfaff-Czarnecka and J. Whelpton, eds. *Nationalism and Ethnicity in a Hindu Kingdom: The Politics of Culture in Contemporary Nepal*. Amsterdam: Harwood Academia Publishers 1997.

Giddens, Anthony. *The Constitution of Society: An Introduction to the Theory of Structuration*. Berkeley: University of California Press 1984.

Gidwani, Vinay. *Capital Interrupted: Agrarian Development and the Politics of Work in India*. Delhi: Permanent Black 2008.

Gidwani, Vinay and Kalyanakrishnan Sivaramakrishnan. "Circular Migration and the Spaces of Cultural Assertion." *Annals of the Association of American Geographers* 9, issue 1 (2003): 186–213.

Giri, B. P. and Prafulla Kar, eds. *Thinking Territory: Some Reflections*. Delhi: Pencraft International 2009.

Godlewska, Anne. *Geography Unbound: French Geographic Science from Cassini to Humboldt*. Chicago: Chicago University Press 1999.

Gogate, Prasad P. and B. Arunachalam. "Area Maps in Maratha Cartography: A Study in Native Maps of Western India." *Imago Mundi* 50 (1998): 126–40.

Gole, Susan. "A Nepali Map of Central Asia." *South Asian Studies* 8 (1993): 81–9.

———. *Indian Maps and Plans: From Earlies Times to the Advent of European Surveys*. Delhi: Manohar 1989.

———. *Maps of Mughal India. Drawn by Col. Jean Baptiste Gentil, Agent for the French Government to the Court of Shuja-ud daula at Faizabad, in 1770*. Delhi: Manohar 1988.
———. *India within the Ganges*. Delhi: Jayaprints 1983.
Gommans, Jos. "The Silent Frontier of South Asia, c. 1100–1800." *JWH* 9, no. 1 (1998): 1–24.
Gordon, Colin, ed. *Power/Knowledge: Selected Interviews and Other Writings, 1972–1977*. New York: Pantheon 1980.
Gordon, Stewart and John F. Richards. 1985. "Kinship and Pargana in eighteenth-century Khandesh." *IESHR* 22, no. 4 (1985): 372–97.
Gottmann, Jean. *The Significance of Territory*. Charlottesville: University Press of Virginia 1973.
Gregory, Derek. *Geographical Imaginations*. London: Blackwell 1995 (1993).
Gregory, Derek and John Urry, eds. *Social Relations and Spatial Structures*. New York: St. Martin's Press 1985.
Grover, B. R. "Nature of the *Dehat-I-Taaluqa* (Zamindari Villages) and the Evolution of the Taaluqdari System during the Mughal Age, Part 2." *IESHR* 2, no. 3 (1964): 259–89.
———. "'Raqba-Bandi' Documents of Akbar's Reign." *PIHRC* 36, no. 2 (1961): 55–60.
Guha, Ramachandra. *Environmentalism: A Global History*. New York: Longman 2000.
Guha, Ramachandra and Madhav Gadgil. *This Fissured Land: An Ecological History of India*. Berkeley: The University of California Press 1992.
Guha, Ranajit. *Elementary Aspects of Peasant Insurgency*. Delhi: Oxford University Press 1983.
———. *A Rule of Property for Bengal: An Essay on the Idea of Permanent Settlement*. 3rd ed. Durham: Duke University Press 1996.
Guha, Sumit. *The Agrarian Economy of the Bombay Deccan, 1818–194*. Delhi: Oxford University Press 1985.
———. "Claims on the Commons: Political Power and Natural Resources in Pre-Colonial India." in *India's Environmental History: Colonialism, Modernity, and the Nation*, vol. 2. Edited by Mahesh Rangarajan and K. Sivaramakrishnan. 327–48. Delhi: Permanent Black 2012.
Guneratne, U. Arjun. *Many Tongues, One People: The Making of Tharu Identity in Nepal*. Ithaca: Cornell University Press 2002.
Gupta, S. P. *The Agrarian System of Eastern Rajasthan*. Delhi: Manohar 1987.
———. "Khasra Documents in Rajasthan." In *Medieval India: A Miscellany*. vol. 4. 168–76. Bombay: Asia Publishing House 1977.
Gupta, S. P. and Sumbul Halim Khan. *Mughal Documents: Taqsim (C. 1649–C. 1800)*. Jaipur: Publication Scheme 1996.
Gupta, Sulekh Chandra. *Agrarian Relations and Early British Rule in India: A Case Study of the Ceded and Conquered Provinces (Uttar Pradesh), 1801–1833*. 2nd Edition, 1995. Delhi: Peoples Publishing House 1963.
Gurkhas. 2 vols. Simla: Government of India Press 1941.
Gurung, Harka. *Maps of Nepal: Inventory and Evaluation*. Bankok: New Orchid Press 1983.
Gutschow, Niels. "Ritual as a Mediator of Space in Kathmandu, Nepal." In *South Asia: 30th International Congress of Human Sciences in Asia and North Africa*, vol. 3. 1–13. Mexico: Collegio De Mexico 1982.
———. "Functions Of Squares in Bhaktapur." In *Ritual Space in India: Studies in Architectural Anthropology*. Edited by Jan Pieper. Max Mueller Bhavan Art and Archaeology Papers. 57–64. Bombay: Max Mueller Bhavan 1980.
Gutschow, Niels and Axel Michels, eds. *The Heritage of the Kathmandu Valley: Proceedings of an International Conference in Lubeck, June 1985*. VGH Wissenschaftsverlag. St. Augustine 1987.
Gutschow, Niels and Bernhard Kolver. *Ordered Space Concepts and Functions in a Town of Nepal*. Weisbaden: Franz Steiner Verlag 1975.
Habib, Irfan. *The Agrarian System of Mughal India*. 2nd ed. Delhi: Oxford University Press 1999.
———. "Reply." *IESHR* 26, no. 3 (1989): 368–72.
———. "Review of Andre Wink's Land and Sovereignty in India: Agrarian Society and Politics Under the Eighteenth Century Maratha Svarajya." *IESHR* 25, no. 4 (1988): 527–31.

———. *An Atlas of the Mughal Empire*. Reprint, Delhi: Oxford University Press (1982) 1983.
———. "Cartography in Mughal India." In *Medieval India: A Miscellany*, vol. 4. 122–38. Bombay: Asia Publishing House 1977.
———. *The Agrarian System of Mughal India*. Bombay: Asia Publishing House 1963.
Habib, Irfan and Tapan Raychaudhuri, eds. *The Cambridge Economic History of India, Vol 1: 1200–1750*. Delhi: Orient Longman 1982.
Hamilton, Walter. *A Geographical, Statistical, and Historical Description of Hindostan and the Adjacent Countries*. 2 vols. Delhi: Oriental Publishers 1971 (1820).
Hannah, Matthew. *Governmentality and the Mastery of Territory in Nineteenth-Century America*. Cambridge: Cambridge University Press 2000.
Harley, John Brian. "Deconstructing the Map." In *Writing Worlds: Discourse, Text and Metaphor in the Representation of Landscape*. Edited by Trevor Barnes and James S. Duncan. 231–47. New York: Routledge 1992.
Harley, John B. and David Woodward, eds. *Cartography in the Traditional Islamic and South Asian Societies*. Vol. 2, part 2 of *The History of Cartography*. Chicago: University of Chicago Press 1987.
———. "An Alternative Route to Mapping History."*Americas*, nos. 5 and 6 (1991): 6–13.
Hasan, Farhat. "The Mughal Fiscal System in Surat and the English East India Company." *MAS* 7, no. 4 (1993): 711–18.
S. Hasan, Mahmud. *An Eighteenth Century Agrarian Manual: Yasin's Dastur-i-Malguzari*. Delhi: Kitab Bhavan 2000.
Hasan, S. Nurul. *Some Thought on Agrarian Relations in Mughal India*. Delhi: People's Publishing House (1973) 1983.
Hasrat, Bikram Jit. *History of Nepal: As Told by its Own and Contemporaries*. Hosiarpur: V. V. Research Institute 1970.
Helgerson, Richard. *Forms of Nationhood: The Elizabethan Writing of England*. Chicago: University of Chicago Press 1992.
———. "Nation or Estate?: Ideological Conflict in the Early Modern Mapping of England." *Cartographica* 30, no. 1 (1993): 68–74.
Hirst, F. C. *Notes on the Revenue Surveys of Bengal, Bihar, Orissa, and Assam*. Calcutta: Thacker, Spink and Company 1912.
Hodgson, Brian H. *Selections from the Records of the Government of Bengal*. Number 27. Calcutta: Calcutta Gazette Office 1857.
———. "On the Administration of Justice in Nepal." *Asiatick Researches* 20 (1836): 94–134.
Hofer, Andras. *The Caste Hierarchy and the State: A Study of the Muluki Ain of 1854*. Innsbruck: Universitatsverlag Wagner 1974.
Hooker, Joseph Dalton. *Himalayan Journals: Notes of a Naturalist in Bengal, the Sikkim and Nepal Himalayas, the Khasi Mountains*. 2 vols. London: John Murray 1855.
Hooper, J. *Final Report on the Settlement of the Basti District*. Allahabad: Government Press 1891.
Hostetler, Laura. *Qing Colonial Enterprise: Ethnography and Cartography in Early Modern China*. Chicago: University of Chicago Press 2001.
Hubbard, Phil, Rob Kitchin, Brendan Bartley and Duncan Fuller, eds. *Thinking Geographically: Space, Theory and Contemporary Human Geography*. London: Continuum 2004.
Hubbard, Phil, Rob Kitchin, Brendan Bartley, Setha Low and Denise Lawrence-Zuniga, eds. *The Anthropology of Space and Place: Locating Culture*. Malden, MA: Blackwell 2003.
Hughes, Donald, ed. *The Face of the Earth: Environment and World History*. Armonk, New York: M. E. Sharpe 1999.
Hunt, Lynn. *The New Cultural History*. Berkeley: University of California Press 1989.
Hunter, W. W., ed. *A Statistical Account of Bengal, vol 13, Tirhut and Champaran*. London: Trubner and Company 1877.
Inden, Ronald. *Imagining India*. London: Blackwell.
Inglis, James. *Tent Life in Tigerland: Sport and Work on the Nepaul Frontier*. London: Sampson Press 1878.

Irschick, Eugene F. *Dialogue and History: Constructing South India, 1795–1895*. Berkeley: University of California Press 1994.
Islam, Sirajul. *The Permanent Settlement in Bengal: A Study of its Operation*. Dacca: Bangla Academy 1979.
Jafri, S. Z. H. "Origins and Growth of Taa'alluqadari Tenures in Awadh." In *Awadh: From Mughal to Colonial Rule*. 73–82. Delhi: Gyan Publishing House 1998.
Jessop, Bob. *State Theory: Putting the Capitalist State in its Place*. University Park, PA: Penn State University Press 1990.
Johnston, R. J. "Territoriality and the State." In *Geography, History and the Social Sciences*. Edited by G. B. Benko and U. Strohmayer. 213–25. Amsterdam: Kluwer 1995.
Joseph, Gilbert M. and Daniel Nugent, eds. *Everyday Forms of State Formation: Revolution and the Negotiation of Rule in Modern Mexico*. Durham: Duke University Press 1994.
Kain, Roger J. P. and Elizabeth Baigent. *The Cadastral Map in the Service of the State*. Chicago: University of Chicago Press 1992.
Kalpagam, U. "Cartography in Colonial India." *EPW* (29 July 1995): 87–98.
Karan, Pradyumna P. *Nepal: A Physical and Cultural Geography*. Lexington: University of Kentucky Press 1960.
Kark, Ruth. "Mamluk and Ottoman Cadastral Surveys and Early Mapping of Landed Properties in Palestine." *Agricultural History* 71, no. 1 (1997): 46–70.
Khan, Gholam Hossein. *Seir Mutaqherin*. 4 vols. Lahore: Sheikh Mubarak Ali 1975 (1902).
Khan, Shaukat Ullah. "Agricultural Statistics of Mughal India: A Reconsideration." *SIH* 13, no. 1 (1997): 121–46.
Khanduri, Chandra. *A Re-Discovered History of Gorkhas*. Delhi: Gyan Sagar Publications 1997.
Kierstead, Thomas. *The Geography of Power in Medieval Japan*. Princeton: Princeton University Press 1992.
King, Geoff. *Mapping Reality: An Exploration of Cultural Cartographies*. New York: St. Martin's Press 1996.
Kirby, Peter W. *Boundless Worlds: An Anthropological Approach to Movement*. New York: Berghahn Books 2009.
Kirkpatrick, William. *An Account of the Kingdom of Nepaul (being the substance of Observations made on a mission to that country in 1793)*. London: William Miller 1811.
Kolver, Bernhard. "A Ritual Map from Nepal." In *Folia Rara: Wolfgang Voigt LXV Diem Celebranti*. Edited by Herbert Franke, Walther Hessig and Wolfgang Treue. Verzeichnis der Orientalischen Handscriften in Deutschland, supplement 19. 68–80. Wiesbaden: Franz Steiner Verlag 1976.
Kolff, Dirk H. A. *Naukar, Rajput, Sepoy: The Ethnohistory of the Military Labour Market of Hindustan, 1450–1850*. Cambridge: Cambridge University Press 2002.
Kopytoff, Igor. "Introduction." In *The African Frontier: The Reproduction of Traditional African Societies*. 3–84. Bloomington: Indiana University Press 1987.
Krauskopf, Giselle, Tej Narain Panjiar and Tek Bahadur Shrestha, eds. *The Kings of Nepal and the Tharu of the Tarai: The Panjiar Collection of Fifty Royal Documents from 1726–1971*. Los Angeles, California: Rusca Press 2000.
Krishna, Sankaran. "Cartographic Anxiety: Mapping the Body Politic in India." In *Challenging Boundaries: Global Flows, Territorial Identities*. Edited by Michael Shapiro and Hayward Alker. 193–214. Minneapolis: University of Minnesota Press 1996.
Kulke, Hermann, ed. *The State in India, 1000–1700*. Delhi: Oxford University Press 1995.
Kumar, Sunil, Munis Faruqui, Richard M. Eaton and David Gilmartin, eds. *Expanding Frontiers in South Asian and World History: Essays in Honour of John F. Richards, Special Issue of Modern Asian Studies*. Cambridge: Cambridge University Press 2009.
Lahiri, Manosi. *Mapping India*. Delhi: Niyogi Publications 2012.
Laxton, Paul and J. H. Andrews. *The New Nature of Maps: Essays in the History of Cartography*. Baltimore, MD: Johns Hopkins University Press 2001.
Lefebvre, Henri. *The Production of Space*. London: Blackwell 1991.

LePatourel, H. E. Jean, Moira H. Long, and May F. Pickles, eds. *Yorkshire Boundaries*. Claremont, Leeds: Yorkshire Archaeological Society 1993.
Levine, Nancy. "Caste, State and Ethnic Boundaries in Nepal." *JAS* 46, no. 1 (1987): 71–88.
Levy, Robert I. *Mesocosm: Hinduism and the Organization of a Traditional Newar City in Nepal*. Berkeley: University of California Press 1990.
Lewis, Martin and Karen Wigen. *The Myth of Continents: A Critique of Metageography*. Berkeley: University of California Press 1997.
Lorimer, Hayden. "Cultural Geography: The Busyness of Being 'More-than Representational.'" *Progress in Human Geography* 29, no. 1 (2005): 83–94.
Ludden, David. *Reading Subaltern Studies: Critical History, Contested Meaning and the Globalization of South Asia*. New Delhi: Permanent Black 2001.
———. *An Agrarian History of South Asia*. Cambridge: Cambridge University Press 1999.
Madan, P. L. "Field-Books and Memoirs: Untapped Source for Historical Research." *The Indian Archives* 33, no. 2 (July–December 1984): 33–40.
———. *Indian Cartography*. Delhi: Manohar 1997.
Majumdar, R. C. "An Account of the Sena Kings of Nepal." *PIHRC* 13 (1929).
Malik, Z. U. "Problems of Fauzdari Administration in Baiswara." *PIHC*, 34th Session, Chandigarh (1973): 211–15.
Malhotra, R. C. *Agricultural Investigations of Morung District (Terai) Kingdom of Nepal*. Kathmandu 1939.
Mann, Michael. "Mapping the Country: European Geography and the Cartographical Construction of India, 1760–1790." *Science, Technology and Society* 8, no. 1 (2003): 25–46.
———. *British Rule on Indian Soil: North India in the First Half of the Nineteenth Century*. Delhi: Manohar 1999.
———. "A Permanent Settlement for the Ceded and Conquered Provinces: Revenue Administration in North India, 1801–33." *IESHR* 32, no. 2 (1995): 245–69.
Mann, Michael. *The Sources of Social Power. Vol. 1. A History of Power from the Beginning to A.D. 1760*. Cambridge: Cambridge University Press 1986.
Marriot, McKim. *India Through Hindu Categories*. Delhi: Vikas 1990.
Marshall, P. J. *Bengal: The British Bridgehead, Eastern India, 1740–1828*. Cambridge: Cambridge University Press 1987.
Martin, R. Montgomery. *The History, Antiquities, Topography and Statistics of Eastern India*. 3 vols. London: William H. Allen & Company 1838.
Massey, Doreen. *For Space*. Thousand Oaks, CA: Sage Publications 2005.
May, John and Nigel Thrift, eds. *Timespace: Geographies of Temporality*. London: Routledge 2001.
McClintock, Anne. *Imperial Leather: Race, Gender, and Sexuality in the Colonial Contest*. New York: Routledge 1995.
McLane, John. *Land and Kingship in Eighteenth-Century Bengal*. Cambridge: Cambridge University Press 1993.
Merrifield, Andrew. "Space and Place: A Lefebvrian Reconciliation." *Transactions of the Institute of British Geographers* 18, no. 4 (1993): 516–31.
Metcalf, Thomas. *Land, Landlords and the British Raj: Northern India in the Nineteenth Century*. Berkeley: University of California Press 1979.
Michael, Bernardo A. "Making Territory Visible: The Revenue Surveys of Colonial South Asia." *Imago Mundi: Journal for the International History of Cartography* 59, no. 1 (2007): 78–95.
———. "Separating the Yam from the Boulder: Statemaking, Space, and the Causes of the Anglo–Gorkha War of 1814–1816." PhD diss., University of Hawaii–Manoa, 2001.
Migdal, Joel. *State in Society: Studying How States and Societies Transform and Constitute One Another*. Cambridge: Cambridge University Press 2001.
———. *Strong Societies and Weak States: State–Society Relations and State Capabilities in the Third World*. Princeton: Princeton University Press 1988.

Migdal, Joel, Atul Kohli and Vivienne Shue, eds. *State Power and Social Forces: Domination and Transformation in the Third World*. Cambridge: Cambridge University Press 1994.

Mikesell, Stephen L. "A Critique of Levy's Theory of the Urban Mesocosm." *CNS* 20, no. 2 (1993): 231–54.

Misra, B. B. *The Judicial Administration of the East India Company in Bengal, 1765–1782*. Delhi: Motilal Banarsidass 1961.

———. *The Central Administration of the East India Company*. Manchester: Manchester University Press 1959.

Mishra, Girish. *Agrarian Problems of Permanent Settlement: A Case Study of Champaran*. New Delhi: Peoples Publishing House 1978.

Mishra, Ratneshwar. "Agrarian Economy of Purnea in the 18th century." *JBRS* 60, nos. 1–4 (1974): 183–9.

Mitchell, Timothy. "The Limits of the State: Beyond Statist Approaches and their Critics." *American Political Science Review* 85, no. 1 (1991): 77–96.

Mojumdar, K. *Anglo–Nepalese Relations in the Nineteenth Century*. Calcutta: Firma K. L. Mukhopadhyaya 1973.

Moll, Herman. *A New Description of England and Wales*. London: C. Rivington 1724.

Mookerji, Radha K. *Indian Land System: Ancient, Medieval and Modern*. Alipore: Bengal Government Press 1940.

Moore, Henrietta. *Space, Text and Gender: An Anthropological Study of the Marakwet in Kenya*. 1986. Revised and reprinted by Guilford Press, 1996.

Moore, Sally F. "Explaining the Present: Theoretical Dilemmas in Processual Anthropology." *American Ethnologist* 14, no. 4 (1987): 727–36.

———. "Epilogue." In *Symbol and Politics in Communal Ideologies*. Edited by Sally F. Moore and Barbara Meyerhoff. 210–39. Ithaca: Cornell University Press 1975.

Moosvi, Shireen. "Aurangzeb's *Farman* to Rasikdas on Problems of Revenue Administration, 1665." In *Medieval India 1: Researches in the History of India, 1200–1750*. Edited by Irfan Habib. 197–208. Delhi: Oxford University Press 1992.

———. *The Economy of the Mughal Empire, c. 1595*. Delhi: Oxford University Press 1987.

Moreland, W. H. *The Agrarian System of Moslem India: A Historical Essay with Appendices*. Cambridge: W. Heffer & Sons 1929.

Morgan, Victor. "The Cartographic Image of 'The Country' in Early Modern England." *Transactions of the Royal Historical Society (Sixth Series)* 29 (1979): 129–54.

Muller, Ulrike. "Interpretation of Cadastral Maps and Land Registers – Examples from the Kathamandu Valley and Gorkha." In *Recent Research on Nepal*. Edited by Klaus Seeland. 141–159. Muchen: Weltforum Verlag 1986.

Mundy, Barbara. *The Mapping of New Spain: Indigenous Cartography and the Maps of the Relaciones Geograficas*. Chicago: University of Chicago Press 1996.

Murton, Brian J. "Changing Land Categories in Interior Tamil Nadu, 1750–1850: Propositions and Implications for the Agricultural System." In *Man, Culture, and Settlement*. Edited by Robert C. Eidt, Kashi N. Singh and Rana P. B. Singh. 31–40. Delhi: Kalyani Publishers 1977.

———. "Key People in the Countryside: Decision-Makers in Interior Tamilnadu in the Late Eighteenth Century." *IESHR* 10, no. 2 (1973): 157–80.

———. "Towards a Deconstruction of Landed Categories in the Late Eighteenth Century British Records in Southern India." In *Contemporary Approaches to Human Geography*. Edited by Rais Akhtar. 101–108. Delhi: APH Publishing Corporation 1997.

Nevill, H. R. *Gorakhpur: A District Gazetteer*, vol. 31, *District Gazetteer of the United Provinces of Agra and Awadh*. Allahabad: Government Press 1909.

Nicholls, George. *Outlines of Indian Geography for the Use of Schools and Colleges in India*. Calcutta: Calcutta School Book Society Press 1849.

———. *That Noble Dream: The "Objectivity Question" and the American Historical Profession.* Cambridge: Cambridge University Press 1988.

O'Brien, Michael. "On Observing the Quicksand." *AHR* 104, no. 4 (1999): 1202–7.

O'Hanlon, Rosalind and David Washbrook. "Histories in Transition: Approaches to the Study of Colonialism and Culture in India." *History Workshop Journal* 32 (1991): 110–27.

Ohnuki-Tierney, Emiko, ed. *Culture Through Time: Anthropological Approaches.* Stanford: Stanford University Press, 1991.

Oldfield, H.A *Sketches from Nepal.* vol. 1. 1880. Reprint, Delhi: Cosmo Publications 1974.

Onta, Pratyoush. "Creating a Brave Nepali Nation in British India: The Rhetoric of *Jati* Improvement, Rediscovery of Bhanubhakta and the Writing of *Bir* History." *SINHAS* 1, no. 1 (1996): 37–76.

———. "Institutional Geography and the Future of Academic History on Nepal." Unpublished paper, page 25.

———. "Rich Possibilities: Notes on Social History in Nepal." *CNS* 21, no. 1 (1994): 1–43.

Ortner, Sherry. *Anthropology and Social Theory: Culture, Power, and the Acting Subject.* Durham: Duke University Press 2006.

Pandian, Anand. *Crooked Stalks: Cultivating Virtue in South India.* Durham: Duke University Press 2009.

Pant, Mahesh Raj. "The Ups and Downs of an Intellectual Pursuit: Towards a History of the Historical Journal *Purnima*." *EBHR*, no. 11 (1996): 27–36.

Papers Respecting the Nepaul Wars. 2 vols. London: J. L. Cox & Sons 1824.

Park, Hyunhee. *Mapping the Chinese and Islamic Worlds: Cross Cultural Exchange in Pre-Modern Asia.* Cambridge: Cambridge University Press, 2012.

Patra, Atul C. *The Administration of Justice under the East-India Company in Bengal, Bihar and Orissa.* London: Asia Publishing House 1962.

Peabody, Norbert W. "*Kota Majajagat*, or the Great Universe of Kota: Sovereignty and Territory in 18th Century Rajasthan." *CIS* (n.s.) 25, no. 1 (1991): 29–56.

Peluso, Nancy L. "Fruit Trees and Family Trees in an Anthropogenic Forest: Ethics of Access, Property Zones, and Environmental Change in Indonesia." *CSSH* 38, no. 3 (1996): 510–47.

———. "Whose Woods are These? Counter-Mapping Forest Territories in Kalimantan, Indonesia." *Antipode* 27, no. 4 (1995): 383–406.

———. *Rich Forests, Poor People: Resource Control and Resistance in Java.* Berkeley: University of California Press 1992.

Pemble, John. *The Invasion of Nepal: John Company at War.* Oxford: Clarendon Press 1971.

———. *The Raj, the Indian Mutiny, and the Kingdom of Oudh, 1801–1859.* Rutherford, NJ: Fairleigh Dickinson University 1977.

Perlin, Frank. "The Precolonial Indian State in History and Epistemology. A Reconstruction of Societal Formation in the Western Deccan from the 15th to the Early 19th Century." In *The Study of the State.* Edited by Henri J. M. Claessen and Peter Skalnik. 275–302. The Hague: Mouton 1981.

Philip, Kavita. *Civilizing Natures: Race, Resources, and Modernity in Colonial South India.* New Brunswick, NJ: Rutgers University Press 2004.

Phillimore, R. H. *Historical Records of the Survey of India.* 4 vols. Dehra Dun: Survey of India 1945–1958.

———. "Three Indian Maps." *Imago Mundi* 9 (1952): 111–14.

Pinch, William. *Peasants and Monks in British India.* Berkeley: University of California Press 1996.

Poovey, Mary. *A History of the Modern Fact: Problems of Knowledge in the Sciences of Wealth and Society.* Chicago: University of Chicago Press 1998.

Pradhan, Kumar. *The Gorkha Conquests.* Delhi: Oxford University Press 1990.

Prakash, Om, ed. *Uttar Pradesh District Gazetteers: Gorakhpur.* Allahabad: Government of Uttar Pradesh 1985.

Pratt, Mary Louise. *Imperial Eyes: Travel Writing and Transculturation.* London: Routledge.

Raj, Kapil. *Relocating Modern Science: Circulation and the Construction of Knowledge in South Asia and Europe, 1650–1900.* New York: Palgrave Macmillan 2010.

Raj, Yogesh. *Expedition to the Nepal Valley: The Journal of Captain Kinloch Related to the Nepal Expedition August 26 – October 17, 1767*. Kathmandu: Jagdamba Prakashan 2012.
Ramble, Charles. "Civic Authority and Agrarian Management in Southern Mustang." *Ancient Nepal* 136 (1994): 89–120.
Ramble, Charles A. E. and Michael Vinding. "The Bem-chag Village Record and the Early History of Mustang District." *Kailash* 13, nos. 1 and 2 (1987): 5–47.
Ramsbotham, R. B. *Studies in the Land Revenue History of Bengal, 1769–87*. London: Oxford University Press 1926.
Ramusack, Barbara. *The Indian Princes and their States*. Cambridge: Cambridge University Press 2004.
Rana, Netra Rajya Laxmi. *The Anglo–Gorkha War of 1814–1816*. Kathmandu: Jore Ganesh Press 1970.
Rangan, Haripriya. "Property vs. Control: The State and Forest Management in the Indian Himalaya." *Development and Change* 28 (1997): 71–94.
Rangarajan, Mahesh and K. Sivaramakrishnan, eds. *India's Environmental History: Colonialism, Modernity, and the Nation*, vol. 2. Delhi: Permanent Black, 2012.
Ravenhill, W.L.D. ed. *Benjamin Donn: A Map of the County of Devon, 1765*. London: Percy Lund, Humphries & Co. 1965.
Raye, N. N. *The Annals of the Early English Settlement in Bihar*. Calcutta: Kamala Book Depot 1927.
Reginald-Hand, J. *Early English Administration of Bihar, 1781–1785*. Calcutta: Bengal Secretariat Press 1894.
Regmi, Dilli R. *Modern Nepal, Vol. 1. Rise and Growth in the Eighteenth Century*. Calcutta: Firma K. L. Mukhopadhyaya 1975.
_____. *Modern Nepal, Vol. 2. Expansion and Climax and Fall*. Calcutta: Firma K. L. Mukhopadyaya 1975.
Regmi, Mahesh C. *Imperial Gorkha: An Account of Gorkhali Rule in Kumaun (1791–1815)*. Delhi: Adroit Publications 1999.
_____. *A Study in Nepali Economic History, 1768–1846*. Delhi: Manjushri 1971.
_____. *Land Tenure and Taxation in Nepal*. Delhi: Manjushri 1978.
_____. *Kings and Political Leaders of the Gorkhali Empire*. Hyderabad: Orient Longman 1995.
_____. *The State and Economic Surplus: Production, Trade and Resource Mobilisation in the Early 19th Century*. Varanasi: Nath Publishing House 1984.
Reilly, R. *Richard Griffith and His Valuations of Ireland: With an Inventory of the Books of the General Valuation of Rateable Property in Ireland*. Baltimore: Genealogical Publishing Co. 2000.
Rennell, James. *Memoir of a Map of Hindustan*. London: W. Bulmer and Co. 1793.
Report On the Reorganization of District Administration in Nepal. Kathmandu 1956. House of Commons Parliamentary Papers, vol. 75.
Return to an Order of the House of Commons, dated 22 July 1853 for a Selection of Papers Illustrative of the Character and Results of the Revenue Survey and Assessment which has been Introduced in the North-West Provinces of Bengal Presidency, Since the year 1833. London 1853. House of Commons Parliamentary Papers, vol. 75.
Ribot, Jesse C. and Nancy Lee Peluso. "A Theory of Access." *Rural Sociology* 68, no. 2 (2003): 153–81.
Riccardi Jr, Theodore. "The Royal Edicts of King Rama Shah of Gorkha." *Kailash* 5, no. 7 (1977): 29–65.
_____. "An Account of Nepal from the Vir Vinod of Shyamaldas." *Kailash* 3, no. 3 (1975): 199–286.
Richards, John F., ed. *Land, Property, and the Environment*. Oakland: ICS Press 2002.
Richards, John F. *The Unending Frontier: An Environmental History of the Early Modern World*. Berkeley: University of California Press 2003.
_____. *The Mughal Empire*. Cambridge: Cambridge University Press 1993.

———. *Document Forms for Official Orders of Appointment in the Mughal Empire*. Cambridge: E. J. Gibb Memorial Trust 1986.
Richards, Thomas. *The Imperial Archive: Knowledge and the Fantasy of Empire*. London: Verso 1993.
Rizvi, S. A. N. "The Mughal Empire and Bureaucracy." In *Aligarh Papers on History: Indian History Congress, 59th Session, Panjabi University, Patiala*. 455–95. Aligarh 1998.
Rizvi, Syed Najmul Raza. "Srinet Zamindars of Sarkar Gorakhpur under the Mughals." *Uttar Pradesh Historical Review* 7 and 8 (1993–5): 35–41.
Rosaldo, Renato. *Culture and Truth: The Remaking of Social Analysis*. Boston: Beacon Press 1989.
Rose, Carol M. *Property and Persuasion: Essays on the History, Theory, and Rhetoric of Ownership*. Boulder: Westview Press 1994.
Rose, Gillian. *Feminism and Geography: The Limits of Geographical Knowledge*. Minneapolis: University of Minnesota Press 1993.
Rundstrom, Robert A. "The Role of Ethics, Mapping and the Meaning of Place in Relations Between Indians and Whites in the United States." *Cartographica* 30, no. 1 (1993): 21–28.
———. "A Cultural Interpretation of Inuit Map Accuracy." *Geographical Review* 80, no. 2 (1990): 155–68.
Sack, Robert. *Human Territoriality: Its Theory and History*. Cambridge: Cambridge University Press 1986.
Safier, Neil. *Measuring the New World: Enlightenment Science and South America*. Chicago: University of Chicago Press 2008.
Sahlins, Marshall D. *Islands of History*. Chicago: University of Chicago Press 1985.
Sahlins, Peter. *Boundaries: The Making of France and Spain in the Pyrenees*. Berkeley: University of California Press 1989.
Said, Edward. *Culture and Imperialism*. New York: Alfred Knopf 1993.
———. "Representing the Colonized: Anthropology's Interlocuters." *Critical Inquiry* 15 (1989): 207–26.
———. *Orientalism*. New York: Vintage 1978.
Samaddar, Ranabir, ed. *Space, Territory and the State: New Readings in International Politics*. Hyderabad: Orient Longman 2002.
Sanwal, B. D. *Nepal and the East India Company*. Bombay: Asia Publishing House 1965.
Saran, P. *The Provincial Government of the Mughals, 1526–1658*. 1941. Reprint, Bombay: Asia Publishing House 1973.
Sarkar, Jadunath. *The India of Aurangzeb: Topographies, Statistics, and Development Compared with the India of Akbar*. Calcutta: Bose Brothers 1901.
Saumarez-Smith, Richard. *Rule by Records: Land Registration and Village Custom in Early British Panjab*. Delhi: Oxford University Press 1997.
Joseph Schwartzberg. "South Asian Cartography." In *The History of Cartography, Vol. 2, Part 2: Cartography in the Traditional Islamic and South Asian Societies*. Edited by John B. Harley and David Woodward. 293–388. Chicago: University of Chicago Press 1987.
Scott, James C. *Seeing Like a State: How Certain Schemes to Improve the Human Condition have Failed*. New Haven: Yale University Press 1998.
———. *The Art of Not Being Governed: An Anarchist History of Upland Southeast Asia*. New Haven: Yale University 2009.
Scott, James C. and Nina Bhatt, eds. *Agrarian Studies: Synthetic Work at the Cutting Edge*. New Haven: Yale University Press 2001.
Sen, Sudipta. *Distant Sovereignty: National Imperialism and the Origins of British India*. New York: Routledge, 2002.
Serajuddin, Alamgir Muhammad. *The Revenue Administration of the East India Company in Chittagong, 1761–1785*. Chittagong, Bangladesh: University of Chittagong 1971.
Sever, Adrian *Nepal Under the Ranas*. New Delhi: Oxford & IBH Publishing Co. 1993.
Seymour, W. A. *A History of the Ordnance Survey*. Kent: William Dawson & Sons 1980.

Sezgin, Fuat. "The Precolumbian Discovery of the American Continent by Muslim Seafarers," *Geschichte des Arabischen Scrifttums* 13 (2006): 1–39.
Shaha, Rishikesh. *Modern Nepal: A Political History, 1769–1885*, vol. 1. Delhi: Manohar 1990.
Sharma, G. D. and J. K. Dhot. "Marathi Records on the State Revenue in Gujarat During the Second Half of the Eighteenth Century." *PIHRC* 49 (1973): 83–98.
Sharma, Kunjar M. "The Economic Theme in Nepali Foreign Policy: An Historical Analysis up to the End of the Anglo–Gorkha War." PhD diss. University of Denver 1973.
Sharma, Pitamber. *Unravelling the Mosaic: Spatial Aspects of Ethnicity in Nepal.* Kathmandu: Himal Books 2008.
Sharma, Pitamber, Narendra Khanal, and Subhash Chaudhary Tharu. *Towards a Federal Nepal: An Assessment of Proposed Models.* Kathmandu: Himal Books 2009.
Sharma, Radha. "Social Configuration in the Three Parganas under British Rule." *The Panjab Past and Present* vol. 23, part 1, serial no. 45 (1989): 81–6.
Sharma, R. K. "Some Aspects of the Land Revenue Records of Udaipur State: A Study of the Karan Mahal Revenue Records of the Rajasthan State Archives." *PIHRC* 49 (1973): 99–108.
Sharma, S. C. *Land-use Survey in Tarai Tract: A Study of Eastern Uttar Pradesh.* Delhi: Concept Publishing House 1991.
Shue, Vivienne. *The Reach of the State: Sketches of the Chinese Body Politic.* Stanford: Stanford University Press 1988.
Siddiqui, Asiya. *Agrarian Change in a Northern Indian State: Uttar Pradesh, 1819–1833.* Oxford: Clarendon Press 1973.
Siddiqui, Noman Ahmad. "The Classification of Villages Under the Mughals." *IESHR* 1, no. 3 (1964): 73–83.
———. "The Fauzdar and Fauzdari Under the Mughals." *Medieval India Quarterly* 4 (1961): 22–35.
Singh, Chetan. *Natural Premises: Ecology and Peasant Life in the Western Himalayas, 1800–1950.* New Delhi: Oxford University Press 1998.
Singh, Kashi N. "The Territorial Basis of Medieval Town and Village Settlement in Eastern Uttar Pradesh, India." *Annals of the Association of American Geographers* 58, no. 2 (1968): 203–20.
Singh, Lekh Raj. *The Tarai Region in U. P.: A Study in Human Geography.* Allahabad: Lal Beni Prasad 1965.
Singh, Rana P. B. "Morphogenesis of the Cultural Landscape: The Case of the Saran Plain, India." In *Man, Culture and Settlement.* Edited by Robert C. Eidt, Kashi N. Singh and Rana P.B. Singh. Delhi: Kalyani Publishers 1977.
Singh, R. L. and Ram Bali Singh. "Spatial Diffusion of Rajput Clan Settlements in a Part of Middle Ganga Valley." In *Readings in Rural Settlement Geography.* Edited by R. L. Singh, Kashi N. Singh and Rana P. B. Singh. Varanasi: National Geographical Society of India 1975.
Singh, R. L. and Rana P. B. Singh. "Evolution of Clan Territorial Units Through Land Occupance in the Middle Ganga Valley." In *Man, Culture and Settlement.* Edited by Robert C. Eidt, Kashi N. Singh, and Rana P.B. Singh. Delhi: Kalyani Publishers 1975.
———. "Some Approaches to the Morphogenesis of Indian Village." In *Man, Culture and Settlement.* Edited by Robert C. Eidt, Kashi N. Singh and Rana P.B. Singh. Delhi: Kalyani Publishers 1975.
Singh, S. N. *History of Tirhut: From Earliest Times to the End of the Nineteenth Century.* Calcutta: Baptist Mission Press 1922.
Singha, Radhika. *A Despotism of Law: Crime and Justice in Early Colonial India.* Delhi: Oxford University Press 1998.
Sinha, C. P. N. *From Decline to Destruction: Agriculture in Bihar during the Early British Rule, 1765–1813.* Cambridge: Cambridge University Press 1997.
———. *The Subah of Allahabad Under the Great Mughals (1580–1707).* Delhi: Jamia Millia Islamia 1974.

Siu, Helen F. and David Faure, eds. *Down to Earth: The Territorial Bond in Southern China*. New Haven: Yale University Press 1995.

Sivaramakrishnan, K. *Modern Forests: Statemaking and Environmental Change in Colonial Eastern India*. Stanford: Stanford University Press 1999.

———. "Transition Zones: Changing Landscapes and Local Authority in Southwest Bengal, 1880s–1920s," in *India's Environmental History: Colonialism, Modernity, and the Nation*, vol. 2. Edited by Mahesh Rangarajan and K. Sivaramakrishnan. 197–245. Delhi: Permanent Black 2012.

———. "British Imperium and Forested Zones of Anomaly in Bengal, 1767–1833." *Indian Economic and Social History Review* 33, no. 3 (1996): 243–82.

Sivaramakrishnan, K. and Arun Agrawal. "Regional Modernities in Stories and Practices of Development." Working Paper 51, Yale Center for International and Area Studies (YCIAS), 1998.

Sivaramakrishnan, K. and Arun Agrawal, eds. *Agrarian Environments: Resources, Representations, and Rule in India*. Durham: Duke University Press 2000.

Skaria, Ajay. *Hybrid Histories: Forests, Frontier, and Wildness in Western India*. Oxford: Oxford University Press 2001.

Skocpol, Theda, Peter Evans and Dietrich Rueschemeyer, eds. *Bringing the State Back In*. Cambridge: Cambridge University Press 1985.

Sletto, Bjorn Ingmunn. "'We Drew What We Imagined': Ethnocartography, Power, and Place-Making in Postcolonial Landscapes." Paper presented at the Conference on Social Histories of Space in Latin America, Yale University, New Haven, Connecticut, 22–3 October 2005.

Slusser, M. S. and G. Vajracharya. *Nepal Mandala – A Cultural Study of the Kathmandu Valley*. 2 vols. Princeton: Princeton University Press 1982.

Smith, Neil. "Geography, Empire and Social Theory." *Progress in Human Geography* 18, no. 4 (1994): 491–500.

Smith, Neil, and Cindi Katz. "Grounding Metaphor: Towards a Spatialized Politics." In *Place and the Politics of Identity*. Edited by Michael Keith and Steve Pile. 67–83. London: Routledge 1993.

Soja, Edward. *Postmodern Geographies: The Reassertion of Space in Contemporary Social Thought*. London: Verso 1988.

Sparke, Matthew. *In the Space of Theory: Postfoundational Geographies of the Nation-State*. Minneapolis: University of Minnesota Press 2005.

———. "Triangulating the borderless world: geographies of power in the Indonesia–Malaysia–Singapore Growth Triangle." *Transactions of the Institute of British Geographers* NS 29 (2004): 485–98.

Stein, Burton. "Idiom and Ideology in Early Nineteenth Century South India." In *Rural India*. Edited by Peter Robb. 23–58. London: Curzon 1983.

———. *Peasant State and Society in Medieval South India*. Delhi: Oxford University Press 1980.

———. *South Indian Temples: An Analytic Reconsideration*.

———. "The Segmentary State: Interim Reflections." *Purusartha* 13 (1991): 217–38.

Steinmetz, George. *State/Culture: State-Formation After the Cultural Turn*. Ithaca: Cornell University Press 1999.

Stern, Philip. *The Company-State: Corporate Sovereignty and the Early Modern Foundations of the British Empire in India*. Oxford: Oxford University Press 2011.

Stevenson-Moore, C. J. *Final Report on the Survey and Settlement Operations in Champaran District, 1892–1899*. Calcutta: Bengal Secretariat Press 1900.

Stiller, Ludwig. *The Silent Cry: The People of Nepal, 1816–1839*. Kathmandu: Sahayogi Prakashan 1976.

———. "Hodgson on Justice." *RRS* 16 (September–October 1984): 139–40.

———. *A Typescript of Microfilms Preserved in the Tribhuvan University Library from Documents in the Archives of India (The Stiller Typescript)*. Vol. 2, June 1973.

———. *The Rise of the House of Gorkha*. Delhi: Manjushri 1973.

Stoler, Laura Ann. "On Degrees of Imperial Sovereignty." *Public Culture* 18, no. 1. (2006): 125–46.

Strathern, Marilyn. *Reproducing the Future: Essays on Anthropology, Kinship and the New Reproductive Technologies*. New York: Routledge 1992.
Sturgeon, Janet C. *Border Landscapes: The Politics of Akha Land Use in China and Thailand*. Seattle: University of Washington Press 2005.
Subrahmanyam, Sanjay. "Review of Shireen Moosvi's The Economy of the Mughal Empire, c. 1595: A Statistical Study." *IESHR* 25, no. 1 (1988): 103–6.
Sutton, Deborah. *Other Landscapes: Colonialism and the Predicament of Authority in Nineteenth-Century South India*. Copenhagen: NIAS Press 2009.
Tagliacozzo, Eric. *Secret Trades, Porous Borders: Smuggling and States Along a Southeast Asian Frontier, 1865–1915*. New Haven: Yale University Press 2005.
Talbot, Cynthia. *Precolonial India in Practice: Society, Region, and Identity in Medieval Andhra*. New York: Oxford University Press 2001.
Tambiah, Stanley J. "What did Bernier Actually Say? Profiling the Mughal Empire." *CIS* (n.s.) 32, no. 2 (1998): 360–86.
———. "The Galactic Polity in Southeast Asia." In *Culture, Thought and Action: An Anthropological Perspective*. 252–86. Cambridge: Harvard University Press 1985.
Taniguchi, Shinkichi. "The *Zamindar's* Estate-Control on the Eve of the Permanent Settlement in Bengal (1793) – A Case-Study of a Middle-Size *Zamindari* in Northern Bengal." *The Calcutta Historical Journal* 18, no. 2 (1996): 1–41.
Thrift, Nigel. "Space: The Fundamental Stuff of Human Geography." In *Key Concepts in Geography*. Edited by Sarah L. Holloway, Stephen P. Rice and Gill Valentine. 95–107. London: Sage Publications 2003.
Thuillier, H. L. and R. Smyth, comps. *A Manual of Surveying for India*. 1851. Reprint, Calcutta: Thacker, Spink and Company 1875.
Tongchai Winichakul. "Siam Mapped: The Making of Thai Nationhood." *The Ecologist* 26, no. 5 (1996): 215–21.
———. *Siam Mapped: The History of the Geo-Body of a Nation*. Honolulu: University of Hawaii Press 1994.
Tooker, Deborah. "Putting the Mandala in its Place: A Practice-based Approach to the Spatialization of Power on the Southeast Asian Periphery." *JAS* 55, no. 2 (1996): 323–58.
Travers, Robert. "'The Real Value of the Lands': The Nawabs, the British and the Land Tax in Eighteenth-Century Bengal." *MAS* 38, no. 3 (July 2004): 517–58.
Trivedi, K. K. "Estimating forests, wastes and fields, c.1600." *Studies in History* (n.s.) 14, no. 2 (1998): 301–11.
———. "Reappraisals of *A'ins* Area Statistics: A Note." *IHR* 25, no. 1 (1998): 45–59.
Tsing, Anna. *Friction: An Ethnography of Global Connection*. Princeton: Princeton University Press 2005.
United Kingdom Parliament. "Report from the Select Committee on the Cadastral Survey; with the Proceedings of the Committee and Appendix." In *Reports from Committees: Eleven Volumes, Session 6 February–7 August 1862*, vol. 6. London: House of Commons 1862.
Turner, Frederick J. *The Significance of the Frontier in American History*. New York: Holt, Reinhart and Winston 1962.
Vaidya, Tulasi Ram. *Jayaprakash Malla: The Brave King of Kantipur, 1736–1767*. Delhi: Anmol Publications 1996.
———. *Prithvinarayan Shah: The Founder of Modern Nepal*. Delhi: Anmol Publications 1993.
———. "The Historiography of Nepal: An Analytical Approach." In *Asian Panorama: Essays in Asian History: Past and Present*. 89–102. Edited by K. M. de Silva et al. Delhi: Vikas 1990.
Vaidya, Tulasi Ram and Tri Ratna Manandhar. *Crime and Punishment in Nepal: A Historical Perspective*. Kathmandu: Bini Vaidya and Purna Devi Manandhar 1985.
Van Schendel, Willem. "Geographies of Knowing, Geographies of Ignorance: Jumping Scale in Southeast Asia." *Environment and Planning D: Society and Space* 20, no. 6 (2002): 647–68.
———. *The Bengal Borderland: Beyond State and Nation in South Asia*. London: Anthem Press 2005.

Vandergeest, Peter and Nancy L. Peluso. "Territorialization and State Power in Thailand." *Theory and Society* 24 (1995): 385–426.
Whitmore, Sarah. *Hybrid Geographies: Natures, Cultures, Spaces*. Delhi: Sage Publications 2002.
Whelpton, John. *Kings, Soldiers and Priests: Nepalese Politics and the Rise of Jang Bahadur Rana, 1830–1857*. New Delhi: Manohar 1991.
Wilson, H. H. *A Glossary of Judicial and Revenue Terms, and of Useful Words Occuring in Official Documents Relating to the Administration of the Government of British India*. Delhi: Motilal Banarsidas (1850) 1968.
Wilson, Jon E. *The Domination of Strangers: Modern Governance in Eastern India, 1780–1835*. New York: Palgrave Macmillan 2008.
Winchester, Angus. *Discovering Parish Boundaries*. Buckinghamshire, UK: Shire Publications 1990.
Wink, Andre. "A Rejoinder to Habib." *IESHR* 26, no. 3 (1989): 363–67.
———. *Land and Sovereignty in India: Agrarian Society and Politics under the Eighteenth-Century Maratha Svarajaya*. Cambridge: Cambridge University Press 1986.
Wolf, Eric. "Facing Power – Old Insights, New Questions." *AA* 92, no. 3 (1990): 586–96.
Wolters, O.W. *History, Culture and Region in Southeast Asia*. Singapore: University of Singapore Press 1982.
Worster, Daniel. *The Ends of the Earth: Perspectives on Modern Environmental History*. Cambridge: Cambridge University Press 1988.
Wyatt, Alexander. *Geographical and Statistical Memoir of the District of Tirhoot*. Calcutta: Calcutta Gazette Office 1854.
———. *Statistics of the Districts of Sarun, consisting of the Sircars of Sarun and Chumparun*. Calcutta: Military Orphan Press 1847.
Young, Crawford. *The African Colonial State in Comparative Perspective*. New Haven: Yale University Press 1994.
Zilli, I. A. "Two Administrative Documents of Akbar's Reign." *PIHC*, 32nd Session, Jabalpur (1979): 367–73.

INDEX

Maps, plates and tables are indicated by bold page numbers.

"absolute space" 107, 187n88
accountants 10, 24, 148n47
account registers 28
Act of Union (1535) 124
Adam, John 8
Adilabad 70
administration of justice 35, 69, 100, 156n24
administrative divisions: agrarian rights and relationships impacting 48; ambiguity of 33, 78; "dependent" *tarafs* of 38; impact of opportunistic practices on 41; intermediate 107; land pattern use impact on 28–9; Mughal 170n4; noncompliance with 33; offices held 109; plasticity of 35, 40; precolonial 77, 82; in precolonial South Asia 67–70, 171n11; reorganizations of 121, 194n162; setting up in Eastern Tarai 33–4, 153n11; villages as building blocks for 100; *see also suba*
Agnew, P. Vans 67
agrarian entitlements: as autonomous 55; in framework of cultures of governance 71, 126; landholder's location in 43; preservation of 110; territorial claims and 14; territory production and 71–4
agrarian environments: overview of 17–18; and the production of space 27–9
agrarian expansion 21, 26, 147n29
agrarian resources: contests over 5–6, 17, 25; cultures of governance and 3, 11; of Tarai 31, 152n4
agriculture: classes of society employed in 24, 149n50; labor 21, 24–5, 148n44, 148n46; *pargana* association with 83; "shifting" 21, 24
"agroforest" 25, 149n54
Ahmad, Qeyamuddin 100, 186n70, 186n73
Ain-i-Akbari 77–8, 177n61, 180n8
Ajabgarh 75

amanat system 34, 35, 153n11, 156n25; *see also* revenue collection
Amar Narayan Temple 51, 162n11
"*ambal/amval*" 110, 189n105
Amended Code of Regulations for the Decennial Settlement of Bengal and Bihar 10
Amini Commission 9, 143nn50–52
Amorha 27, 76, 151n71, 175n52
Amudarya **113**
Anderson, Adam 125
Anglo–Bhutan border 105, 187n86
Anglo–Gorkha boundary **4**; agrarian space production in 28; ambiguity of 28–9; ambiguity of administrative divisions of 33; Champaran–Tarriani 11–12; Company records about 53, 163n28; composition of 5; cultures of governance impacting 3, 5; delineation of 12, 127; demarcating 93–8, 182n35; forest–field–waste mosaics on 25–27; Gorakhpur–Butwal 4, 11–12; Gorkhali investigations regarding 44; labor patterns along 24, 149n49; "principle of limitation" 8, 142n44; Purnea-Morung area disputes 76; representation and organization of 14; territorial overlaps along 38, 158n46; Tirhut-Sarlahi area disputes 76
Anglo–Gorkha War 11–14; accounts of 13, 144n71, 144nn66–7; as a "diagnostic event" 14, 144nn70–71
archives: territorial 11, 143n59
area studies approaches 5, 140n26
Argha 18
Asafuddaulah 54, 58, 62, 166n61, 167n84; *see also* Awadh
ascetics 22, 147n30
Asia, maps valued in 92, 181n18
asli 69
Athbazar 118

Athgaon 79
Atlas of England and Wales, An (Saxton) 89, 180n6
Atlas of India project 185n60
Atlas of the Mughal Empire, An (Habib) 87, 88, 180n5
Australia 5, 122, 140n23, 194n165
Awadh **101**; cedes Gorakhpur to the Company 49, **50**; cultivation incentives of 27; dominant land holding groups in 51; forgery in 80, 178n78; *maafi* in 52–4, 163n25; migration from 24; *nawab* of 18, 145n10; as overlords along Gorakhpur–Butwal frontier 60, **61**; as overlords of Palpa 58–9, 166n61; Palpa's payments to in arrears 51, 162n7; Ratanpur Bansi of 62; revenue register transfers by 76; Treaty of Cession 80; *see also* Asafuddaulah

Babra 18, 76
Baghdad **113**
Bahadur, Kalyan Singh 36
Bandipur **119**
Banjaras 21, 147n31
Banke-Bardia 118
Bansi: *see* Ratanpur Bansi
Baroda 98, 125
Barour 103
Barrow, Ian xiii, 140n22, 142n37, 185n58
Bayly, Christopher 24–5, 90, 180n9
Beames, John 69–70, 82–3, 172n17
Beg, Mirza Abdulla 40–43, 75, 159nn54–5, 160n66, 160n74
Beg, Qulb Ali 40
Begum, Bahu 80, 178n75
Beli 118
Belwa 36, 156n29
Bengal: Bettiah as refractory dependent of 36; under British rule 38; Company acquirement of 14; famine 21, 147n28; fixed divisions regulation 10; Islam in 18, 146n13; Mir Jafar of 40, 158n53; Mir Kasim of 40; Permanent Settlement 150n63; revenue collection in 11; territorial transfers in 107, 187n89
Bengal Judicial Consultations 107, 188n94
Bentley, Charles 104–5
Bettiah: Babra conquered by 76; boundary disputes with Palpa 56, 165n54; claimed by Gorkhalis 37, 157–8n43; land disputes between rajas and priests of 80, 178n77;

land dispute witnesses of 45; little kingdoms of Tanahu and 36; raj of 153n9, 156n26; refusal of aid to Hem Karna Sen 40, 158n48; subdued by Bengal 156n28; *tappas* claimed by 40, 157n39; *see also* Singh, Bir Kishor; Singh, Jugal Kishor
Bhabar 19
Bhagulpoor **102**
Bhaju, Maniraj 51, 63–4, 66, 169n106
Bhangarh 75
bhardars 34, 154n14
Bhargava, Meena 25
Bhutan 104
Bihar: Buchanan-Hamilton on 105, 187n84; Company acquirement of 14; fixed divisions regulation 10; Gaya district of 107, 188nn92–3; Gentil's map of **90**; Permanent Settlement 150n63; revenue collection in 11; spatiality of 77, 176n59; territorial transfers in 107
Bijay 41
Binayakpur 60, 62, 71
birt landholders 52, 56, 163n20, 165n47
Blochmann, H. 69
block formulation 121, 194n161
Board of Revenue 9–10
Boileau, John Peter 95, **97**, 182n34
boundaries 4–5
Boundary Commission (1837) 124
boundary vs. frontier delineation 93
Bradshaw, Paris 24, 26, 44, 148m48, 150n62; investigation of *maafi* lands 54
bribery 77, 81–2
British defeat of Gorkhalis by 8
Brooke, Thomas 42
Brooke, William 43
Buchanan-Hamilton, Francis: anxiety of regarding surveys 9; on Bansi waste lands 27; on Dholiya Bhandar 65; on Gorakhpur tenants 22, 148n39; on local maps 187n87; map making by 114, 192nn135–6; on *pahikasht* cultivators 24; on Purnea 106–7; Ratanpur Bansi survey of 19, 146n16; on record keeping in Lucknow 56; on *thanas* 105, 187n84
Burack, Natalie 73, 79, 101, 106
Bureau of Census and Statistics 118–19
Burghart, Richard 3, 74–5, 84, 126, 138n11
Burwa 41
Butsilla 76
Butwal: Gorkha claiming rights to 55, 59, 164n40, 166n72; government

management of 51, 161n6; labor flight from 24, 148n44; migration to 27; value of at Company acquisition 53
Butwal–Nawalparsi region 22, 148n41
Butwal Tarai 38, 51, 54, 60–62; *see also* Palpa
Bykuntpur 104

cadastral mapping and property rights 7
cadastral surveys 117–18, 193n152
calendars xiv
"cartographic anxiety" 99, 185n64
cartography: criticism of 6–7, 141–2n36, 142n39; methodological implications 7; multiple histories in 11, 143n62; and spatiality 6–11, 142n37
castes 21, 70
cattle 21, 26, 149n59, 150n64
Ceded and Conquered districts 49, 107, 161nn2–3
Census Enumeration Abstracts (1831) 124
Central Asia, Nepali map of **113**
Central Nepal **114**
Cerdanya 92
Chahar Gulshan 92
chakla 67, 170n4
Chakrabarti, Animesh 109, 188n98
Champaran **90**; frontier *parganas* of 18; geography of 31, 151n2; land ambiguities in 33, 153n9; migration from to Tarriani 19; oppressive conditions in 24, 148n46; population of 21, 146n27; revenue collection in 31; soil of 19; subdivision of 107, 188n91; Tanahu claims in 36, 156–7nn31–2; "waste land" in 26
Champaran–Tarriani frontier **32**; agrarian expansion in 21, 147nn29–30; boundary demarcation of 95, 182nn34–5; constitution of order on 31; cultures of governance and illegible landscapes on 33–6; as disputed area 11–12; disputed villages on **45**; irrigation problems of 19; little kingdoms of Bettiah and Tanahu 36–7; local agency role and additional territorial disputes 46–7; Makwani Raj and *pargana* Tauter/Thathar 37–8; role of local forces 33; *tappa* Rautahat, *pargana* (Gadh) Simraon 38–44, **39**; *tappa* Rautahat and Nannor's entangled edges 44–6; "Tarriani" boundary and 18
Chaudhari, Bikha 41, 46, 159n56
Chaudhari, Hem, Shah's *lal mohar* to **23**
Chaudhari, Jhungha 169n101

Chaudhari, Jurawan 63, 95, 169n105, 183n41
chaurasi 83, 179n90
Chigwan 36, 76, 157n35
Chilli 111, 191n120
China 11, 143n60
Chittagong 76, 174n50
Circular Orders by the Sudder Board of Revenue, North West Provinces Addressed to Commissioners of Revenue on Records and Registration 10
Clive, Robert 99, 185n63
Cohn, Bernard S. 87, 196n28
Colebrooke, Edward 49
Colgong 102
colonial boundary formation 2
colonialism: goals of 6, 8; works on 141n34
"commercialization of power" 69, 171n15
concessional cultivation 51, 162n12
Counties (Detached Parts) Act of 1844 123, 195n6
Craib, Raymond xiii, 141n30, 141n36
Crawford, John 31
crops 19
cultural histories: perspective of 14, 144n71; on statemaking 3, 138–9n13
culture: approaches to 3, 139n14; defined 3; power and history interwoven with 3, 139n15; process-oriented approach to 3
cultures of governance: agrarian resources in 3, 25; conceptual framework of 71; on the Gorakhpur–Butwal frontier 55–7; and illegible landscapes on Champaran–Tarriani frontier 33–6; land use patterns impacted by 28; marked by territorial intermixture 41; plasticity of institutional arrangements in 34; rent-free grants in 53–54; shaped by agrarian entitlements 126; in states and statemaking 3–6; and territory production in South Asia 71–84

dakhili 69
Dang 111, 191n120
Dang highlands 38, 158n46
"Dangols" 117, 193n145
Dangs 98
dasturs 69, 171n7
Deccan 67, 92
Deokhori 63
Deokhori-Sheoraj 63, 80
"*dependent*" *tarafs* 38
DesChene, Mary 13–14
Devi, Rajrajeshwari 167, 167n86

Dhading District 118, **119**
Dhebrua (*tappa*) 24, 63–4
Dholiya Bhandar 65, 75–6, 170n120
dhungo 59, 110, 167n76, 190n108
diara disputes 76, 93, 174n51, 181–2n27
Dimiya 106, 187n87
Dinajpore survey 102
Dirks, Nicholas B. 87
district boundaries 108
Divided Parishes Acts 124
diwani: *see* revenue administration
Doars 105, 187n86
Dowdeswell, George 6
Down Survey 124
Duara, Prasenjit 11, 143n62

Eastern Tarai: districts of 18, 31; labor importation in 22; population of 21; revenue collection in 33–5, 153nn11–12, 155n20; Tharus fled 22, 24; *see also* Gorkha; Tarai
Eaton, Richard 18, 146n13
Edney, Matthew 98, 184n56
elephants 21, 37–8, 51, 160n66
Elliot, H. M. 69–70, 83, 93, 179n90, 181n21
Elliott, Charles 74, 173n35
English East India Company: acquisition of Ceded and Conquered districts by 49, 161n2; on ambiguity of Anglo–Gorkha frontier 33; attacked by Gorkhali troops 66; Butwal value at Company acquisition 53; Champaran ruled by 18; claims on Palpa 59, 167n75; claims on Sheroraj 63; claims to Butwal 55; clandestine meetings of 34; "Collectorships" of 105, 187n80; concern about discernible political boundaries 94; dispute investigations of 44, 47; Gorakhpur ceded to 18, 49, **50**, 62; Gorkha territory disputes 2, 7, 38; inheritance of entitlements and territorial disputes by 4; involvement with Sheoraj 62; *jangalbari pattas* issued by 27, 151n72; jurisdiction problems of 24; *kham* management by 161n6; labor flight to territories of 24, 148n44; labor movements of 24, 148n46; land use patterns found by 28, 151n74; Matka directly managed by 62, 168n91; Nannor ruled by 18, 145n9; outstanding issues of in 1780s 41, 159n58; Permanent Settlement and 33, 152n8; Rautahat handed over to Gorkha by 40, 158n50; records on Anglo–Gorkha 53,
163n28; Regulation 11 107; Regulations 7 and 9 of 100, 185nn66–7; rent-free lands of 53–6; response to Mirza Abdulla Beg 43; revenue collection by 11, 31, 50–51, 152n5; sharing authority over Tauter 38; spatial anxiety in 104; state, sovereignty and political power 125, 195n23; territorialization of power by 101; territorial sovereignty of 38; territory of 6, 10, 14, 18, 31, **32**, 37; Treaty of Cession 80; treaty with *nawab* of Awadh 18, 145n10; vision of 8–9, 59, 81, 87, 100; war declared by 12; "waste land" mentions by 25–6, 28, 149n56; *see also* maps, surveys and boundaries, making states legible
entitlements: changing nature of 33, 36, 43, 74; land tenure 3, 4; overview of precolonial 72; thwarting of elite's 27; unenforced 72
environment: *see* agrarian environment
environmental history 17, 145nn2–3
estates (*mahals*) 10
ethnosociology 84, 179n102
Europe, as context for cartography 98

famine 21, 28, 147n28
farming: *see* agriculture
fauzdar 31, 152n3
fiscal relationships 73, 173n34
"*fitna*" 172–3n26
Fitzpatrick, J. 103
"fixed principles" 8
forest–field–waste mosaics 25–8
forests **13**, 19–22, 40, **116**
forgery 80–81, 178n78
Fort of Someshwar 36–7
forts 81–2, 88, **88**, 92
Foxcroft, George 41, 159n62
France 94, 182n28
Francis, Philip 9, 143n52
Franklin, J. 67
Fraser, Alexander 20
"frontier" 17, 145n4
frontier vs. boundary delineation 93
Frykenberg, Robert 76, 175n54
"fugitive landscapes" 5, 141n30
Futtehpoor Singheea 103
Futtehpur 101, **103**

Gadh Simraon 110
Gardner, Edward 115
Garhwal 12, 54–5

INDEX 225

Geertz, Clifford 196n28
gender, spatiality and 5, 140n23
Gentil, Jean Baptiste **90**, 90–91, 180nn10–11
Geo-Body of Nepal **120**, 121, **121**
geography 5, 98, 140n27
Ghazi ka Thana 75
Ghewra 47, 161n79
Gholam Hazrat 26–7
Giri, Laxman: responsibilities of 160n67; revenue contracts of 34, 152n4, 154n16; violent death of 44, 47, 160n67
Golding, Edward 40, 159n53
Gole, Susan 92, 192n140
Gorakhpur: abolished 107, 188n90; Amorha 76, 175n52; ceded to the Company 18, 49, **50**, 62; Company creation of state employees in 164n42; Khairigarh detached from 80; labor migration to 22; *maafi* in 53–4, 56, 163n27; northern boundary *tappas* of 24; *parganas* reverting back to 63; reconfigured tenurial relationships in 56, 165n47; rent-free lands in 54–6; soil of 146n15; tenant behaviour 22, 148n39; *thana* divisions of **106**; waste lands of 26–7, 150n64; *zamindar* types in 52, 162n16
Gorakhpur–Butwal: agrarian expansion in 21, 147nn29–30; boundary demarcation of 95, 182nn34–5; as disputed territory 11–12; land conditions in 27; soil of 19; "Tarriani" boundary and 18; territory of 18
Gorakhpur–Butwal frontier **50**, **61**; Bansi 60; Binayakpur 60; the Butwal Tarai 60–62; cultures of governance and illegible landscapes on 55–7; Khajahani (Bhandar) 60; Matka 60, 62, 167nn79–81; nature of disputes along 56–7; other *tappas* 65; Palpa Raj 57–9; sources of social power on 51–5; structure of territory on 60–65; *tappa* Sheoraj 62–5; Tilpur 60; *zamindars* in 52
Gordon, Stewart 70
Gorkha: attempts to authenticate rent free-lands 55, 164n37; boundary demarcation by 191n122; boundary dispute investigations by 93, 181n25; claiming rights to Butwal 59, 166n72; claims to hill kingdoms 167n73; claim to Rautahat 41–3; complaints against officials of 77, 175n56; defeat of by British 8; disputed villages of 47, 161n79; English East India Company territory disputes 2, 7, 38; expelled from Ramnagar area 97, 184n47; imperialism 3, 138n11; inheritance of entitlements and territorial disputes by 4; jusrisdictional themes in documents of 189n101; labor movements of 24, 148n46; land grants 26; Makwanpur conquered by 22; mapping 109–21; Pyuthana forcibly incorporated by 62, 111; Rana rule in 111–12; Rautahat ruled by 18, 145n9; reinstated Palpali rights to Matka 62; relations with Palpa 58–9, 166n63; rent-free lands in 74; state income sources 57, 165n56; territorial expansion of 11, 143–4n63; Treaty of Friendship 196n34; troops of attack the Company 66; villages occupied by 44, **45**; *see also* Eastern Tarai districts; Tarai
Gorkha–Sikkim boundary 95, 182n35
Goruckpoor [Gorakhpur], district of **20**
Gosains 22, 147n32, 147n35
governmentality 11
Grant, P. Warden 54
Great Britain, administrative geography of 123–5, 194–5n4
"Greater Nepal" 11, 143–4n63
Great Trigonometrical Survey (GTS) 99
Griffith, Richard 124, 195n11
Grover, R. R. 70
Gulmi 18, 60, 62, 79–80, 167n81, 168n87
Gurdhan **91**
Gurung, Harka 117
Gurung, Narsing 35

Habib, Irfan 69, 72, 88–9, 172–3nn26–7
Hajipur 83
Hamilton, Walter 99
Hamrah 79, 177n71
Harley, John Brian 6–7, 141n35
Haryana 69
Hasanpur Maghar 76
Hastings, Warren 9, 43, 143n52
Haveli 103
Haveli Gorakhpur 76
Haveli Harhara 76
Herat **113**
Helgerson, Richard 98, 184n54
hill kingdoms: disputes between 65; given to Palpali raj 60; as Gorkha's territorial possessions 11, 18; military campaigns against 58
Hindus 21, 147n31
Hodgson, Brian 92, 111, 117, 192n138

Hodgson Collection 115
Hunter, W. W. 25, 149n56
Hutundah 103
Huzar Tukee 102
Huzrut, Mooftee Gholam [Mufti Ghulam Hazrat] 51–2
"hybrid maps" 91, 180n11
Hyderabad 125

ijara system 34–5, 77, 153n11, 155–6n24, 176n57; *see also* revenue collection
"imperial space" 94
importation of labor 22
Inclosure Acts 124
Inden, Ronald 126, 196n30
India 7, 22
Indo–Nepal Trade and Transit treaties 1
inheritable tenures 74
inheritance of entitlements by Gorkha and the Company 4
"inner logic" activities 76, 175n54
institutional infrastructure of territorial governance 4
"intermediate space" 71, 172n25
"invisible city" 4, 139n18
Irish Townland surveys 124, 195n11

Jafar, Mir 40, 158n53
Jaffarabad **79**
jagera lands 57, 165n56
James, Henry 124, 195n7
jangalbari pattas 27, 151n72
Jaunpur **101**
Jhamuna 110, 190n115
Jubal 72–4, **73**, 173n31
judges 35
judicial system 31, 35, 107, 110, 189n107

Kabul **113**
Kandahar **113**
Kangra Fort 82
Kankjole 102, 103
Karan, Pradyumna 118, 121, 194n160
Kark, Ruth 77, 176n60
Kashinath, *thanadar* of Chitwa 66
Kashmir 91–2, **113**, 180n15
Kasim, Mir 40
Kathila 76
Kathmandu: British Resident appointed to 12; commissions of inquiry by 35, 155n23; factional politics in 34; local officials' activities 34; recall of Tharus 23, 24; role of elite of 31; warnings to landholders from 22, 148n38
Katz, Cindi 107, 187n88
Khairigarh 76, 80, 174n50
Khajahani 75–6
Khajahani Bhandar 60, 65, 170n117
Khan, Ali Quli 40, 158–9n53, 158n48
Khan, Alivardi 36
Khan, Kasim Ali 40
Khan, Mohammad Ashraf 36–7
Khan, Shaukat Ullah 78, 177n64
Khanchi 18, 170n118
Khatri, Dashrath 35, 109, 155n20, 189n102
Khatri, Gaj Singh 22, 55, 147n37, 164n38
Khawas, Mahima 34
Khawas, Tribhuwan 35
Kheri 29
khidmatguzari (service tenures) 3
khudkasht cultivators 24, 149n49, 149n53
Khuronsa 75
Kieghly, J. I. 9, 142n49
kipat tenure 193n152
Kishungunj 101, 186n75
Kooch Behar **104**
Kuch Bihar 104
Kumaon 12, 54, 164n37
Kunwar, Chandra Bir 109
Kurruckpoor 102
Kuttear 103

labor: agrarian 21–5; flight of 24, 41, 148n44; importation of 21; means of securing 28, 56, 151n73; paucity of 17, 22, 25, 28
Lahore **88–9**
landed rights, complex expression of 52, 163n19
land grants: context of 43; to encourage cultivation 26, 149–50n60; Gorkhali officials role in 31, 152n4; under King Girbana Juddha Bikram Shah 31; by the kings of Makwanpur 22, 147n32; to officials 34, 154n14; political relation reconstituted by 58; *see also* "waste lands"
land rights 9, 43, 45
land-use patterns: in Butwal Tarai 52; cultures of governance impacted by 28; found by the Company 28; political power impacted by 28; precolonial 71, 172n23; in Simraon 26; of "waste lands" 25
law, preservation of 6, 31, 69

Lefebvre, Henri 4, 139n19, 140n23
Limbu tribal leaders 111
Lindesay, G. 13
linguistic regions 83, 195n25
"little kingdoms" 126, 196n28
Local Government (Scotland) Act of 1889 124
Lodweh 102

maafi 3, 52–6, 74–5, 163n24, 164n38
Mackenzie, Holt 100, 185n66
Maghar, *thana* of 105
Mahalwara 118
Mahesh Chandra Regmi 110
Mahottari District 22
Majhar 65, 170n116
Majhowa 18, **79**, 145n9
Makwanpur: conquest by Gorkha 22, 76; copper plate grant by raja of 40; districts controlled by 37, 157n42; incorporation into Gorkhali Empire 38
malaria 21, 28
malguzari (tenure by revenue collection arrangements) 3
Malhotra, R. C. 118, 193n153
Maljhamuna 110, 190n115
Manbhoom district 107, **108**
Mando 78, **79**
Mann, Michael 2
"map-mindedness" 98, 184n56
Mapping India (Lahiri) 184n55
maps, surveys and boundaries, making states legible 87–122; "absolute space" 107, 187n88; of Asia 92, 181n18; Bandipur **119**; Bihar **90**; block formulation 121, 194n161; cadastral surveys 117–18, 193n152; Central Nepal **114**; definition of maps 87, 179–80n3; demarcating the Anglo–Gorkha boundary 93–8, 182n35; detached lands in 100, 186n73; Dhading District 118, **119**; Dinajpore survey 102; early European 92, 181n17; Geo-Body of Nepal **120**, 121, **121**; Gorkhali territories 109–21; Great Trigonometrical Survey (GTS) 99; Gurdhan **91**; "hybrid maps" 91, 180n11; "imperial space" 94; indigenous maps and representations of territory 87–93, 117, 192n141; indigenous traditions 112, 191n129; Lahore and Multan **88–9**; map types 87; Maratha maps 91–2; *naqsha* compass projects in North India 98–104, 184n50; Nepali map of Central Asia **113**; organizing principle behind 96–7; *pargana* maps 100, **101–4**; physical demarcation of boundaries 93, 94, 181n21; pictographic 117; process of 99–100, 185n61, 186n74; projects of legibility and simplification 122, 194n164; Regulations 7 and 9 of the Company 100, 185nn66–7; reordering territory 104–9, 188n98; revenue surveys 100–104, 185n65; Survey of India 117–18, 192n142; *thana* divisions of Gorakhpur **106**; topographic map of Southeastern Nepal **116**, 117; Western Nepal **115**
Maratha maps 92
Marwar ra Parganan ri Vigat (Nainsi) 83
Matka (*taluqa*) 56, 60, 62, 75, 79–80, 167nn79–81
mauzas 69
Mehsi 18
memorialization of important personages 83
Meshed **113**
Metcalf, Charles 8
Mewa 110
Mewa Gadh Simraon 110, 190n115
Michael, Bernardo A. 32, 39, 50, 61, 73, 79, 101
Michael, Saramma 4, 61
Michael, Sharon 4, 50
Mirchwar 71
Mirserai 107, 188n95
Mitchell, Timothy 128
Moglan 22, 34, 155n23, 160n69
Moll, Herman 123
Monckton, John 44
Montgomerie, Archibald 9–10, 26
Morang–Purnea 95
Moreland, W. H. 69
Morung 22, 147–8n37
Mudhwal **79**
Mughal Empire: administrative divisions in 69, 170n4; *Ain-i-Akbari* 77–8, 177n61, 180n8; *Atlas* (Habib) 87, 88–9, 180n5; boundaries and internal divisions of **68**; *Chahar Gulshan* 92; Company inheritance from 14; fiscal units in 69; importance of military in 76; labor mobility during 70–71; map of Lahore and Multan **88–9**; province divisions in 67; revenue collection in 77–8, 175n55; *see also* precolonial territorial divisions, disjointed spaces of

Mukwanpoor **13**
Multan **88–9**, 90
Municipal Corporations Act (1835) 124
munsifi (judicial divisions) 107, 188n92
Mureeahoo **101**
Muslims 21, 51, 147n31
Mustang 111
Mysore 9, 125

Nadir Shah 71
nagadi pattas 161n6
Nannor 18, 44–6, 145n9, 150n62, 151n2; *see also* Simraon
Naqsha compass projects in North India 98–104, 184n50
Nausai 118
Nawabgunj 80, 178n75
nawab of Awadh: *see* Awadh
Nawalpur 118
Nepal: economic blockade on 1; geo-body of **120**, 121, **121**; government departments for source materials 2, 137n7; Nepal–German Manuscript Preservation Project 3, 138n10; scholarly works on 2–3, 137–8n8, 138n11, 138n12; topographic map of Southeastern **116**; "unification" in nationalist historiography 138n9; Western portion **115**
Netwar 71
Nipaul Tarriani and Zillah Sarun boundary **18**
"non-state spaces" 5, 140–41n29

Ochterlony, David **12**, 82, 179n86; leadership of 12; routes toward Mukwanpoor **13**
oppression by *amils* (revenue collectors) 22
Ordnance Survey 124
Ordnance Survey Act of 1841 124
"The Origins of Subdivisions in Bengal" 109, 188n98
Orissa 14, 75; Permanent Settlement 150n63
Orme, Robert 99, 185n63
orthographic practices, lack of standardized 81, 178n81
Otroj 72–4, **73**
Ottoman cadastral surveys 77, 176n60
overlords 75

Pachrauta 38, **39**, 40–41, 95, 183n38
Padhya, Brahmanand 34
pahikasht cultivators 24–5, 149n49, 149n53
Pakistan 7
Palestine 176n60

Palpa: in arrears to Awadh 51, 162n7; Awadh as overlords of 58–9, 166n61; boundary disputes with Satasi and Bettiah 56, 165n51; Chauhan Rajputs of 57; claims to Matka 60, 62, 79, 168n87; Gorkhalis claims as overlords of 55, 164n40; Gorkha reinstates rights to Matka 62; Khanchi transferred to 65; Majhar claim of 79–80; Mukund Sen I 57–8, 166n58; officials reinstated 51, 162n10; raja arrest 24; Raj of 57–9; relations with Gorkha 58, 75, 166n63; rent-free grants to 53; revenue collection in 50–51, 161n6; rulers of 53, 163n30; subdivision of 118; territory of 18, **20**, 37, **50**; vulnerability of 58; *see also* Butwal Tarai
Pande, Dalabhanjan 51, 82, 166n72, 169n108
Pande, Damodar 59
Pandit, Ranganath 31, 152n4, 169n108
Pandit, Sri Krishen 31, 152n4
parganas: defined 122; impact of revenue administration on 70; land use patterns effecting 71; maps of 100, **101–4**; in Mughal Empire 67–8, 171n5; officials of 69; representations of in everyday life 82–4; revenue accounts of 9, 10; *see also raqbabandi* records
Parvat *thum* 118
patwaris (village accountants) 10, 24, 148n47
Pemberton, J. J. 102–4
pergunnahs: *see parganas*
Perlin, Frank 4, 67, 139n18
Permanent Settlement 31, 33, 150n63, 152n8
Petty, William 124
Phillimore, R. H. 92
Pickersgill, Joshua 95, 182n34
"planetary consciousness" 98
pluralism, in history writing 3
police divisions (*thanas*) 100–101, 103, 105, **106**, 122, 187n83
political power: dispersed 57; land use patterns impacted by 28; reactions to 27; role of in statemaking 11; shared sovereignty and 74, 98
political relationships 4
political strategies 22
political transformation 121
postage stamps **121**
Powakhalee 101, 103, **103**
Powell, B. H. Baden 72, 173n28
power 6, 47, 64, 81, 141n31

INDEX   229

Pratt, Mary Louise 98
precolonial territorial divisions, disjointed spaces of: administrative divisions in South Asia 67–70, 171n11; agrarian entitlements and territory production 71–4; cultures of governance and territory production in 71–84; documenting territory 77–81; rent-free (*maafi*) grants 74–5; representation of *parganas* in everyday life 82–4; territorial rearrangements 75–7; territorial significance of forts 81–2; *see also* Mughal Empire; space and spatiality; territory
"principle of limitation" 8, 142n44
property rights 4, 7, 72, 139n21, 173n28
Pudukkottai 173–4n37
Purbutpara 102
Purnea 93, 100–101, **103**, 106–7, 181n26
Purnea frontier 28, 151n74
Purnea-Morung area disputes 76
Pyuthana 18, 62, 65, 111

Qing Empire 112, 191n131

Rai, Shitab 36
Raijhamuna 110, 190n115
Rai tribal leaders 111
raiyati 69
rajas 52, 162n16
Rajasthan 75, 177
Raj Bandh 44, **45**
Rama Shah 93
Ramnagar 26, 97, 149n58, 183n44, 184n47
Ramsay, G. 192n142
Rana, Bir Shamsher 111
Rana, Jang Bahadur Rana 97, 111
Rana period 111
Rangpur **104**
Raniganj 107, 188n94
Rani Pakeer 80
raqbabandi records 77, 176n59; *see also parganas*; *tappas*
Raree **101**
Ratanpur Bansi **61**; Company settlement with 150–51n69; in Company territory 18; district change of 76; fiscal ties to Company 63; *maafi* lands in 53; marshy lakes of 146n16; northern reaches of 148n48; *pahikasht* in *thanas* of 24; transfer of Matka from 60; villages of 151n71; waste lands in 27
Raut, Bassun 45–6

Rautahat: Beg's entitlement claim to 75; in Champaran–Tarriani 18; creation of 145n9; dispute over 37–41; entangled edges of 44–6; geography of 75, 151n2; granted to Gorkha 150n62; land grant holders in 31, 152n4; (re)constitution of 38–44; territorial information about 110, 190–91n117; territorial rearrangement of 118, 193n157; *see also* Simraon
rebellion of Raja Chait Singh 43, 159n64
records: keeping of 9–10, 56, 164n42; manipulation of 54, 56, 80, 164–5n44
Regmi, Mahesh C. 3, 138nn10–11
Regmi, Mahesh Chandra 109
Regmi Research Collection (RRC) 3, 77, 138n10
Regmi Research Series (*RRS*) 3, 77, 138n10
Rennell, James 99, 184n57
rent-free lands (*lakhiraj*) 10, 53–4; dynamics surrounding 173n37; types of 74; *see also maafi*
Report on the Administration of Bengal 122, 194n166
Resolution of the Revenue Department 100, 186n71
revenue collection: avoidance of 24, 77, 148n47; from Bir Kishor Singh 33, 153n9; commissions of inquiry about 35, 155n23; by the Company 11, 31, 152n5; concealment of resources regarding 26; in disputed territories 46, 160–61n74; in Eastern Tarai 33–5, 153nn11–12, 155n20; grazing taxes 149n59; Hem Chaudhari's rights to **23**; impact on *pargana* organization 70, 100; jurisdictional fluctuations in 69, 171n15; migration to avoid 24; Mughal 77–8, 175n55; official types supervising 69; oppression by 22, 34–5, 154–5n18, 189n102; organization of 9; Otroj's 72; in Palpa 50–51; *parganas* as units for 67; resistance to 25, 33; in Sheoraj 63, 64; by *subbas* 152n3; systems of 34–5, 153n11, 168n94; *see also* revenue records
revenue contracts 34, 154n16
revenue records: manipulation of 77; precolonial 77–8, 81, 176n58; reconfiguration of lands in 78; systematization of 79, 81; territory divisions in 9–10, 38; transfers between 76; *see also* revenue collection
Richards, John F. 70

Richards, Thomas 11, 143n59
rights and privileges: historical view of 3–4;
    works on 4, 139n20; *see also* property
    rights
Robinson, Arthur 6–7
Rohtas 75, 174n40
Rongopur [Rangpur] 106
Routledge, John 27
Roy, William 124
rule of law 101, 125, 186n76

Sadr Board of Revenue 10
Sahlins, Peter 92, 94
Said, Edward W. 87
Sallyan 111, 191n120
Sangrampur 78
Sansar Chand 82
Saran, P. 69
sardars 22, 147n37
Sarkar, Jadunath 69
sarkar officials 69
Satasi 56, 79, 118, 165n51
Saxton, Christopher 89, 123, 180n6
Schwartzberg, Joseph 91, 93, 180n11, 181n19
Scott, David 24, 148nn47–8
Scott, James C. 5, 140–41n29, 194n164
Seherwa 80
Sen, Har Kumar Dat 36
Sen, Hem Karna 40, 158nn48–9
Sen, Lal Ran Bahadur 50–51
Sen, Mahadat 54, 58, 60, 62, 166n61, 167n84
Sen, Mukun, II 60
Sen, Mukund, I 57–8, 166n58
Sen, Prithvipal: execution of 51, 59, 71,
    145n12, 166n71; labor force loss by 22;
    royal decree to 54
Sen, Rattan 54
Sen, Survir 56, 165n52
Sen, Tej Pratap 95, 183n41
Sen, Vinayak 58
Shah, Bhavnanni 159n58
Shah, Hastidal 109
Shah, King Girbana Juddha Bikram 31
Shah, King Prithvinarayan 37, 41, 111,
    166n63
Shah, Pratap Singh, *lal mohar* of to
    Chaudhari **23**
Shah, Ran Badhadur 18, 145n12
Shah, Ran Bahadur **42**; assassination of 59,
    166n71; Chilli rendered independent
    of Dang by 111; downfall of 193n144;
    eldest wife of 167n86; land survey by 117;
    marriage of 58; misappropriation
    charges by 35
Shah, Rudra Vir 82, 109
Shah, Sher Bahadur 35
Shah, Tej Bahadur 111
Sheoraj: *see tappa* Sheoraj
Sherwill, James Lind 102
Sherwill, W. S. 102
Shitab Rai 40, 156n29
Shore, John 33, 105
Siam 5
Sidhua Jobna 75
Silhet 76
Simraon: as Champaran *pargana* 18; granted
    to Oulb Ali Beg 40; joint ownership of
    38; land use patterns in 26; location and
    internal divisions of **39**; overview of
    158n47; *tappas* of 145n9, 151n2; *see also*
    Nannor; Rautahat
Simrown 102
Singh, Abdhut 36–7
Singh, Bir Kishor: claim to Belwa annulled 36,
    156n29; claim to Rautahat 40, 158nn50–
    51; land claims of 44–5, 150n63; revenue
    engagements of 33, 153n9, 160n74;
    Simraon claim of 26; *see also* Bettiah
Singh, Dhrub 36, 40
Sing[h], Moorid Beiji 56, 165n52
Singh, Pahalwan 165n48
Singh, Prithvipat 27, 151n71
Singh, Raja Chait 43, 159n64
Singh, Ranjit 82
Singh, Sarabjit 27, 151n69, 151n71, 163n21
Singh, Shivnath 46–7
Singh, Sri Krishen 33
Singh, Zalim 27, 151n71
Singheea 101, **103**
Singh, Jugal Kishor 36, 37, 40–41, 158n53; *see
    also* Bettiah
Sirmur 72–4, **73**, 173n31
Sivaramakrishnan, K. 25, 149n54
Skaria, Ajay 98
Smith, Neil 7, 107, 142n42, 187n88
social forces 2, 6, 7, 70
social groups: of Anglo–Gorkha Tarai 21;
    geographical expression of 70, 172n18;
    "inner logic" activities with the Company
    76, 175n54; state boundary discontinuity
    and 70
social power, sources of on Gorakhpur–Butwal
    frontier 51–5
social reality 3

social theory and spatiality 5, 7, 140n23
society as process 2
socio-political forces 17
soil 19, 146n15
Soja, Edward W. 123
Song Yun 112
Soogaon 78
Soojainnuggur 103
Southeastern Nepal, topographic map of **116**
sovereigns 54
space and spatiality: agrarian environments and 27–9; binding and marking 5; capacity to bound and mark 87; cartography and 6–11, 142n37; colonial anxieties about 6; content formed by cultures of governance and agrarian entitlements 71; defined 1, 5; discontinuous administrative divisions and 41; gender and 5, 140n23; imagined permanence of 126; "jurisdictional sovereignty" as basis for 123, 194n2; Lefebvre on 5, 140n23; "non-state spaces" 5, 140–41n29; overlords having multiple claims on 75; place contrasted with 5, 140n25; "principle of limitation" 8, 142n44; in Pudukkottai 173–4n37; rearrangement of 43–4; relationship network impacting on 46; in revenue records 9–10; role of tax-exempt lands in 41; "territorial sovereignty" as basis for 123, 194n2; *see also* precolonial territorial divisions, disjointed spaces of
statemaking 1–6, 137n6, 138–9n13
state patronage 22
state–society relations: works on distinctions between 2, 137n4
States Reorganization Act (1956) 195n25
Stein, Burton 126, 196n29
Stiller, Ludwig 13, 95, 182n36
structure of the book 14–15
"subaltern" history and culture, works on 2, 137n6
suba 41, 67, 75, 77, 80, 83, 90, 174n40, 176n59; *see also* administrative divisions
subba 35, 152nn3–4, 156n25, 161n80
surveying practices 9
Survey of India **88**, 117–18, **119**, 192n142

talluqdars 10, 52, 60, 162–3n18
taluqa 69
Tambiah, Stanley 126, 196n30
Tanahu 36–7, 156–7nn31–2

tappas 10, 69, 71, 171n6; *see also raqbabandi* records; *specific tappas*
tappa Sheoraj 62–5, 78, 80, 168n94, 168nn100–101, 169n110
tarafs 69
Tarai: agrarian resources of 31, 152n4; districts of 18; environment and society 18–21; exports of 20; Gorkhalis claim to *tappas* of 37, 157n43; labor importation by 22; land disputes in 57, 76, 175n53; land grants in 22; land use patterns in 71, 172n23; locality description 144n64; military expeditions into 37, 157–8n43; overview of 17; present day 18, 145n8; under Rana rule 111–12, 191n126; territorial frontier of 11; territory divisions in 110, 190n111; Tharu cultivators in 51; *see also* Eastern Tarai; Gorkha
Tarikh-i-Qal'ah-i- Kashmir 91
"Tarriani" 18, 21, 145n7
Tauter 37–38, 75, 157n41
tax-exempt lands 41
temples 51, 83, 162n11
Terae **97**
territory: archives of 11, 143n59; defined 5, 140n22; divisions of in revenue records 9–10; documenting of 77–8; geography as physically dividing 83; mark of agrarian dynamism on 25; plasticity in 6, 14; precolonial divisions of 4–5; rearrangements of 75–7, 121, 188n98; representation of 14; theme exploration 5, 140n27; *see also* Burghart, Richard; precolonial territorial divisions, disjointed spaces of
thana: *see* police divisions
Thapa, Achal 35, 155n19
Thapa, Amar Singh: as commander on Gorakhpur–Butwal frontier 64; efforts to capture fort Kangra 81–2; governing Palpali territory 51, 162n8; Kathmandu suspicious of 178n85; loss of face by 179n86; mapmakers employed by 112; offers to farm the Butwal *zamindari* 168n91; ordered to take over Butwal lowlands 166n72; Sheoraj activities of 169n111
Thapa, Bhim Sen **12**; land grant holdings of 31, 152n4; linear boundaries understood by 95, 182n36; retributions unleashed by 18, 51, 145n12, 162n8, 166n71; treaty ratification failure 12

Thapa, Chandra Bir 35, 155n20
Nyan Singh Thapa 82
Thapa, Parshuram 35, 155n20
Tharu 21–3, 26, 150n61
Tharu, Kashi Gurau 97
Thongchai Winichakul 5
Thuillier, H. L. 102, 187n78
thums 190n111
Tibrikote *thum* 118
Tilpur 60, 62, 65
Tirhut 38, 40, 100, 158n48, 160n71, 186n72
Tirhut–Saptari–Mahottari 95, 182n35
Tirhut-Sarlahi area disputes 76
Tithe Commutation Act (1836) 124
transliteration xv
Travers, Robert 9, 143n52
Treaty of Cession 80
Treaty of Friendship 196n34
Treaty of Sugauli 12, 144n67
tribute collection 2, 14–15, 33, 37–8, 46

"unification" 3, 138n9, 138n11
United States Agency for International Development (USAID) 118
Upadhyaya, Chandra Shekhar 95
Upadhyaya, Dinanath: alledged bribe by 41, 159n57; dual offices of 109; as faction leader 41, 159n58; presents Gorkhali land claims 37–8, 81; Rautahat land holdings of 31, 152n4; revenue engagements of 34, 154n15
Upadhyaya, Vrajvilas 34, 154n15

Vaishnavaite abbots 22
Village Development Committee (VDC) 194n162
villages (*mauzas*) 10
Vir Vinod (Shyamaldas) 128

"waste lands": cultivated on concessional terms 51, 162n12; of Eastern Tarai 34, 153n13; enormity of 149n56; "intermediate space" and 71, 172n25; land use patterns of 25–8; *maafi* grants regarding 54; precolonial 71; tax evasion and 177n64; terms implications 149n55; *see also* land grants
water rights 151n69, 161n79
Waugh, Andrew 192n142
Western Himalayas 72, 173n30
wildlife 20–21, 27
Wilford, Francis 112
Wolters, O. W. 126, 196n30
Woodward, David 6–7
Wroughton, Robert 76, 175n52
Wyatt, Alex 100, 186n72

Young, John 44

zamindars 10, 52, 162n16
Ziauddin, Sheikh 41, 159n57
Zillah Sarun and Nipaul Tarriani boundary **18**
"zones of anomaly" 5, 141n30

www.ingramcontent.com/pod-product-compliance
Lightning Source LLC
Chambersburg PA
CBHW021824300426
44114CB00009BA/314